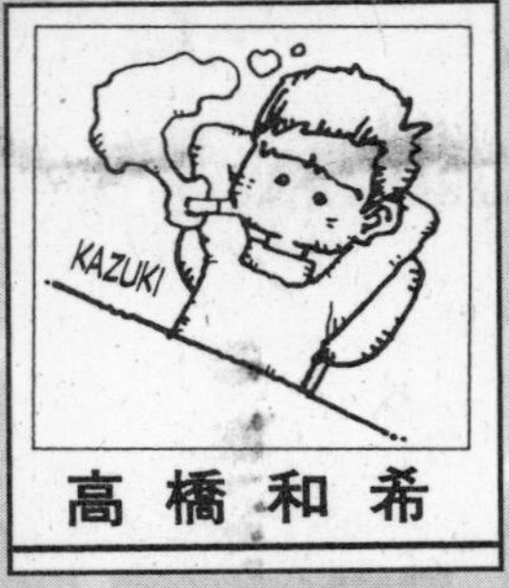
KAZUKI
高橋和希

KAZUKI TAKAHASHI
I'M WORKING HARD TO GET THE STUDIO DICE WEBSITE UP AND RUNNING SO IT CAN GO LIVE IN MAY! IT'S HTTP://STUDIO-DICE.COM. COME CHECK OUT DRAWINGS OF JADEN, SOME WEIRD ANIME AND OTHER STUFF!

KAZUKI TAKAHASHI
Artist/author Kazuki Takahashi first tried to break into the manga business in 1982, but success eluded him until *Yu-Gi-Oh!* debuted in the Japanese *Weekly Shonen Jump* magazine in 1996. *Yu-Gi-Oh!*'s themes of friendship and fighting, together with Takahashi's weird and imaginative monsters, soon became enormously successful, spawning a real-world card game, video games, and four anime series (two Japanese *Yu-Gi-Oh!* series, *Yu-Gi-Oh! GX* and *Yu-Gi-Oh! 5D's*). A lifelong gamer, Takahashi enjoys Shogi (Japanese chess), Mahjong, card games, and tabletop RPGs, among other games.

NAOYUKI KAGEYAMA
Naoyuki Kageyama was born April 12, 1969, which makes him an Aries, and is originally from Tokyo, Japan. He is the recipient of an honorable mention for the 1990 *Weekly Shonen Jump* Hop Step Award for his work *Mahou No Trump* (Magic Trump) and started drawing *Yu-Gi-Oh! GX* for *Monthly V Jump* in February 2006. Kageyama is a baseball fan and his favorite team is the Seibu Lions.

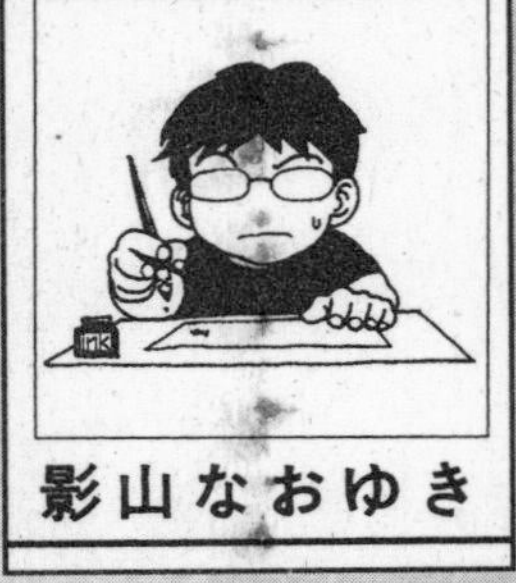
ink
影山なおゆき

NAOYUKI KAGEYAMA
I'M PROUD TO ANNOUNCE THAT THE LAST CHAPTER IN VOLUME 7 MARKS THE 50TH CHAPTER IN THE SERIES. NOOOOBODY WOULD CONGRATULATE ME FOR IT, SO AFTER I FINISHED DRAWING IT, I PARTIED ALL BY MYSELF (*LAUGHS*).

YU-GI-OH! GX Volume 7
SHONEN JUMP Manga Edition

ORIGINAL CONCEPT/SUPERVISED BY
KAZUKI TAKAHASHI

STORY AND ART BY
NAOYUKI KAGEYAMA

Translation & English Adaptation/Taylor Engel and Ian Reid, HC Language Solutions
Touch-up Art & Lettering/John Hunt
Designer/Ronnie Casson
Editor/Mike Montesa

Published by VIZ Media, LLC
P.O. Box 77010
San Francisco, CA 94107

10 9 8 7 6 5 4 3 2 1
First printing, August 2011

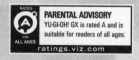

PARENTAL ADVISORY
YU-GI-OH! GX is rated A and is
suitable for readers of all ages.
ratings.viz.com

www.viz.com

www.shonenjump.com

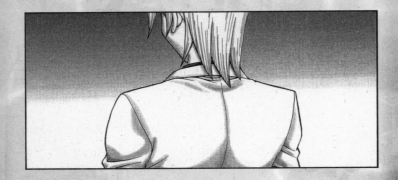

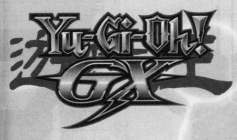

VOLUME 7
King Atticus's
True Power

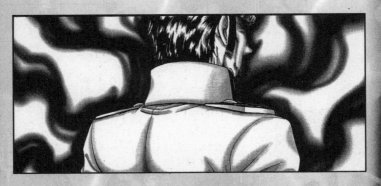

**Story & Art by
NAOYUKI
KAGEYAMA**

**Original Concept/
Supervised by
KAZUKI
TAKAHASHI**

THE STORY SO FAR

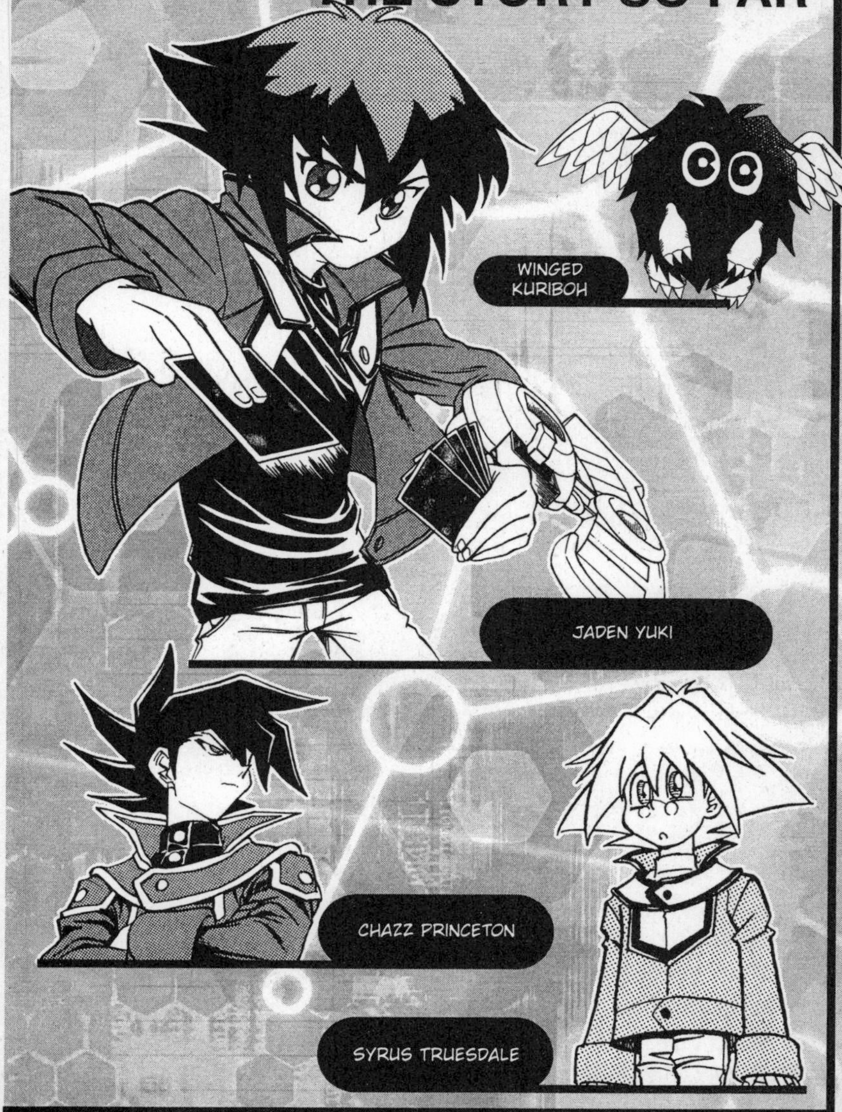
WINGED KURIBOH
JADEN YUKI
CHAZZ PRINCETON
SYRUS TRUESDALE

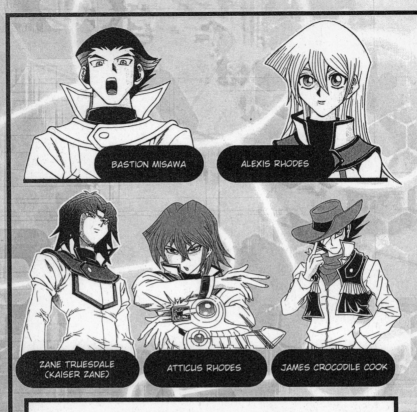

BASTION MISAWA

ALEXIS RHODES

ZANE TRUESDALE
(KAISER ZANE)

ATTICUS RHODES

JAMES CROCODILE COOK

ON AN ISLAND IN THE SOUTHERN SEA STANDS AN ACADEMY WHERE THE NEXT GENERATION OF DUELISTS IS TRAINED. IT IS CALLED DUEL ACADEMY!

JADEN YUKI LEARNED ABOUT THE EXCITEMENT OF DUELING THROUGH AN ENCOUNTER WITH DUEL WORLD CHAMPION, KOYO HIBIKI. ENTRUSTED WITH HIBIKI'S DECK, JADEN TAKES ON ALL CHALLENGERS AT THE ACADEMY IN ORDER TO BECOME A TRUE DUELIST!

THE TOURNAMENT FOR THE RIGHT TO DUEL KAISER ZANE IS OVER. WITH A NEW DECK IN HAND, JADEN RESOLVES TO FIGHT THE BLACK SHADOW THAT'S AFTER THE SPIRIT CARDS. IN THE MIDST OF ALL THIS, FOUR AMERICAN DUELISTS ARRIVE FOR AN EXCHANGE BATTLE. SOON AFTER, CROCODILE, ONE OF THE FOUR, CHALLENGES ALEXIS'S BROTHER ATTICUS TO A DUEL. EVEN AS CROCODILE TURNS UP THE HEAT, ATTICUS KEEPS HIS COOL. WHAT IS HIS REAL POWER?!

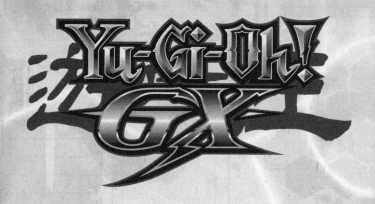

Volume 7: King Atticus's True Power

CONTENTS

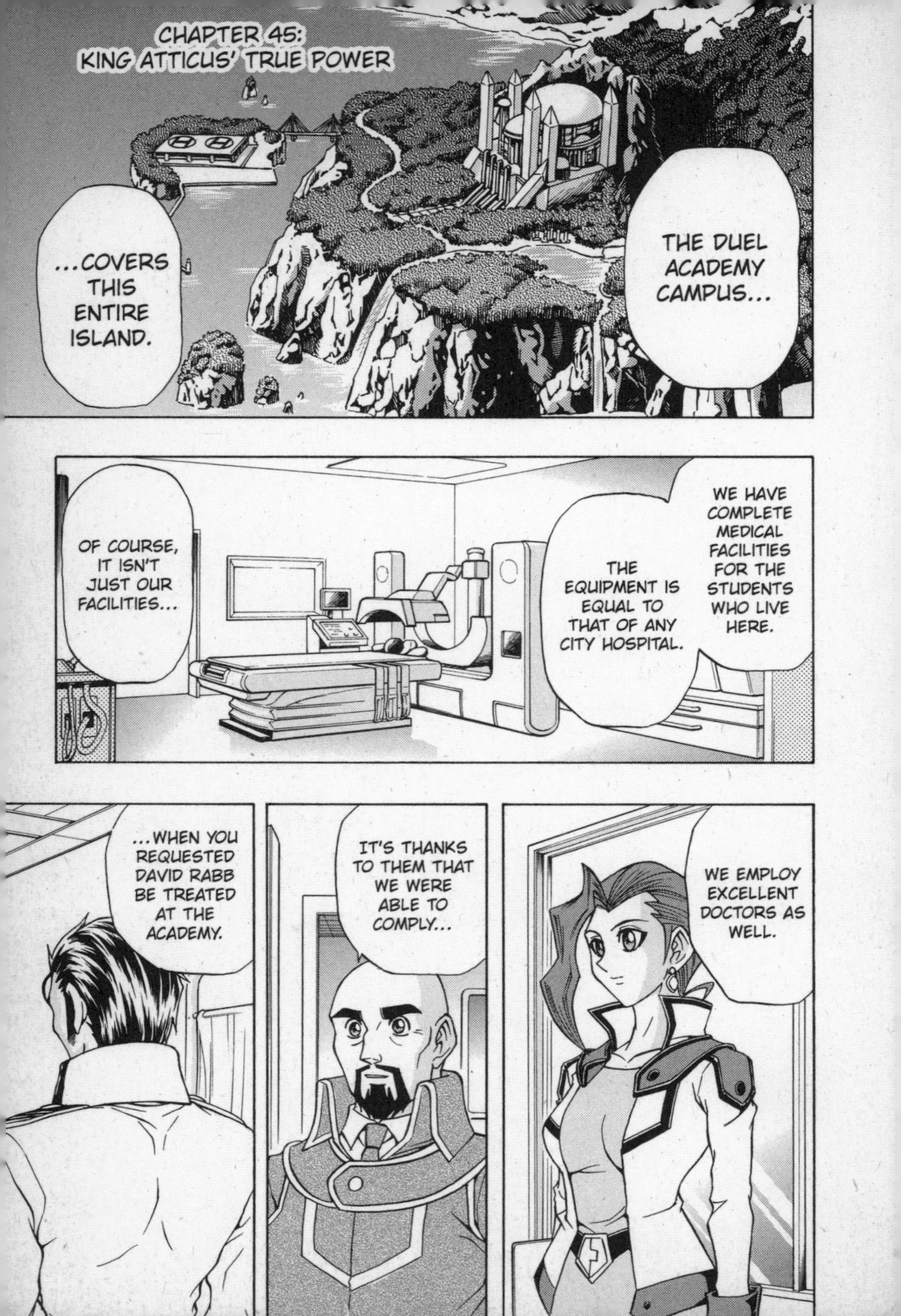
CHAPTER 45: KING ATTICUS' TRUE POWER
THE DUEL ACADEMY CAMPUS...
...COVERS THIS ENTIRE ISLAND.
WE HAVE COMPLETE MEDICAL FACILITIES FOR THE STUDENTS WHO LIVE HERE.
THE EQUIPMENT IS EQUAL TO THAT OF ANY CITY HOSPITAL.
OF COURSE, IT ISN'T JUST OUR FACILITIES...
WE EMPLOY EXCELLENT DOCTORS AS WELL.
IT'S THANKS TO THEM THAT WE WERE ABLE TO COMPLY...
...WHEN YOU REQUESTED DAVID RABB BE TREATED AT THE ACADEMY.

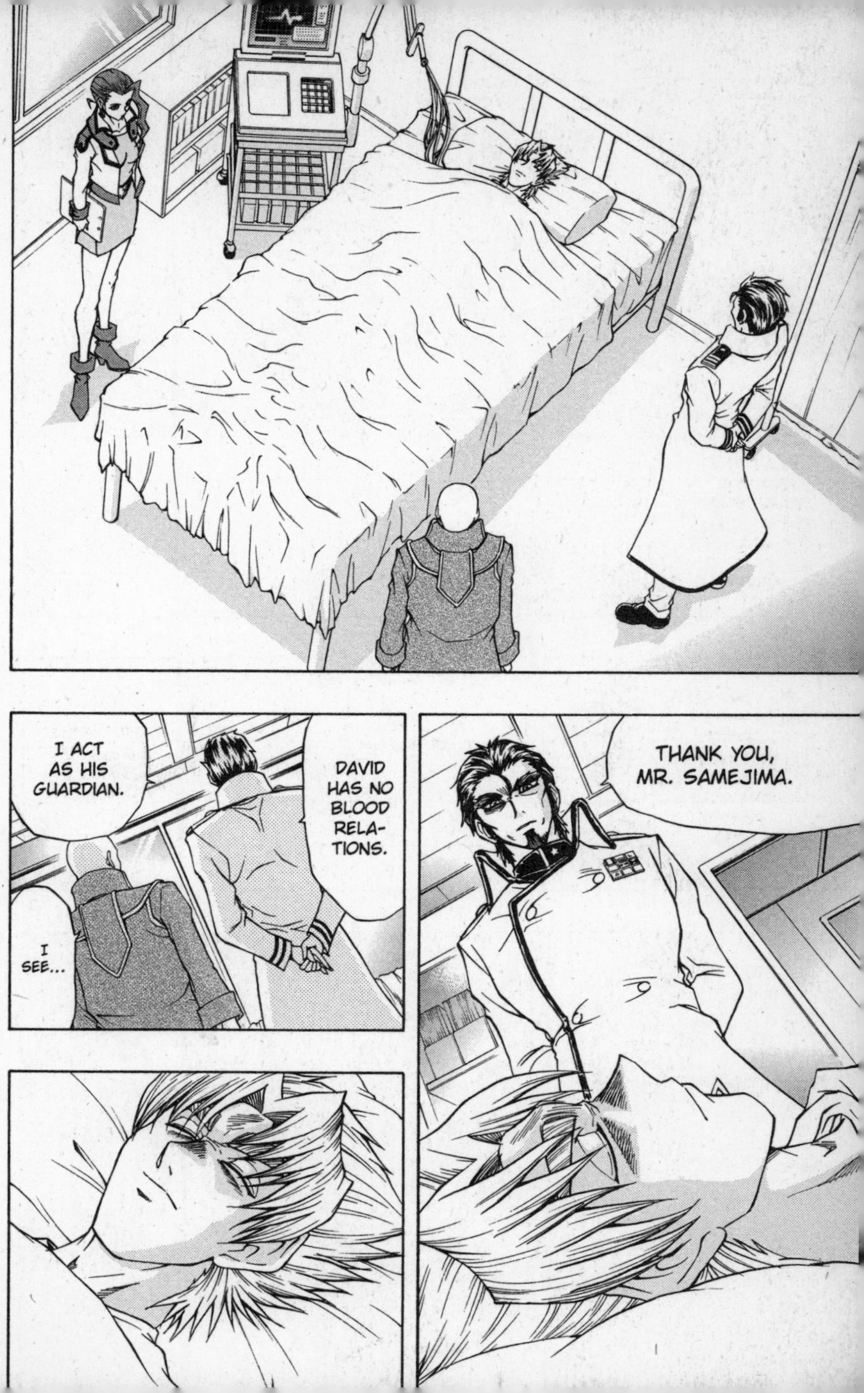
THANK YOU, MR. SAMEJIMA.
DAVID HAS NO BLOOD RELATIONS.
I ACT AS HIS GUARDIAN.
I SEE...

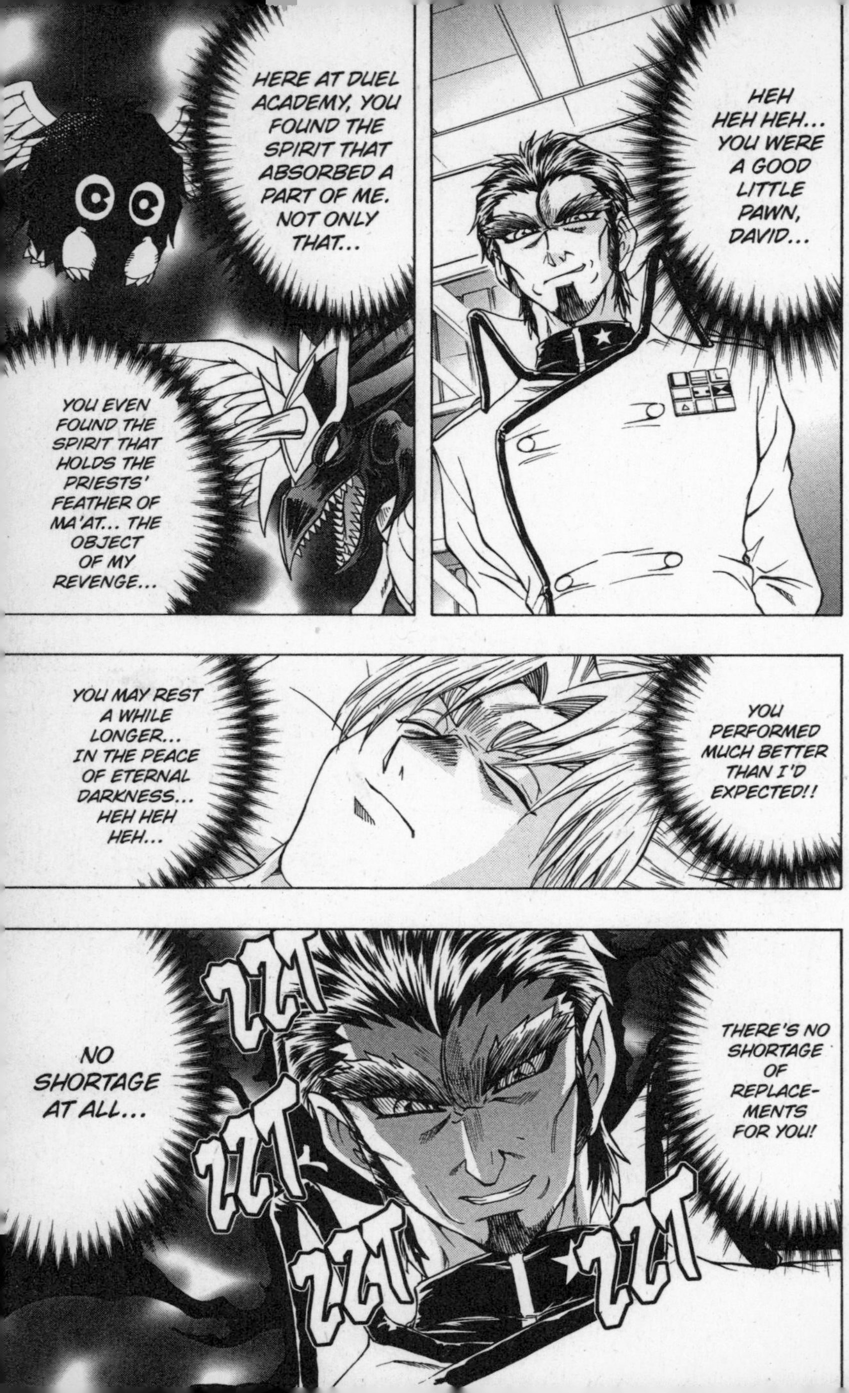
HEH HEH HEH... YOU WERE A GOOD LITTLE PAWN, DAVID...
HERE AT DUEL ACADEMY, YOU FOUND THE SPIRIT THAT ABSORBED A PART OF ME. NOT ONLY THAT...
YOU EVEN FOUND THE SPIRIT THAT HOLDS THE PRIESTS' FEATHER OF MA'AT... THE OBJECT OF MY REVENGE...
YOU PERFORMED MUCH BETTER THAN I'D EXPECTED!!
YOU MAY REST A WHILE LONGER... IN THE PEACE OF ETERNAL DARKNESS... HEH HEH HEH...
THERE'S NO SHORTAGE OF REPLACE-MENTS FOR YOU!
NO SHORTAGE AT ALL...

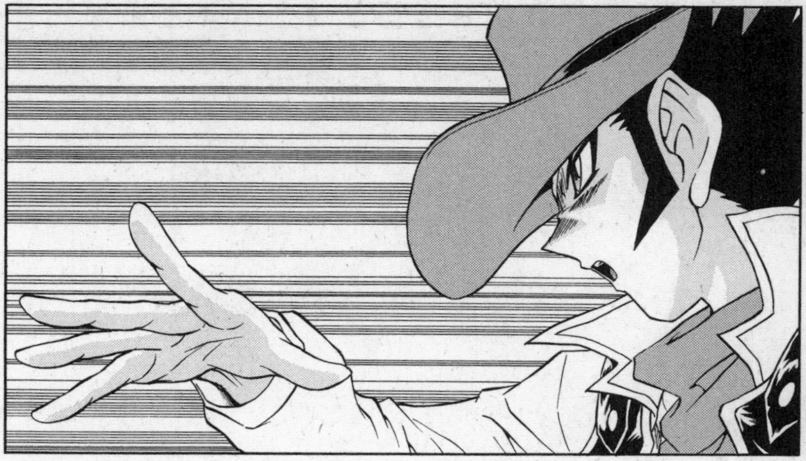

CHAPTER 45: KING ATTICUS' TRUE POWER

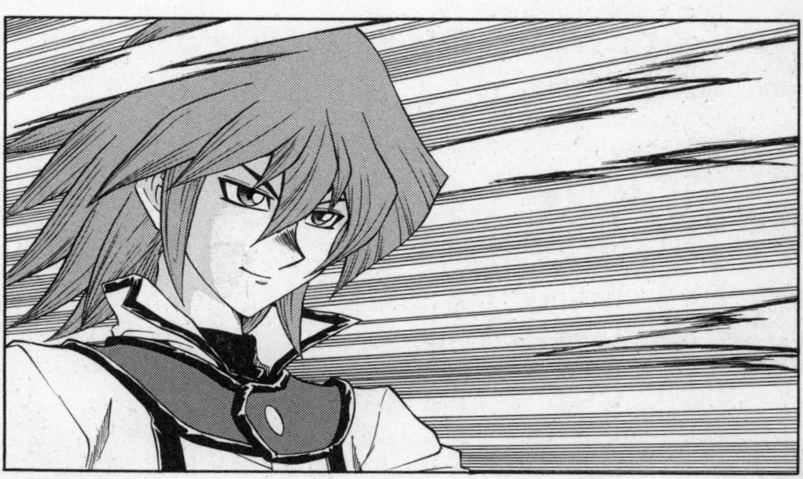

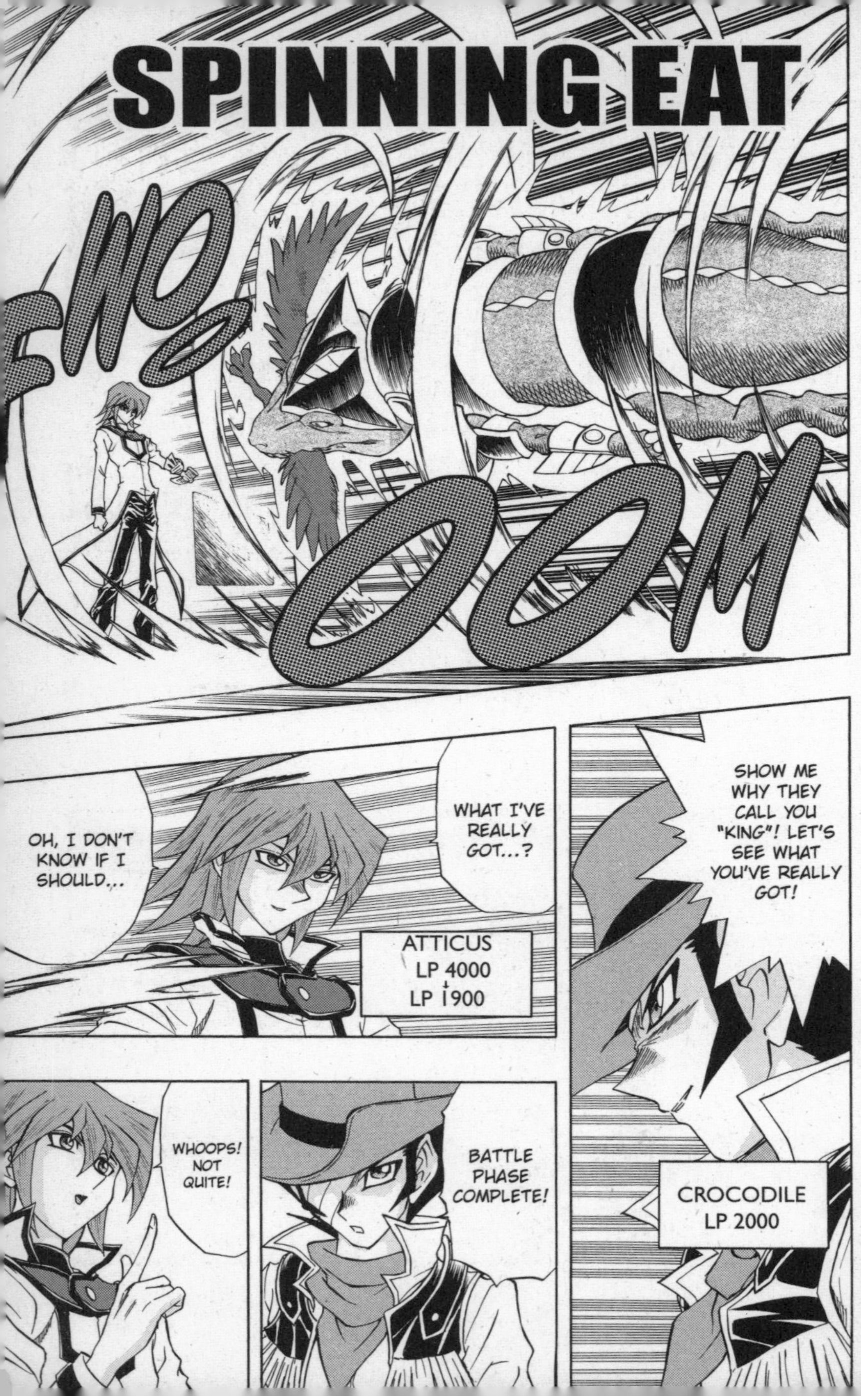
SPINNING EAT
FWOOOM
SHOW ME WHY THEY CALL YOU "KING"! LET'S SEE WHAT YOU'VE REALLY GOT!
CROCODILE
LP 2000
WHAT I'VE REALLY GOT...?
OH, I DON'T KNOW IF I SHOULD...
ATTICUS
LP 4000
↓
LP 1900
BATTLE PHASE COMPLETE!
WHOOPS! NOT QUITE!

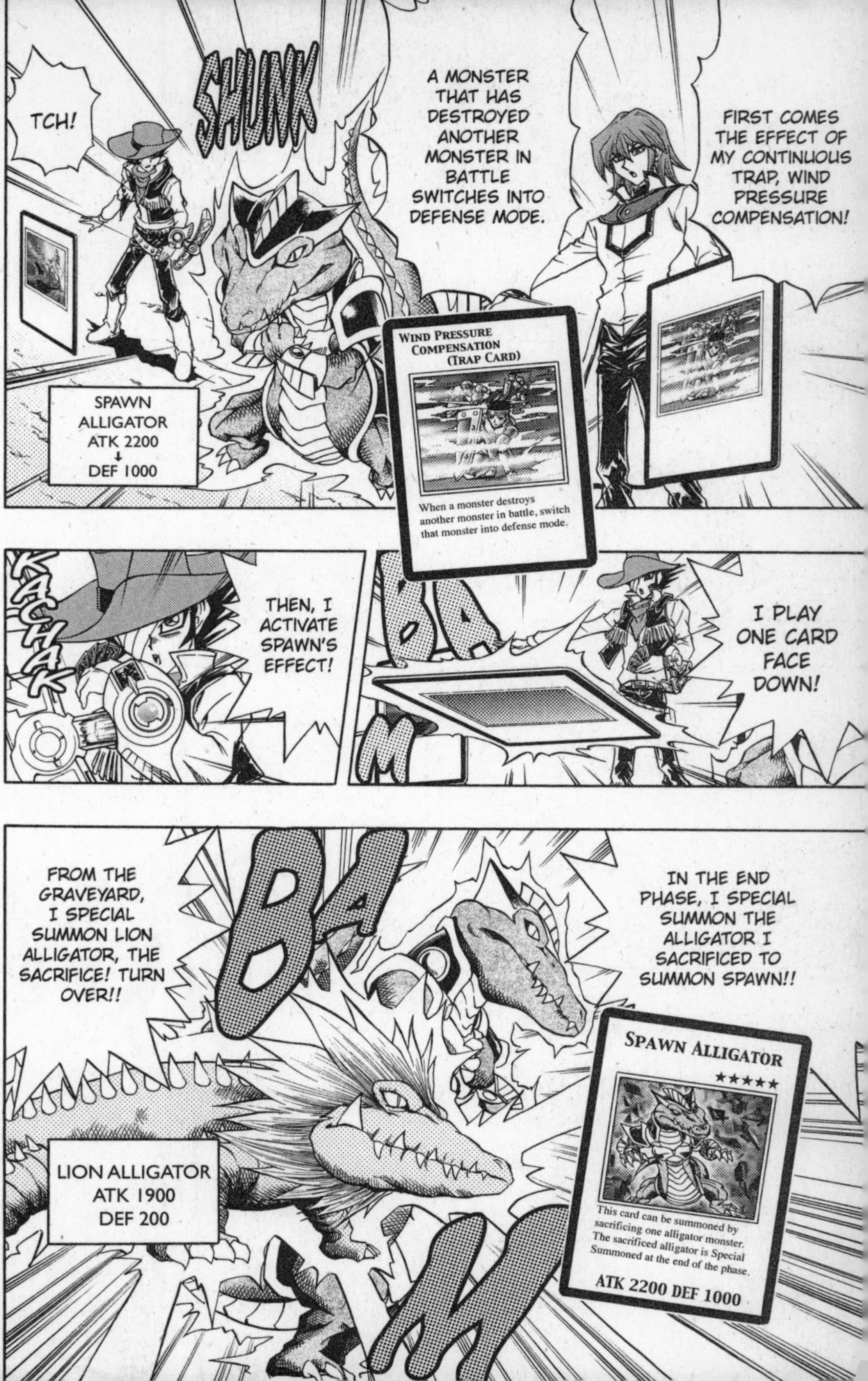
FIRST COMES THE EFFECT OF MY CONTINUOUS TRAP, WIND PRESSURE COMPENSATION!
A MONSTER THAT HAS DESTROYED ANOTHER MONSTER IN BATTLE SWITCHES INTO DEFENSE MODE.
SHUNK
TCH!
SPAWN ALLIGATOR ATK 2200 ↓ DEF 1000
WIND PRESSURE COMPENSATION (TRAP CARD)
When a monster destroys another monster in battle, switch that monster into defense mode.
I PLAY ONE CARD FACE DOWN!
BAM
THEN, I ACTIVATE SPAWN'S EFFECT!
KACHAK
IN THE END PHASE, I SPECIAL SUMMON THE ALLIGATOR I SACRIFICED TO SUMMON SPAWN!!
SPAWN ALLIGATOR
★★★★★
This card can be summoned by sacrificing one alligator monster. The sacrificed alligator is Special Summoned at the end of the phase.
ATK 2200 DEF 1000
BAM
FROM THE GRAVEYARD, I SPECIAL SUMMON LION ALLIGATOR, THE SACRIFICE! TURN OVER!!
LION ALLIGATOR ATK 1900 DEF 200

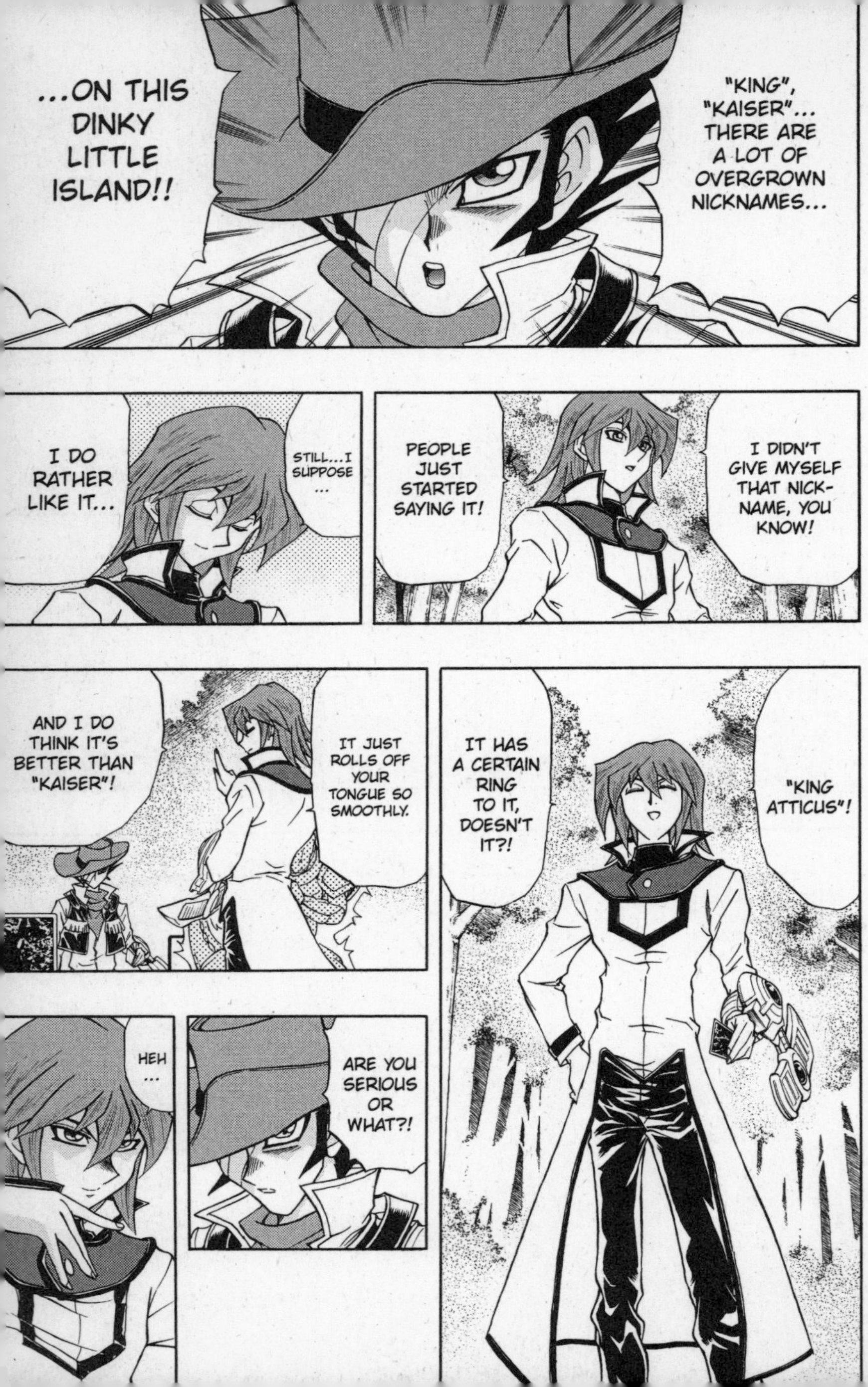
"KING", "KAISER"... THERE ARE A LOT OF OVERGROWN NICKNAMES...
...ON THIS DINKY LITTLE ISLAND!!
I DIDN'T GIVE MYSELF THAT NICK-NAME, YOU KNOW!
PEOPLE JUST STARTED SAYING IT!
STILL...I SUPPOSE ...
I DO RATHER LIKE IT...
"KING ATTICUS"!
IT HAS A CERTAIN RING TO IT, DOESN'T IT?!
IT JUST ROLLS OFF YOUR TONGUE SO SMOOTHLY.
AND I DO THINK IT'S BETTER THAN "KAISER"!
ARE YOU SERIOUS OR WHAT?!
HEH ...

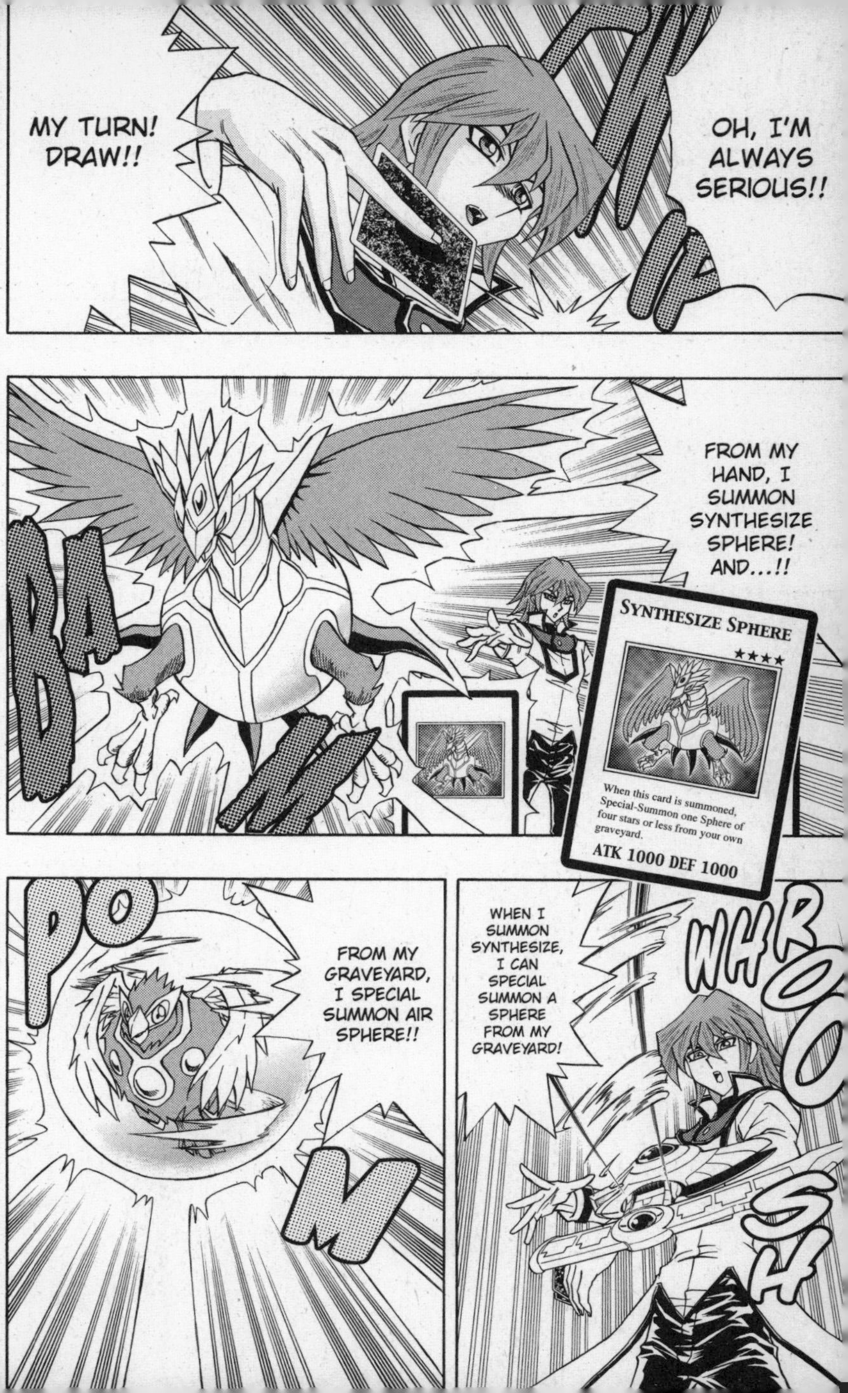
OH, I'M ALWAYS SERIOUS!!
MY TURN! DRAW!!
FROM MY HAND, I SUMMON SYNTHESIZE SPHERE! AND...!!
SYNTHESIZE SPHERE
★★★★
When this card is summoned, Special-Summon one Sphere of four stars or less from your own graveyard.
ATK 1000 DEF 1000
BAM
WHROOSH
WHEN I SUMMON SYNTHESIZE, I CAN SPECIAL SUMMON A SPHERE FROM MY GRAVEYARD!
FROM MY GRAVEYARD, I SPECIAL SUMMON AIR SPHERE!!
POM

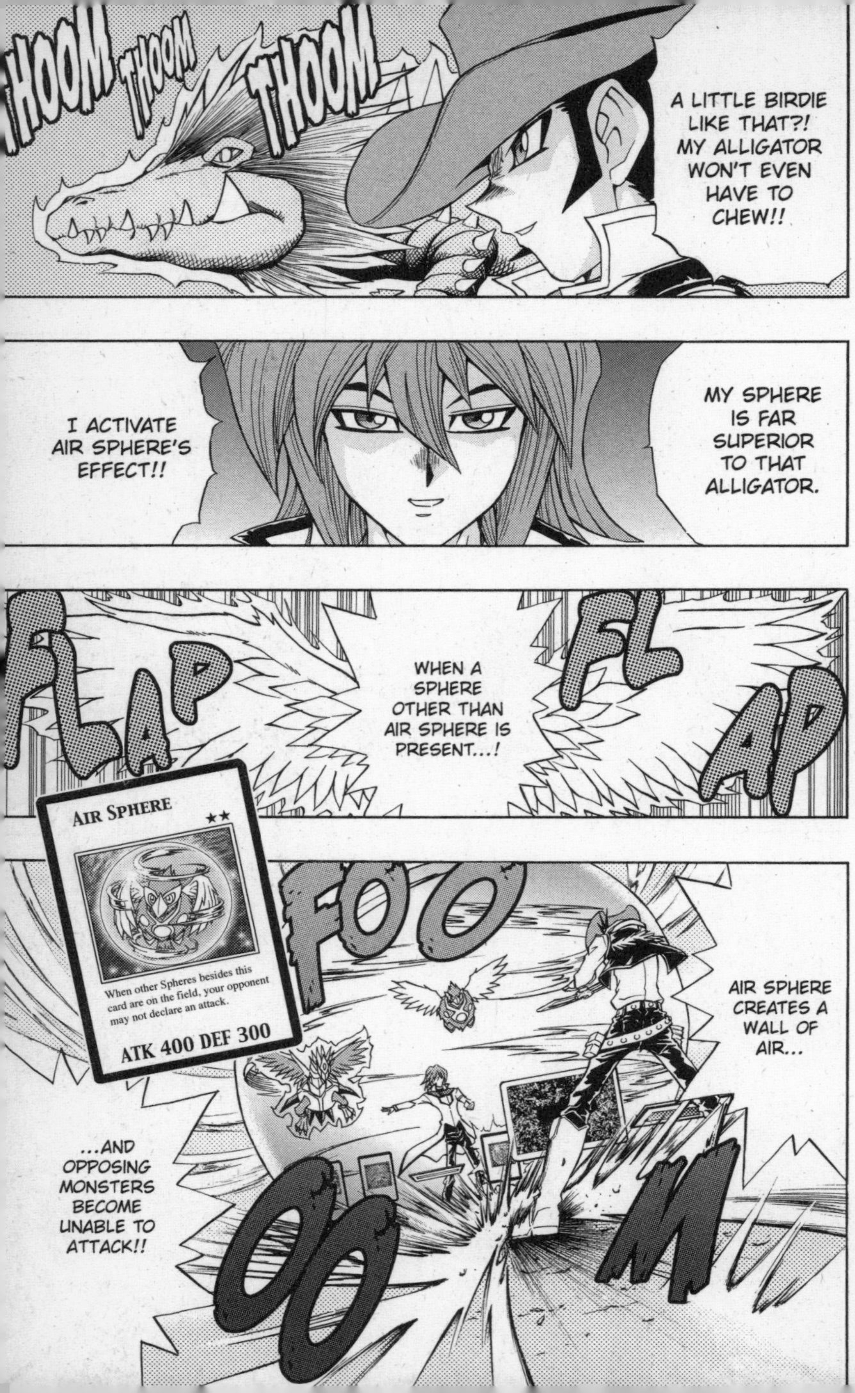
A LITTLE BIRDIE LIKE THAT?! MY ALLIGATOR WON'T EVEN HAVE TO CHEW!!
THOOM
THOOM
THOOM
MY SPHERE IS FAR SUPERIOR TO THAT ALLIGATOR.
I ACTIVATE AIR SPHERE'S EFFECT!!
FL AP
WHEN A SPHERE OTHER THAN AIR SPHERE IS PRESENT...!
FLAP
AIR SPHERE CREATES A WALL OF AIR...
FOOOOM
AIR SPHERE
★★
When other Spheres besides this card are on the field, your opponent may not declare an attack.
ATK 400 DEF 300
...AND OPPOSING MONSTERS BECOME UNABLE TO ATTACK!!

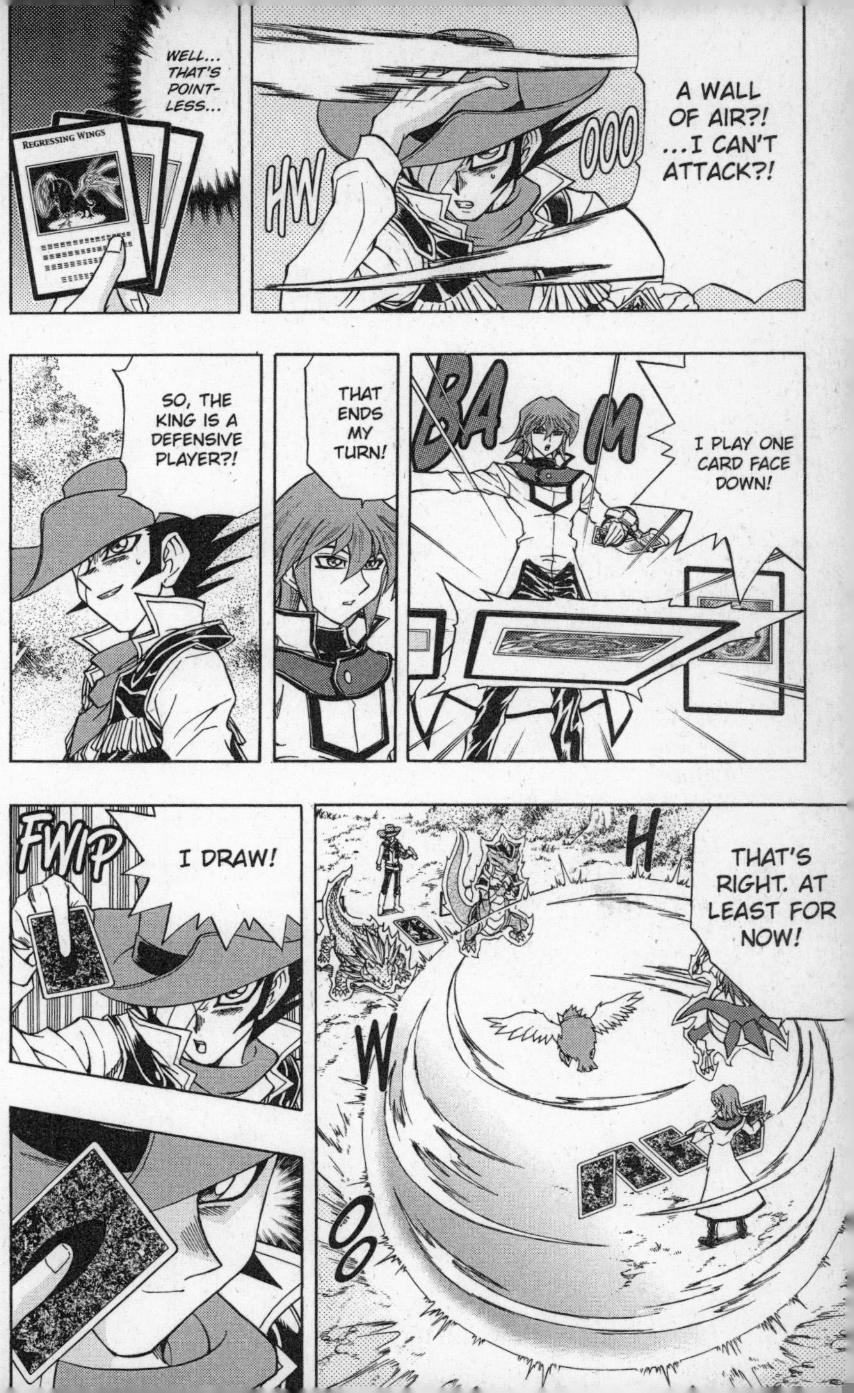
HWOOO
A WALL OF AIR?! ...I CAN'T ATTACK?!
WELL... THAT'S POINTLESS...
REGRESSING WINGS
BAM
I PLAY ONE CARD FACE DOWN!
THAT ENDS MY TURN!
SO, THE KING IS A DEFENSIVE PLAYER?!
THAT'S RIGHT. AT LEAST FOR NOW!
FWIP
I DRAW!

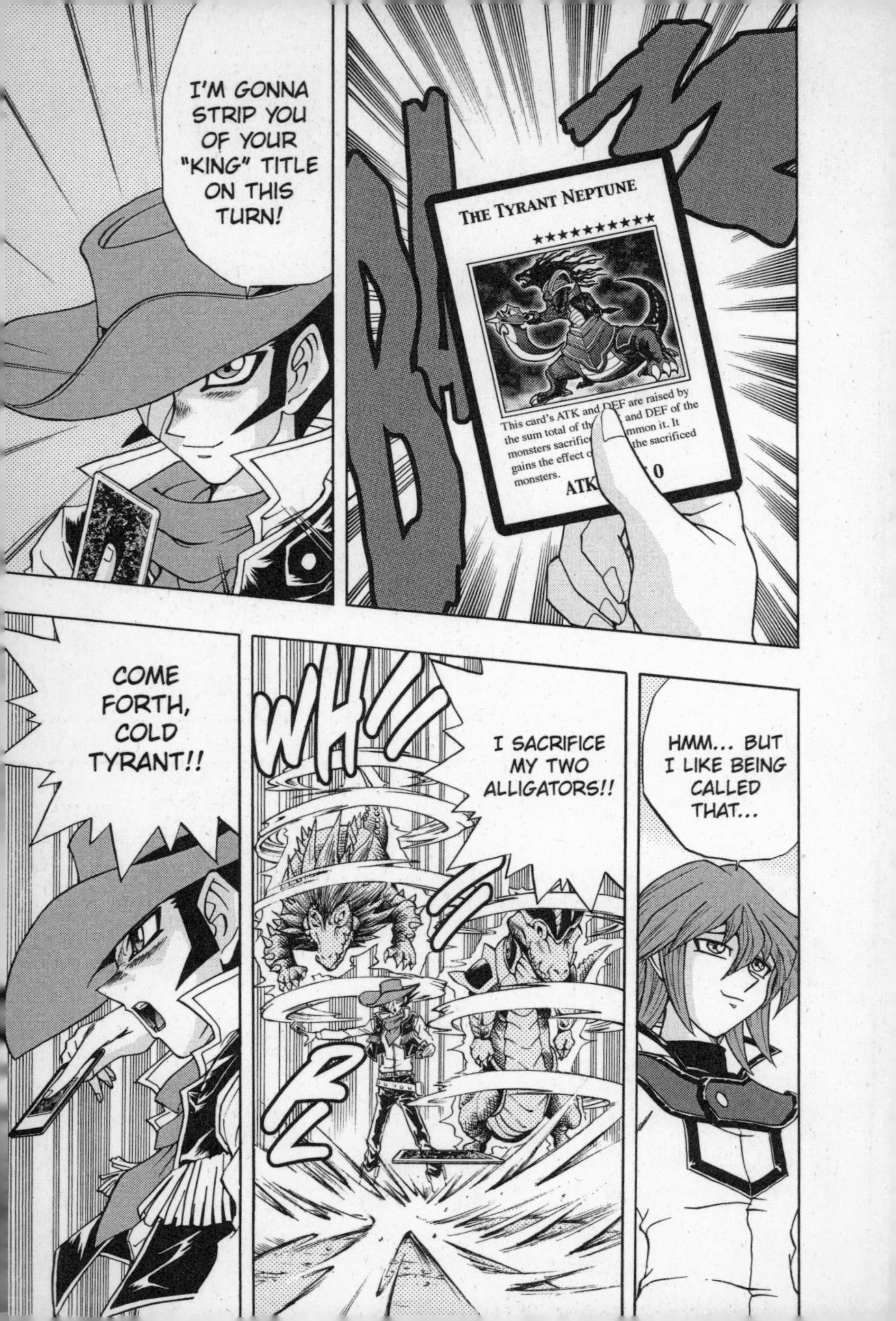
THE TYRANT NEPTUNE
I'M GONNA STRIP YOU OF YOUR "KING" TITLE ON THIS TURN!
HMM... BUT I LIKE BEING CALLED THAT...
I SACRIFICE MY TWO ALLIGATORS!!
COME FORTH, COLD TYRANT!!

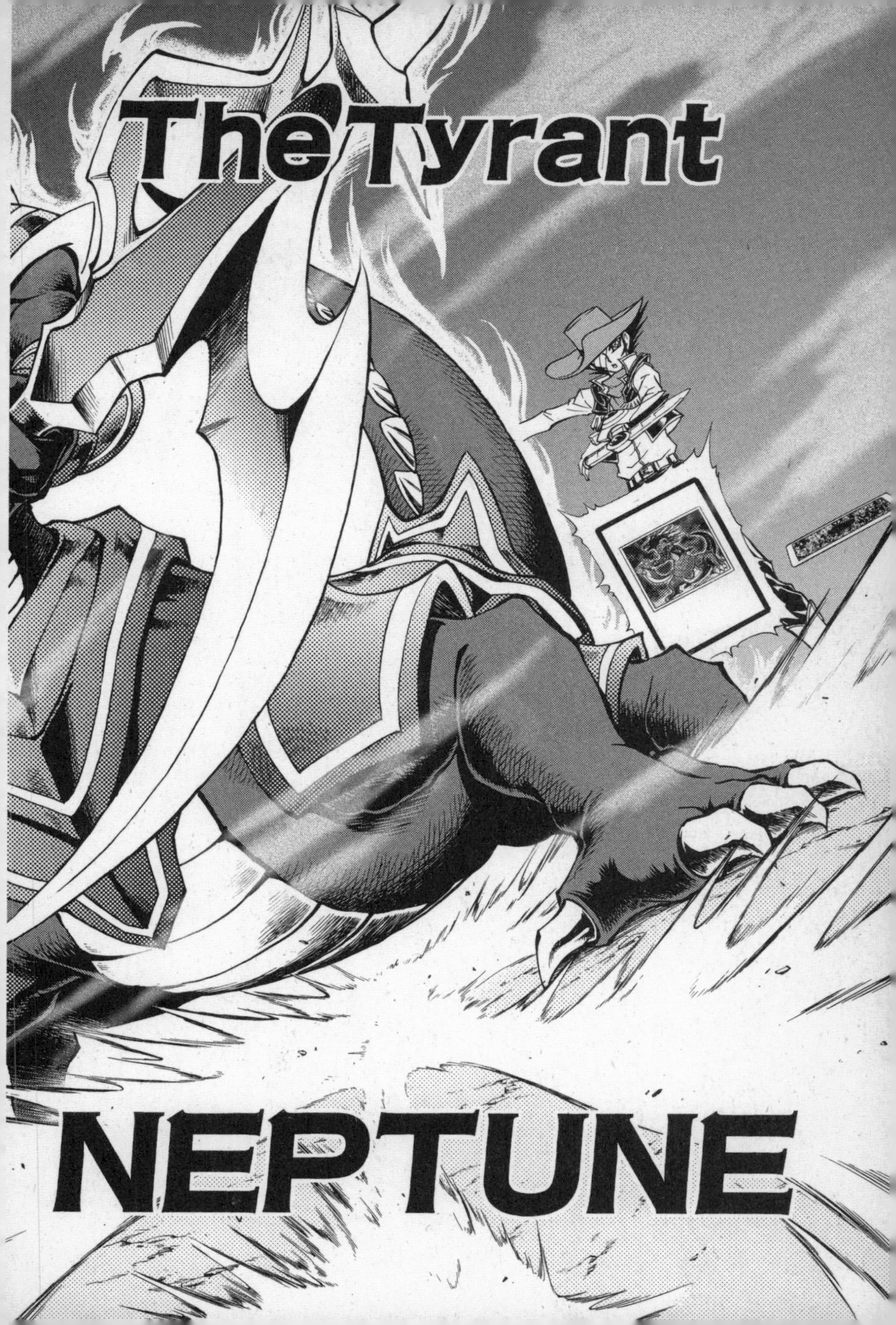

The Tyrant
NEPTUNE

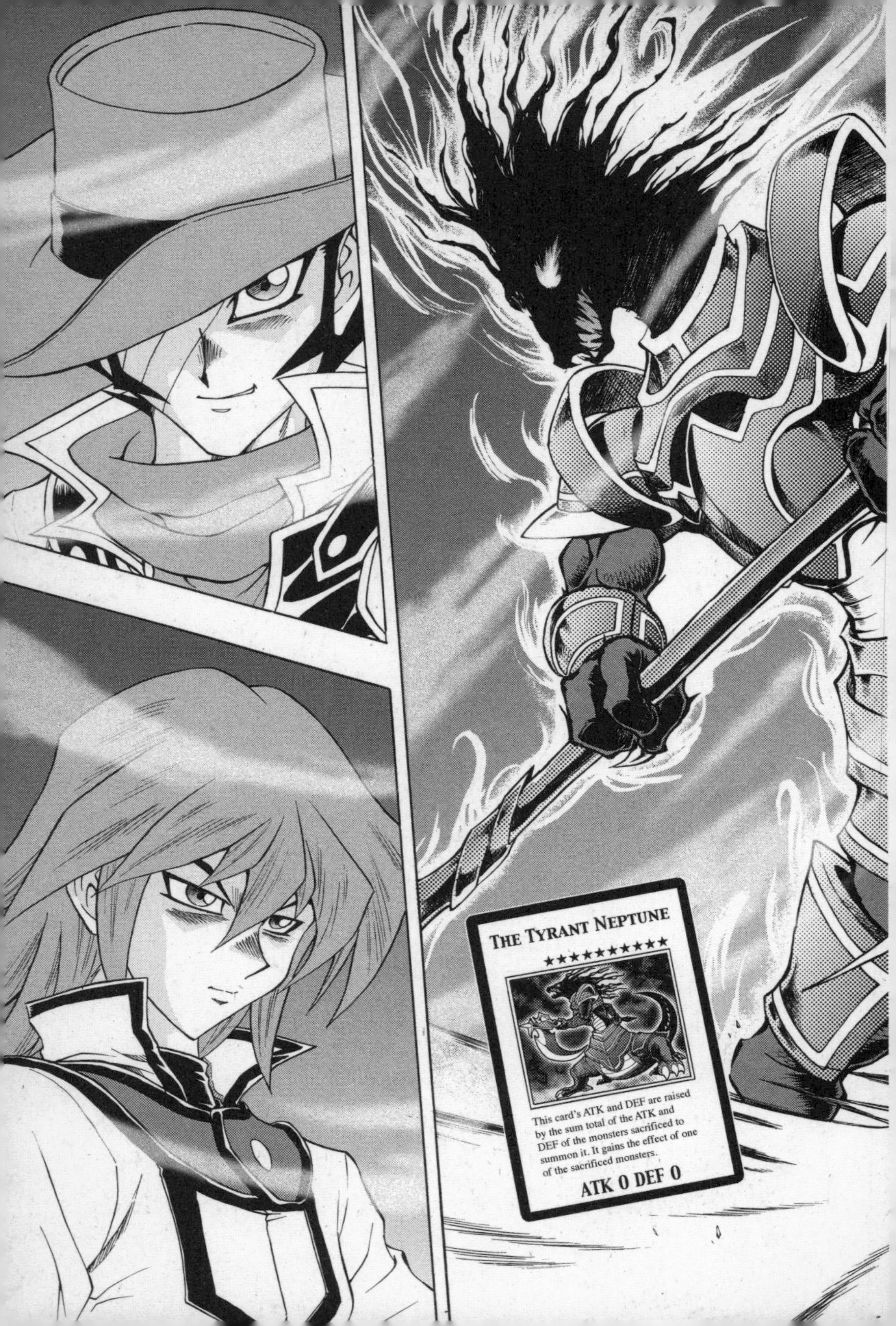
The Tyrant Neptune
★★★★★★★★★★
This card's ATK and DEF are raised by the sum total of the ATK and DEF of the monsters sacrificed to summon it. It gains the effect of one of the sacrificed monsters.
ATK 0 DEF 0

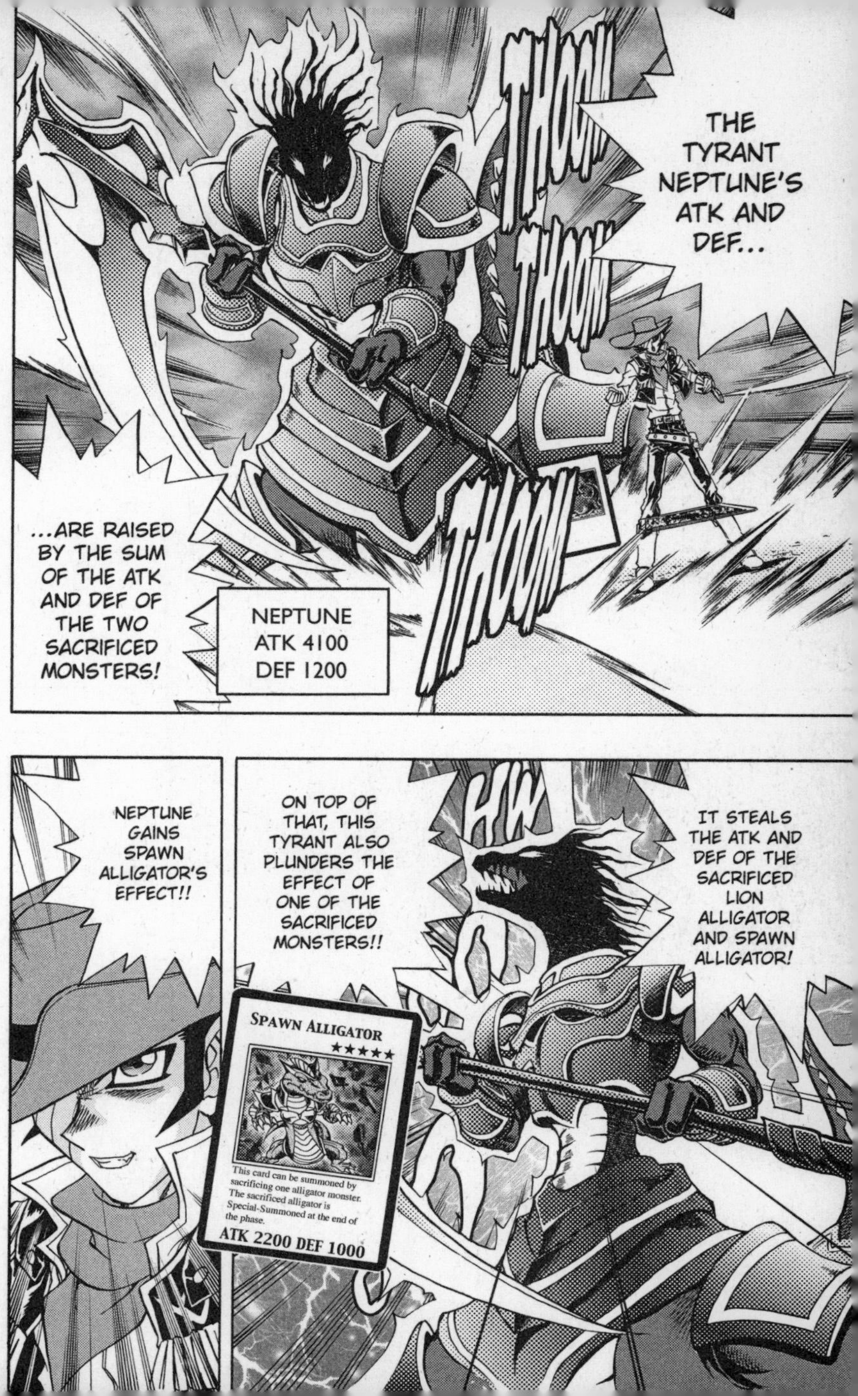
THE TYRANT NEPTUNE'S ATK AND DEF...
THOOM
THOOM
THOOM
...ARE RAISED BY THE SUM OF THE ATK AND DEF OF THE TWO SACRIFICED MONSTERS!
NEPTUNE ATK 4100 DEF 1200
IT STEALS THE ATK AND DEF OF THE SACRIFICED LION ALLIGATOR AND SPAWN ALLIGATOR!
ON TOP OF THAT, THIS TYRANT ALSO PLUNDERS THE EFFECT OF ONE OF THE SACRIFICED MONSTERS!!
SPAWN ALLIGATOR
★★★★★
This card can be summoned by sacrificing one alligator monster. The sacrificed alligator is Special-Summoned at the end of the phase.
ATK 2200 DEF 1000
NEPTUNE GAINS SPAWN ALLIGATOR'S EFFECT!!

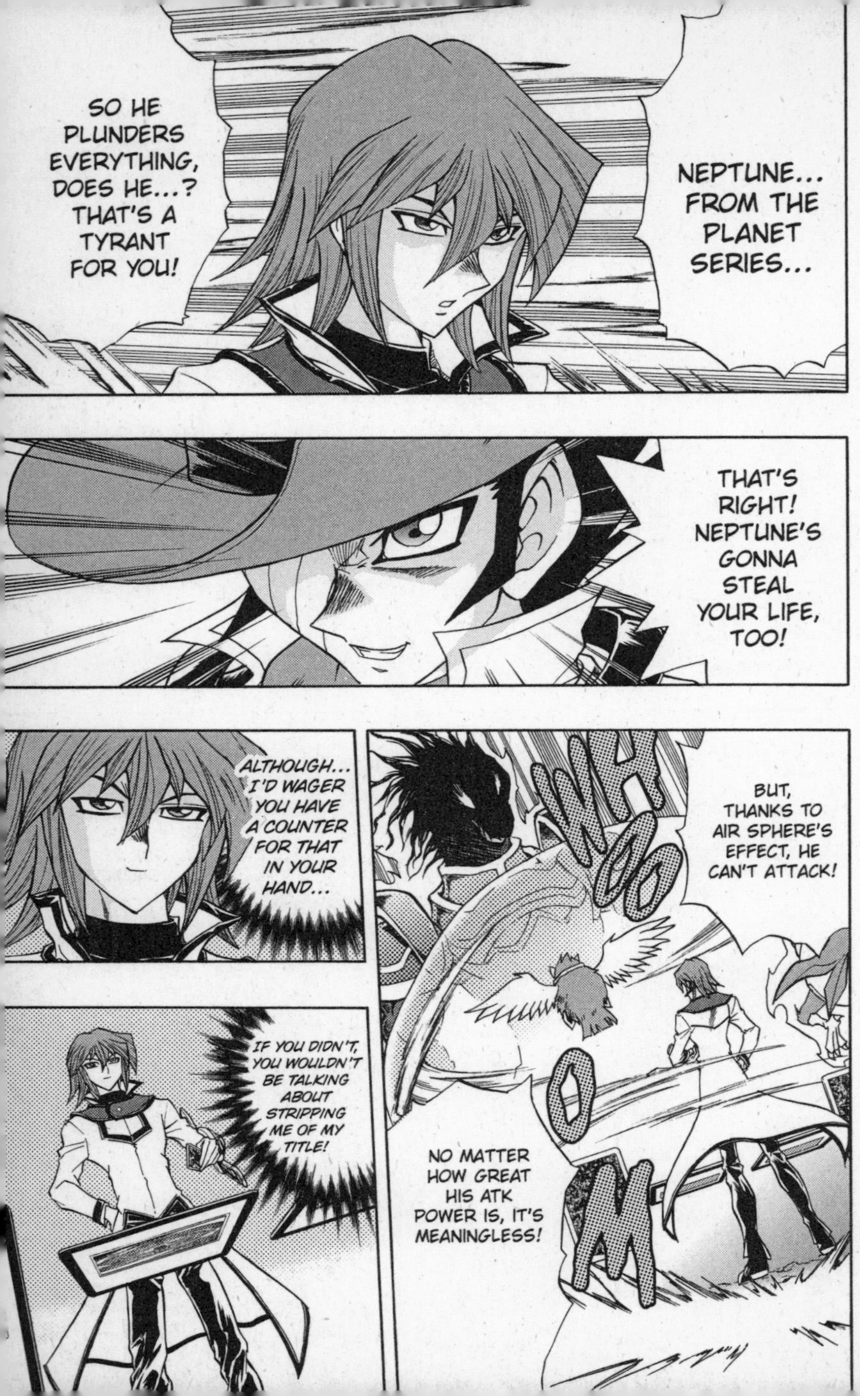
NEPTUNE... FROM THE PLANET SERIES...
SO HE PLUNDERS EVERYTHING, DOES HE...? THAT'S A TYRANT FOR YOU!
THAT'S RIGHT! NEPTUNE'S GONNA STEAL YOUR LIFE, TOO!
BUT, THANKS TO AIR SPHERE'S EFFECT, HE CAN'T ATTACK!
WHOOOM
NO MATTER HOW GREAT HIS ATK POWER IS, IT'S MEANINGLESS!
ALTHOUGH... I'D WAGER YOU HAVE A COUNTER FOR THAT IN YOUR HAND...
IF YOU DIDN'T, YOU WOULDN'T BE TALKING ABOUT STRIPPING ME OF MY TITLE!

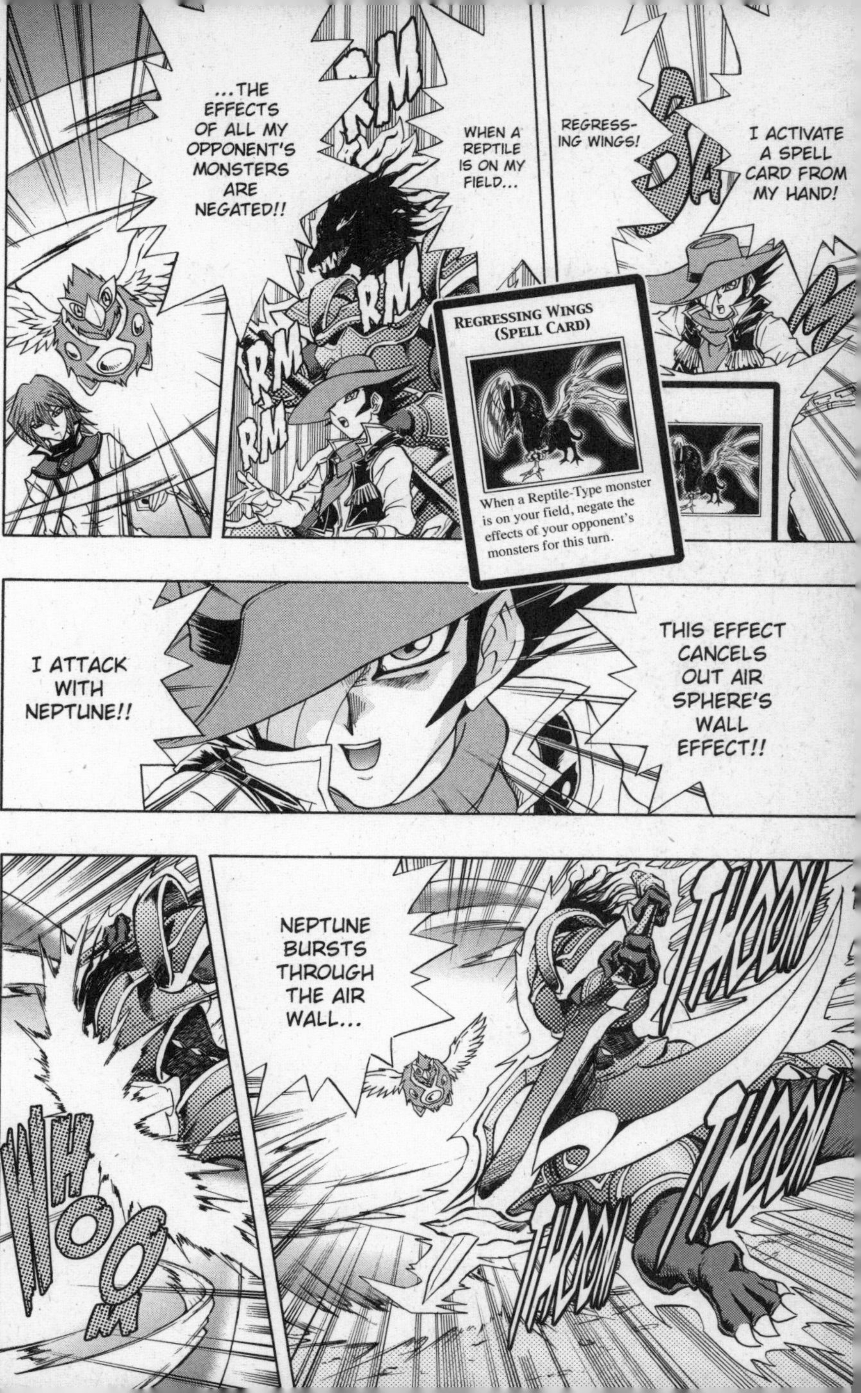
I ACTIVATE A SPELL CARD FROM MY HAND!
REGRESSING WINGS!
WHEN A REPTILE IS ON MY FIELD...
...THE EFFECTS OF ALL MY OPPONENT'S MONSTERS ARE NEGATED!!
REGRESSING WINGS (SPELL CARD)
When a Reptile-Type monster is on your field, negate the effects of your opponent's monsters for this turn.
THIS EFFECT CANCELS OUT AIR SPHERE'S WALL EFFECT!!
I ATTACK WITH NEPTUNE!!
NEPTUNE BURSTS THROUGH THE AIR WALL...
THOOM
THOOM
THOOM

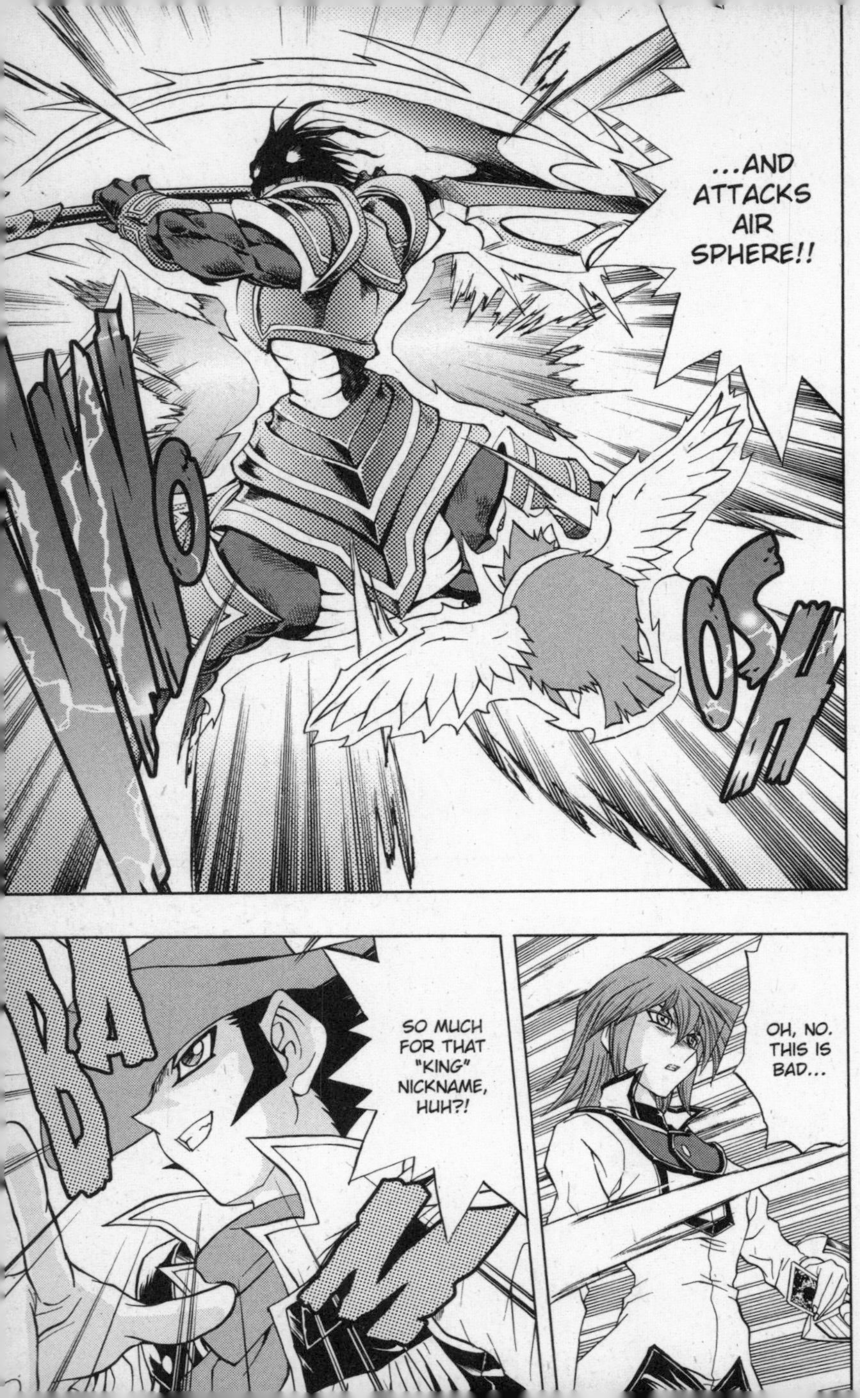
...AND ATTACKS AIR SPHERE!!
OH, NO. THIS IS BAD...
SO MUCH FOR THAT "KING" NICKNAME, HUH?!

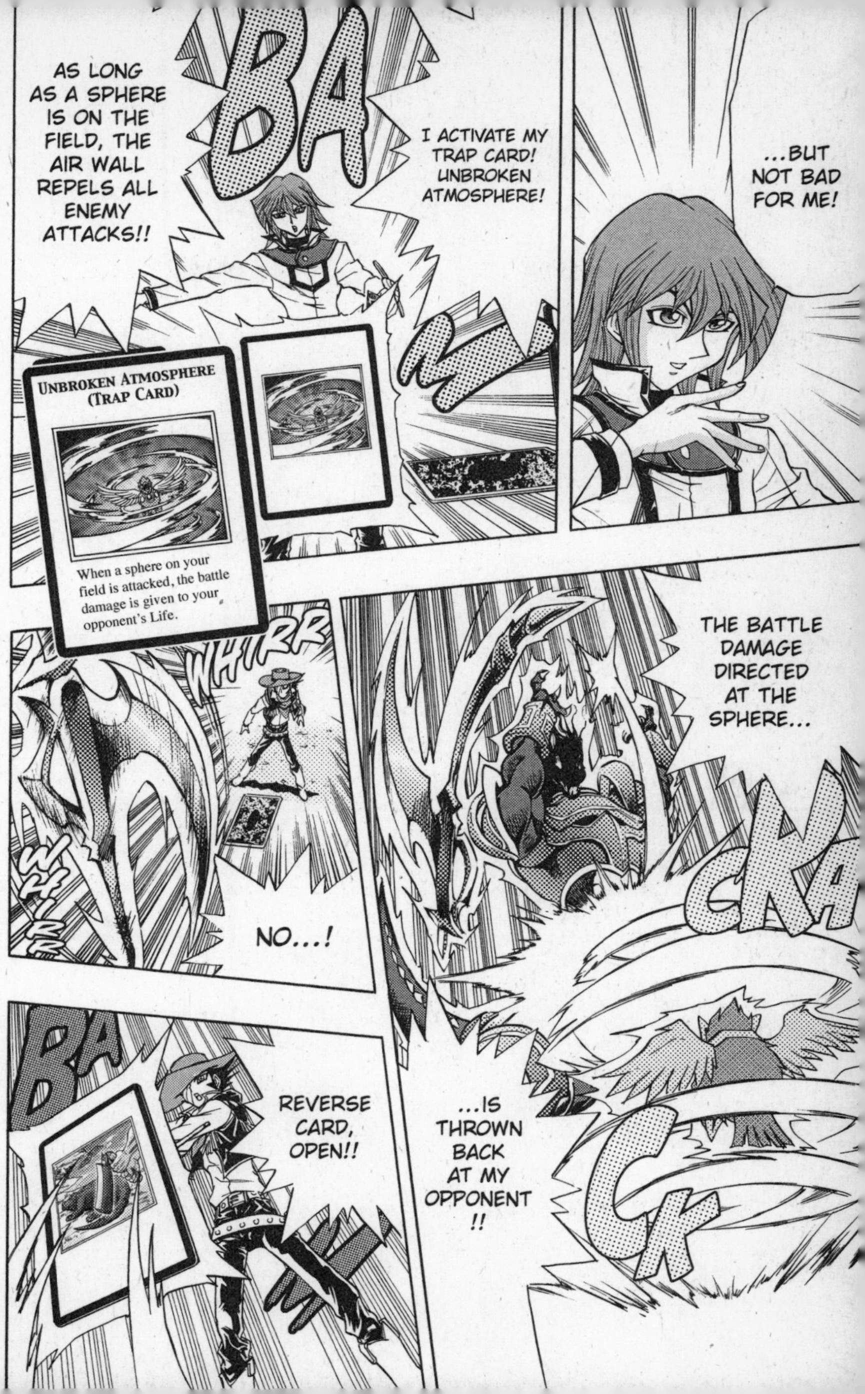
...BUT NOT BAD FOR ME!
MY
BA
I ACTIVATE MY TRAP CARD! UNBROKEN ATMOSPHERE!
AS LONG AS A SPHERE IS ON THE FIELD, THE AIR WALL REPELS ALL ENEMY ATTACKS!!
UNBROKEN ATMOSPHERE (TRAP CARD)
When a sphere on your field is attacked, the battle damage is given to your opponent's Life.
THE BATTLE DAMAGE DIRECTED AT THE SPHERE...
CKA
...IS THROWN BACK AT MY OPPONENT!!
CK
WHIRR
NO...!
WHIRR
BA
REVERSE CARD, OPEN!!

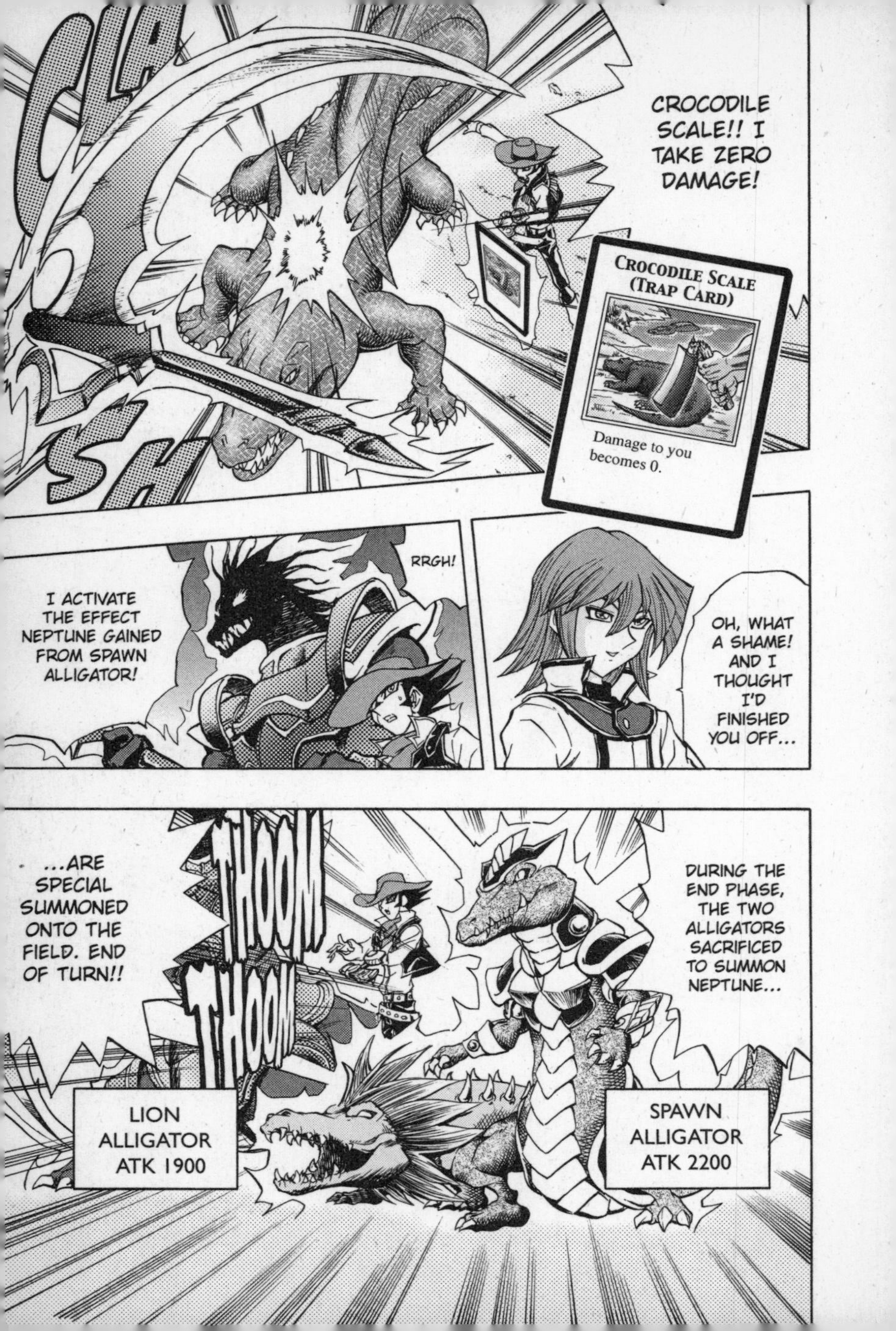
CLASH
CROCODILE SCALE!! I TAKE ZERO DAMAGE!
Crocodile Scale (Trap Card)
Damage to you becomes 0.
OH, WHAT A SHAME! AND I THOUGHT I'D FINISHED YOU OFF...
RRGH!
I ACTIVATE THE EFFECT NEPTUNE GAINED FROM SPAWN ALLIGATOR!
DURING THE END PHASE, THE TWO ALLIGATORS SACRIFICED TO SUMMON NEPTUNE...
THOOM
THOOM
...ARE SPECIAL SUMMONED ONTO THE FIELD. END OF TURN!!
SPAWN ALLIGATOR ATK 2200
LION ALLIGATOR ATK 1900

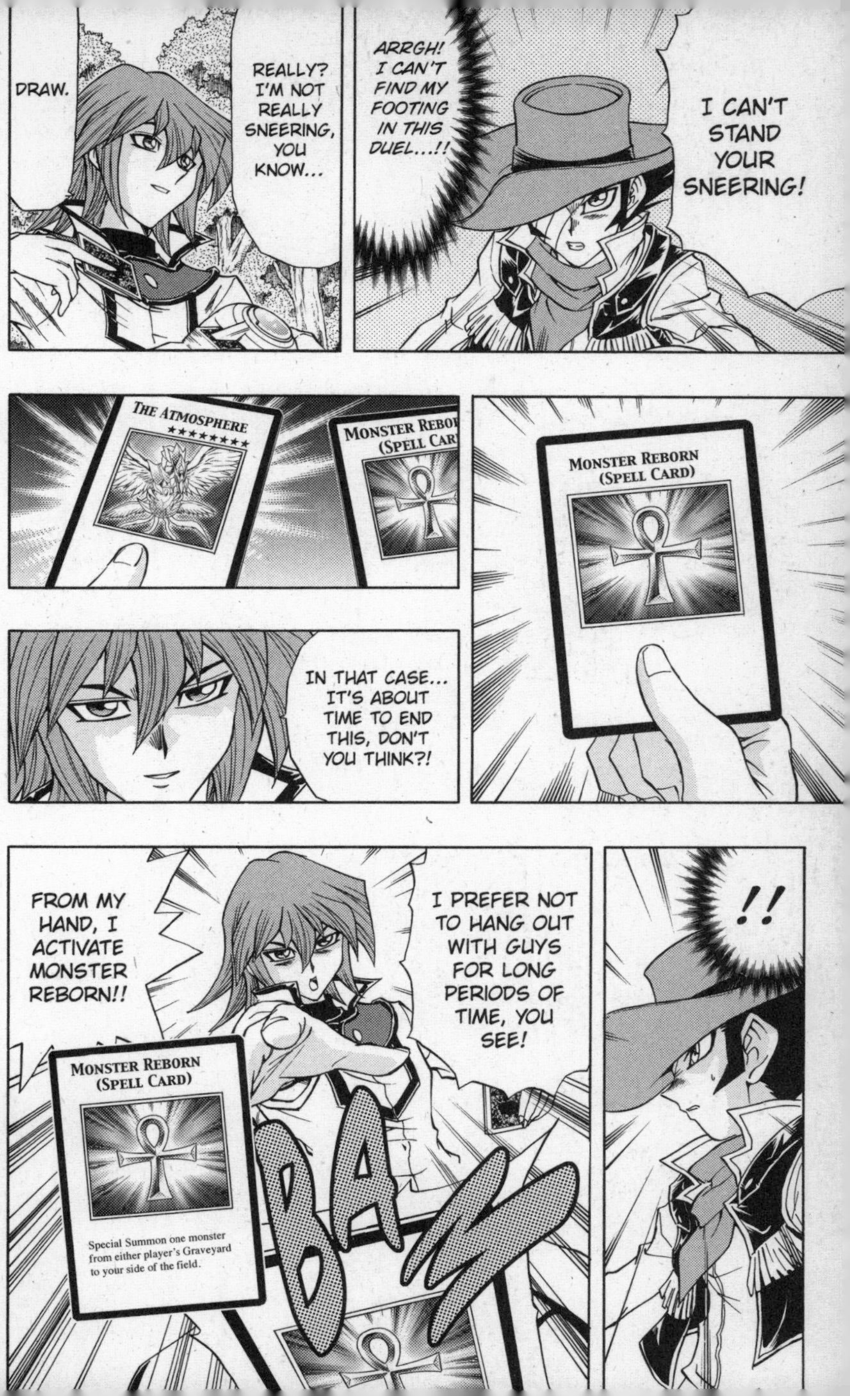
I CAN'T STAND YOUR SNEERING!
ARRGH! I CAN'T FIND MY FOOTING IN THIS DUEL...!!
REALLY? I'M NOT REALLY SNEERING, YOU KNOW...
DRAW.
MONSTER REBORN (SPELL CARD)
THE ATMOSPHERE
MONSTER REBOR (SPELL CAR
IN THAT CASE... IT'S ABOUT TIME TO END THIS, DON'T YOU THINK?!
!!
I PREFER NOT TO HANG OUT WITH GUYS FOR LONG PERIODS OF TIME, YOU SEE!
FROM MY HAND, I ACTIVATE MONSTER REBORN!!
MONSTER REBORN (SPELL CARD)
Special Summon one monster from either player's Graveyard to your side of the field.

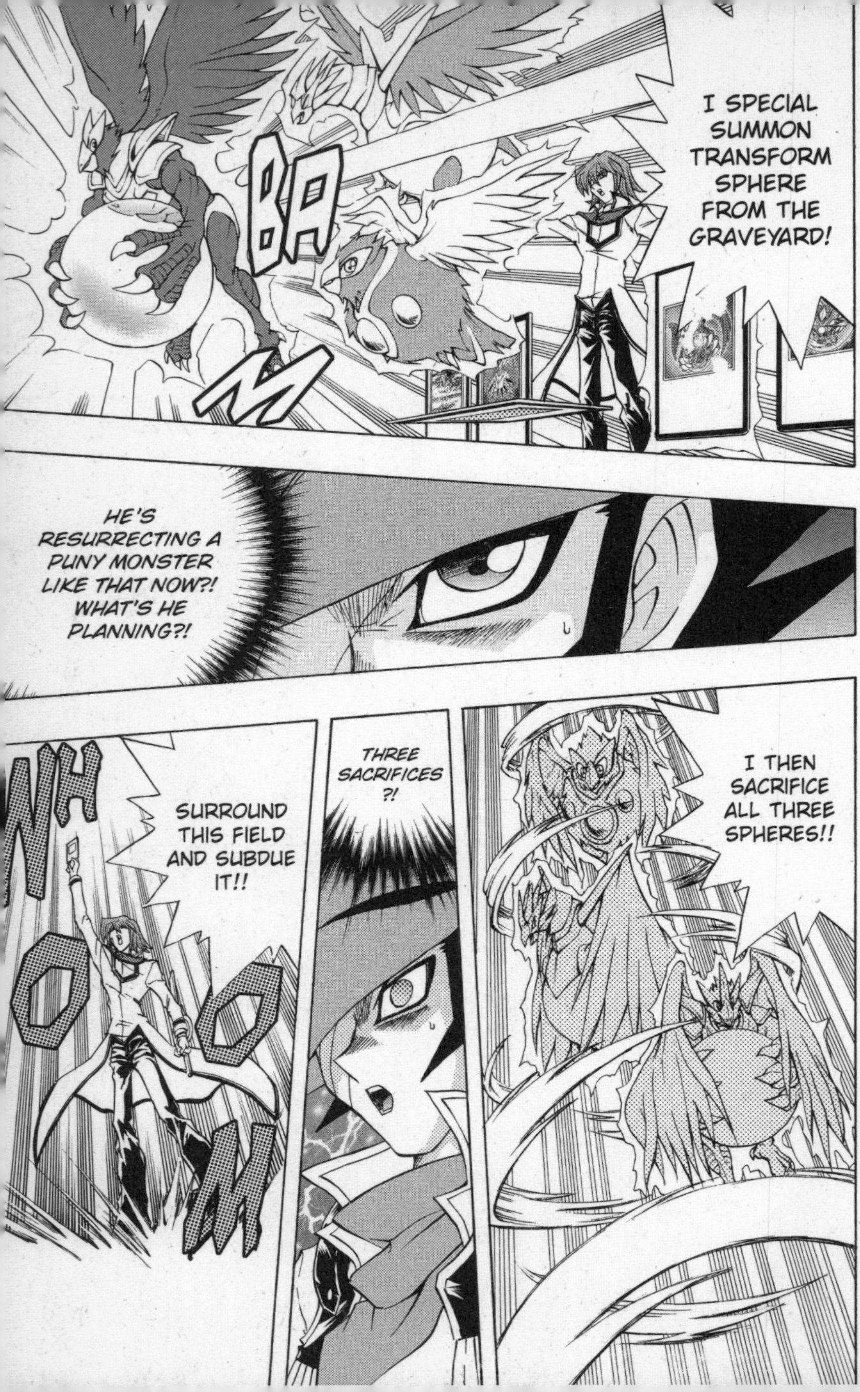
I SPECIAL SUMMON TRANSFORM SPHERE FROM THE GRAVEYARD!
BAM
HE'S RESURRECTING A PUNY MONSTER LIKE THAT NOW?! WHAT'S HE PLANNING?!
I THEN SACRIFICE ALL THREE SPHERES!!
THREE SACRIFICES ?!
SURROUND THIS FIELD AND SUBDUE IT!!
WHOOM

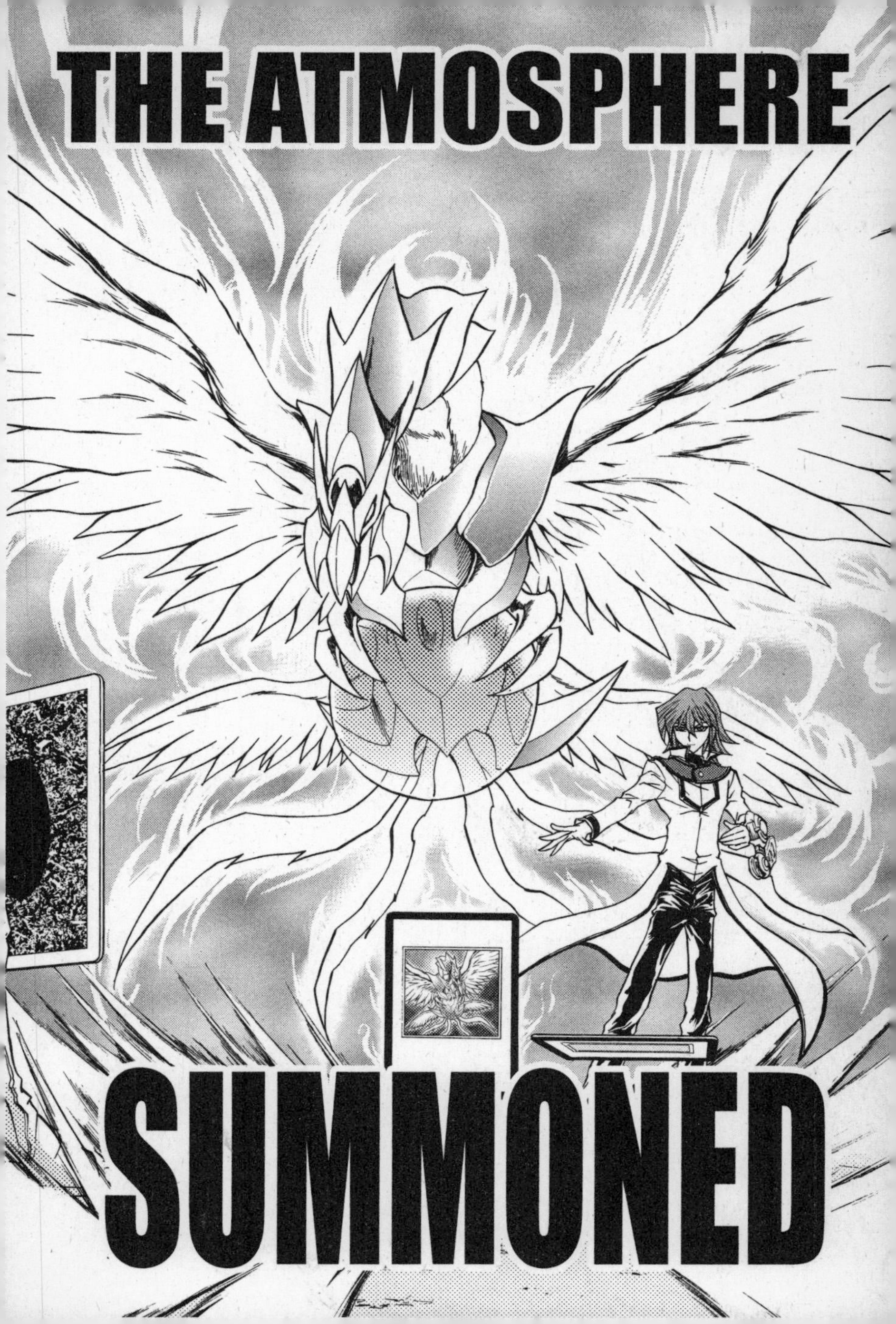
THE ATMOSPHERE
SUMMONED

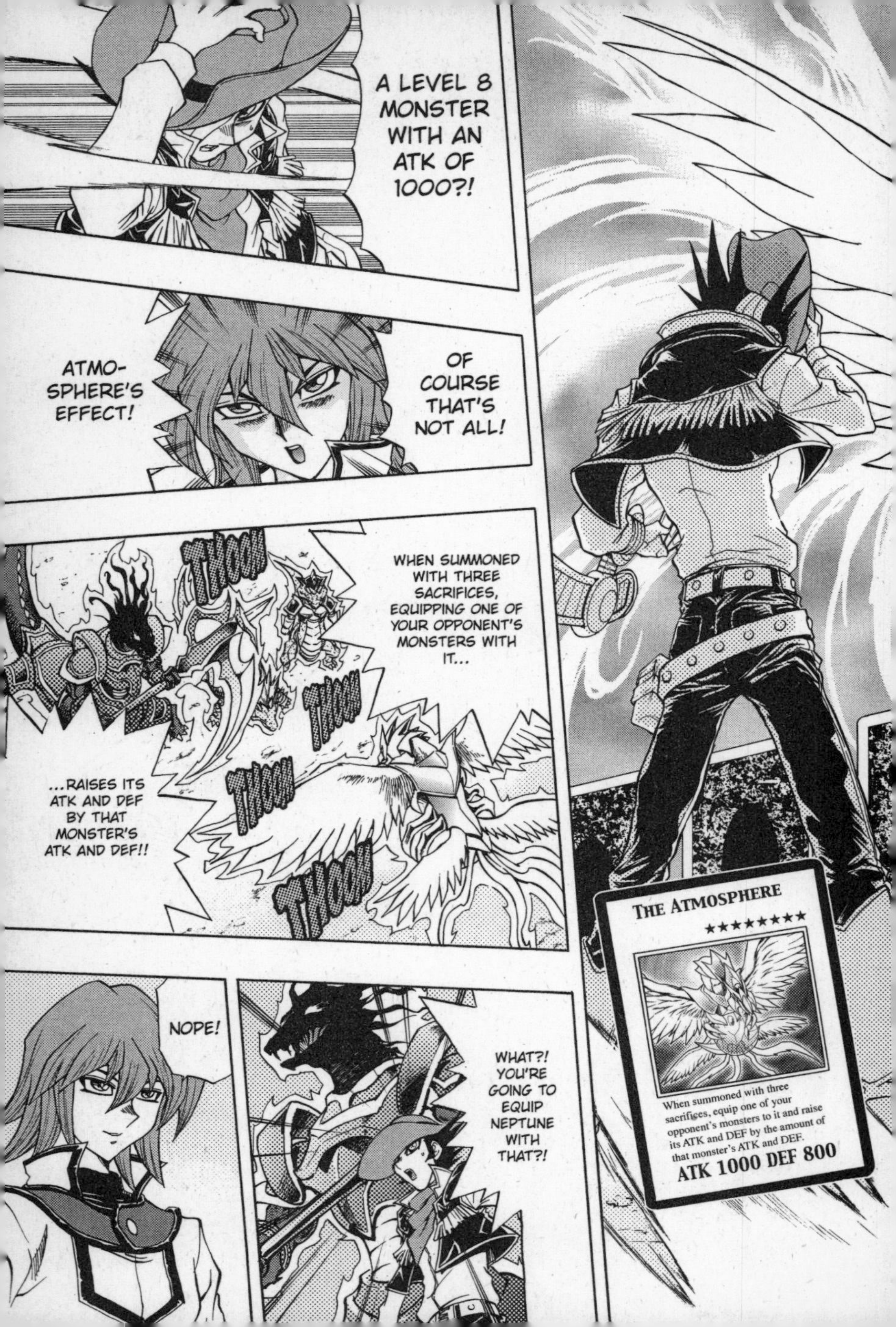
THE ATMOSPHERE
★★★★★★★★
When summoned with three sacrifices, equip one of your opponent's monsters to it and raise its ATK and DEF by the amount of that monster's ATK and DEF.
ATK 1000 DEF 800
A LEVEL 8 MONSTER WITH AN ATK OF 1000?!
OF COURSE THAT'S NOT ALL!
ATMO-SPHERE'S EFFECT!
THOOM
WHEN SUMMONED WITH THREE SACRIFICES, EQUIPPING ONE OF YOUR OPPONENT'S MONSTERS WITH IT...
THOOM
THOOM
...RAISES ITS ATK AND DEF BY THAT MONSTER'S ATK AND DEF!!
THOOM
WHAT?! YOU'RE GOING TO EQUIP NEPTUNE WITH THAT?!
NOPE!

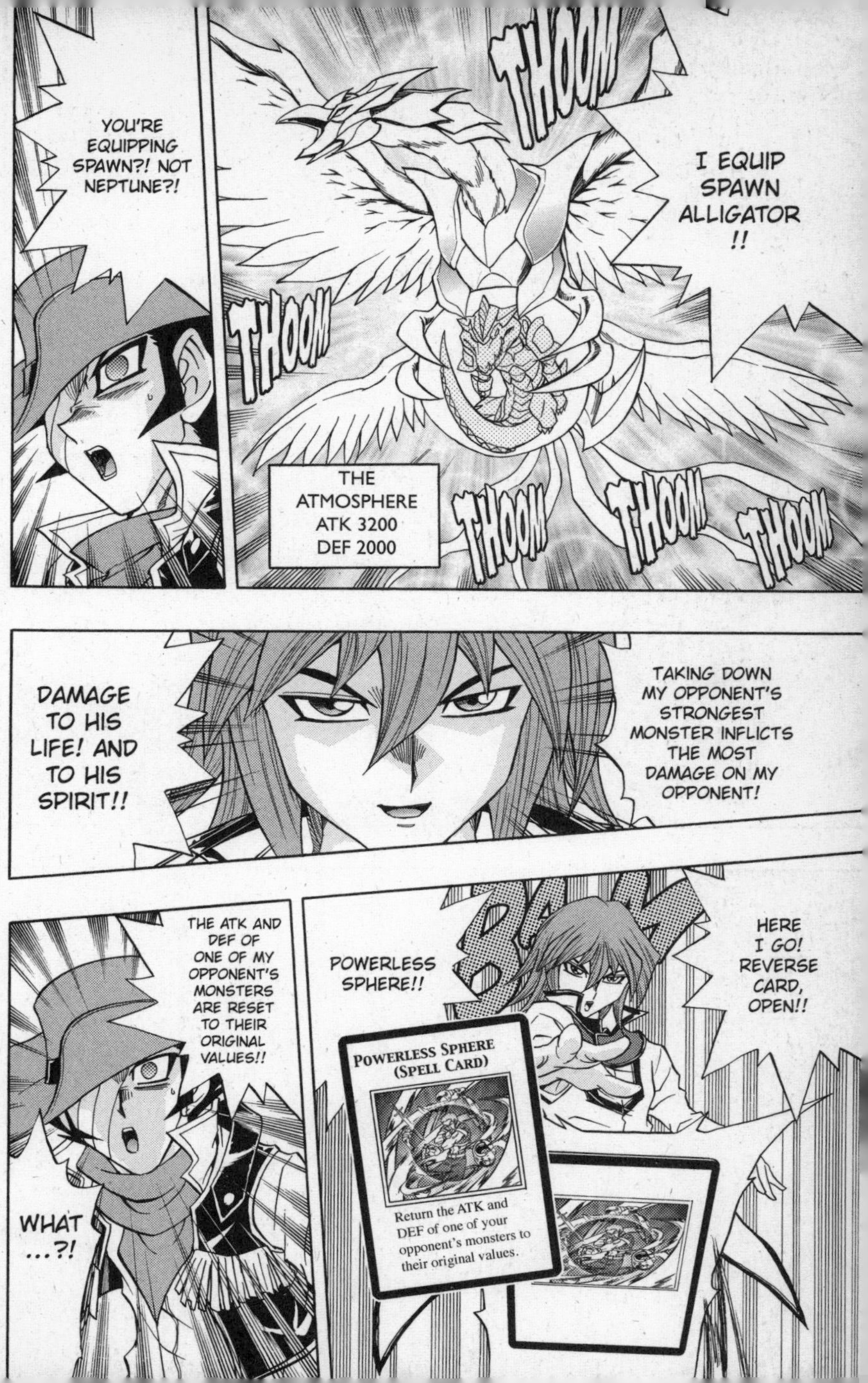
THOOM
I EQUIP SPAWN ALLIGATOR !!
THOOM
THE ATMOSPHERE ATK 3200 DEF 2000
THOOM
THOOM
THOOM
YOU'RE EQUIPPING SPAWN?! NOT NEPTUNE?!
TAKING DOWN MY OPPONENT'S STRONGEST MONSTER INFLICTS THE MOST DAMAGE ON MY OPPONENT!
DAMAGE TO HIS LIFE! AND TO HIS SPIRIT!!
HERE I GO! REVERSE CARD, OPEN!!
POWERLESS SPHERE!!
POWERLESS SPHERE (SPELL CARD)
Return the ATK and DEF of one of your opponent's monsters to their original values.
THE ATK AND DEF OF ONE OF MY OPPONENT'S MONSTERS ARE RESET TO THEIR ORIGINAL VALUES!!
WHAT ...?!

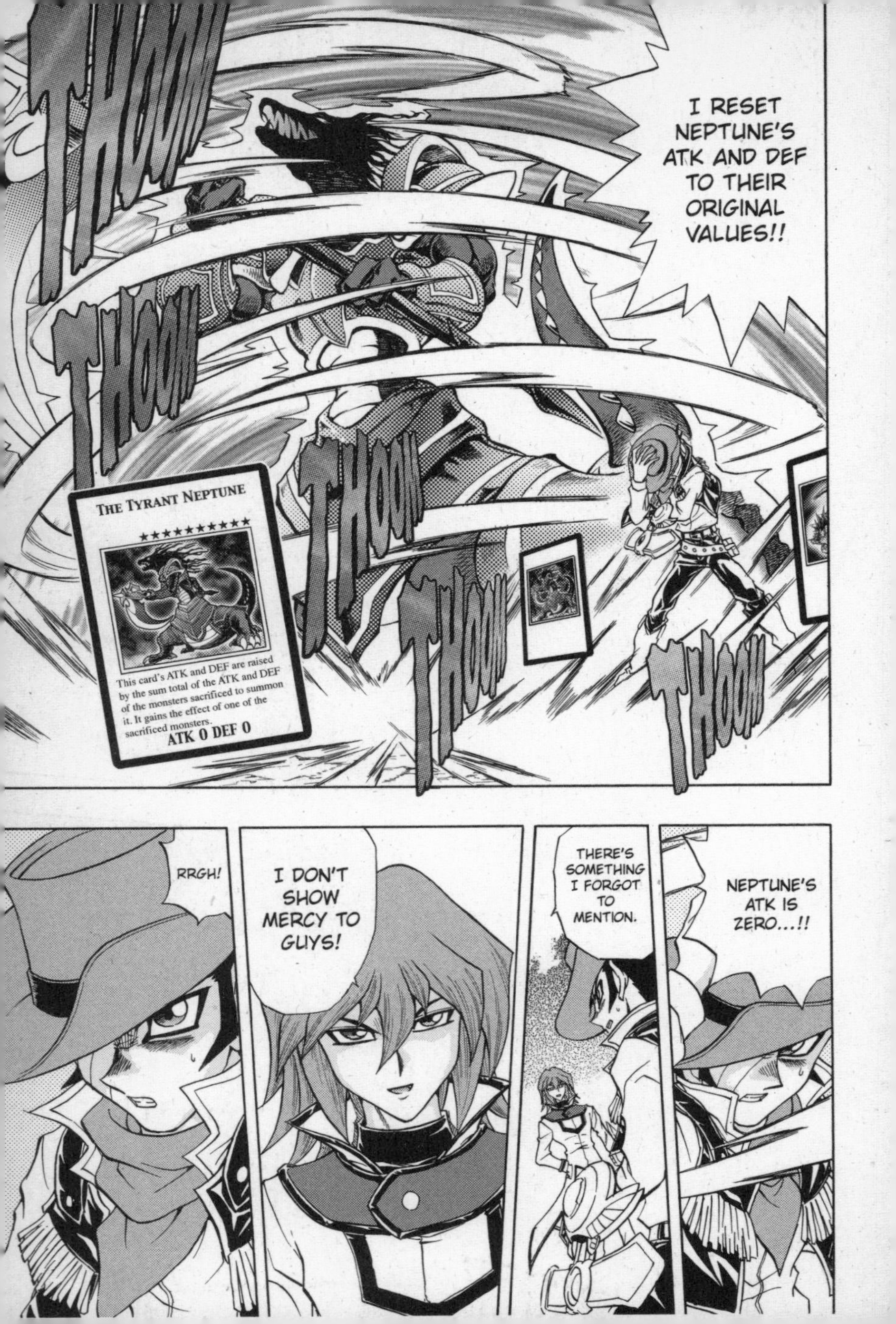
I RESET NEPTUNE'S ATK AND DEF TO THEIR ORIGINAL VALUES!!
THOOM
THOOM
THOOM
THOOM
THOOM
THOOM
THE TYRANT NEPTUNE
This card's ATK and DEF are raised by the sum total of the ATK and DEF of the monsters sacrificed to summon it. It gains the effect of one of the sacrificed monsters.
ATK 0 DEF 0
NEPTUNE'S ATK IS ZERO...!!
THERE'S SOMETHING I FORGOT TO MENTION.
I DON'T SHOW MERCY TO GUYS!
RRGH!

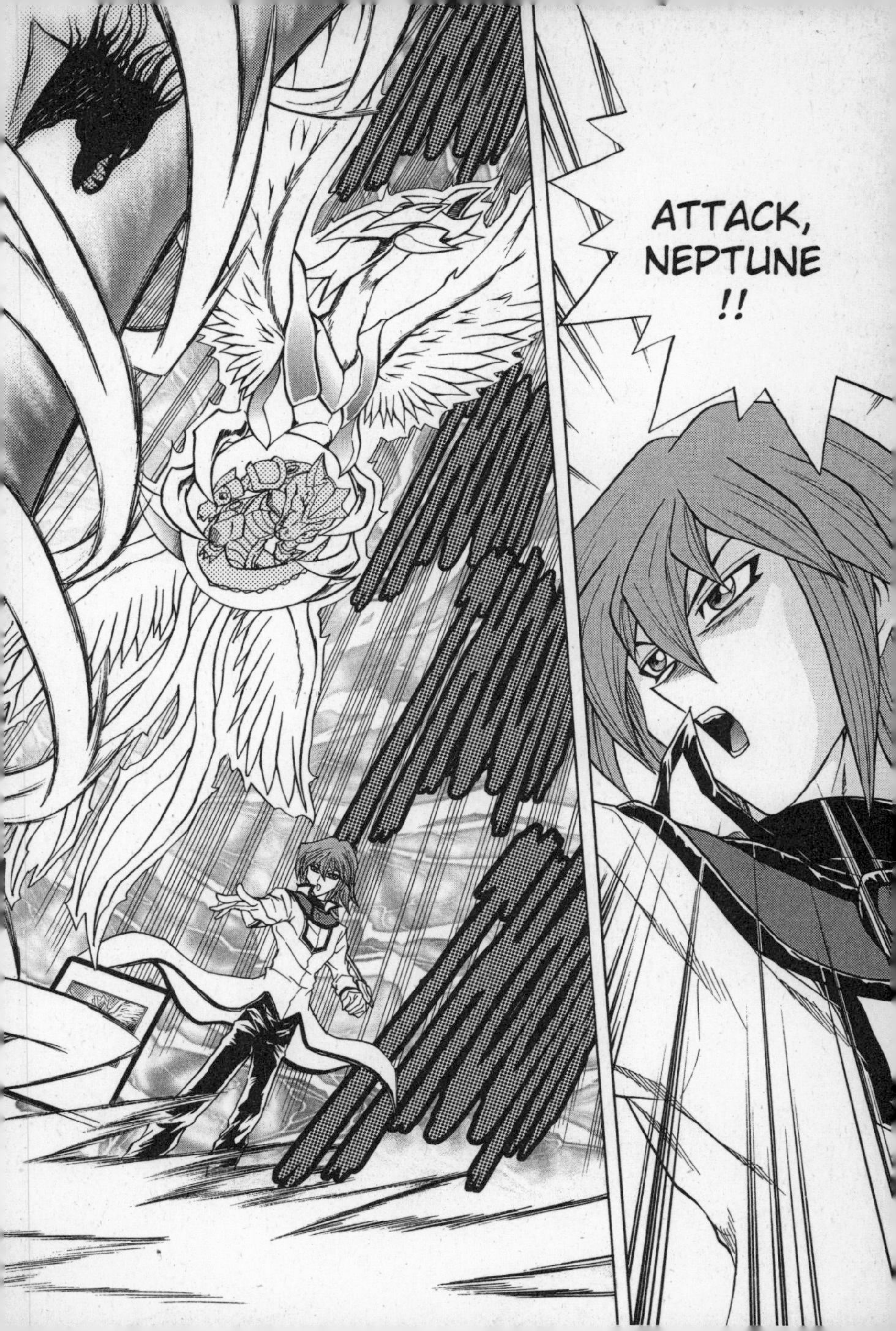
ATTACK, NEPTUNE !!

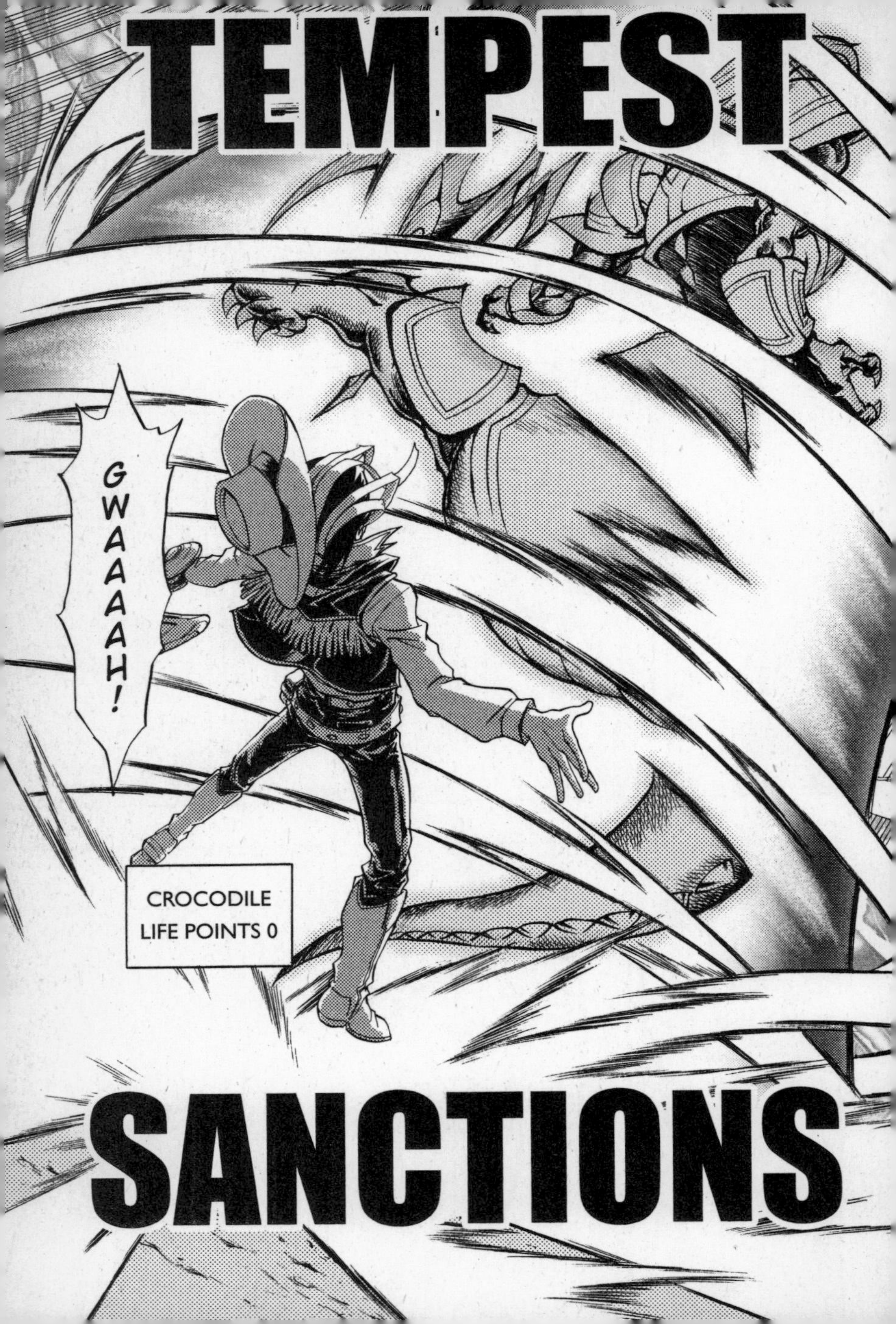
TEMPEST
GWAAAAAH!
CROCODILE
LIFE POINTS 0
SANCTIONS

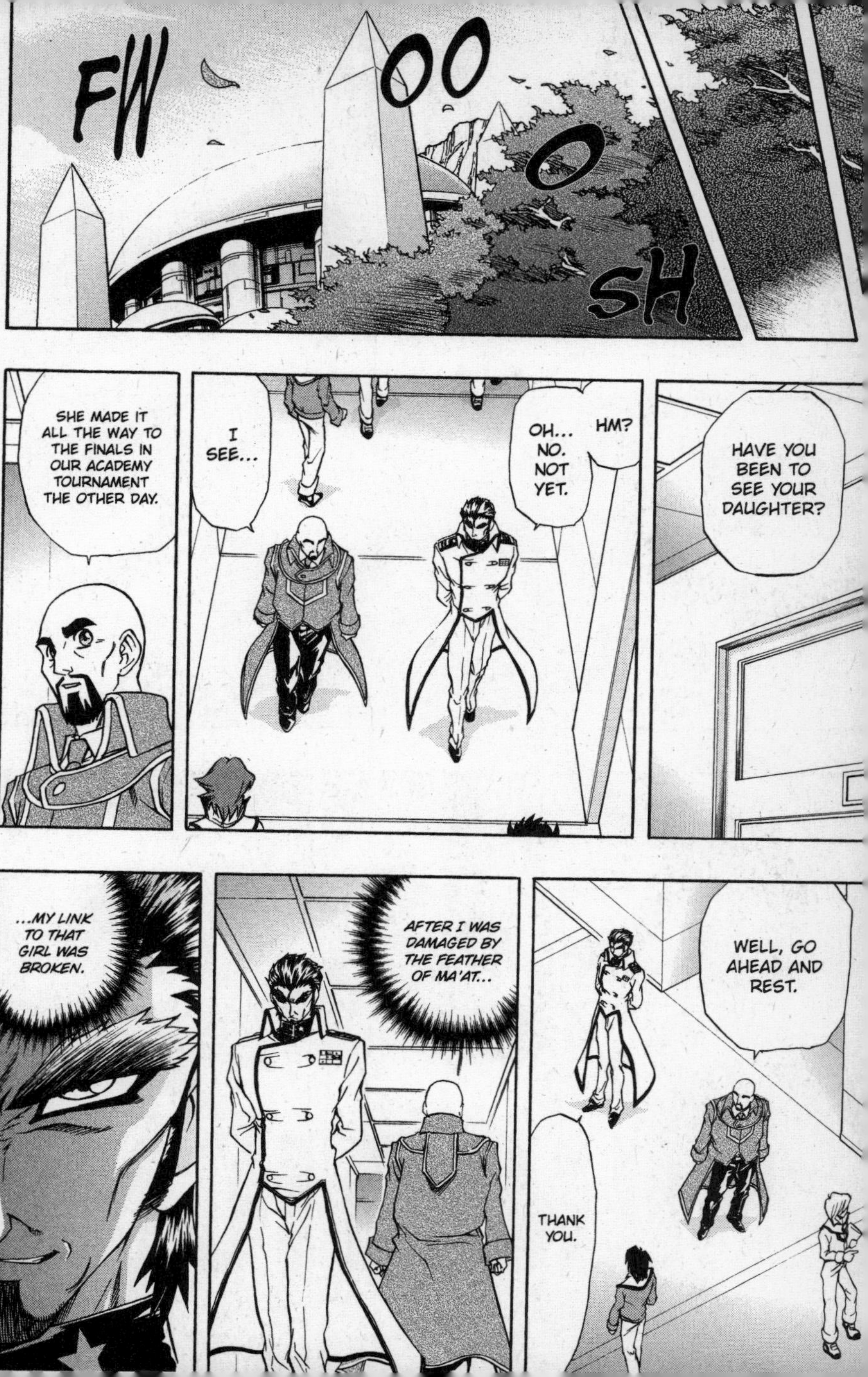
FWOOOSH
HAVE YOU BEEN TO SEE YOUR DAUGHTER?
HM?
OH... NO. NOT YET.
I SEE...
SHE MADE IT ALL THE WAY TO THE FINALS IN OUR ACADEMY TOURNAMENT THE OTHER DAY.
WELL, GO AHEAD AND REST.
THANK YOU.
AFTER I WAS DAMAGED BY THE FEATHER OF MA'AT...
...MY LINK TO THAT GIRL WAS BROKEN.

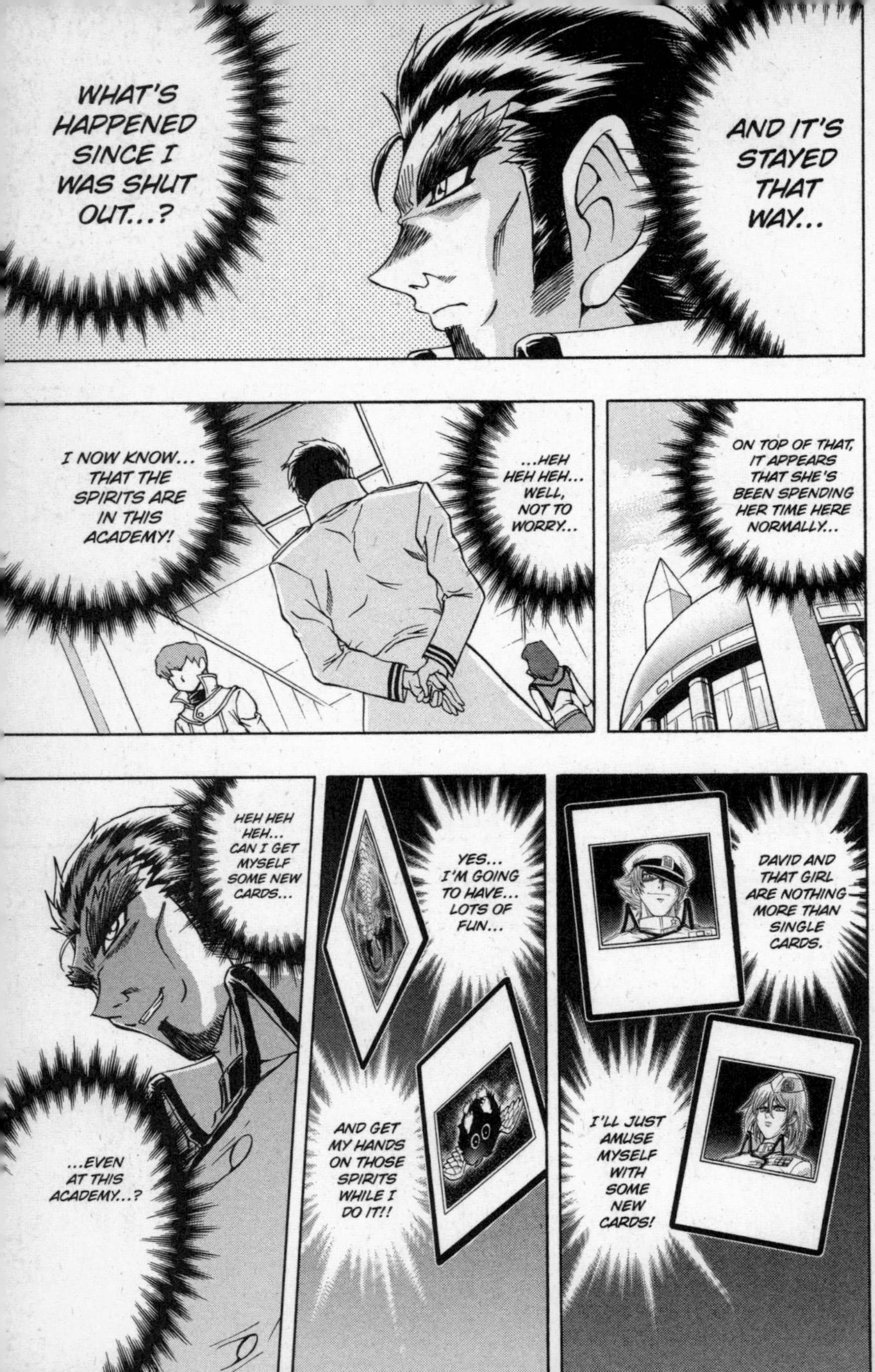
AND IT'S STAYED THAT WAY...
WHAT'S HAPPENED SINCE I WAS SHUT OUT...?
ON TOP OF THAT, IT APPEARS THAT SHE'S BEEN SPENDING HER TIME HERE NORMALLY...
...HEH HEH HEH... WELL, NOT TO WORRY...
I NOW KNOW... THAT THE SPIRITS ARE IN THIS ACADEMY!
DAVID AND THAT GIRL ARE NOTHING MORE THAN SINGLE CARDS.
I'LL JUST AMUSE MYSELF WITH SOME NEW CARDS!
YES... I'M GOING TO HAVE... LOTS OF FUN...
AND GET MY HANDS ON THOSE SPIRITS WHILE I DO IT!!
HEH HEH HEH... CAN I GET MYSELF SOME NEW CARDS...
...EVEN AT THIS ACADEMY...?

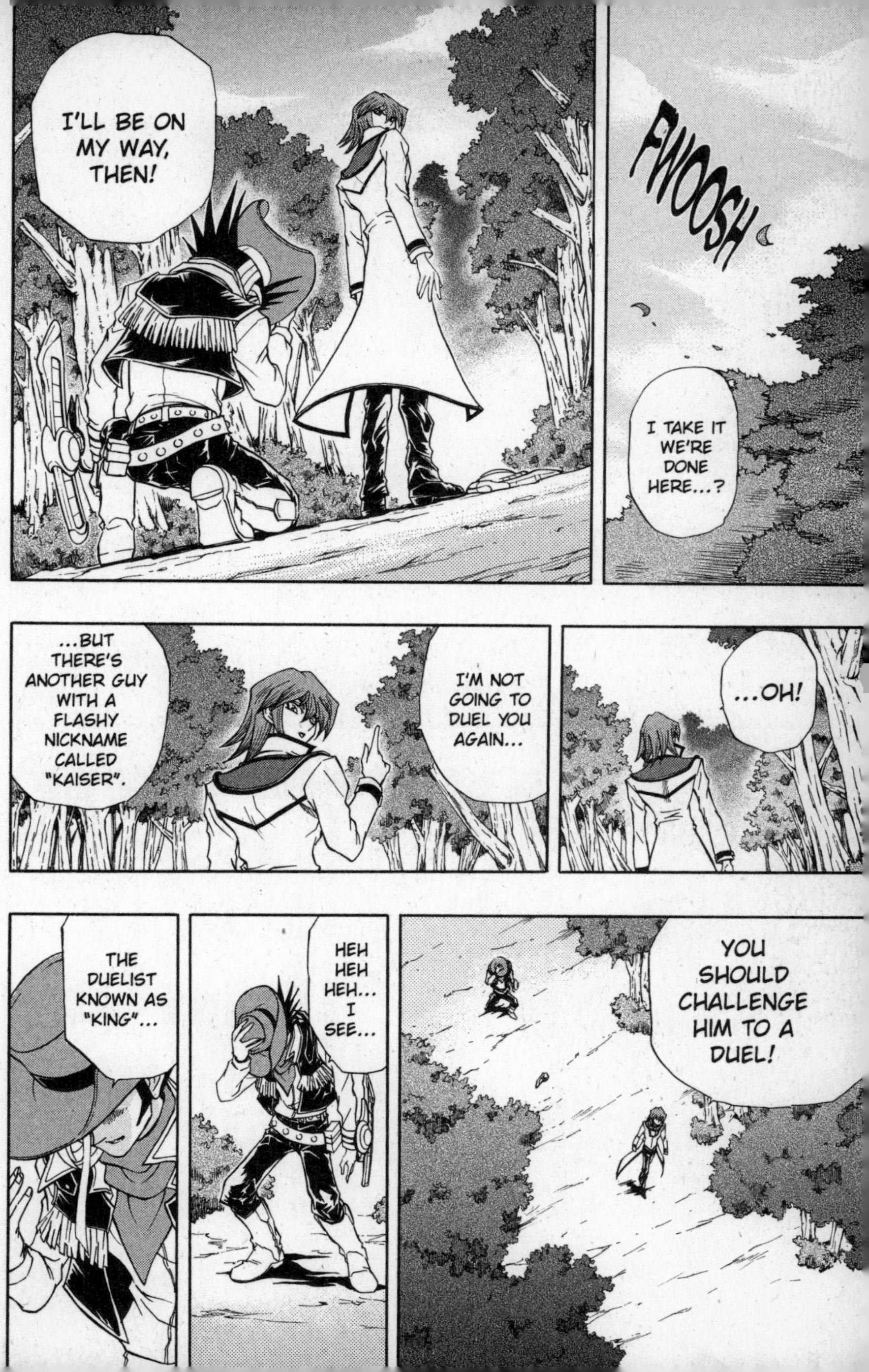
FWOOSH
I TAKE IT WE'RE DONE HERE...?
I'LL BE ON MY WAY, THEN!
...OH!
I'M NOT GOING TO DUEL YOU AGAIN...
...BUT THERE'S ANOTHER GUY WITH A FLASHY NICKNAME CALLED "KAISER".
YOU SHOULD CHALLENGE HIM TO A DUEL!
HEH HEH HEH... I SEE...
THE DUELIST KNOWN AS "KING"...

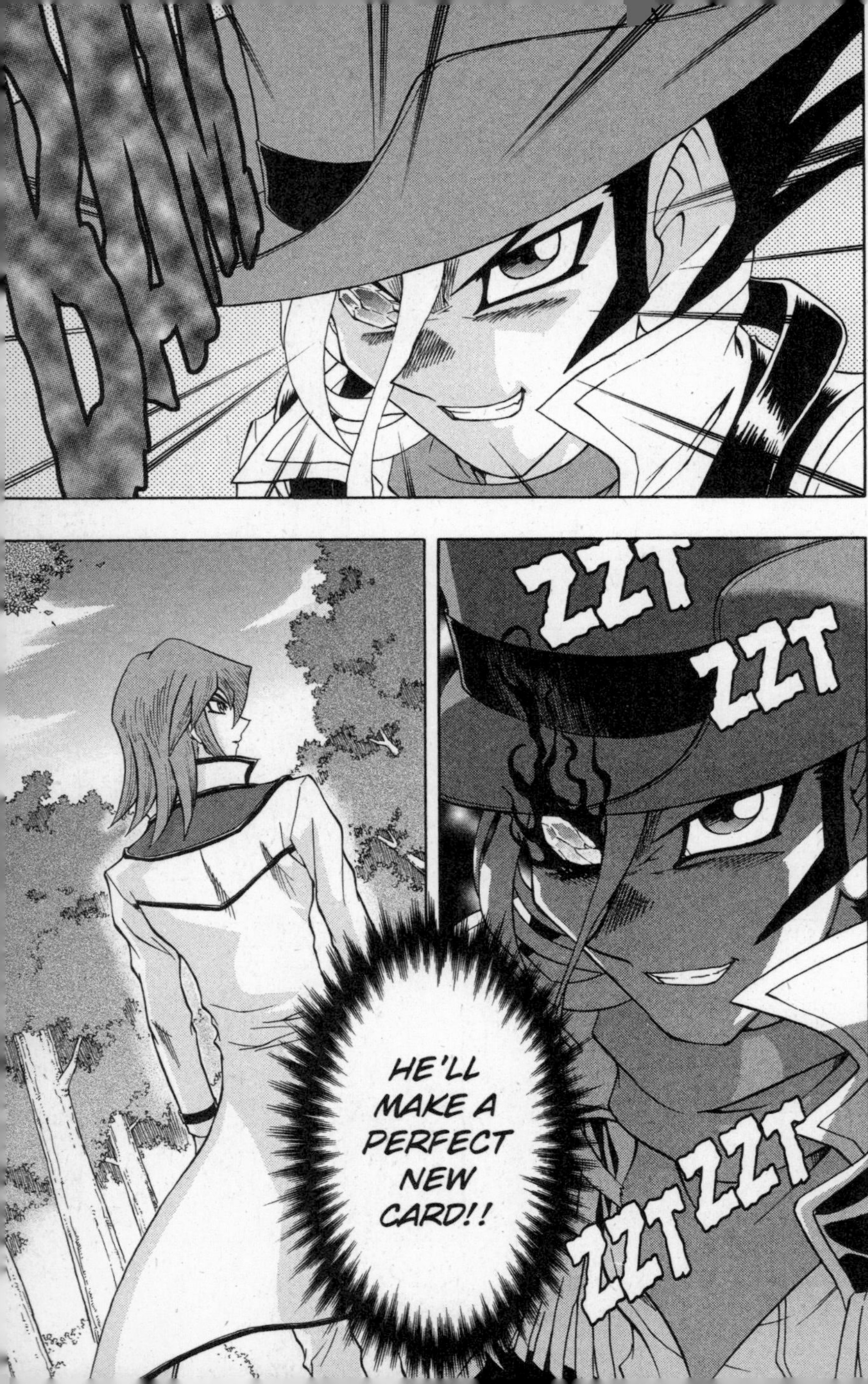
ZZT
ZZT
HE'LL MAKE A PERFECT NEW CARD!!
ZZT ZZT ZZT

THE YU-GI-OH! MOVIE
ONE DAY IN JANUARY, 2010.
I WENT TO THE PREVIEW OF THE FINISHED MOVIE, WHICH WAS HELD FOR THE PROJECT STAFF.
WHOA! WINGED KURIBOH LOOKS REAL!
MAN, WAS IT FUN...
MURMUR
3D IS AWE-SOME!
MURMUR
I DIDN'T THINK THEY'D JUMP OUT THAT FAR...
MR. TAKAHASHI SEEMED HAPPY WITH IT, TOO.
MURMUR
MURMUR
YOU WERE IN CHARGE OF THE PART WHERE YUGI DRAWS, WEREN'T YOU, MR. TAKAHASHI?!
KAZUKI
YES, THAT'S IT! I'M JUST GLAD I DIDN'T GET IN THE WAY OF MR. KAGAMI'S DRAWINGS...
YOU DREW TWO OR THREE CUTS, DIDN'T YOU?! WHERE WERE THEY?!
CHATTER
CHATTER
I'LL WATCH FOR THEM AT THE THEATER.
CHATTER
...
I DON'T KNOW WHAT THE OTHER ONES WERE...

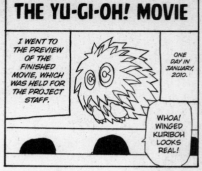

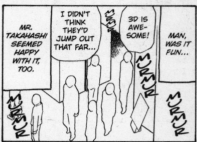

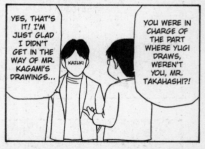

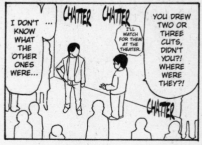

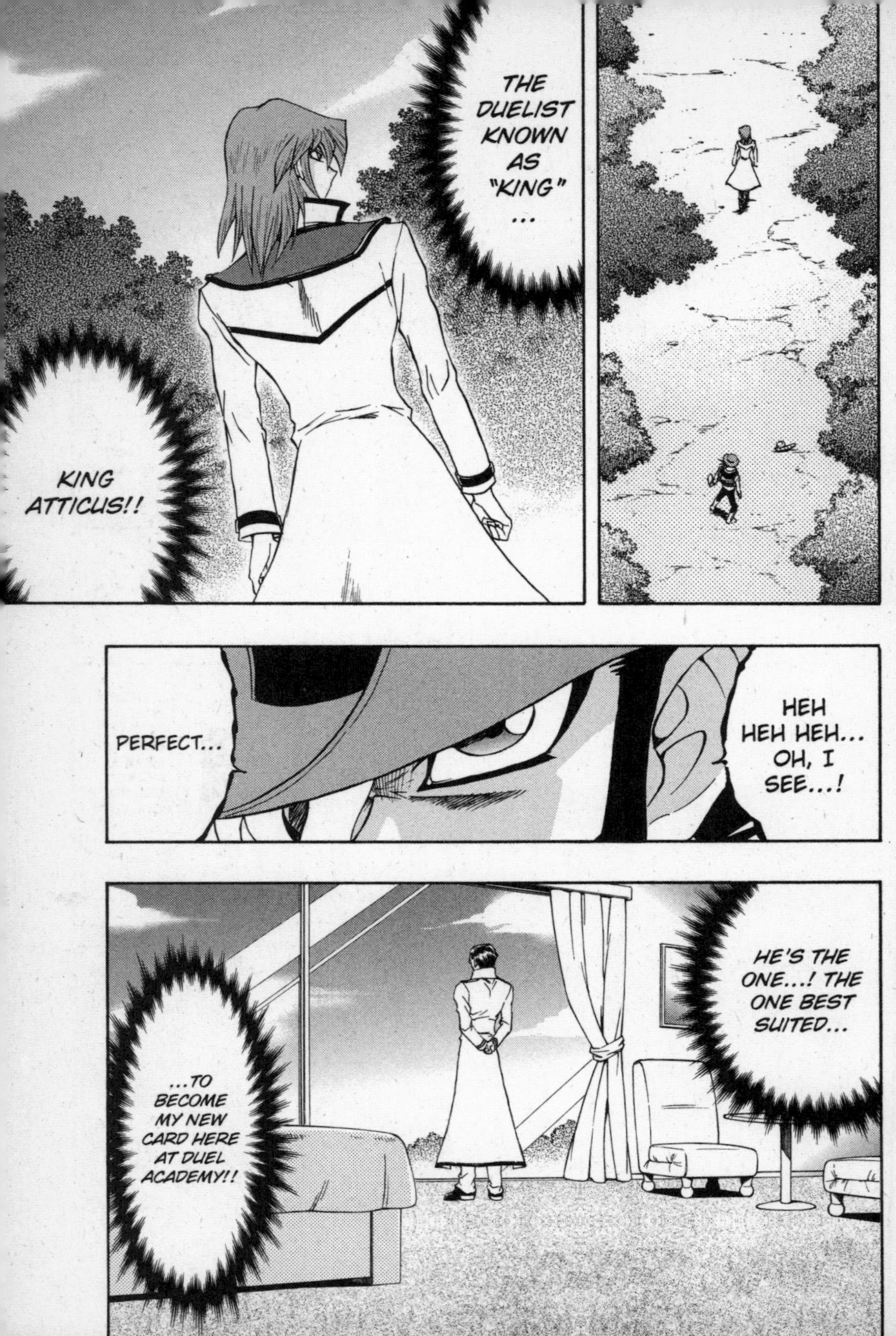
THE DUELIST KNOWN AS "KING" ...
KING ATTICUS!!
HEH HEH HEH... OH, I SEE...!
PERFECT...
HE'S THE ONE...! THE ONE BEST SUITED...
...TO BECOME MY NEW CARD HERE AT DUEL ACADEMY!!

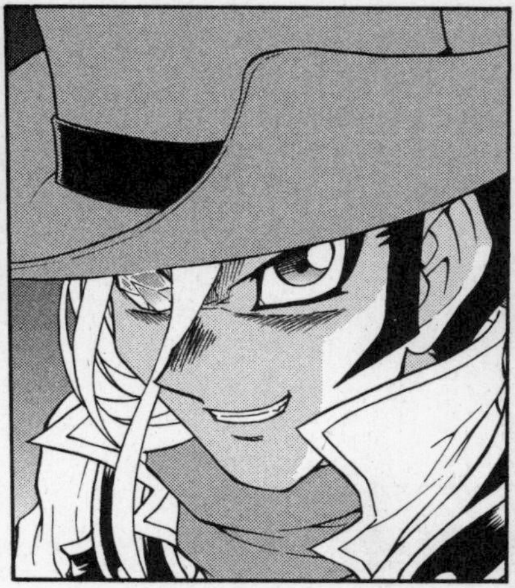

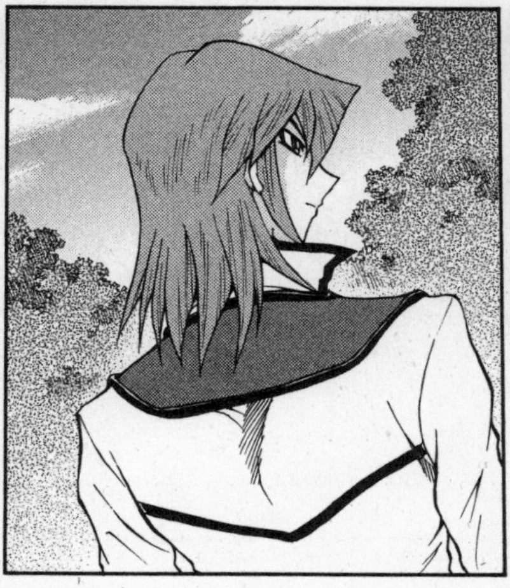

CHAPTER 46: TAG DUEL!!

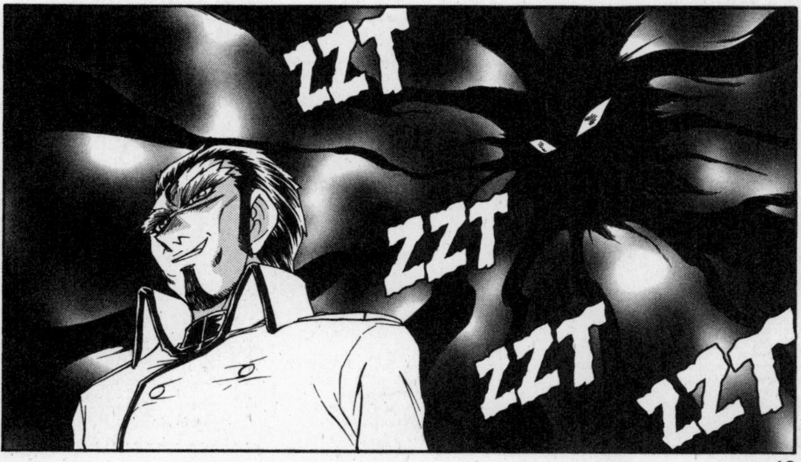
ZZT
ZZT
ZZT
ZZT

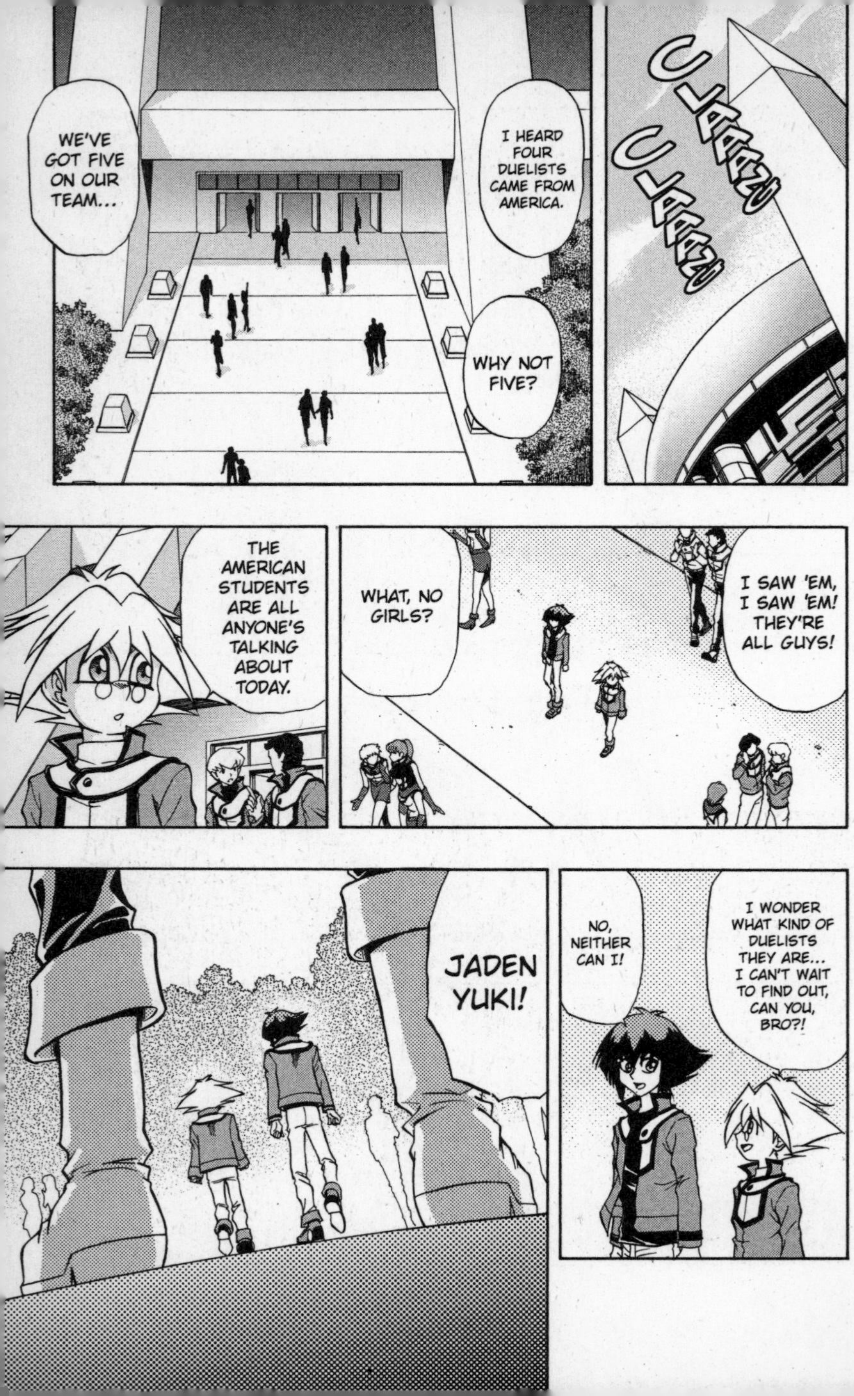
CLAAAZU
CLAAAZU
I HEARD FOUR DUELISTS CAME FROM AMERICA.
WHY NOT FIVE?
WE'VE GOT FIVE ON OUR TEAM...
I SAW 'EM, I SAW 'EM! THEY'RE ALL GUYS!
WHAT, NO GIRLS?
THE AMERICAN STUDENTS ARE ALL ANYONE'S TALKING ABOUT TODAY.
I WONDER WHAT KIND OF DUELISTS THEY ARE... I CAN'T WAIT TO FIND OUT, CAN YOU, BRO?!
NO, NEITHER CAN I!
JADEN YUKI!

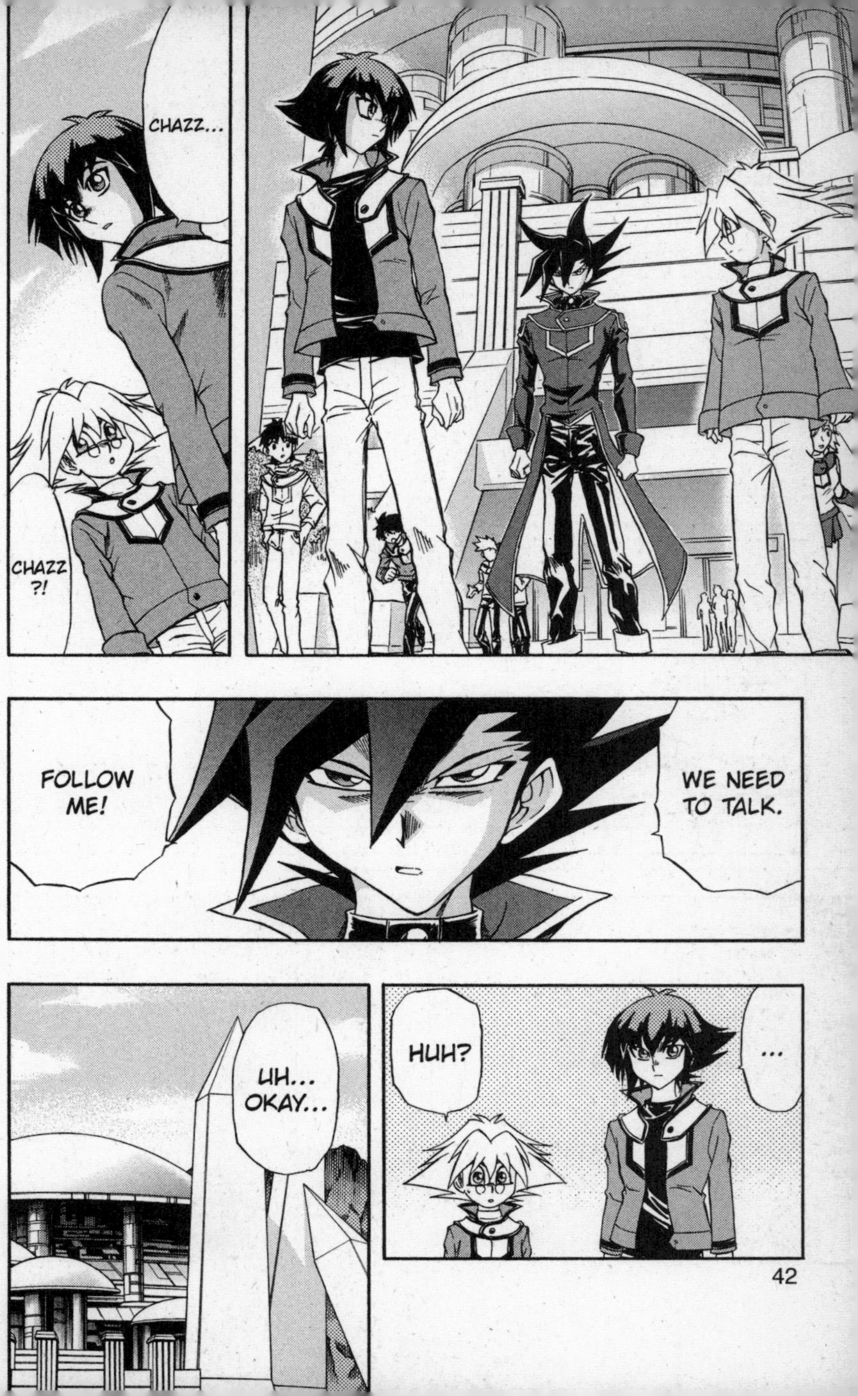
CHAZZ...
CHAZZ ?!
WE NEED TO TALK.
FOLLOW ME!
...
HUH?
UH... OKAY...

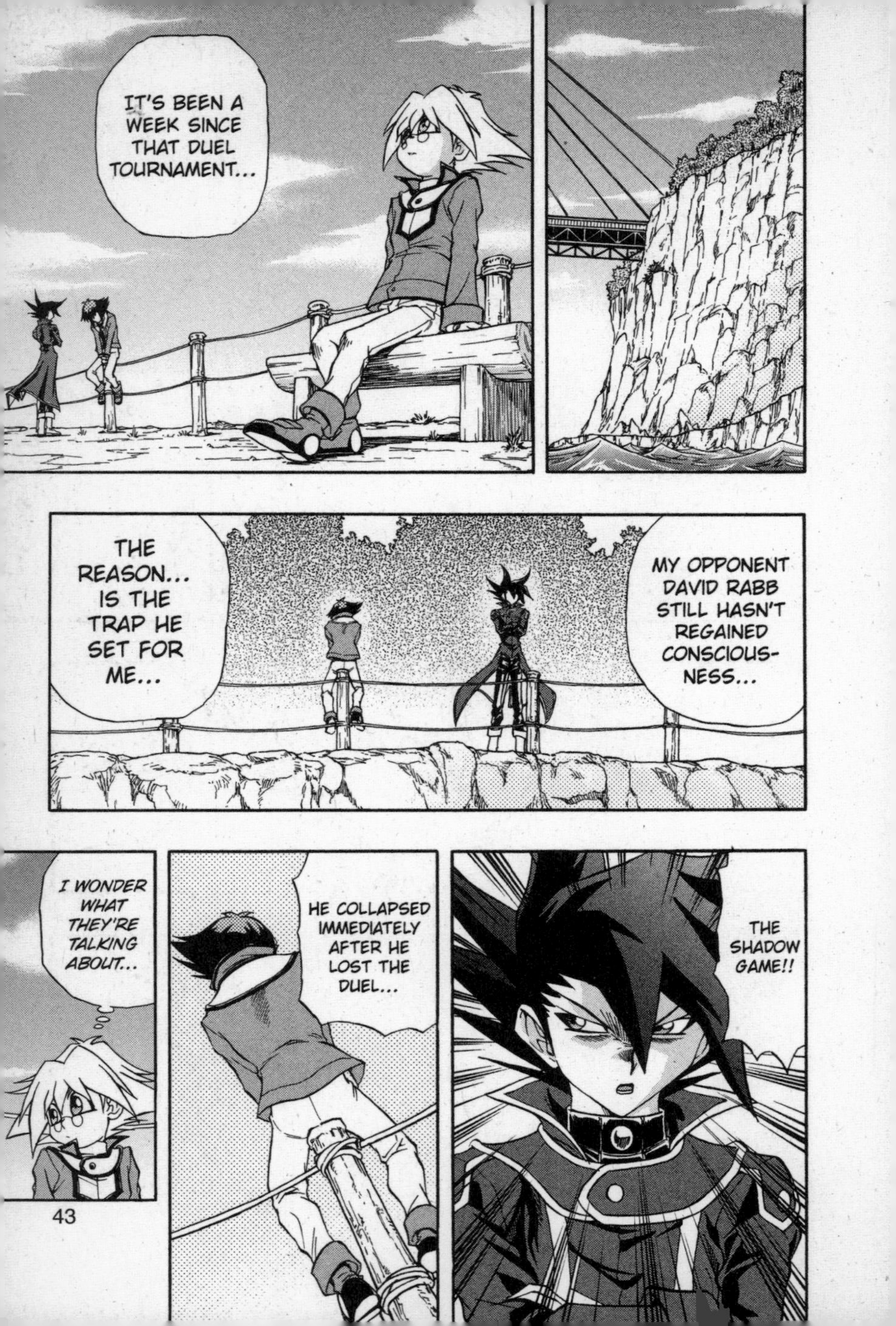
IT'S BEEN A WEEK SINCE THAT DUEL TOURNAMENT...
MY OPPONENT DAVID RABB STILL HASN'T REGAINED CONSCIOUS-NESS...
THE REASON... IS THE TRAP HE SET FOR ME...
THE SHADOW GAME!!
HE COLLAPSED IMMEDIATELY AFTER HE LOST THE DUEL...
I WONDER WHAT THEY'RE TALKING ABOUT...

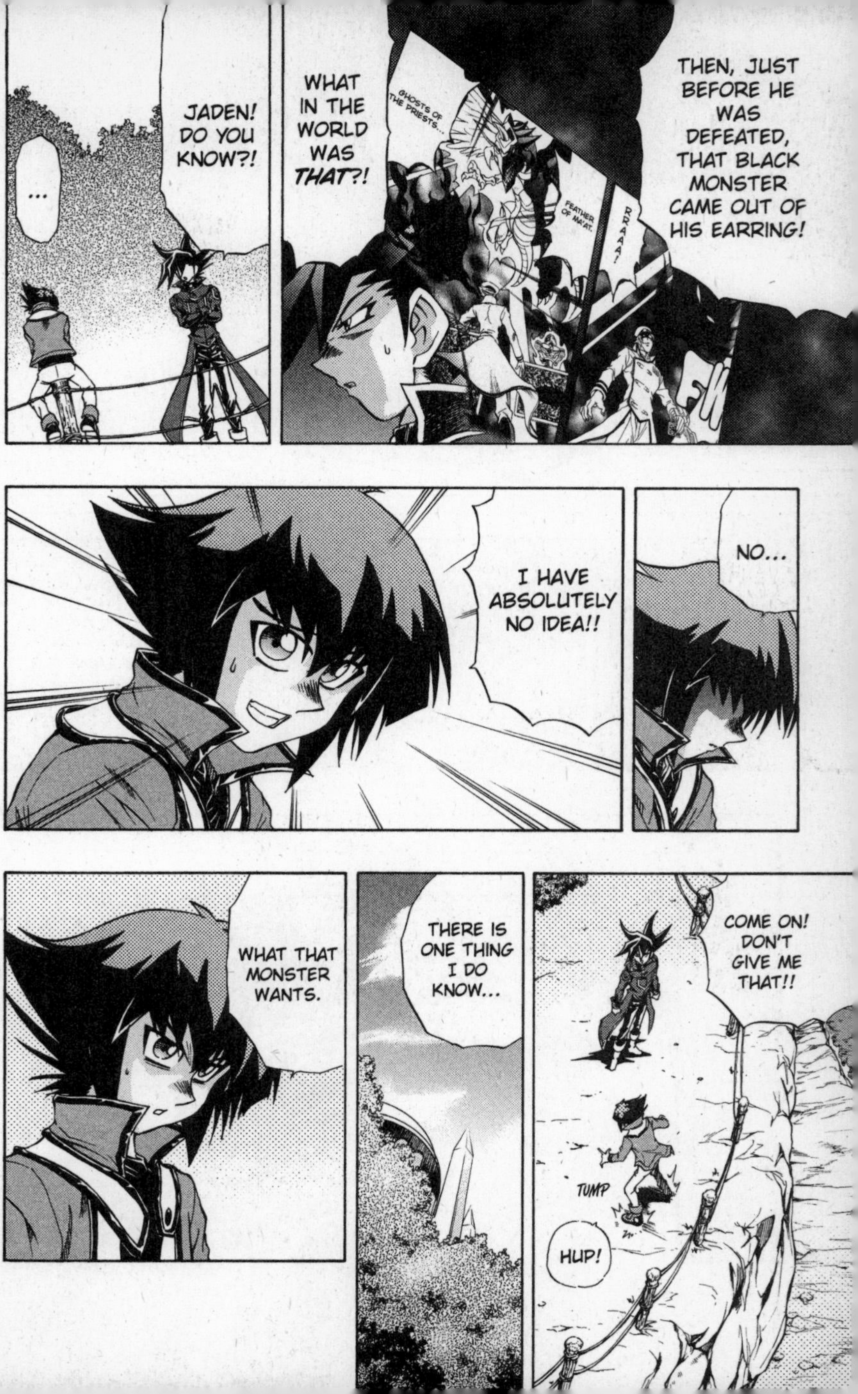
THEN, JUST BEFORE HE WAS DEFEATED, THAT BLACK MONSTER CAME OUT OF HIS EARRING!
RRAAA!
FEATHER OF MA'AT.
GHOSTS OF THE PRIESTS...
WHAT IN THE WORLD WAS *THAT*?!
JADEN! DO YOU KNOW?!
...
NO...
I HAVE ABSOLUTELY NO IDEA!!
COME ON! DON'T GIVE ME THAT!!
TUMP
HUP!
THERE IS ONE THING I DO KNOW...
WHAT THAT MONSTER WANTS.

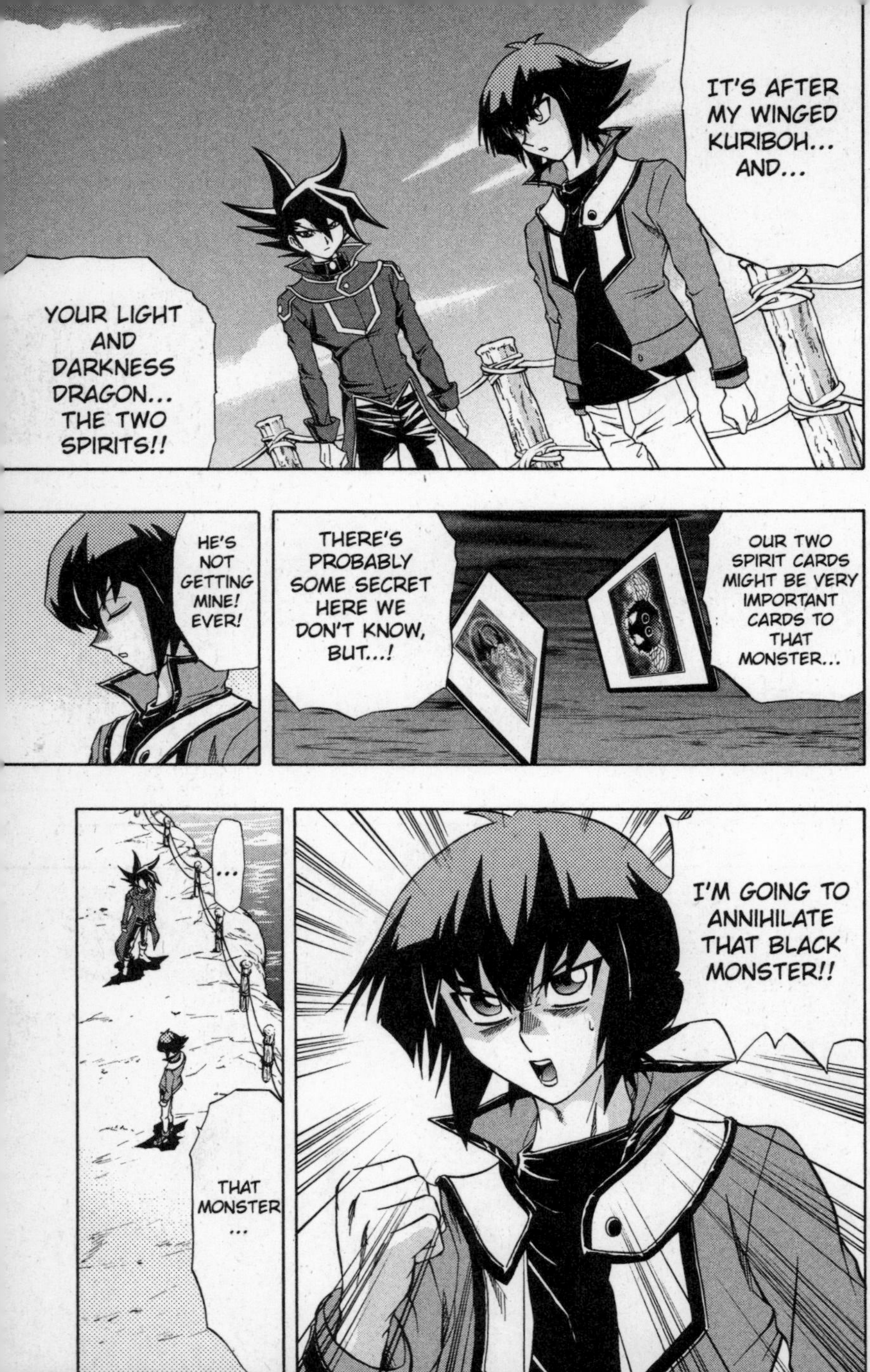
IT'S AFTER MY WINGED KURIBOH... AND...
YOUR LIGHT AND DARKNESS DRAGON... THE TWO SPIRITS!!
OUR TWO SPIRIT CARDS MIGHT BE VERY IMPORTANT CARDS TO THAT MONSTER...
THERE'S PROBABLY SOME SECRET HERE WE DON'T KNOW, BUT...!
HE'S NOT GETTING MINE! EVER!
I'M GOING TO ANNIHILATE THAT BLACK MONSTER!!
...
THAT MONSTER ...

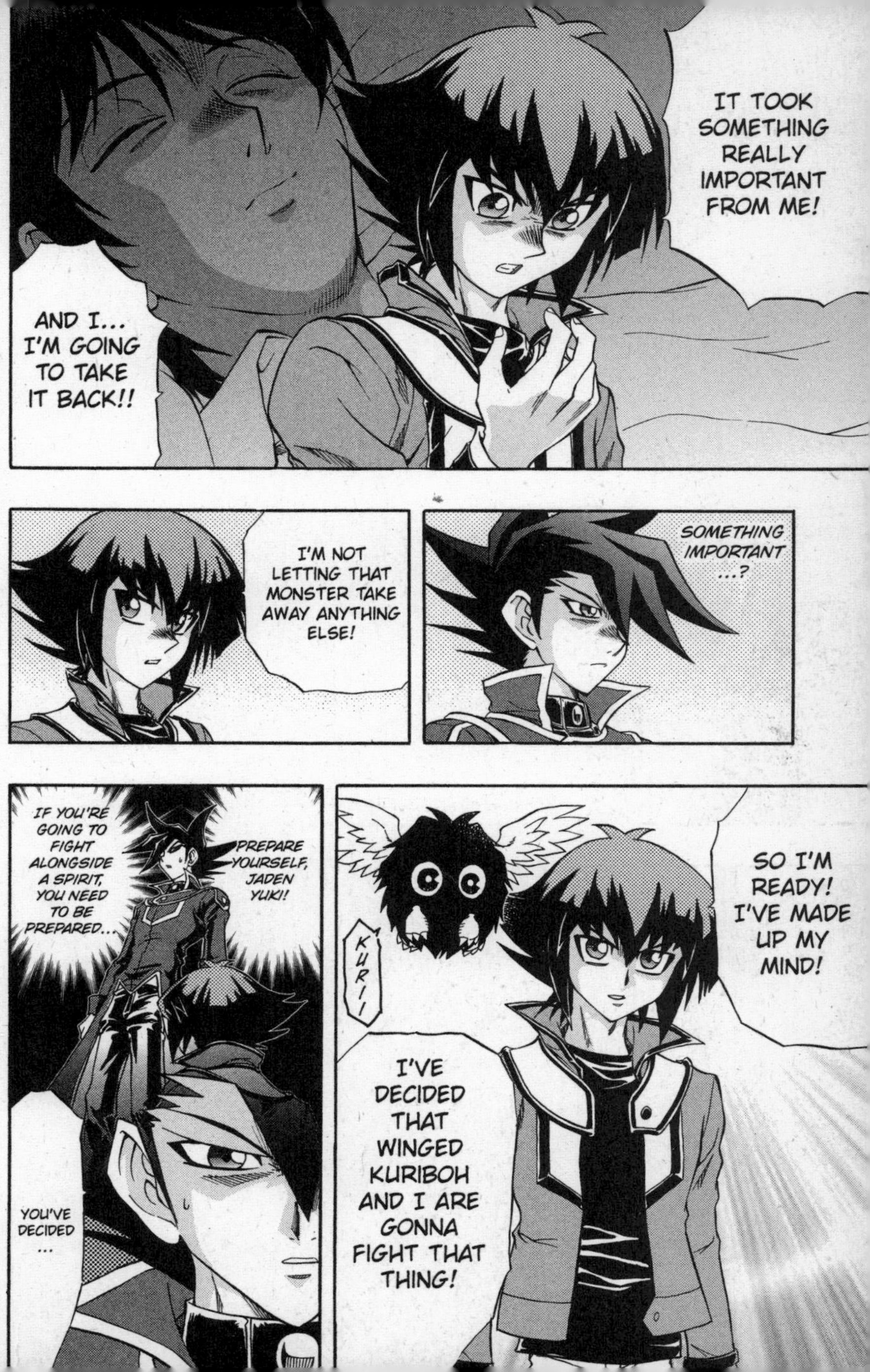
IT TOOK SOMETHING REALLY IMPORTANT FROM ME!
AND I... I'M GOING TO TAKE IT BACK!!
SOMETHING IMPORTANT ...?
I'M NOT LETTING THAT MONSTER TAKE AWAY ANYTHING ELSE!
SO I'M READY! I'VE MADE UP MY MIND!
KURI!
I'VE DECIDED THAT WINGED KURIBOH AND I ARE GONNA FIGHT THAT THING!
PREPARE YOURSELF, JADEN YUKI!
IF YOU'RE GOING TO FIGHT ALONGSIDE A SPIRIT, YOU NEED TO BE PREPARED...
YOU'VE DECIDED ...

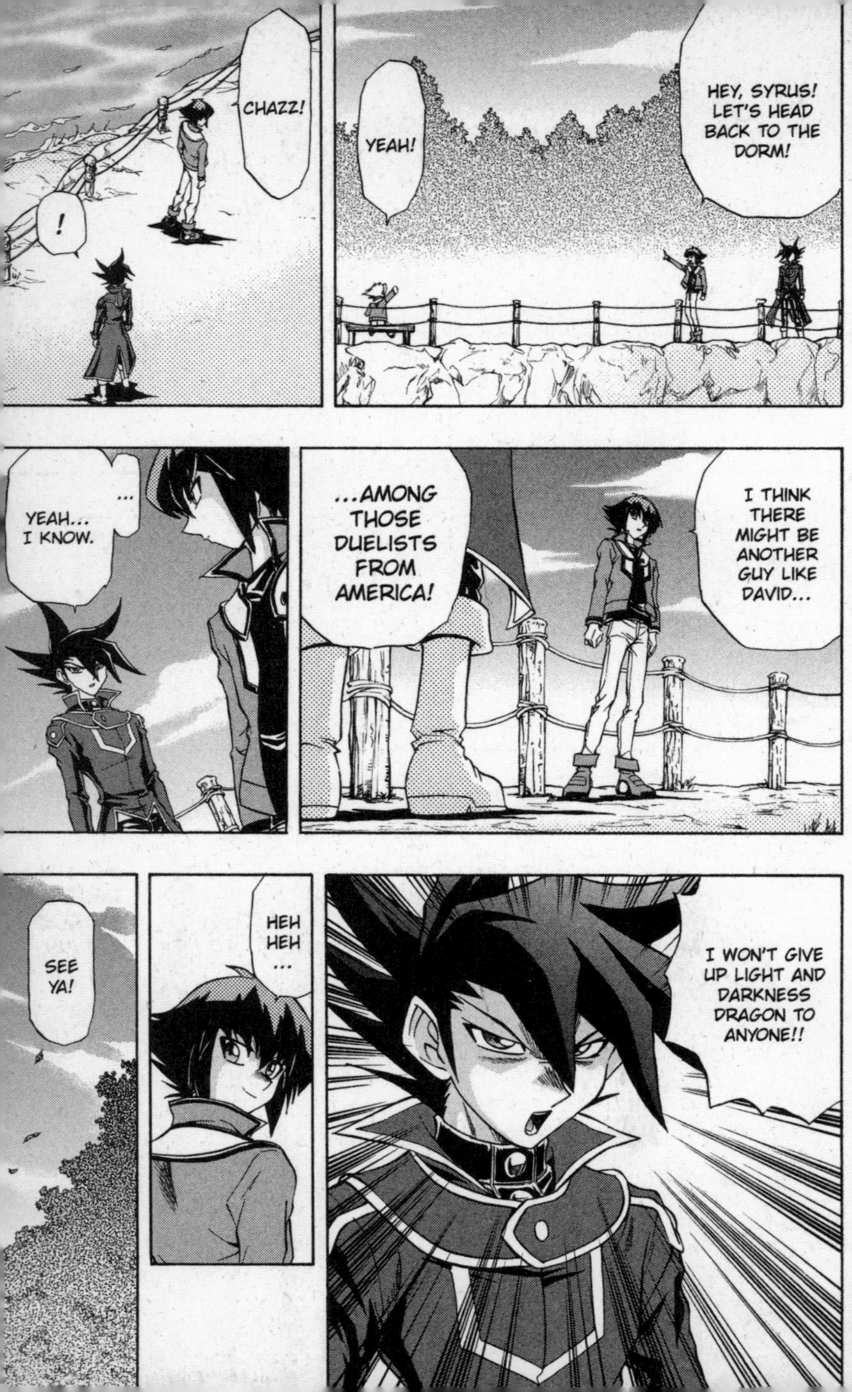
HEY, SYRUS! LET'S HEAD BACK TO THE DORM!
YEAH!
CHAZZ!
!
I THINK THERE MIGHT BE ANOTHER GUY LIKE DAVID...
...AMONG THOSE DUELISTS FROM AMERICA!
...
YEAH... I KNOW.
I WON'T GIVE UP LIGHT AND DARKNESS DRAGON TO ANYONE!!
HEH HEH ...
SEE YA!

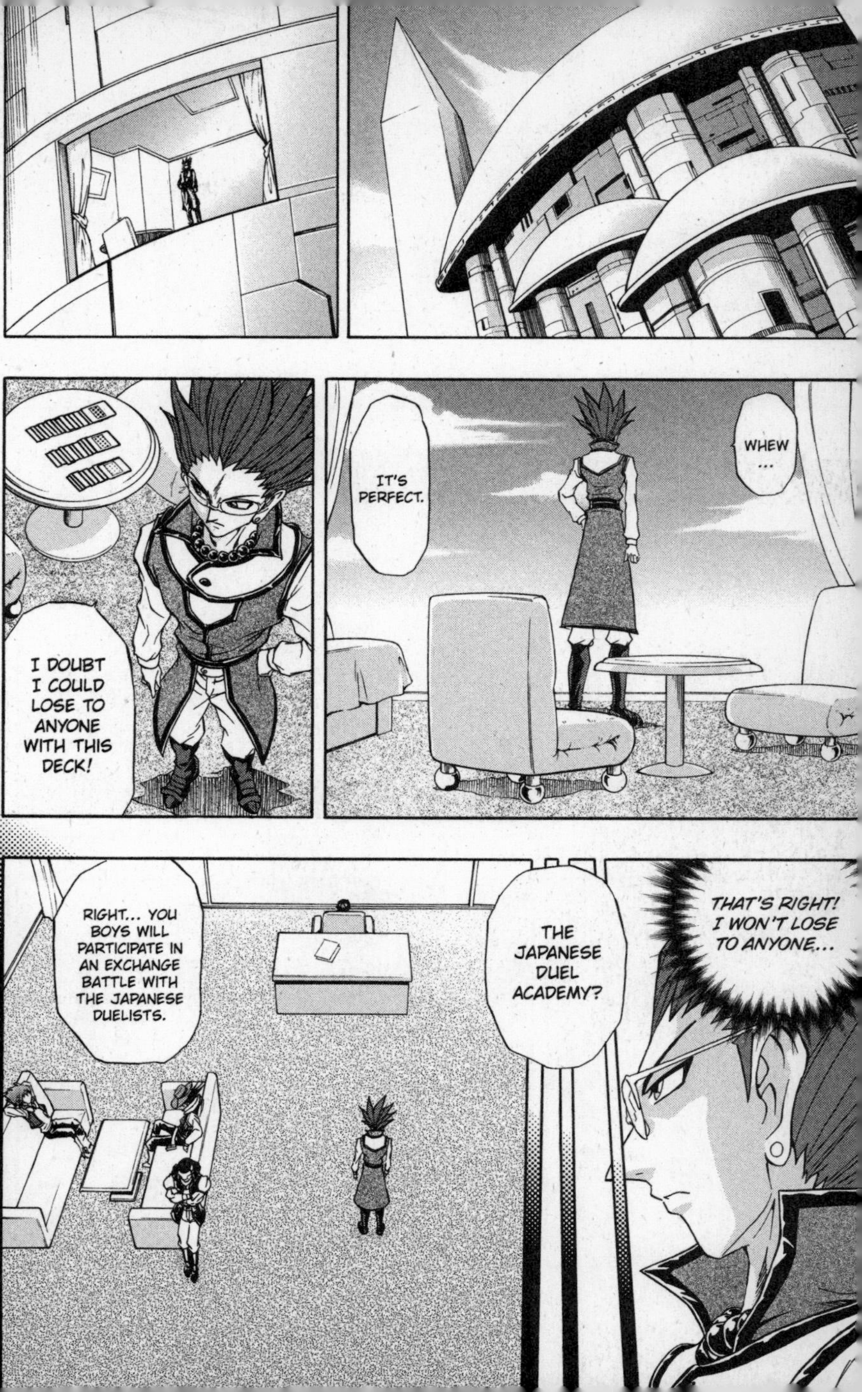
WHEW...
IT'S PERFECT.
I DOUBT I COULD LOSE TO ANYONE WITH THIS DECK!
THAT'S RIGHT! I WON'T LOSE TO ANYONE...
THE JAPANESE DUEL ACADEMY?
RIGHT... YOU BOYS WILL PARTICIPATE IN AN EXCHANGE BATTLE WITH THE JAPANESE DUELISTS.

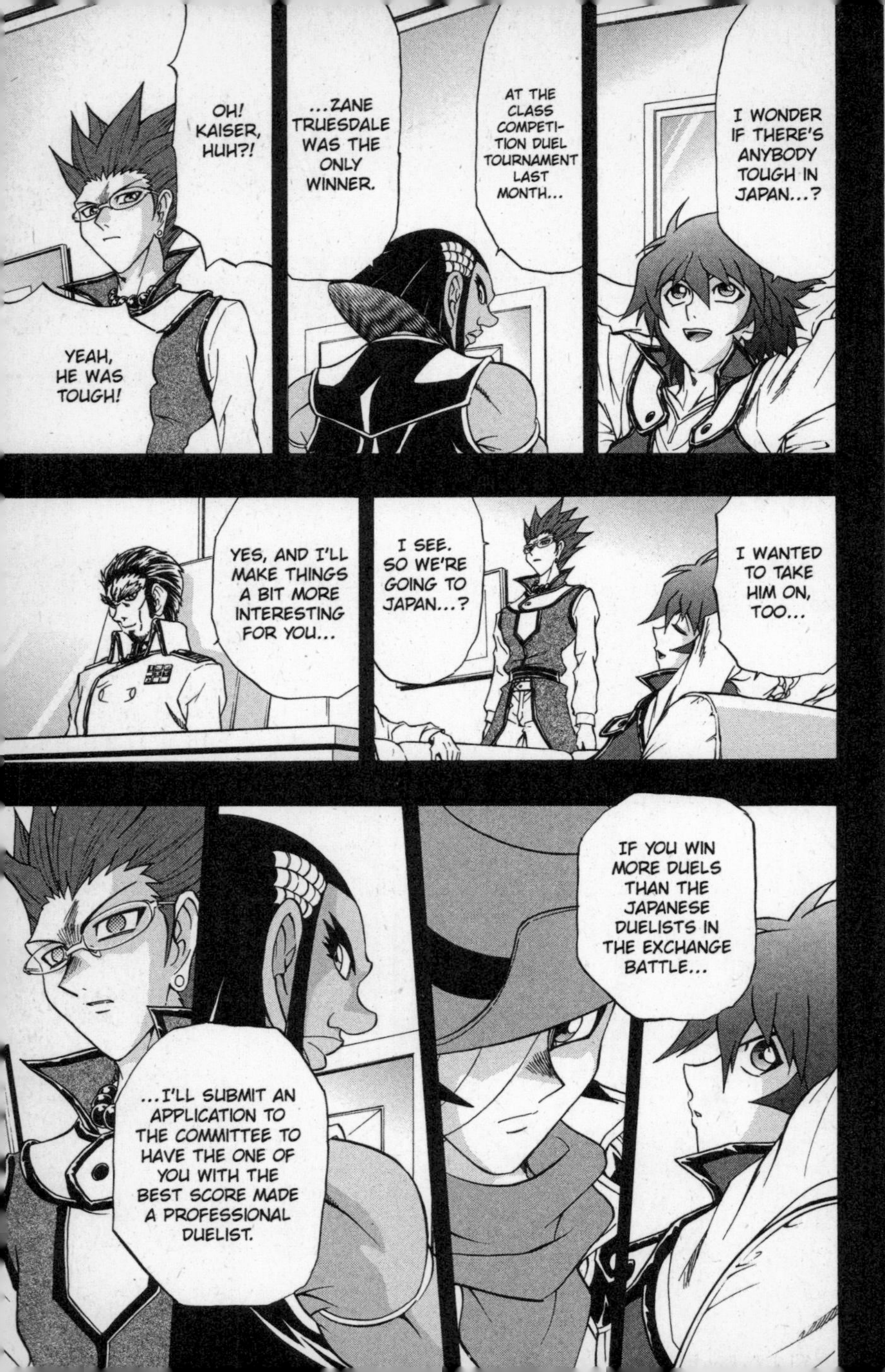
I WONDER IF THERE'S ANYBODY TOUGH IN JAPAN...?
AT THE CLASS COMPETI-TION DUEL TOURNAMENT LAST MONTH...
...ZANE TRUESDALE WAS THE ONLY WINNER.
OH! KAISER, HUH?!
YEAH, HE WAS TOUGH!
I WANTED TO TAKE HIM ON, TOO...
I SEE. SO WE'RE GOING TO JAPAN...?
YES, AND I'LL MAKE THINGS A BIT MORE INTERESTING FOR YOU...
IF YOU WIN MORE DUELS THAN THE JAPANESE DUELISTS IN THE EXCHANGE BATTLE...
...I'LL SUBMIT AN APPLICATION TO THE COMMITTEE TO HAVE THE ONE OF YOU WITH THE BEST SCORE MADE A PROFESSIONAL DUELIST.

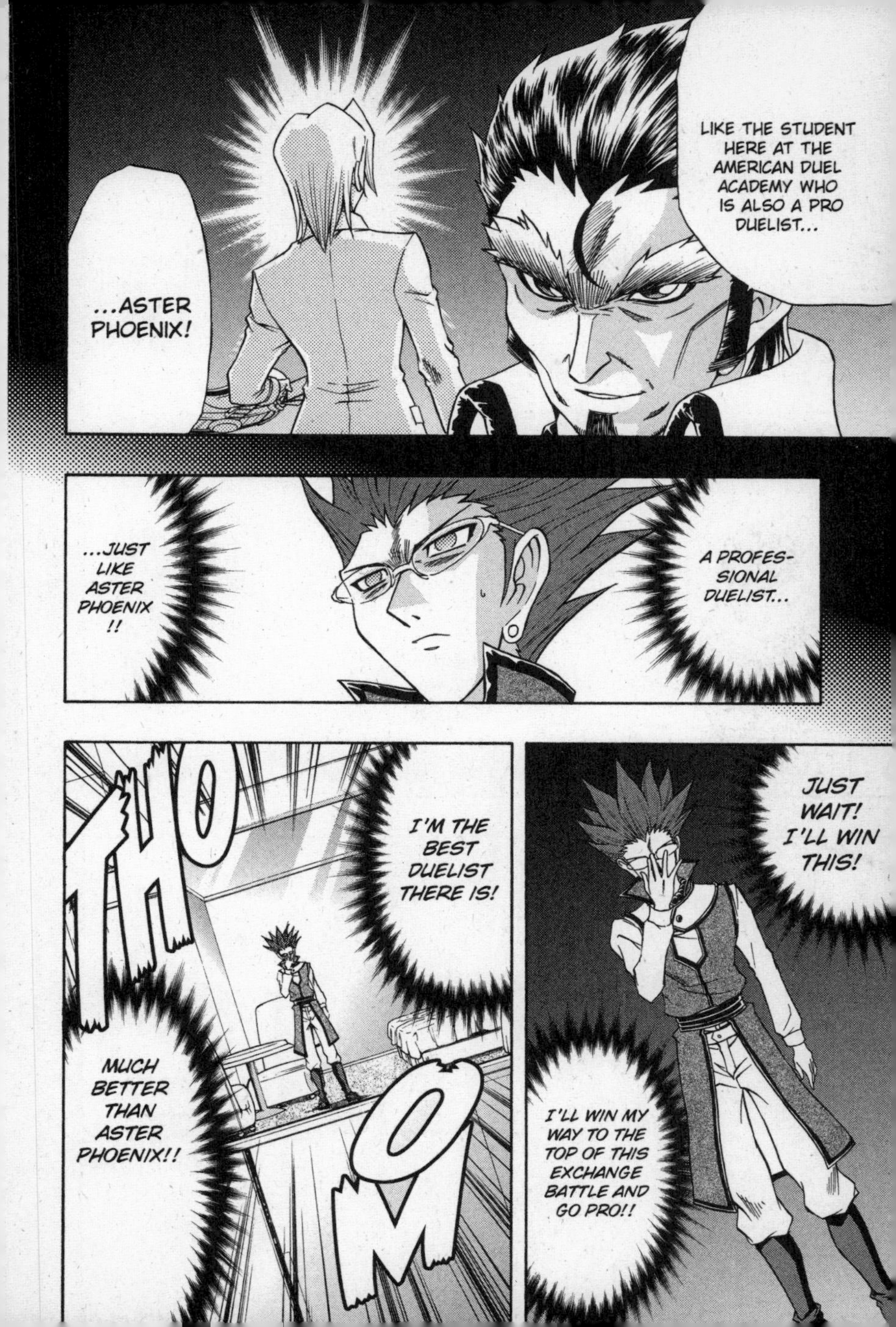
LIKE THE STUDENT HERE AT THE AMERICAN DUEL ACADEMY WHO IS ALSO A PRO DUELIST...
...ASTER PHOENIX!
A PROFES-SIONAL DUELIST...
...JUST LIKE ASTER PHOENIX !!
JUST WAIT! I'LL WIN THIS!
I'LL WIN MY WAY TO THE TOP OF THIS EXCHANGE BATTLE AND GO PRO!!
I'M THE BEST DUELIST THERE IS!
MUCH BETTER THAN ASTER PHOENIX!!
THOOM

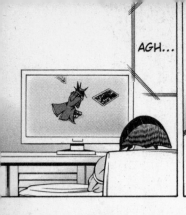

AGH...

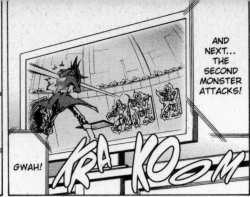

AND NEXT... THE SECOND MONSTER ATTACKS!

GWAH!

KRA KOOM

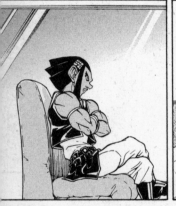

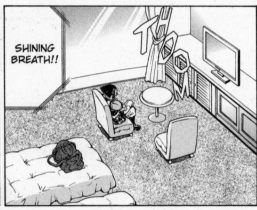

SHINING BREATH!!

THOOM

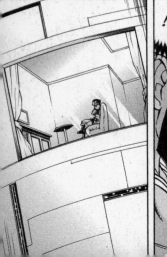

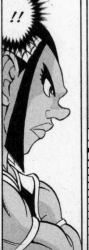

!!

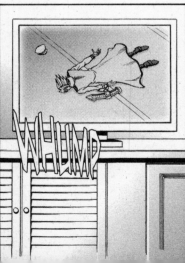

WHUMP

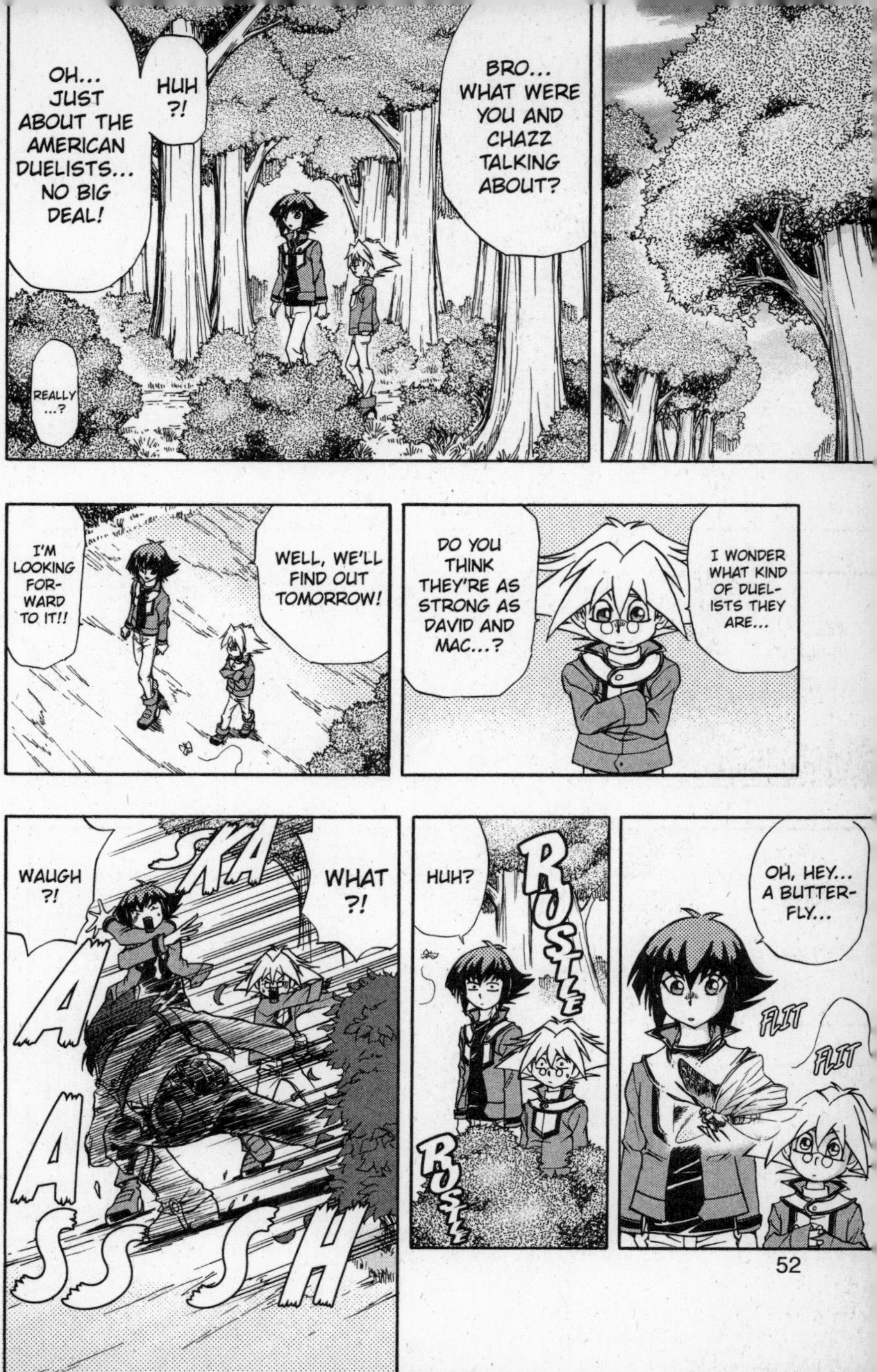
BRO... WHAT WERE YOU AND CHAZZ TALKING ABOUT?
HUH ?!
OH... JUST ABOUT THE AMERICAN DUELISTS... NO BIG DEAL!
REALLY ...?
I WONDER WHAT KIND OF DUEL-ISTS THEY ARE...
DO YOU THINK THEY'RE AS STRONG AS DAVID AND MAC...?
WELL, WE'LL FIND OUT TOMORROW!
I'M LOOKING FOR-WARD TO IT!!
OH, HEY... A BUTTER-FLY...
FLIT
FLIT
RUSTLE
HUH?
RUSTLE
WHAT ?!
WAUGH ?!
SKAAASSSH

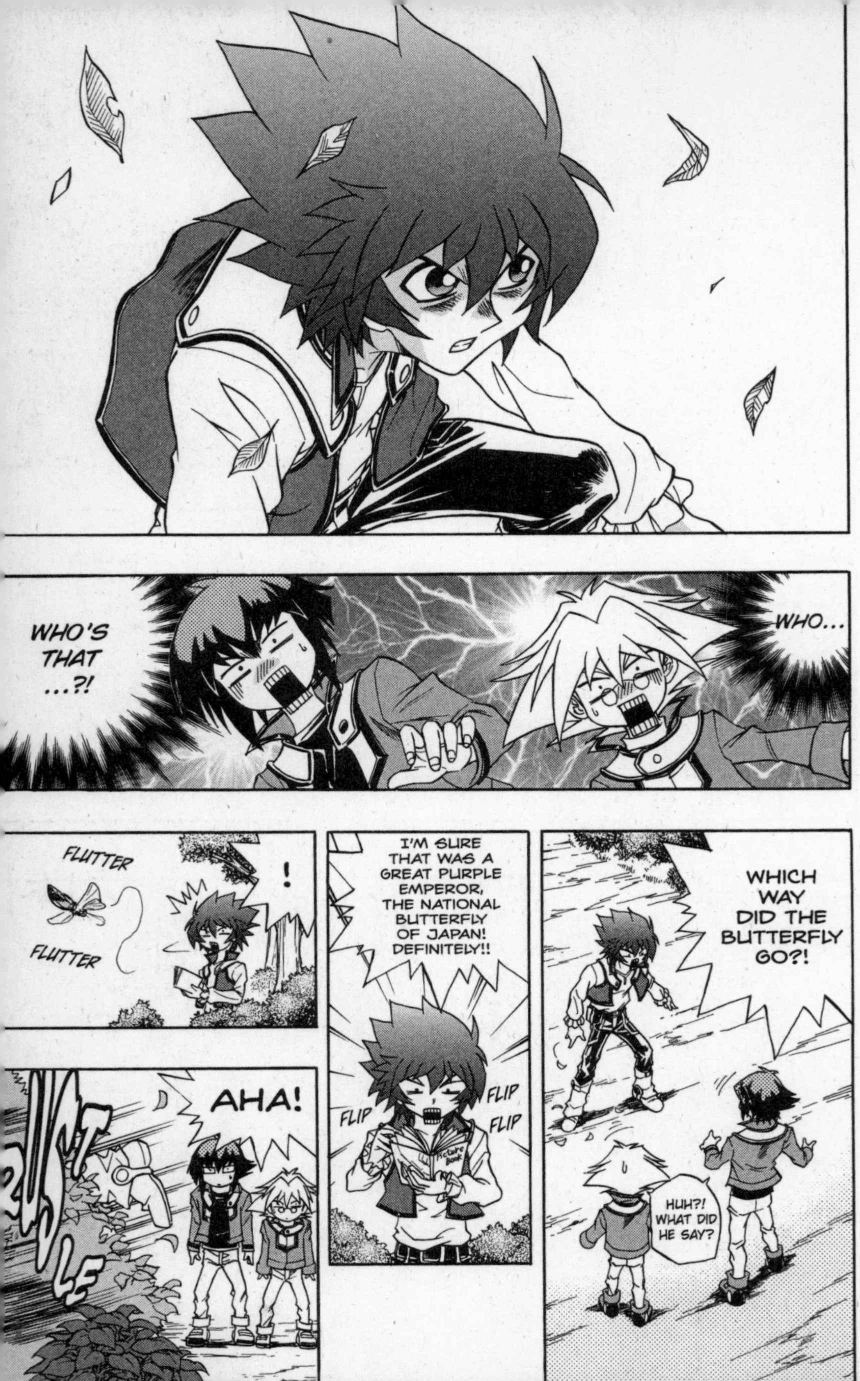
WHO...
WHO'S THAT ...?!
WHICH WAY DID THE BUTTERFLY GO?!
HUH?! WHAT DID HE SAY?
I'M SURE THAT WAS A GREAT PURPLE EMPEROR, THE NATIONAL BUTTERFLY OF JAPAN! DEFINITELY!!
FLIP
FLIP
FLIP
Picture Book
!
FLUTTER
FLUTTER
AHA!
RUSTLE

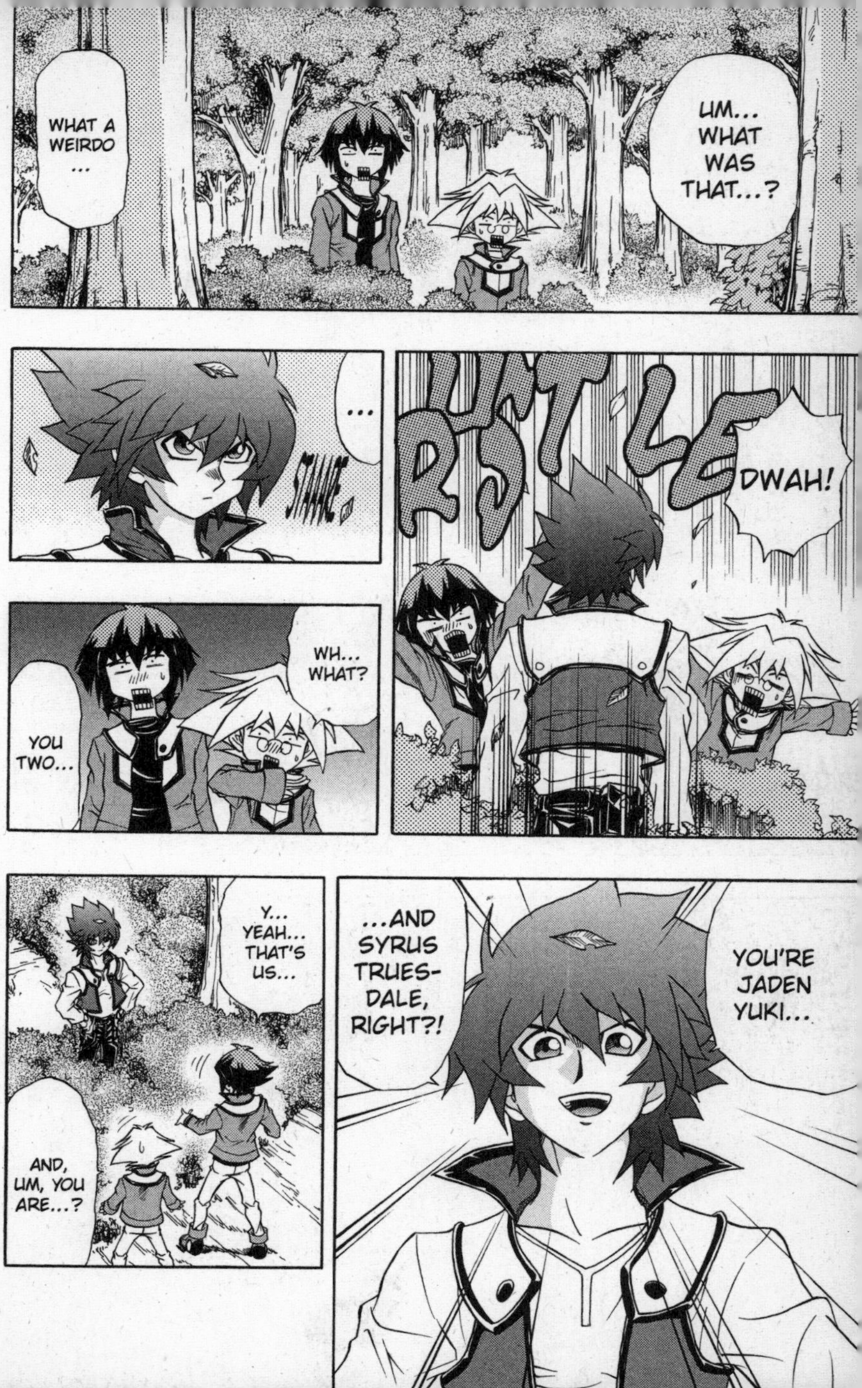
UM... WHAT WAS THAT...?
WHAT A WEIRDO ...
RUSTLE
DWAH!
...
STARE
WH... WHAT?
YOU TWO...
YOU'RE JADEN YUKI...
...AND SYRUS TRUES-DALE, RIGHT?!
Y... YEAH... THAT'S US...
AND, UM, YOU ARE...?

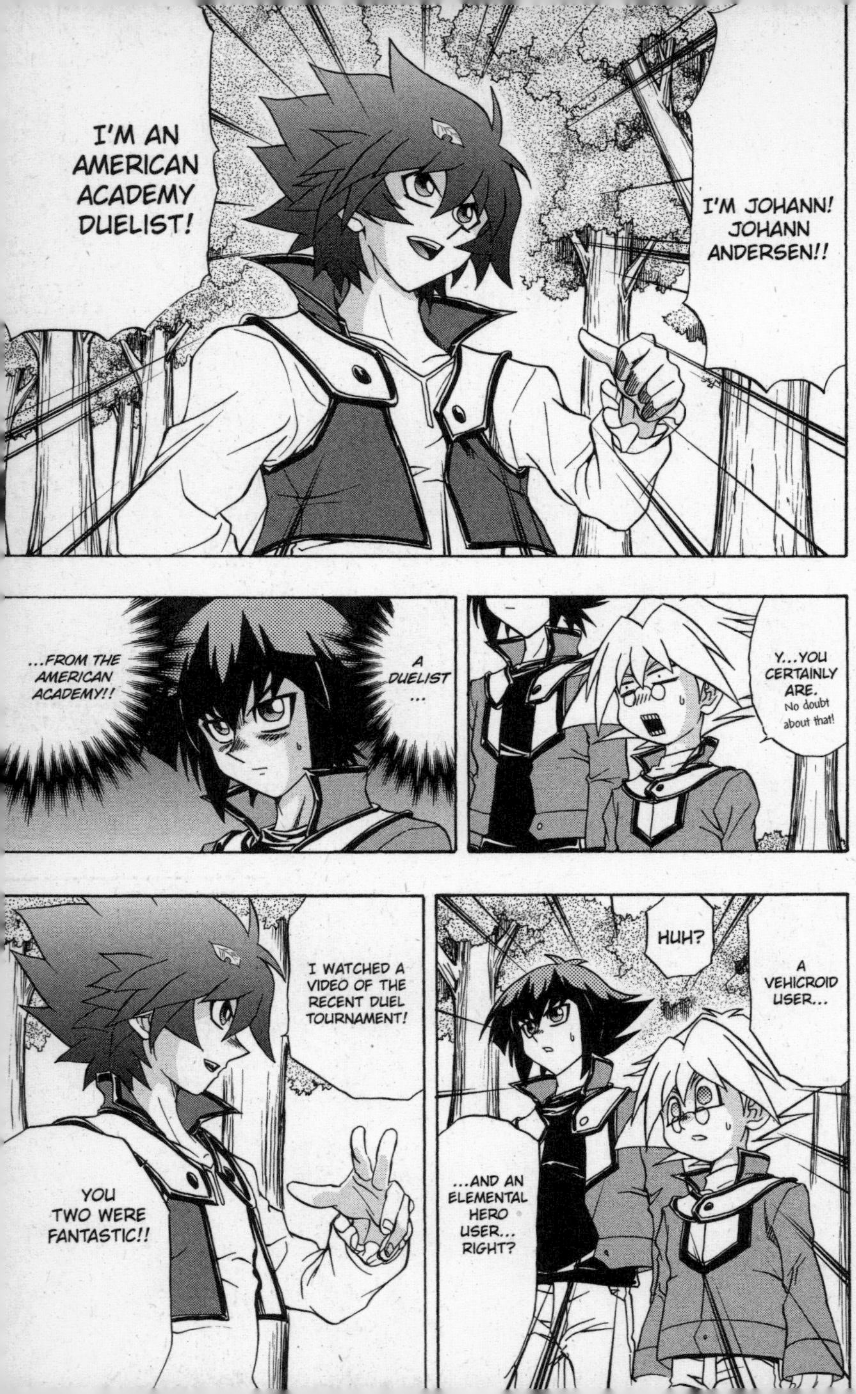
I'M JOHANN! JOHANN ANDERSEN!!
I'M AN AMERICAN ACADEMY DUELIST!
Y...YOU CERTAINLY ARE.
No doubt about that!
A DUELIST ...
...FROM THE AMERICAN ACADEMY!!
HUH?
A VEHICROID USER...
...AND AN ELEMENTAL HERO USER... RIGHT?
I WATCHED A VIDEO OF THE RECENT DUEL TOURNAMENT!
YOU TWO WERE FANTASTIC!!

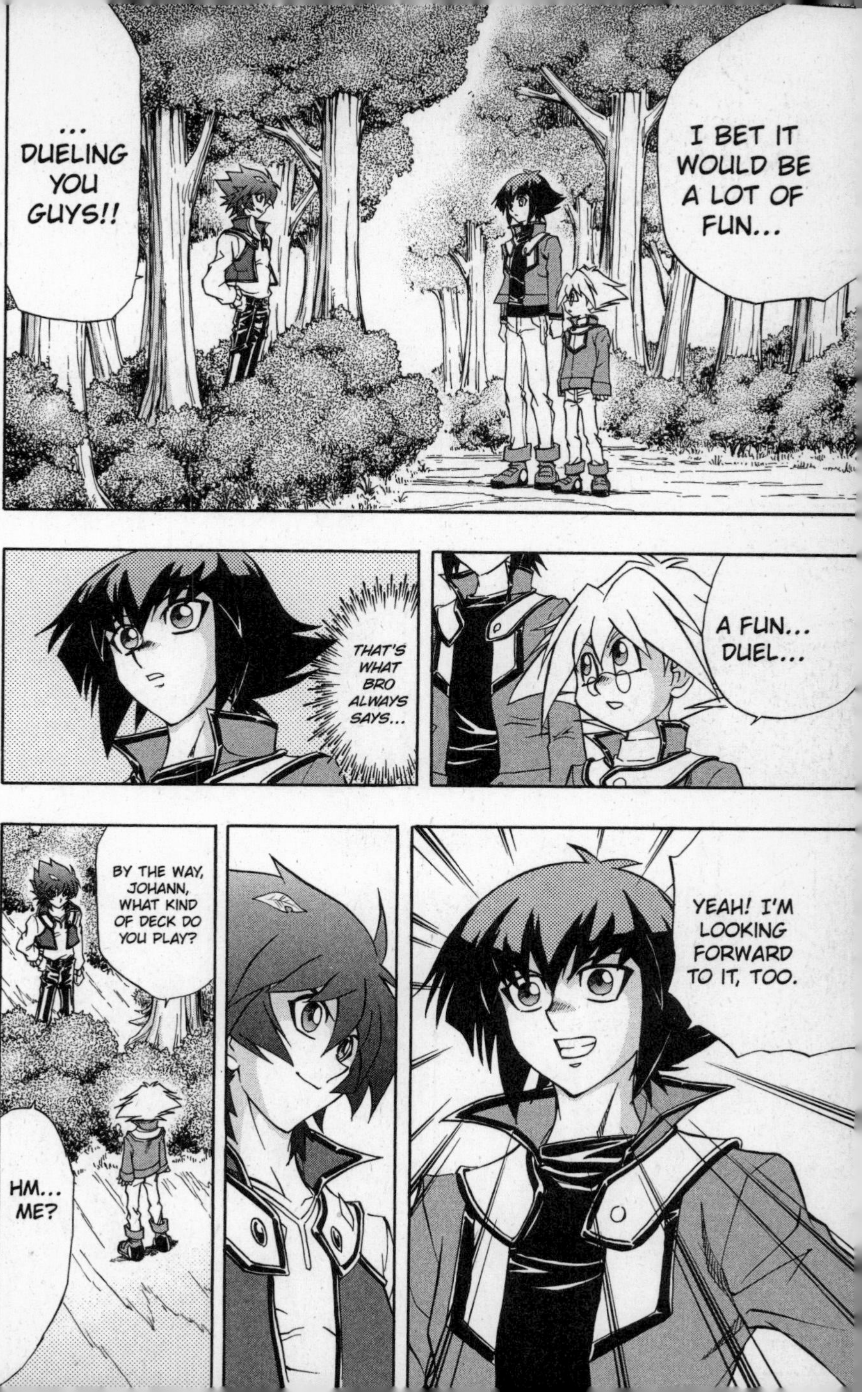
I BET IT WOULD BE A LOT OF FUN...
... DUELING YOU GUYS!!
A FUN... DUEL...
THAT'S WHAT BRO ALWAYS SAYS...
YEAH! I'M LOOKING FORWARD TO IT, TOO.
BY THE WAY, JOHANN, WHAT KIND OF DECK DO YOU PLAY?
HM... ME?

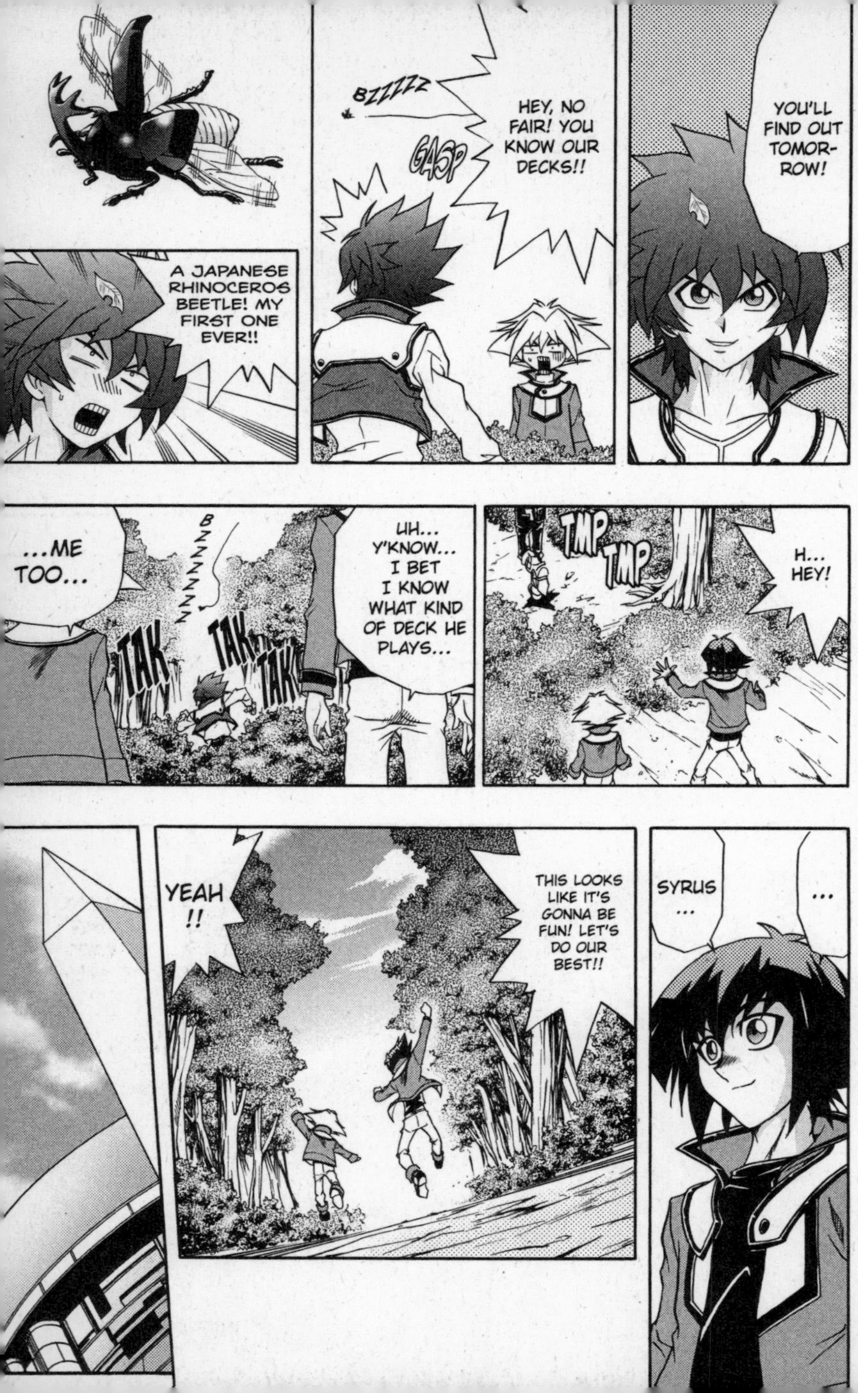
YOU'LL FIND OUT TOMORROW!
BZZZZZ
HEY, NO FAIR! YOU KNOW OUR DECKS!!
GASP
A JAPANESE RHINOCEROS BEETLE! MY FIRST ONE EVER!!
H... HEY!
TMP TMP
UH... Y'KNOW... I BET I KNOW WHAT KIND OF DECK HE PLAYS...
BZZZZZZZ
...ME TOO...
TAK TAK TAK
...
SYRUS ...
THIS LOOKS LIKE IT'S GONNA BE FUN! LET'S DO OUR BEST!!
YEAH !!

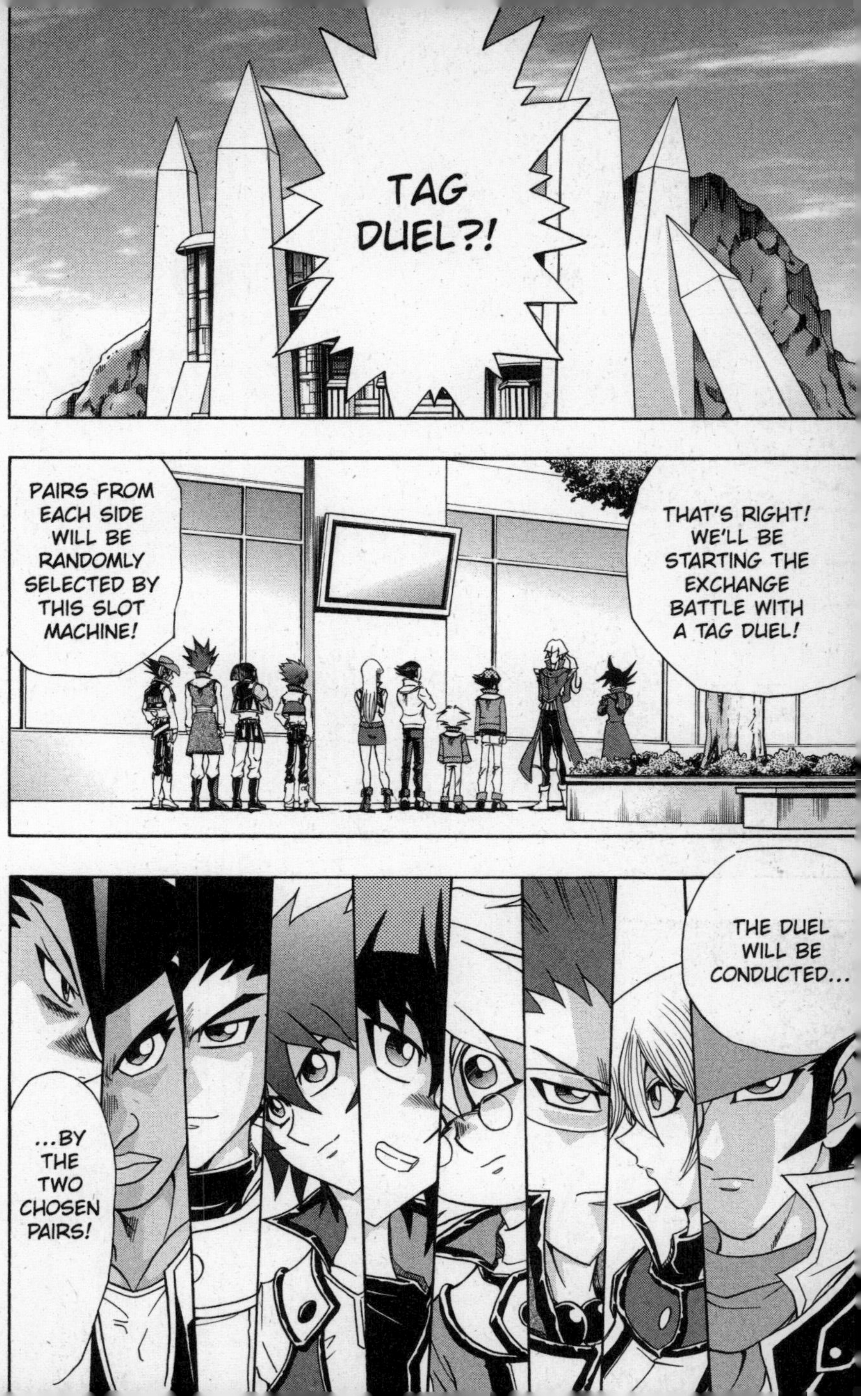
TAG DUEL?!
THAT'S RIGHT! WE'LL BE STARTING THE EXCHANGE BATTLE WITH A TAG DUEL!
PAIRS FROM EACH SIDE WILL BE RANDOMLY SELECTED BY THIS SLOT MACHINE!
THE DUEL WILL BE CONDUCTED...
...BY THE TWO CHOSEN PAIRS!

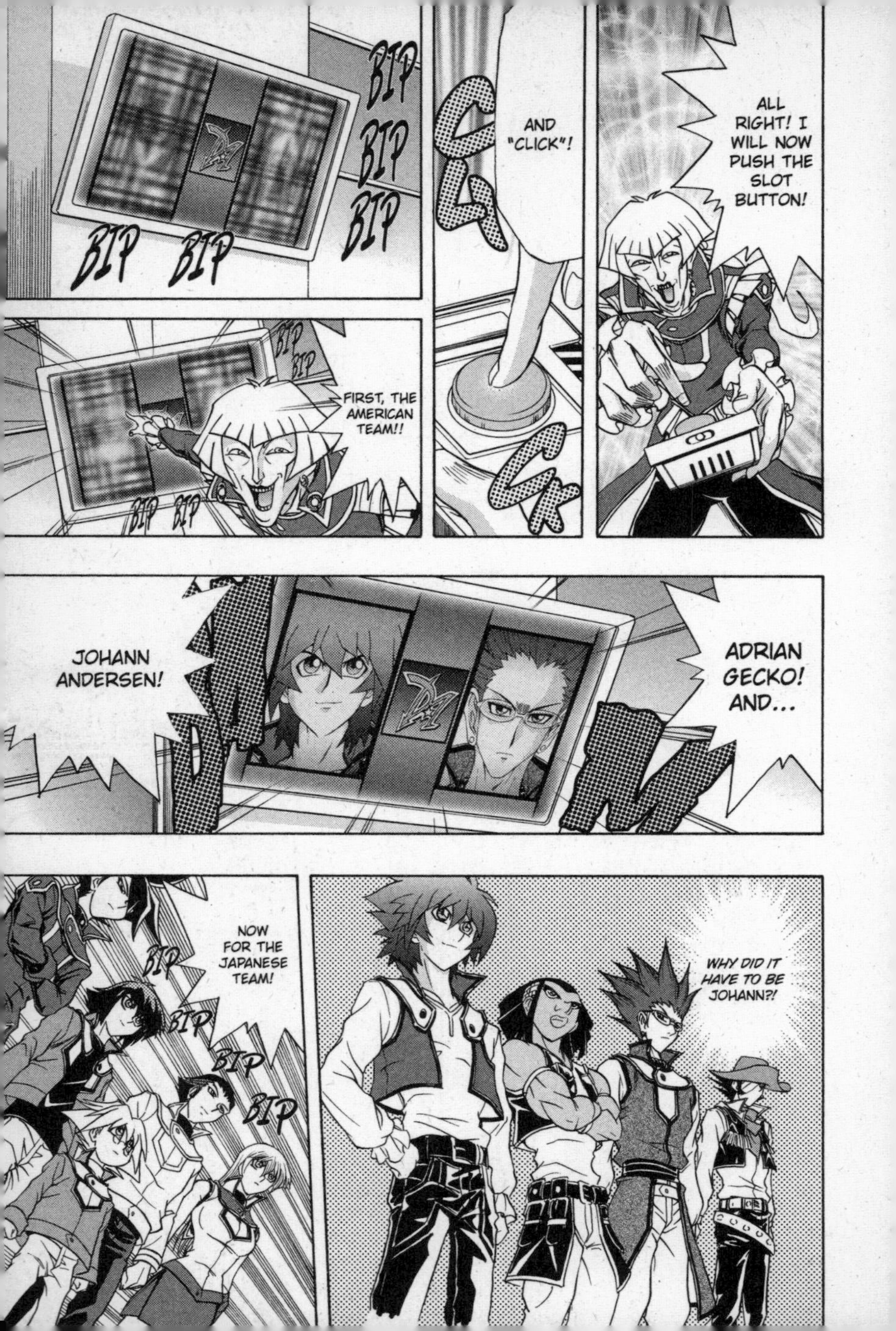
ALL RIGHT! I WILL NOW PUSH THE SLOT BUTTON!
AND "CLICK"!
BIP BIP BIP BIP BIP
BIP BIP
FIRST, THE AMERICAN TEAM!!
BIP BIP
ADRIAN GECKO! AND...
JOHANN ANDERSEN!
WHY DID IT HAVE TO BE JOHANN?!
NOW FOR THE JAPANESE TEAM!
BIP BIP BIP BIP

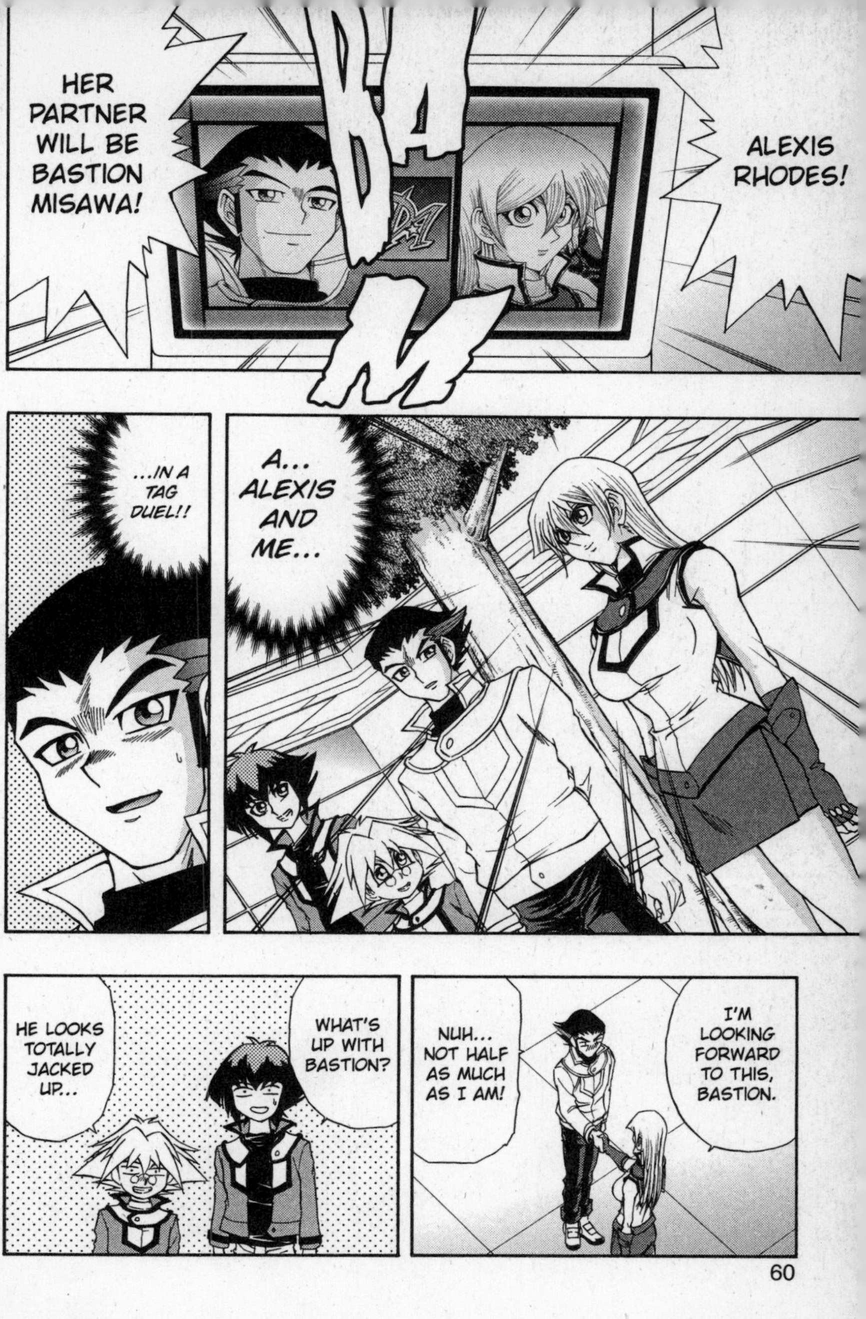
ALEXIS RHODES!
HER PARTNER WILL BE BASTION MISAWA!
BAM
A... ALEXIS AND ME...
...IN A TAG DUEL!!
I'M LOOKING FORWARD TO THIS, BASTION.
NUH... NOT HALF AS MUCH AS I AM!
WHAT'S UP WITH BASTION?
HE LOOKS TOTALLY JACKED UP...

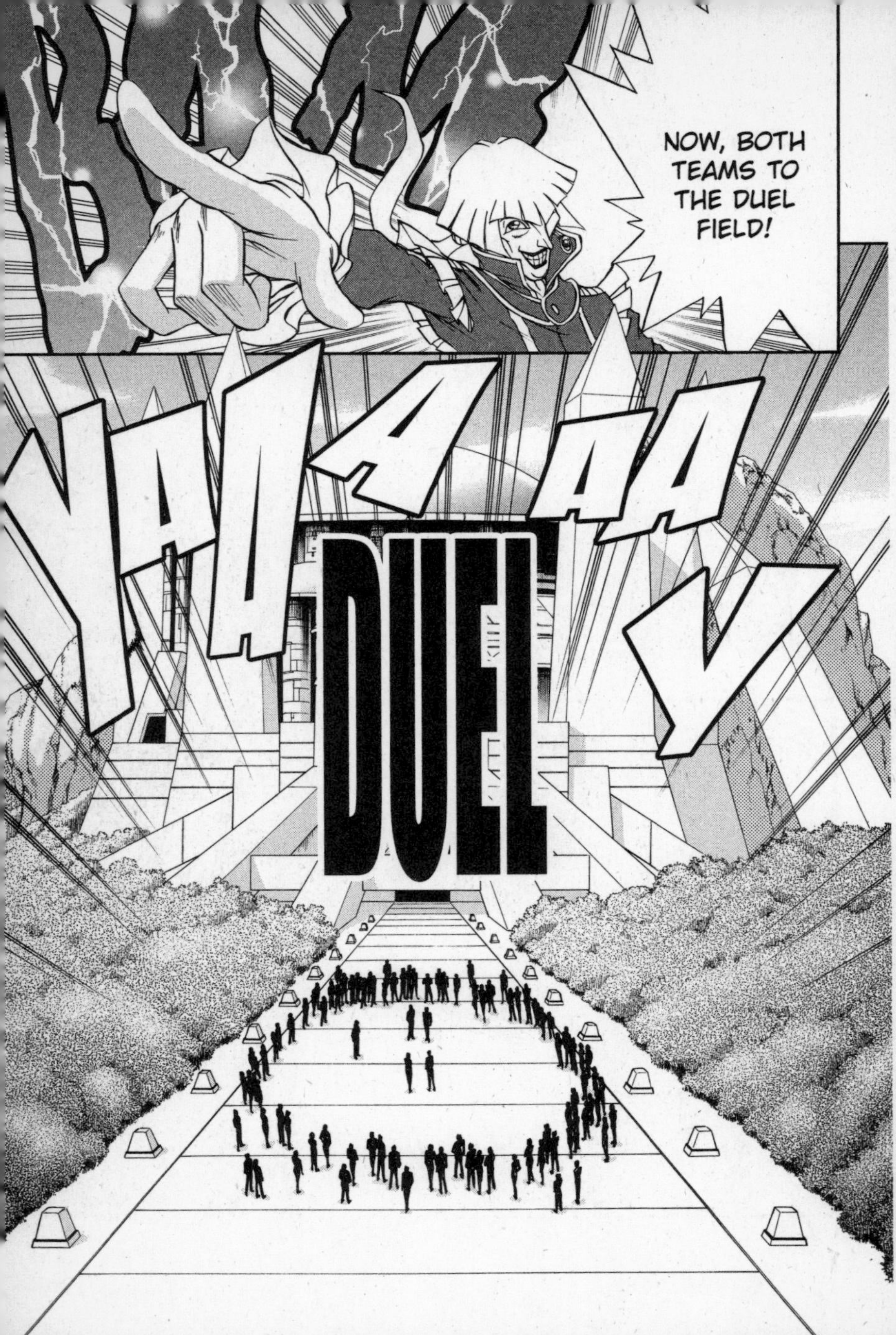
NOW, BOTH TEAMS TO THE DUEL FIELD!
YAAAAAY
DUEL

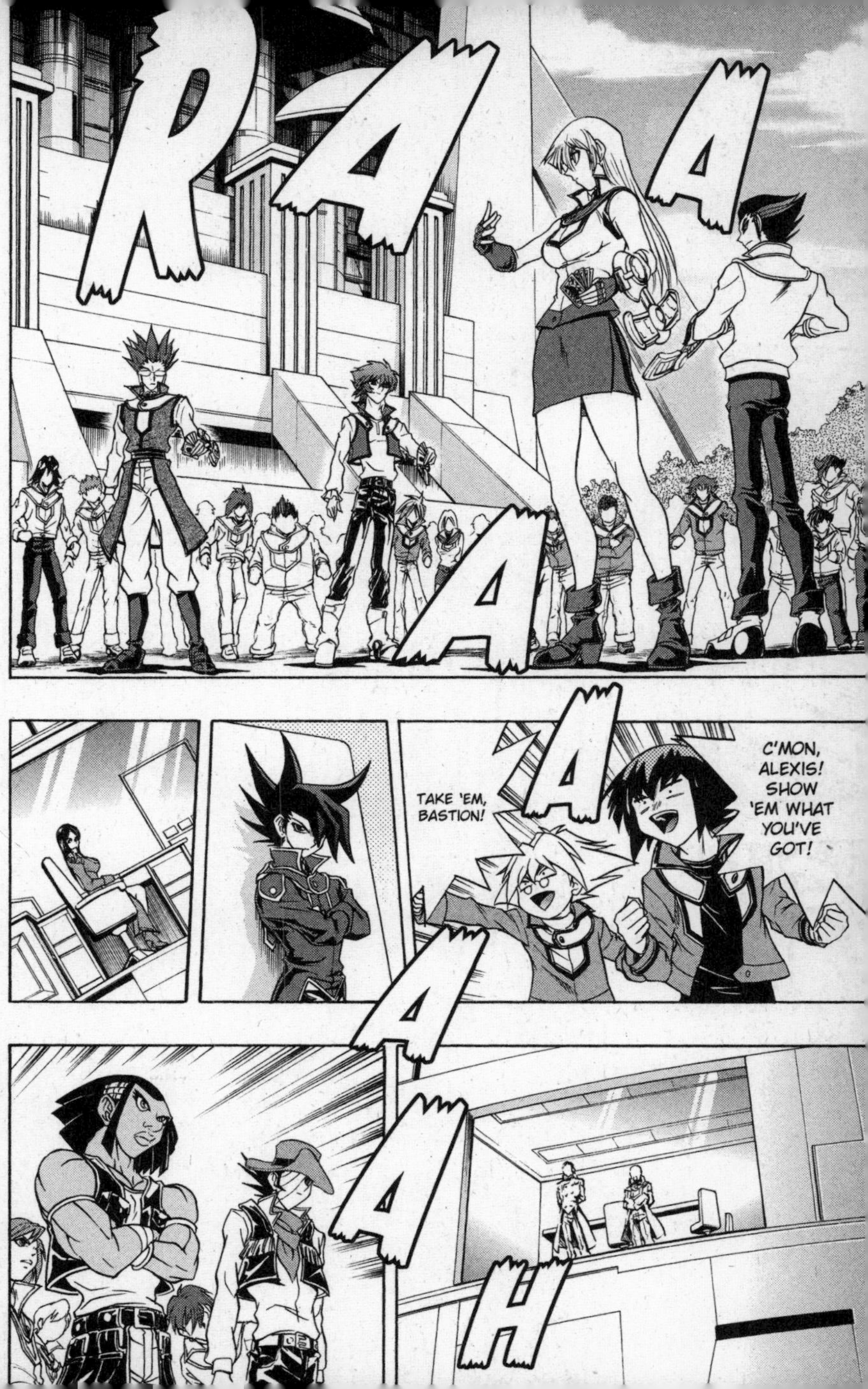
RAAAAAAH
C'MON, ALEXIS! SHOW 'EM WHAT YOU'VE GOT!
TAKE 'EM, BASTION!

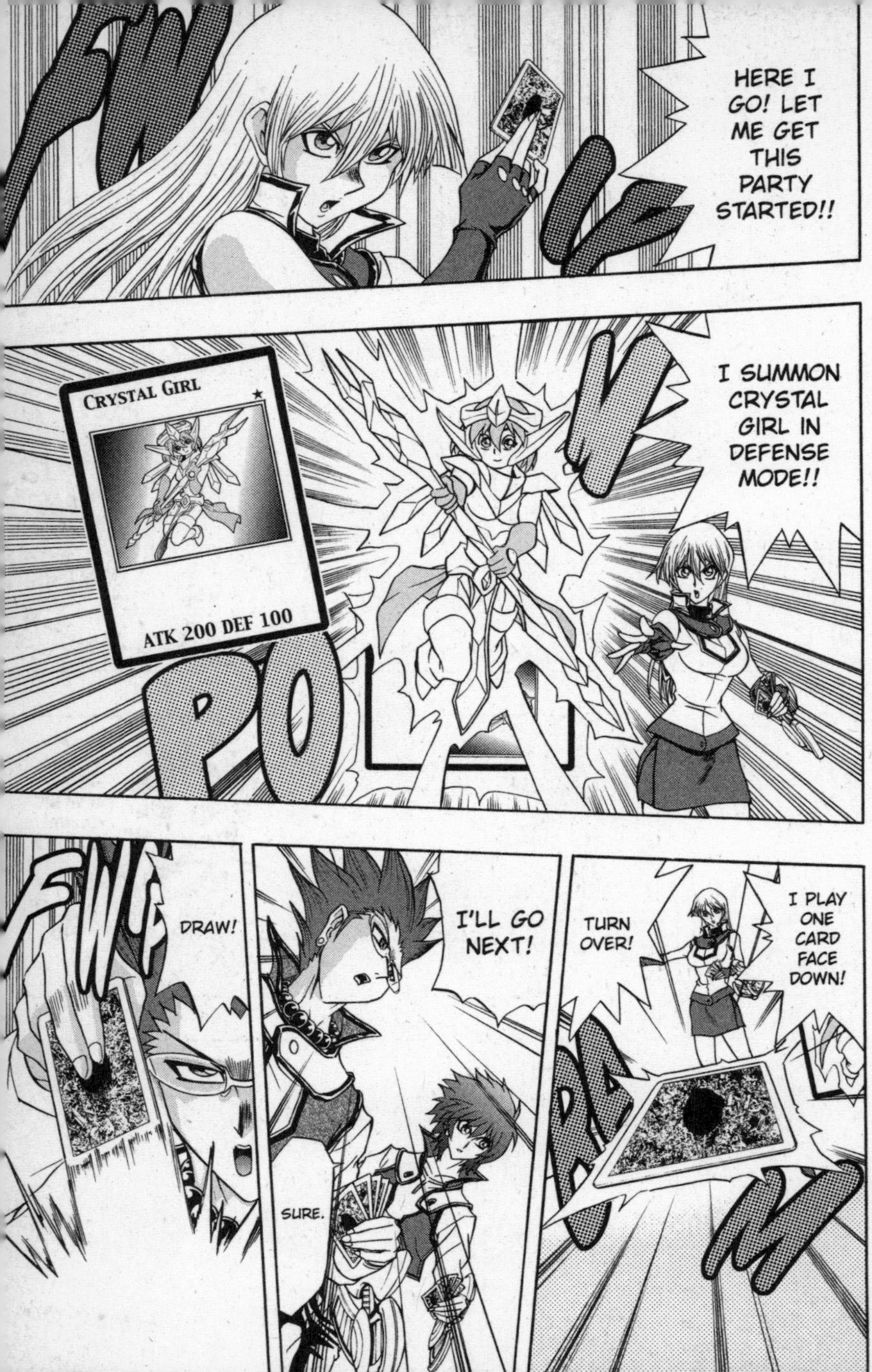
HERE I GO! LET ME GET THIS PARTY STARTED!!
I SUMMON CRYSTAL GIRL IN DEFENSE MODE!!
CRYSTAL GIRL
ATK 200 DEF 100
I PLAY ONE CARD FACE DOWN!
TURN OVER!
I'LL GO NEXT!
SURE.
DRAW!

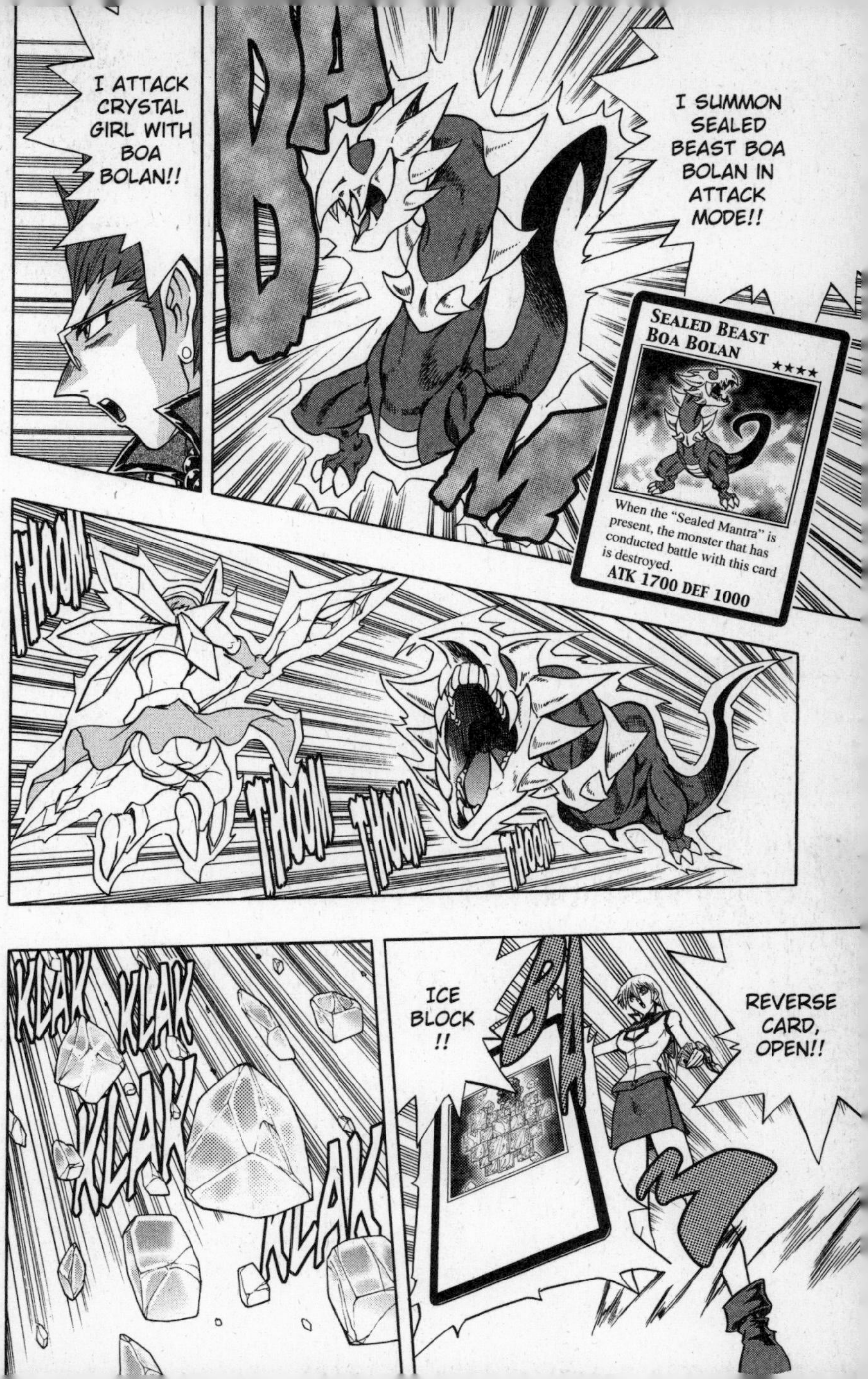
I SUMMON SEALED BEAST BOA BOLAN IN ATTACK MODE!!
BAM
SEALED BEAST BOA BOLAN
When the "Sealed Mantra" is present, the monster that has conducted battle with this card is destroyed.
ATK 1700 DEF 1000
I ATTACK CRYSTAL GIRL WITH BOA BOLAN!!
THOOM
THOOM
THOOM
THOOM
REVERSE CARD, OPEN!!
ICE BLOCK!!
BAM
KLAK KLAK
KLAK
KLAK

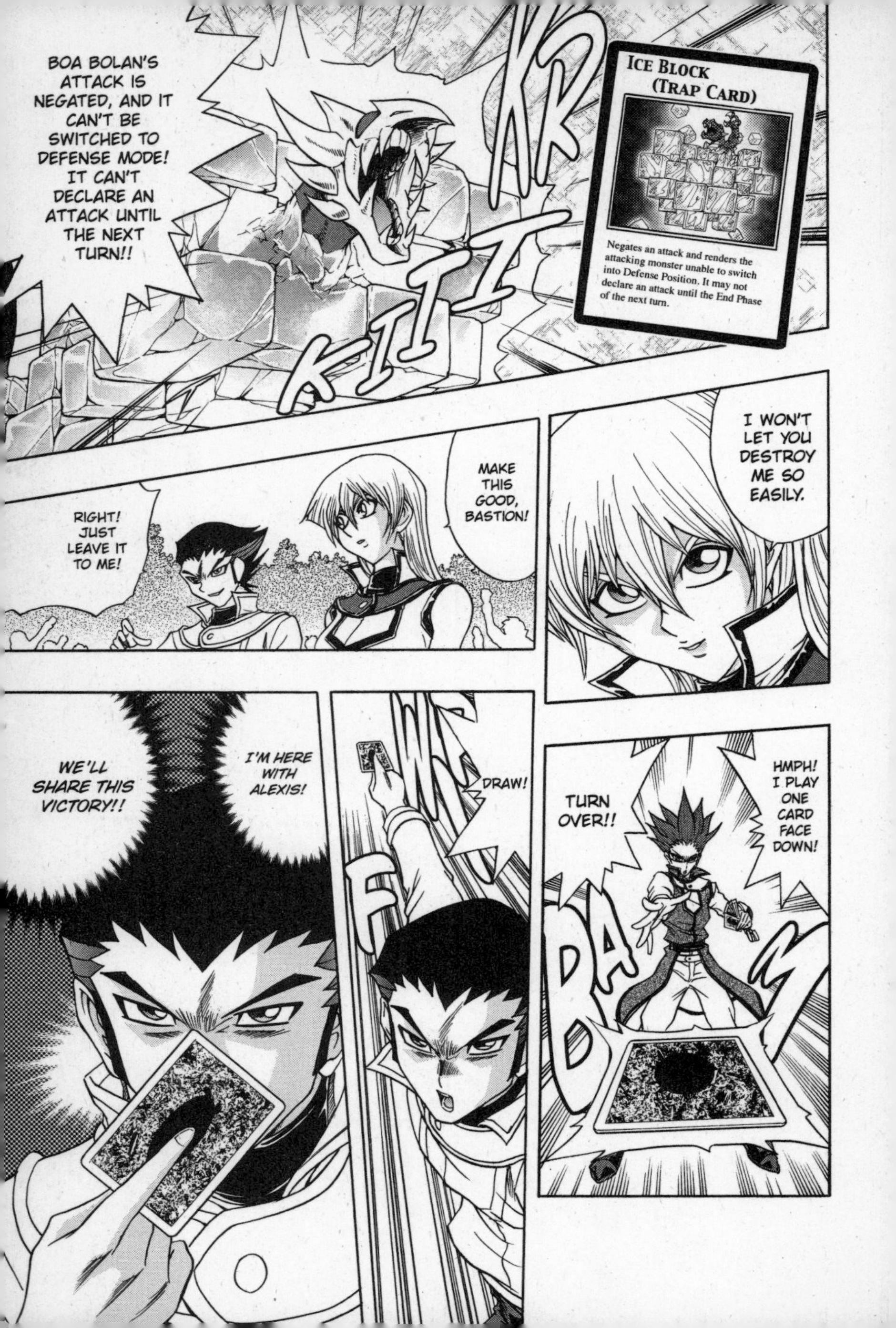
ICE BLOCK (TRAP CARD)
Negates an attack and renders the attacking monster unable to switch into Defense Position. It may not declare an attack until the End Phase of the next turn.
BOA BOLAN'S ATTACK IS NEGATED, AND IT CAN'T BE SWITCHED TO DEFENSE MODE! IT CAN'T DECLARE AN ATTACK UNTIL THE NEXT TURN!!
I WON'T LET YOU DESTROY ME SO EASILY.
MAKE THIS GOOD, BASTION!
RIGHT! JUST LEAVE IT TO ME!
HMPH! I PLAY ONE CARD FACE DOWN!
TURN OVER!!
DRAW!
I'M HERE WITH ALEXIS!
WE'LL SHARE THIS VICTORY!!

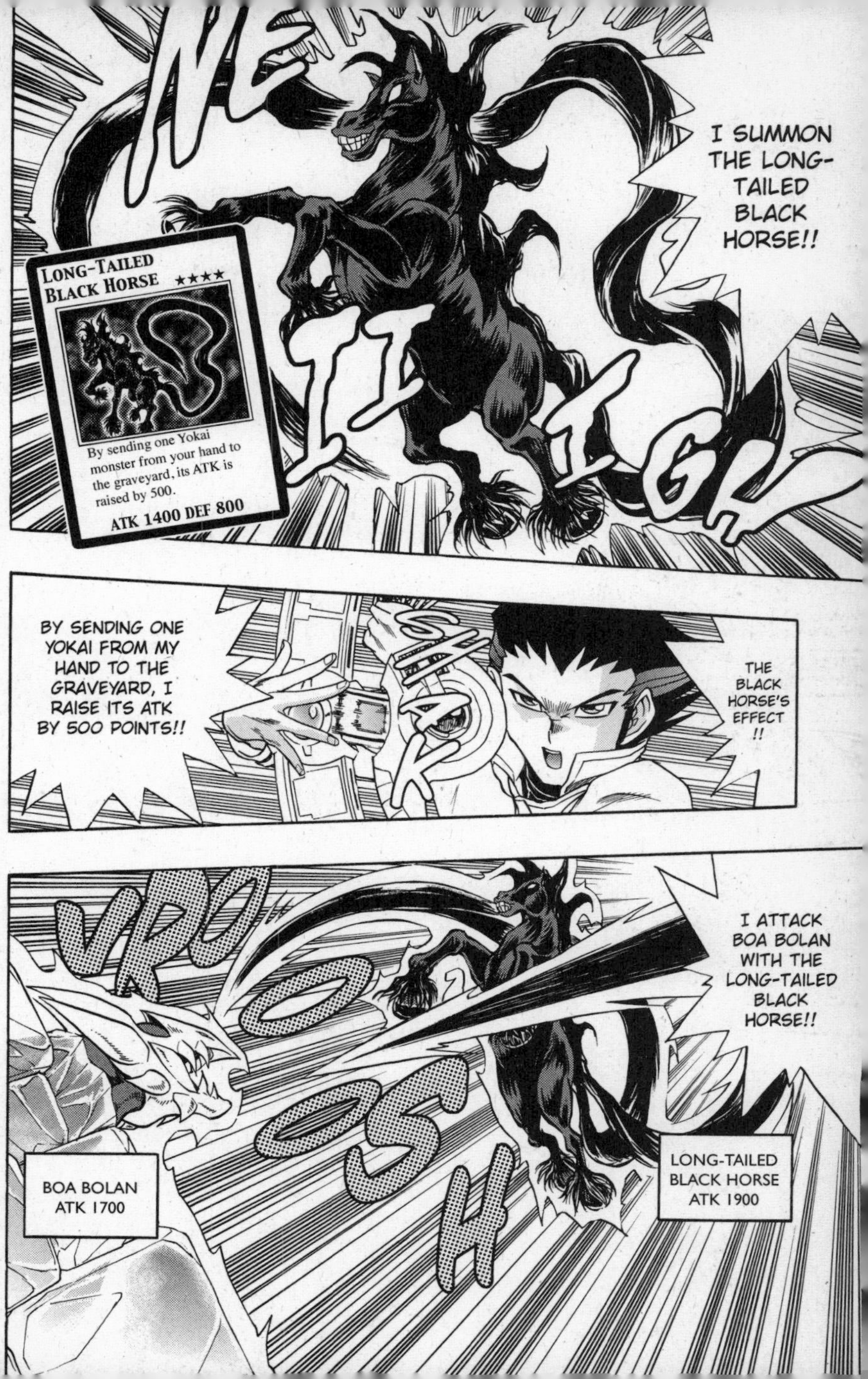
I SUMMON THE LONG-TAILED BLACK HORSE!!
NEIIIGH
LONG-TAILED BLACK HORSE ★★★★
By sending one Yokai monster from your hand to the graveyard, its ATK is raised by 500.
ATK 1400 DEF 800
THE BLACK HORSE'S EFFECT!!
SHAK
BY SENDING ONE YOKAI FROM MY HAND TO THE GRAVEYARD, I RAISE ITS ATK BY 500 POINTS!!
I ATTACK BOA BOLAN WITH THE LONG-TAILED BLACK HORSE!!
VROOOSH
LONG-TAILED BLACK HORSE ATK 1900
BOA BOLAN ATK 1700

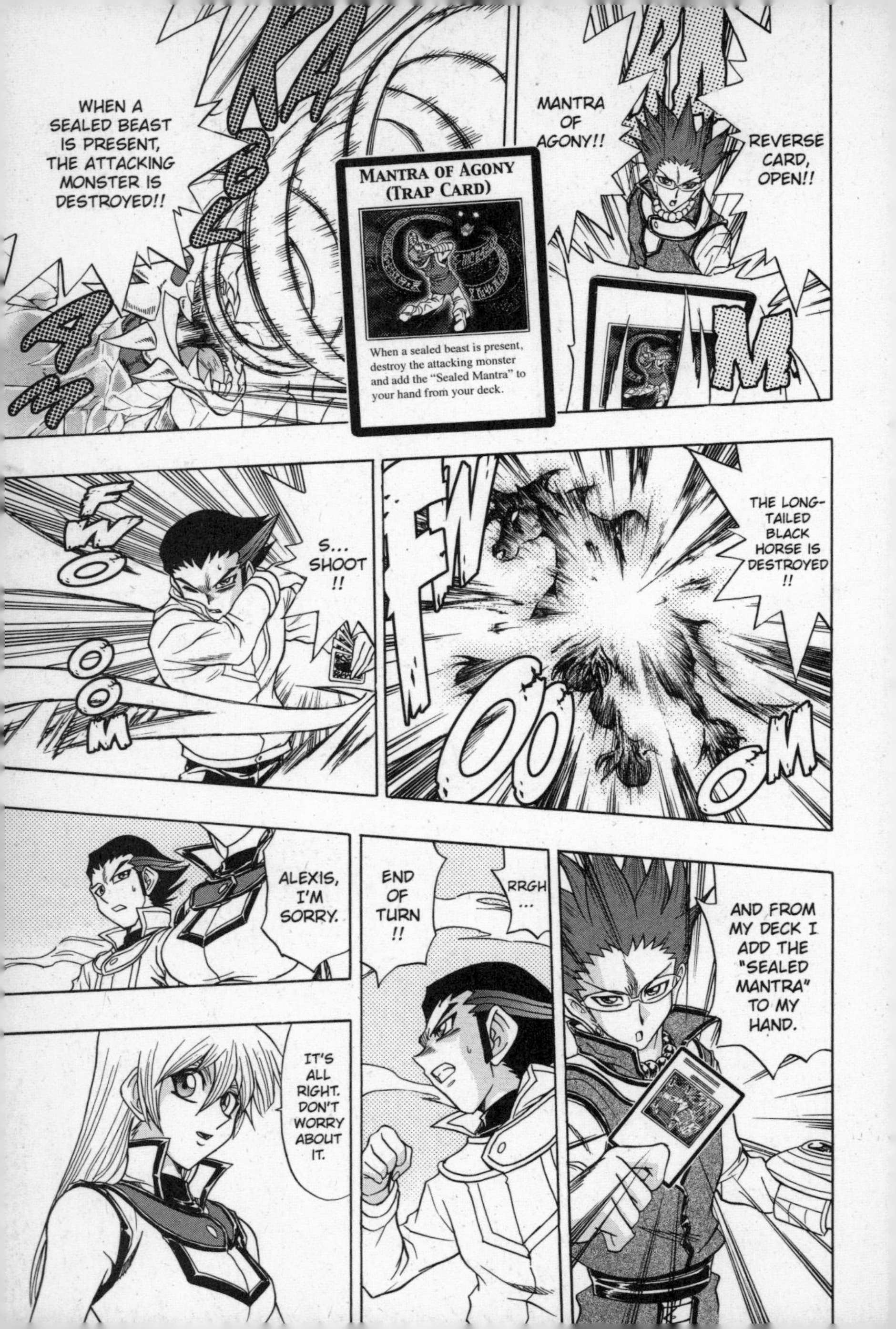
REVERSE CARD, OPEN!!
MANTRA OF AGONY!!
MANTRA OF AGONY
(TRAP CARD)
When a sealed beast is present, destroy the attacking monster and add the "Sealed Mantra" to your hand from your deck.
WHEN A SEALED BEAST IS PRESENT, THE ATTACKING MONSTER IS DESTROYED!!
FWOOOM
THE LONG-TAILED BLACK HORSE IS DESTROYED!!
FWOOOM
S... SHOOT!!
AND FROM MY DECK I ADD THE "SEALED MANTRA" TO MY HAND.
RRGH...
END OF TURN!!
ALEXIS, I'M SORRY.
IT'S ALL RIGHT. DON'T WORRY ABOUT IT.

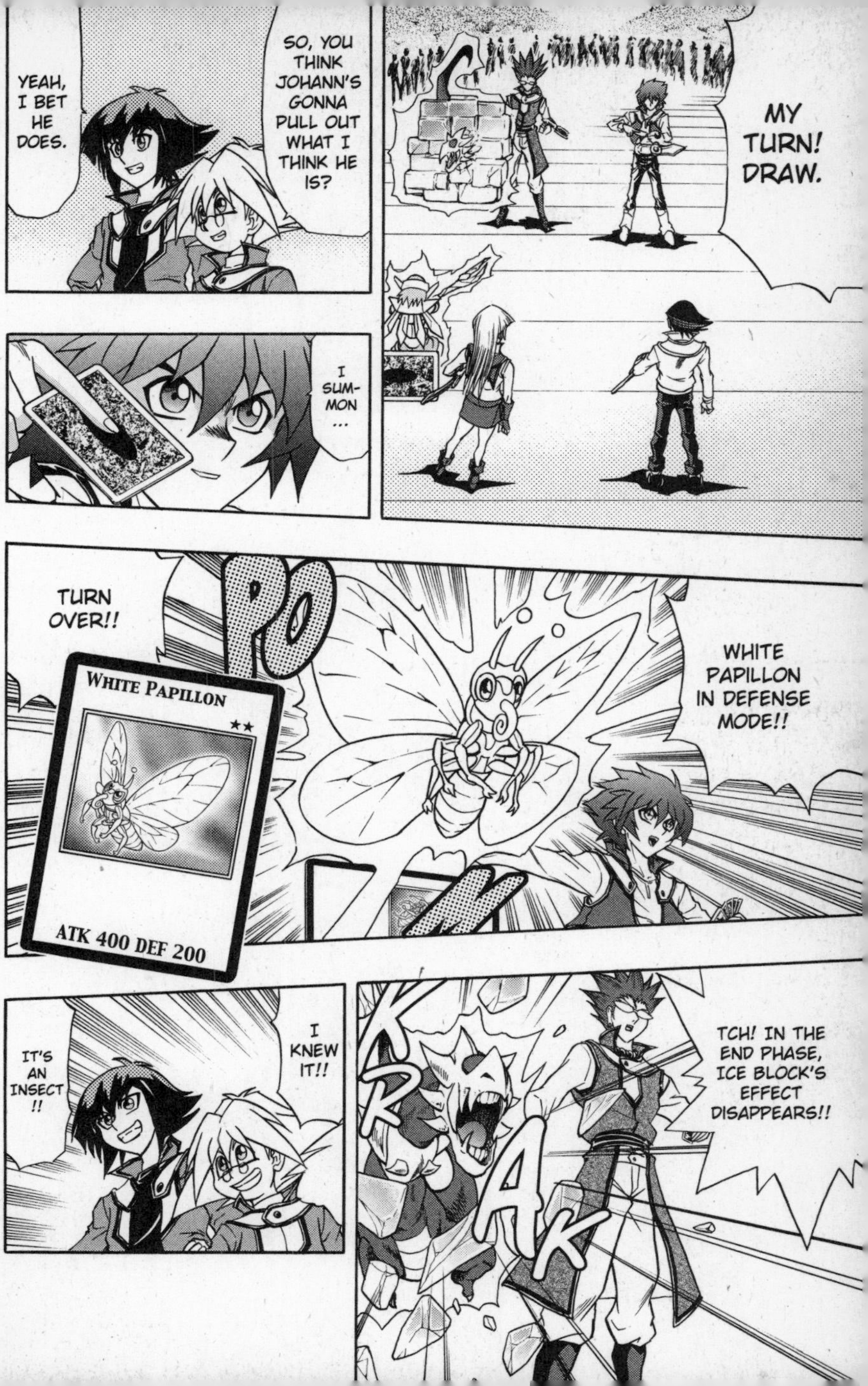
MY TURN! DRAW.
SO, YOU THINK JOHANN'S GONNA PULL OUT WHAT I THINK HE IS?
YEAH, I BET HE DOES.
I SUM-MON...
WHITE PAPILLON IN DEFENSE MODE!!
PO
TURN OVER!!
WHITE PAPILLON
ATK 400 DEF 200
TCH! IN THE END PHASE, ICE BLOCK'S EFFECT DISAPPEARS!!
KRAK
I KNEW IT!!
IT'S AN INSECT!!

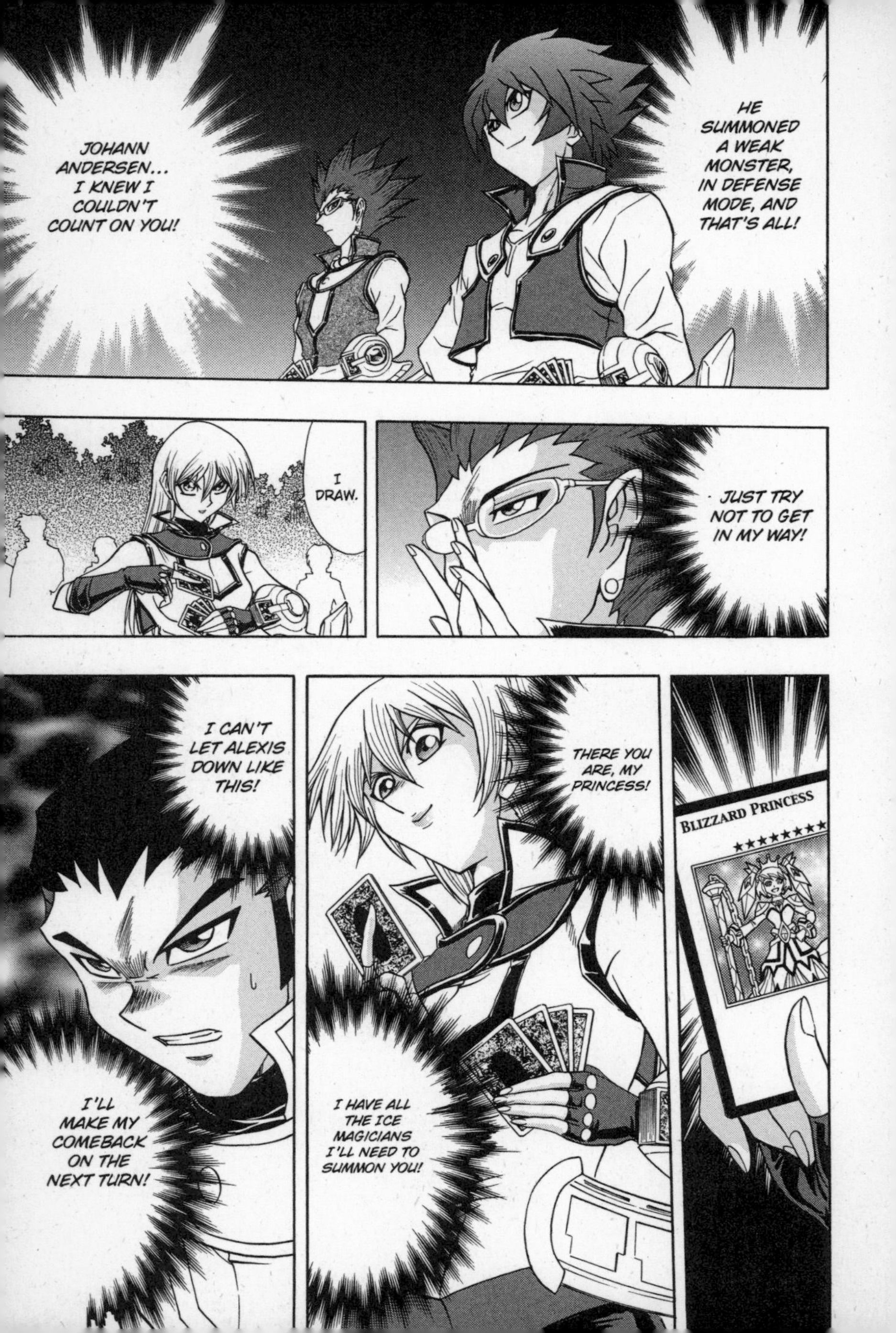
HE SUMMONED A WEAK MONSTER, IN DEFENSE MODE, AND THAT'S ALL!
JOHANN ANDERSEN... I KNEW I COULDN'T COUNT ON YOU!
JUST TRY NOT TO GET IN MY WAY!
I DRAW.
BLIZZARD PRINCESS
THERE YOU ARE, MY PRINCESS!
I HAVE ALL THE ICE MAGICIANS I'LL NEED TO SUMMON YOU!
I CAN'T LET ALEXIS DOWN LIKE THIS!
I'LL MAKE MY COMEBACK ON THE NEXT TURN!

THE MOVIE PREMIERE!

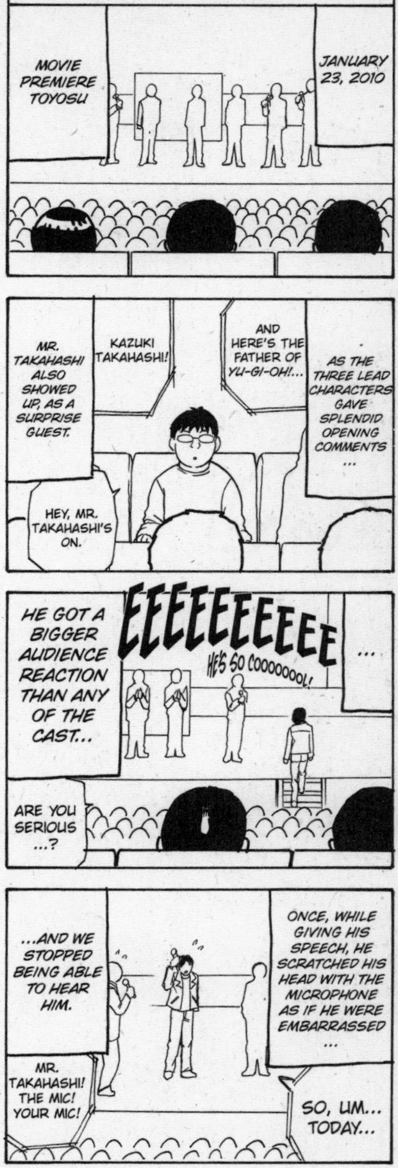
JANUARY 23, 2010
MOVIE PREMIERE TOYOSU
AS THE THREE LEAD CHARACTERS GAVE SPLENDID OPENING COMMENTS ...
AND HERE'S THE FATHER OF YU-GI-OH!...
KAZUKI TAKAHASHI!
MR. TAKAHASHI ALSO SHOWED UP, AS A SURPRISE GUEST.
HEY, MR. TAKAHASHI'S ON.
...
EEEEEEEEEEE
HE'S SO COOOOOOOL!
HE GOT A BIGGER AUDIENCE REACTION THAN ANY OF THE CAST...
ARE YOU SERIOUS ...?
ONCE, WHILE GIVING HIS SPEECH, HE SCRATCHED HIS HEAD WITH THE MICROPHONE AS IF HE WERE EMBARRASSED ...
SO, UM... TODAY...
...AND WE STOPPED BEING ABLE TO HEAR HIM.
MR. TAKAHASHI! THE MIC! YOUR MIC!

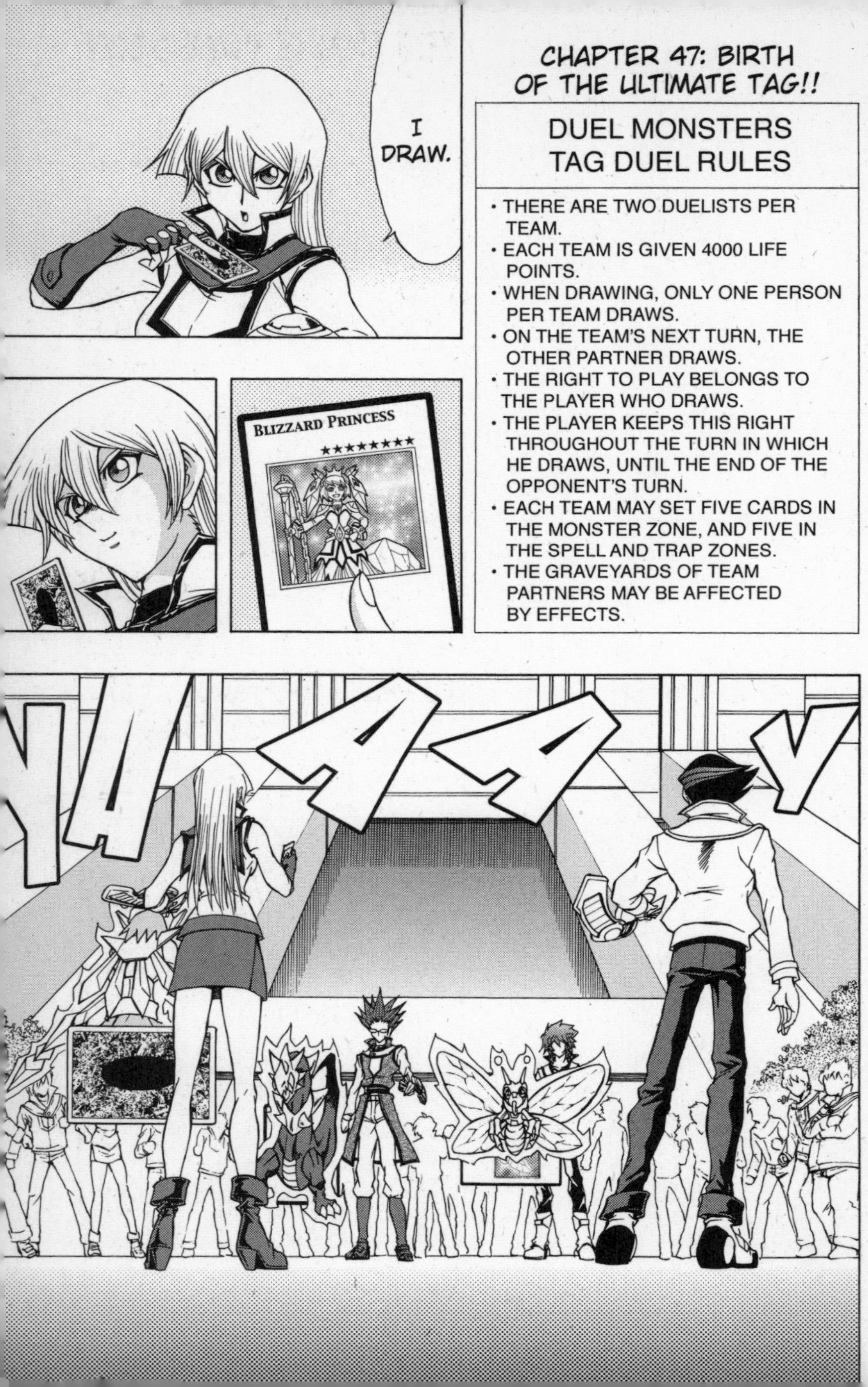
CHAPTER 47: BIRTH OF THE ULTIMATE TAG!!
DUEL MONSTERS TAG DUEL RULES
• THERE ARE TWO DUELISTS PER TEAM.
• EACH TEAM IS GIVEN 4000 LIFE POINTS.
• WHEN DRAWING, ONLY ONE PERSON PER TEAM DRAWS.
• ON THE TEAM'S NEXT TURN, THE OTHER PARTNER DRAWS.
• THE RIGHT TO PLAY BELONGS TO THE PLAYER WHO DRAWS.
• THE PLAYER KEEPS THIS RIGHT THROUGHOUT THE TURN IN WHICH HE DRAWS, UNTIL THE END OF THE OPPONENT'S TURN.
• EACH TEAM MAY SET FIVE CARDS IN THE MONSTER ZONE, AND FIVE IN THE SPELL AND TRAP ZONES.
• THE GRAVEYARDS OF TEAM PARTNERS MAY BE AFFECTED BY EFFECTS.
I DRAW.
BLIZZARD PRINCESS
YAAAY

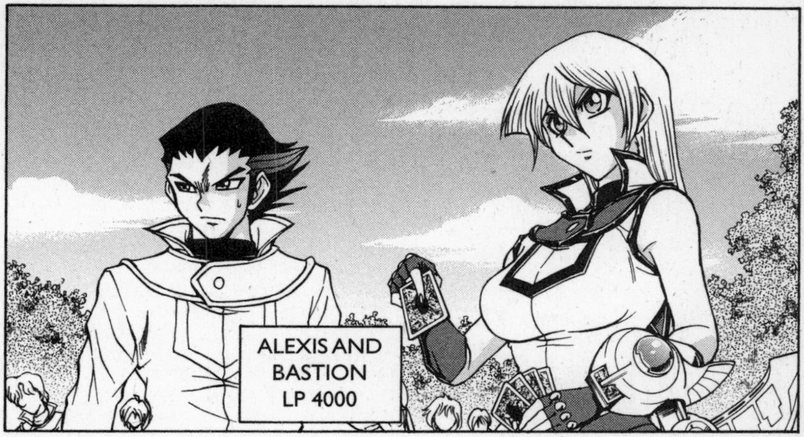
ALEXIS AND
BASTION
LP 4000

CHAPTER 47:
BIRTH OF THE ULTIMATE TAG!!

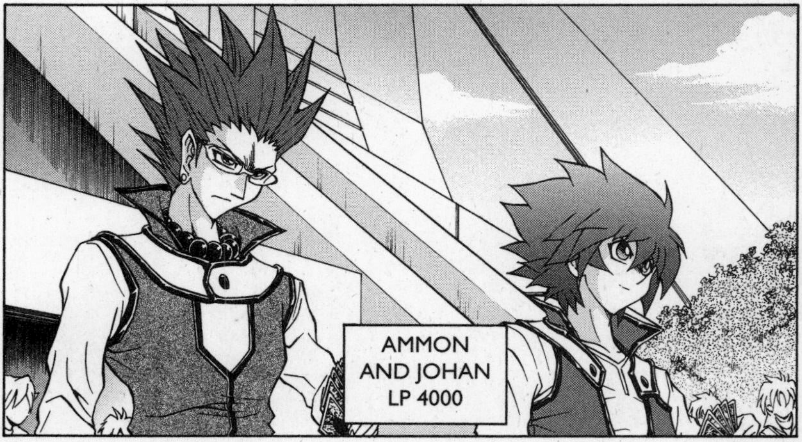
AMMON
AND JOHAN
LP 4000

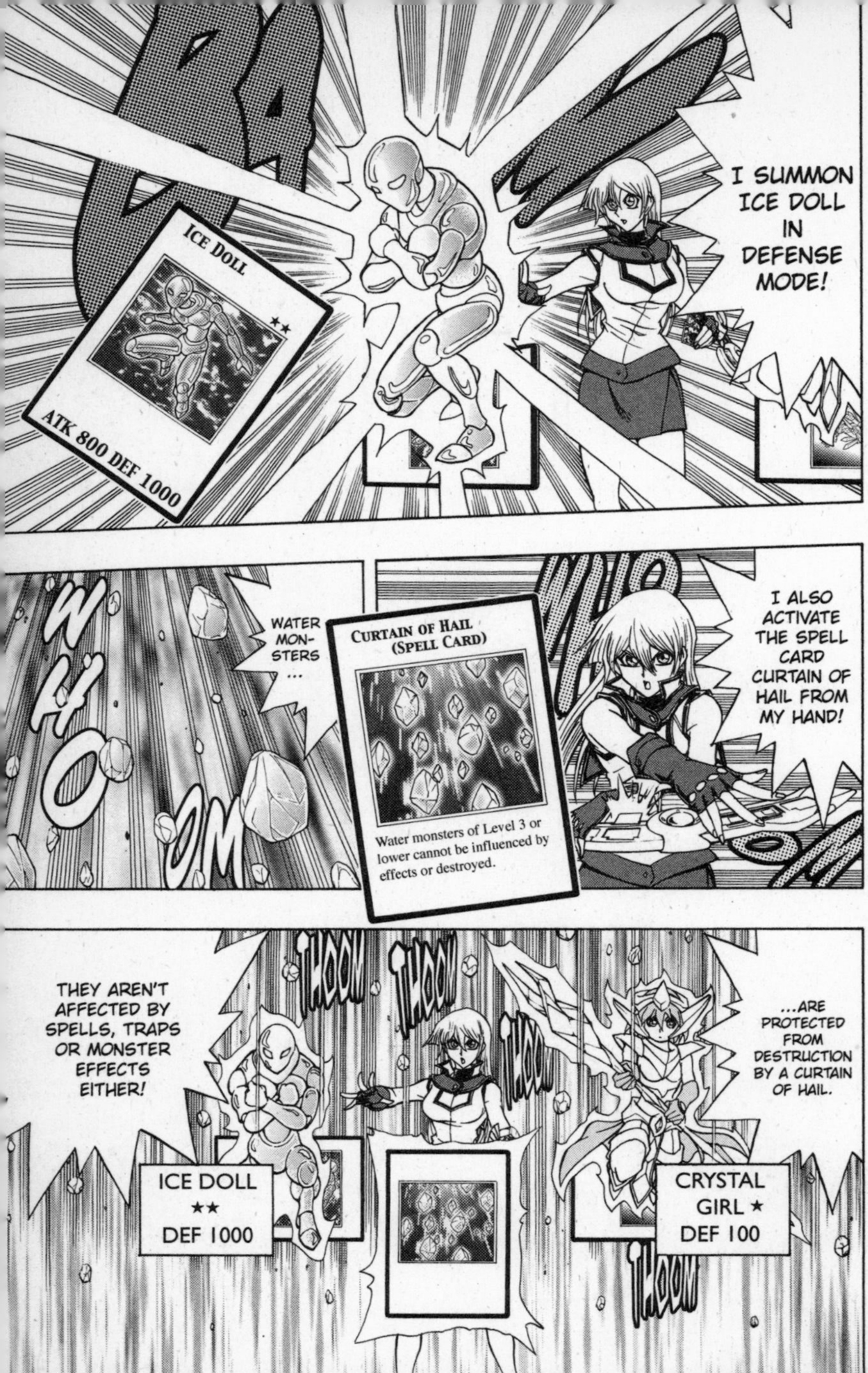
I SUMMON ICE DOLL IN DEFENSE MODE!
ICE DOLL
★★
ATK 800 DEF 1000
I ALSO ACTIVATE THE SPELL CARD CURTAIN OF HAIL FROM MY HAND!
CURTAIN OF HAIL (SPELL CARD)
Water monsters of Level 3 or lower cannot be influenced by effects or destroyed.
WATER MONSTERS ...
WHOOM
...ARE PROTECTED FROM DESTRUCTION BY A CURTAIN OF HAIL.
THEY AREN'T AFFECTED BY SPELLS, TRAPS OR MONSTER EFFECTS EITHER!
THOOM
THOOM
THOOM
THOOM
CRYSTAL GIRL ★
DEF 100
ICE DOLL
★★
DEF 1000

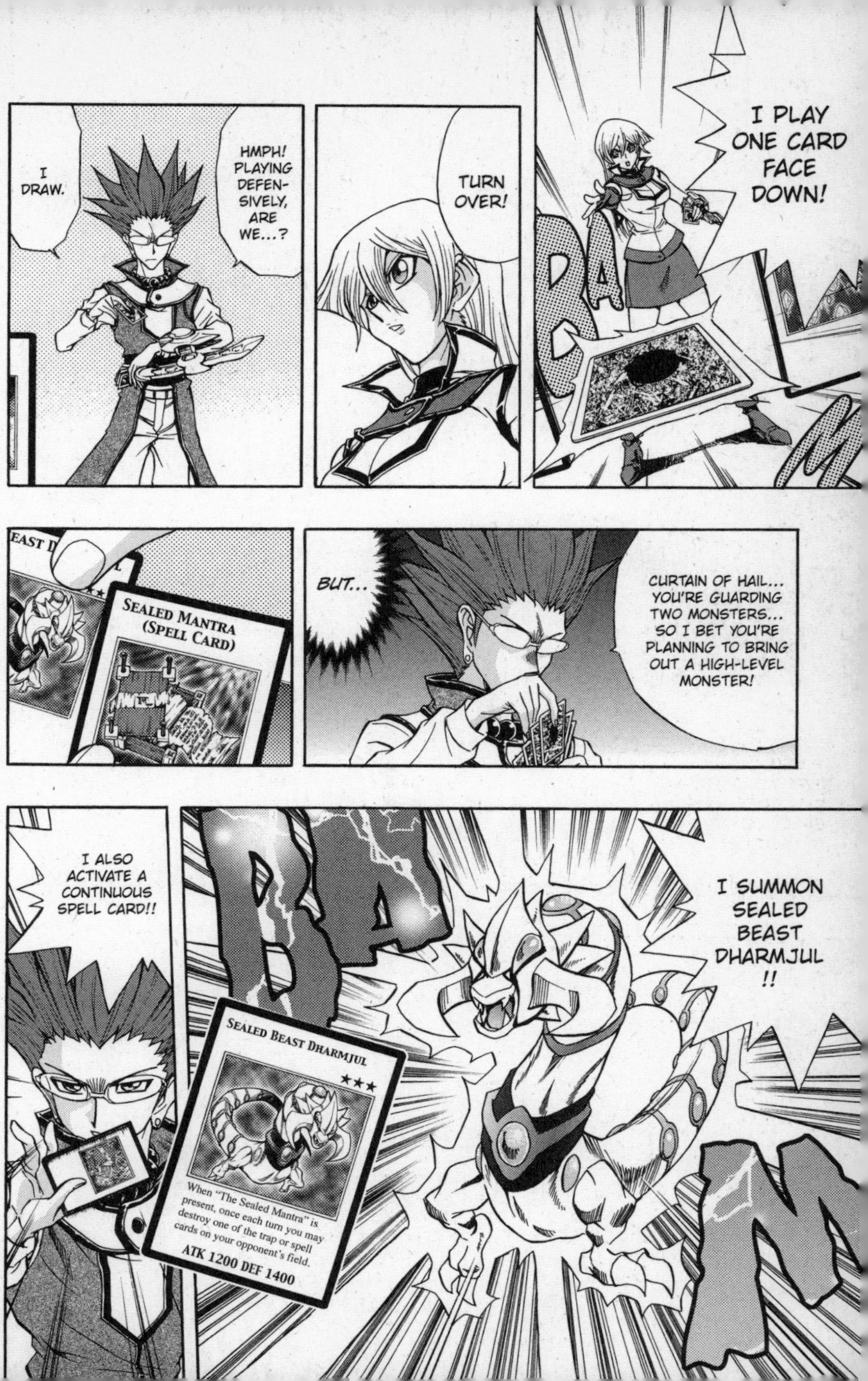
I PLAY ONE CARD FACE DOWN!
TURN OVER!
HMPH! PLAYING DEFENSIVELY, ARE WE...?
I DRAW.
CURTAIN OF HAIL... YOU'RE GUARDING TWO MONSTERS... SO I BET YOU'RE PLANNING TO BRING OUT A HIGH-LEVEL MONSTER!
BUT...
SEALED MANTRA (SPELL CARD)
I SUMMON SEALED BEAST DHARMJUL !!
SEALED BEAST DHARMJUL
When "The Sealed Mantra" is present, once each turn you may destroy one of the trap or spell cards on your opponent's field.
ATK 1200 DEF 1400
I ALSO ACTIVATE A CONTINUOUS SPELL CARD!!

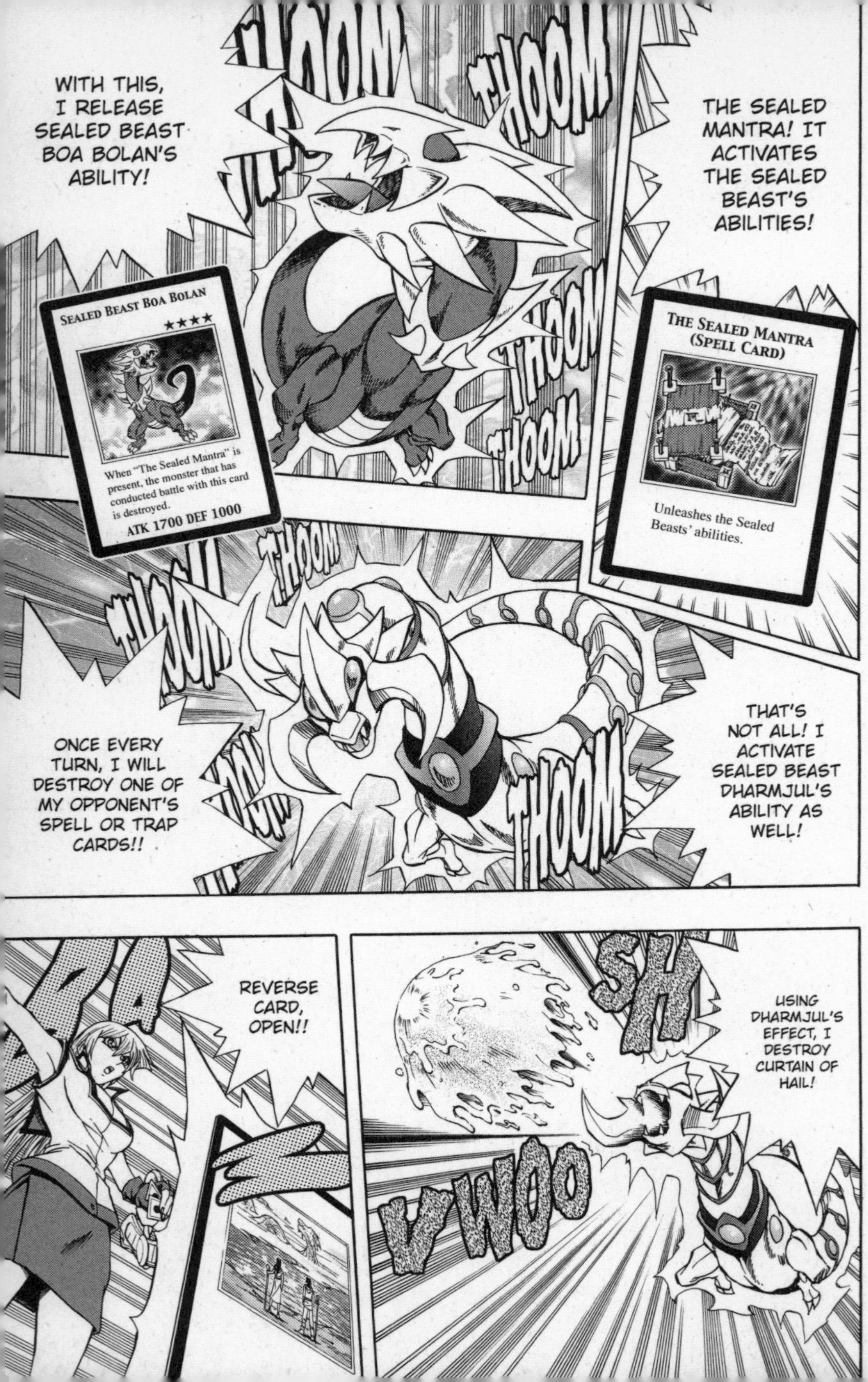
THE SEALED MANTRA! IT ACTIVATES THE SEALED BEAST'S ABILITIES!
THE SEALED MANTRA (SPELL CARD)
Unleashes the Sealed Beasts' abilities.
THOOM
THOOM
THOOM
THOOM
WITH THIS, I RELEASE SEALED BEAST BOA BOLAN'S ABILITY!
SEALED BEAST BOA BOLAN
★★★★
When "The Sealed Mantra" is present, the monster that has conducted battle with this card is destroyed.
ATK 1700 DEF 1000
THAT'S NOT ALL! I ACTIVATE SEALED BEAST DHARMJUL'S ABILITY AS WELL!
THOOM
THOOM
ONCE EVERY TURN, I WILL DESTROY ONE OF MY OPPONENT'S SPELL OR TRAP CARDS!!
USING DHARMJUL'S EFFECT, I DESTROY CURTAIN OF HAIL!
SH
VWOO
REVERSE CARD, OPEN!!

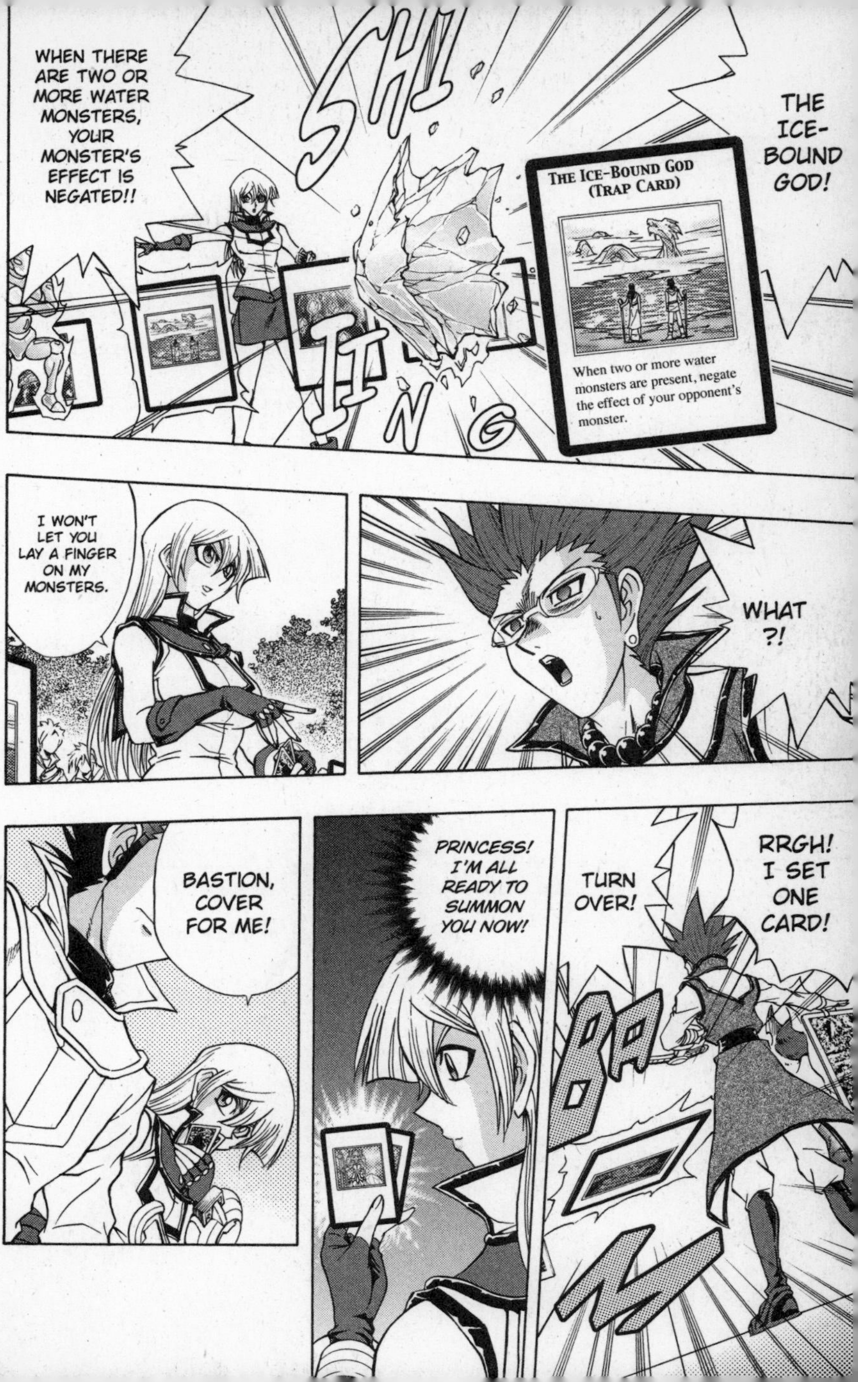
THE ICE-BOUND GOD!
THE ICE-BOUND GOD
(TRAP CARD)
When two or more water monsters are present, negate the effect of your opponent's monster.
SHI
II
N
G
WHEN THERE ARE TWO OR MORE WATER MONSTERS, YOUR MONSTER'S EFFECT IS NEGATED!!
WHAT ?!
I WON'T LET YOU LAY A FINGER ON MY MONSTERS.
RRGH! I SET ONE CARD!
TURN OVER!
BA
M
PRINCESS! I'M ALL READY TO SUMMON YOU NOW!
BASTION, COVER FOR ME!

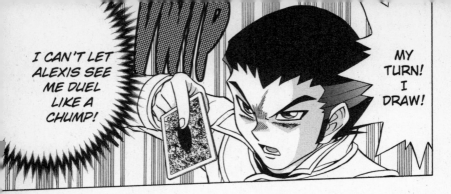

I CAN'T LET ALEXIS SEE ME DUEL LIKE A CHUMP!

MY TURN! I DRAW!

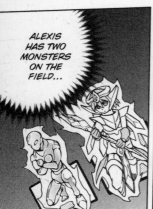

ALEXIS HAS TWO MONSTERS ON THE FIELD...

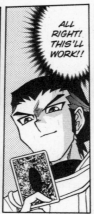

ALL RIGHT! THIS'LL WORK!!

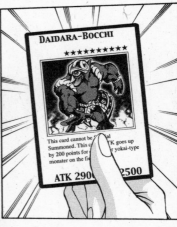

DAIDARA-BOCCHI

★★★★★★★★★★★

This card cannot be Normal Summoned. This card's ATK goes up by 200 points for each yokai-type monster on the field.

ATK 2900   2500

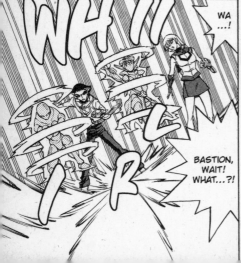

WA...!

HUH?!

BASTION, WAIT! WHAT...?!

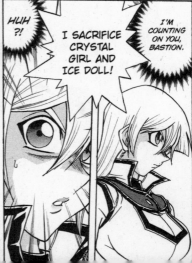

I SACRIFICE CRYSTAL GIRL AND ICE DOLL!

I'M COUNTING ON YOU, BASTION.

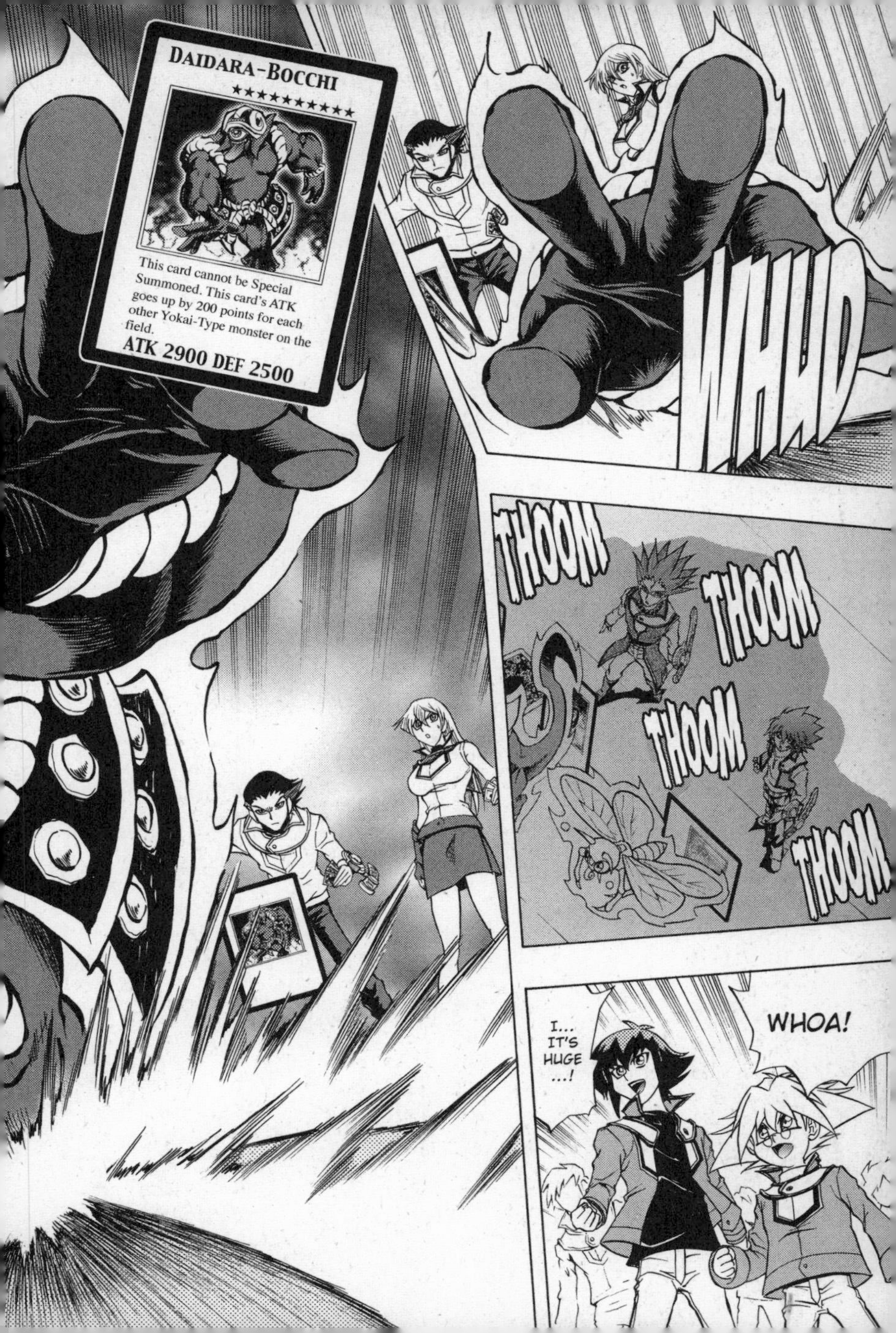
WHUD
THOOM
THOOM
THOOM
THOOM
WHOA!
I... IT'S HUGE ...!
DAIDARA-BOCCHI
This card cannot be Special Summoned. This card's ATK goes up by 200 points for each other Yokai-Type monster on the field.
ATK 2900 DEF 2500

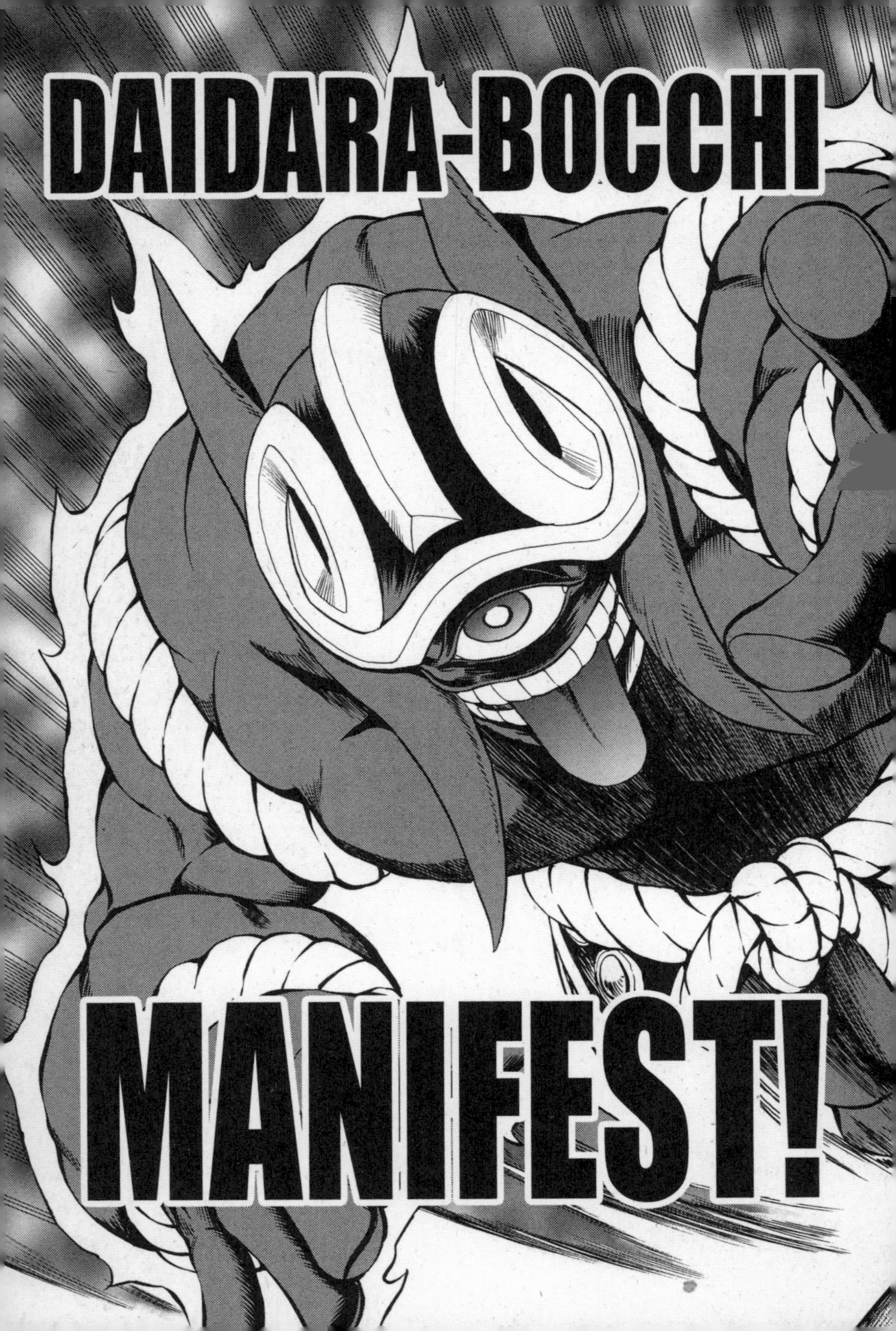
DAIDARA-BOCCHI
MANIFEST!

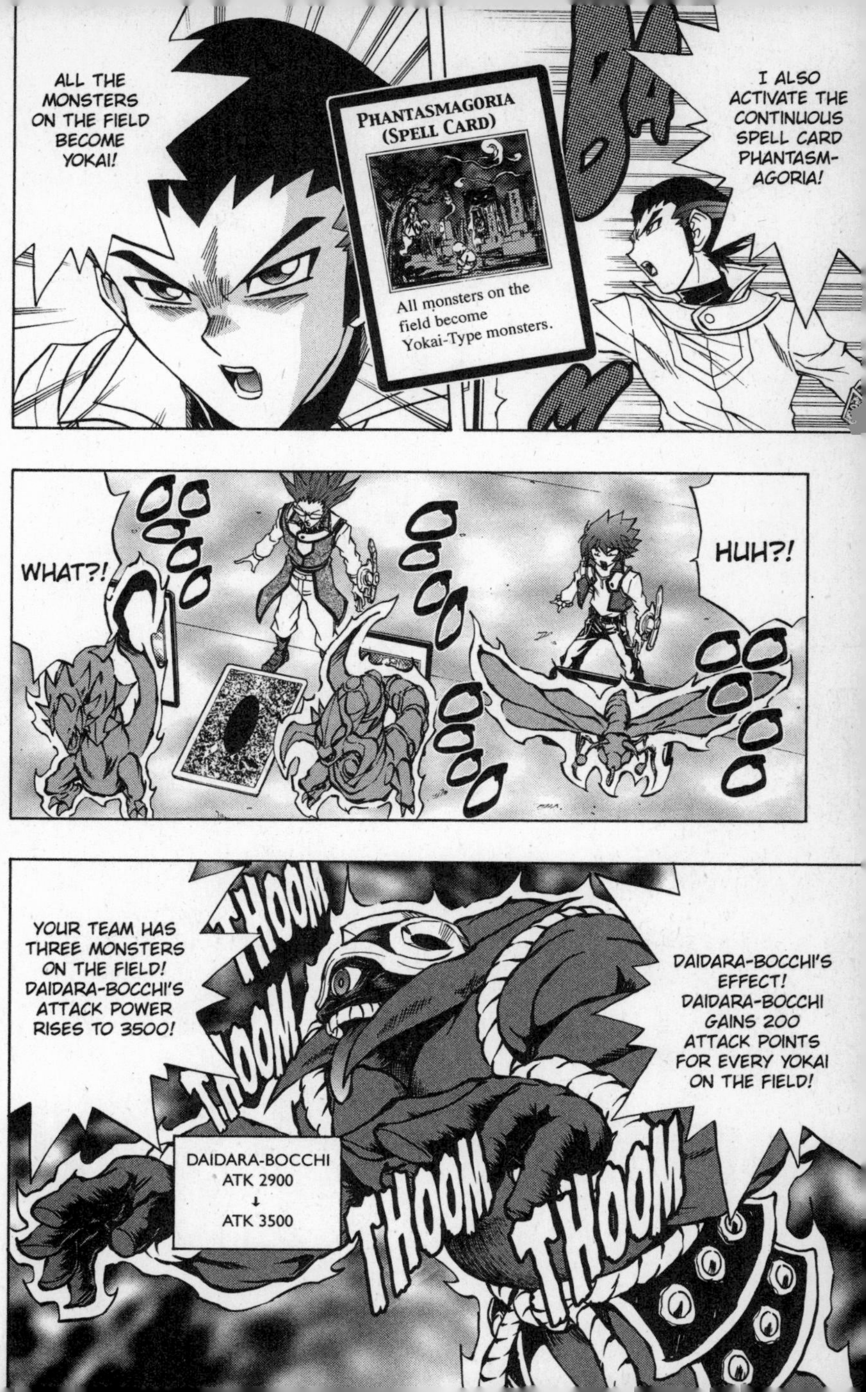
I ALSO ACTIVATE THE CONTINUOUS SPELL CARD PHANTASM-AGORIA!
BAM
PHANTASMAGORIA (SPELL CARD)
All monsters on the field become Yokai-Type monsters.
ALL THE MONSTERS ON THE FIELD BECOME YOKAI!
HUH?!
OOOO
OOOO
OOOO
WHAT?!
DAIDARA-BOCCHI'S EFFECT! DAIDARA-BOCCHI GAINS 200 ATTACK POINTS FOR EVERY YOKAI ON THE FIELD!
THOOM
THOOM
THOOM
THOOM
THOOM
THOOM
DAIDARA-BOCCHI ATK 2900 ↓ ATK 3500
YOUR TEAM HAS THREE MONSTERS ON THE FIELD! DAIDARA-BOCCHI'S ATTACK POWER RISES TO 3500!

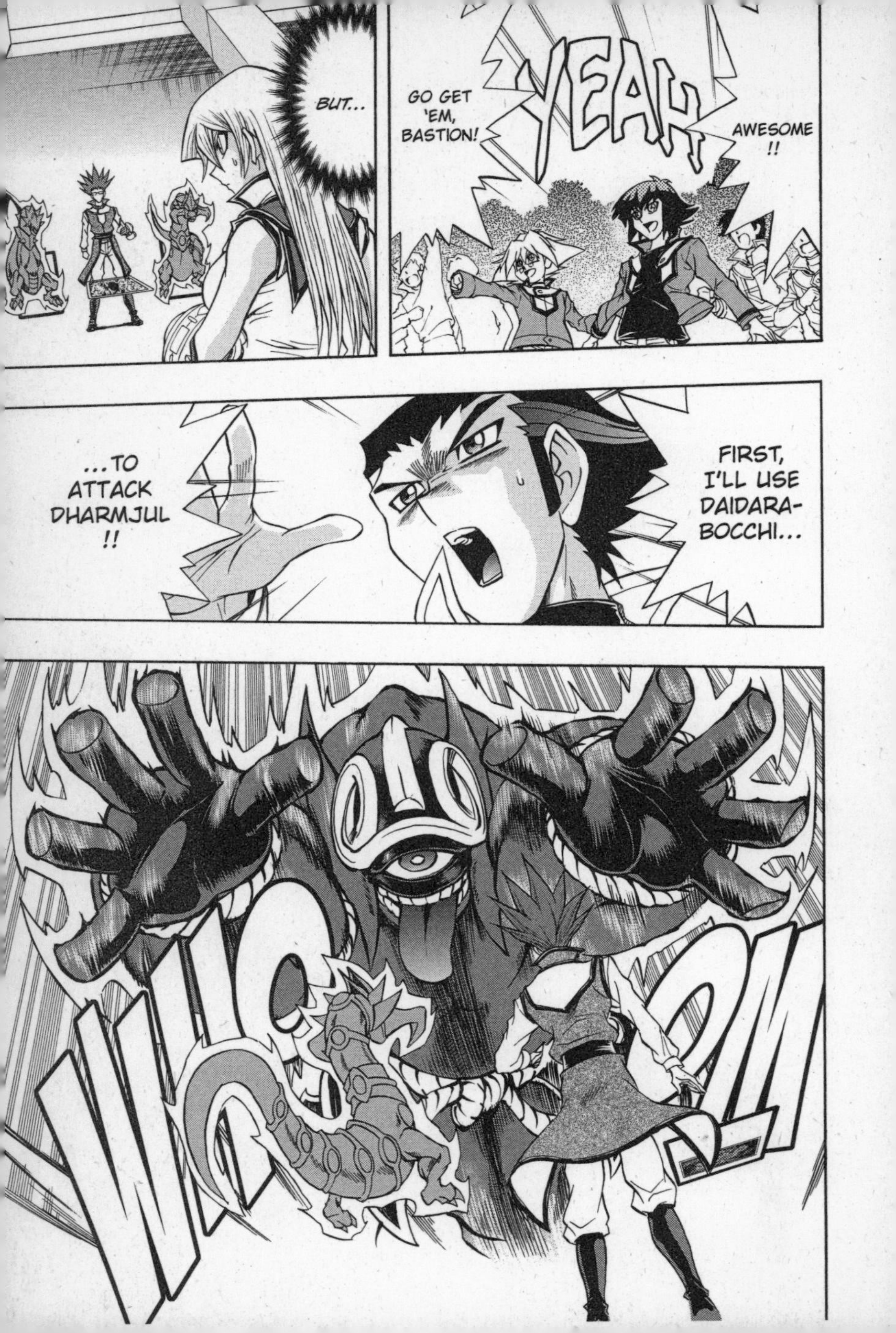
YEAH
AWESOME !!
GO GET 'EM, BASTION!
BUT...
FIRST, I'LL USE DAIDARA-BOCCHI...
...TO ATTACK DHARMJUL !!

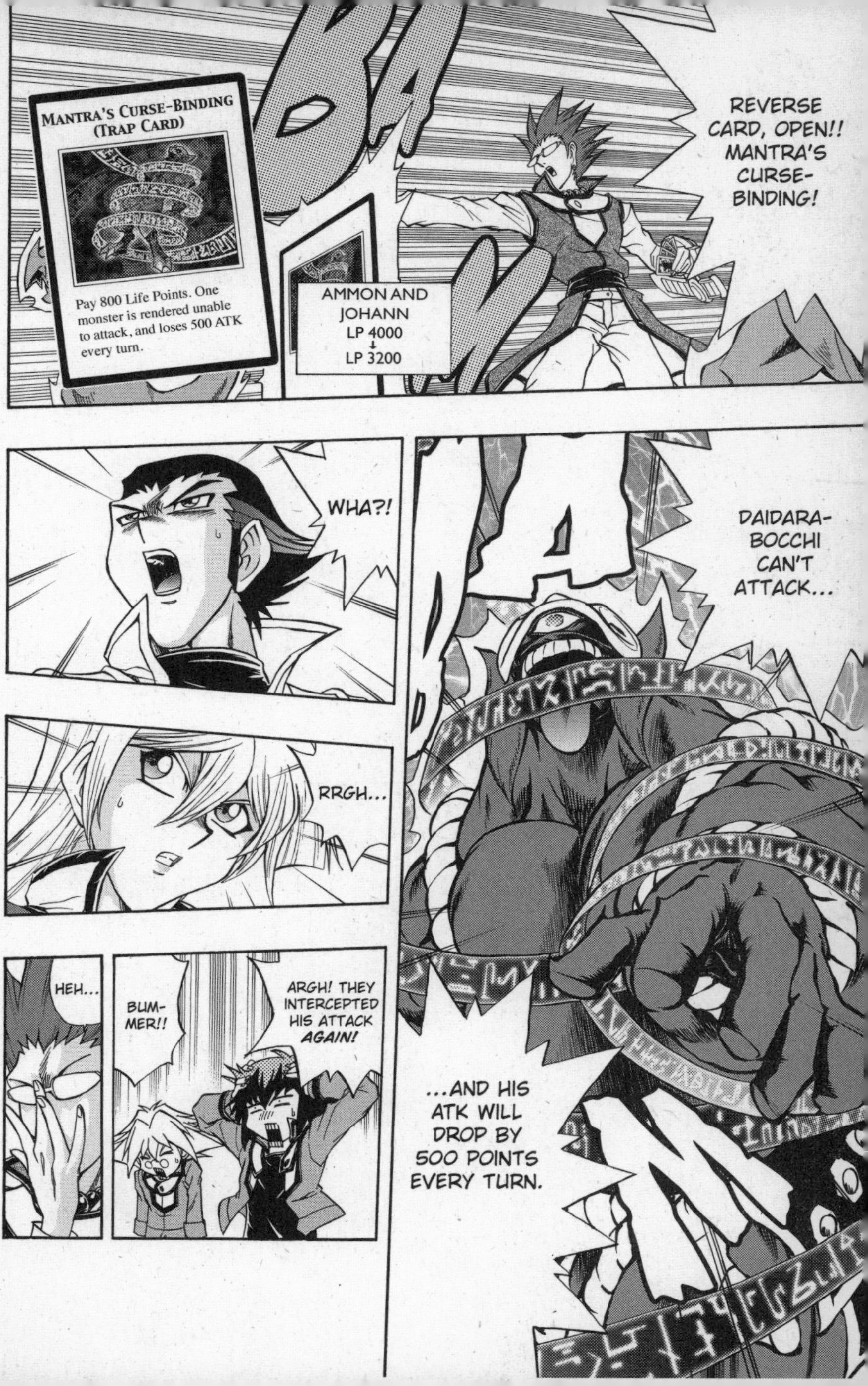
REVERSE CARD, OPEN!! MANTRA'S CURSE-BINDING!
MANTRA'S CURSE-BINDING (TRAP CARD)
Pay 800 Life Points. One monster is rendered unable to attack, and loses 500 ATK every turn.
AMMON AND JOHANN LP 4000 ↓ LP 3200
DAIDARA-BOCCHI CAN'T ATTACK...
...AND HIS ATK WILL DROP BY 500 POINTS EVERY TURN.
WHA?!
RRGH...
ARGH! THEY INTERCEPTED HIS ATTACK *AGAIN!*
BUM-MER!!
HEH...

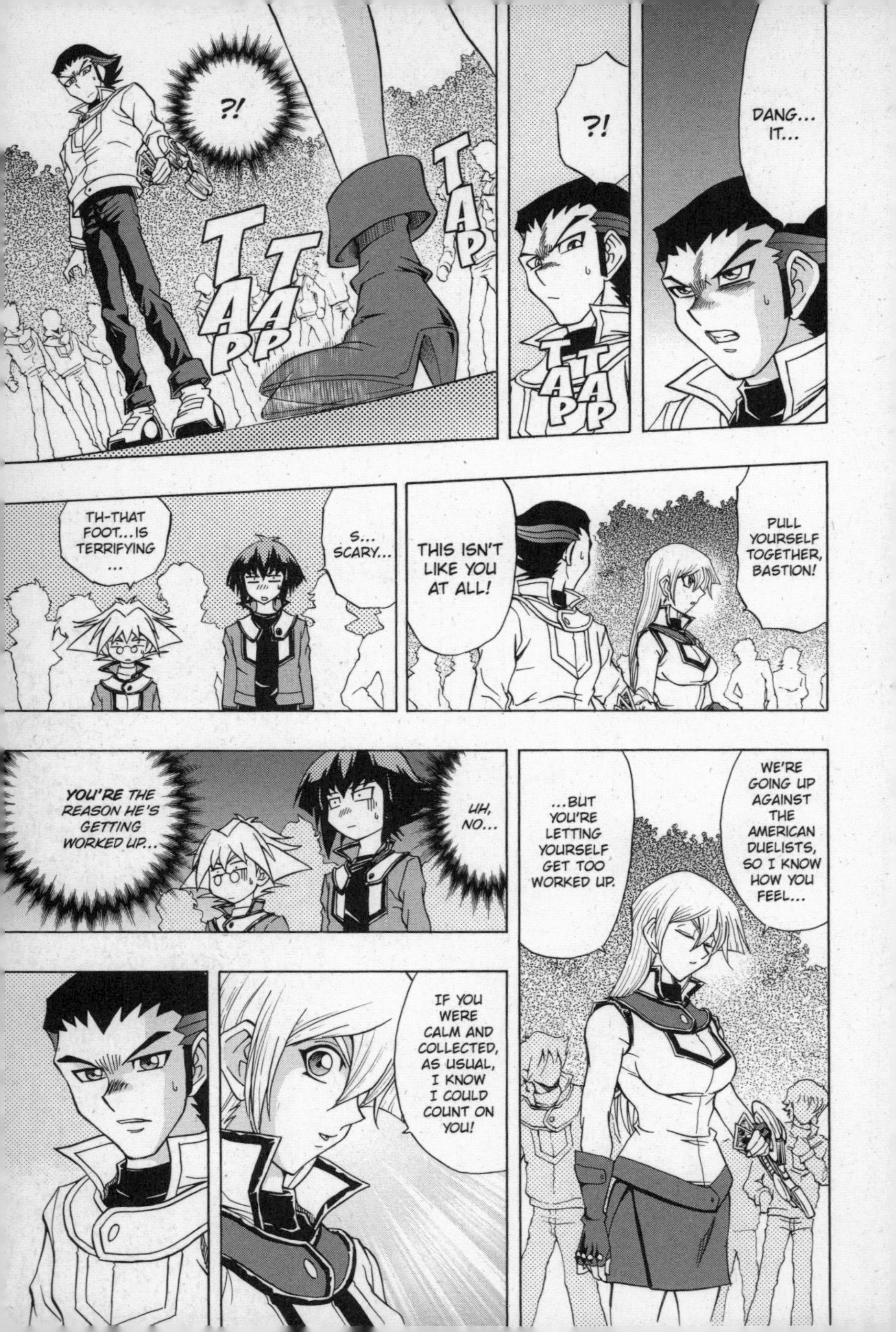
DANG... IT...
?!
TAP TAP
?!
TAP
TAP
TAP
PULL YOURSELF TOGETHER, BASTION!
THIS ISN'T LIKE YOU AT ALL!
S... SCARY...
TH-THAT FOOT...IS TERRIFYING ...
WE'RE GOING UP AGAINST THE AMERICAN DUELISTS, SO I KNOW HOW YOU FEEL...
...BUT YOU'RE LETTING YOURSELF GET TOO WORKED UP.
UH, NO...
YOU'RE THE REASON HE'S GETTING WORKED UP...
IF YOU WERE CALM AND COLLECTED, AS USUAL, I KNOW I COULD COUNT ON YOU!

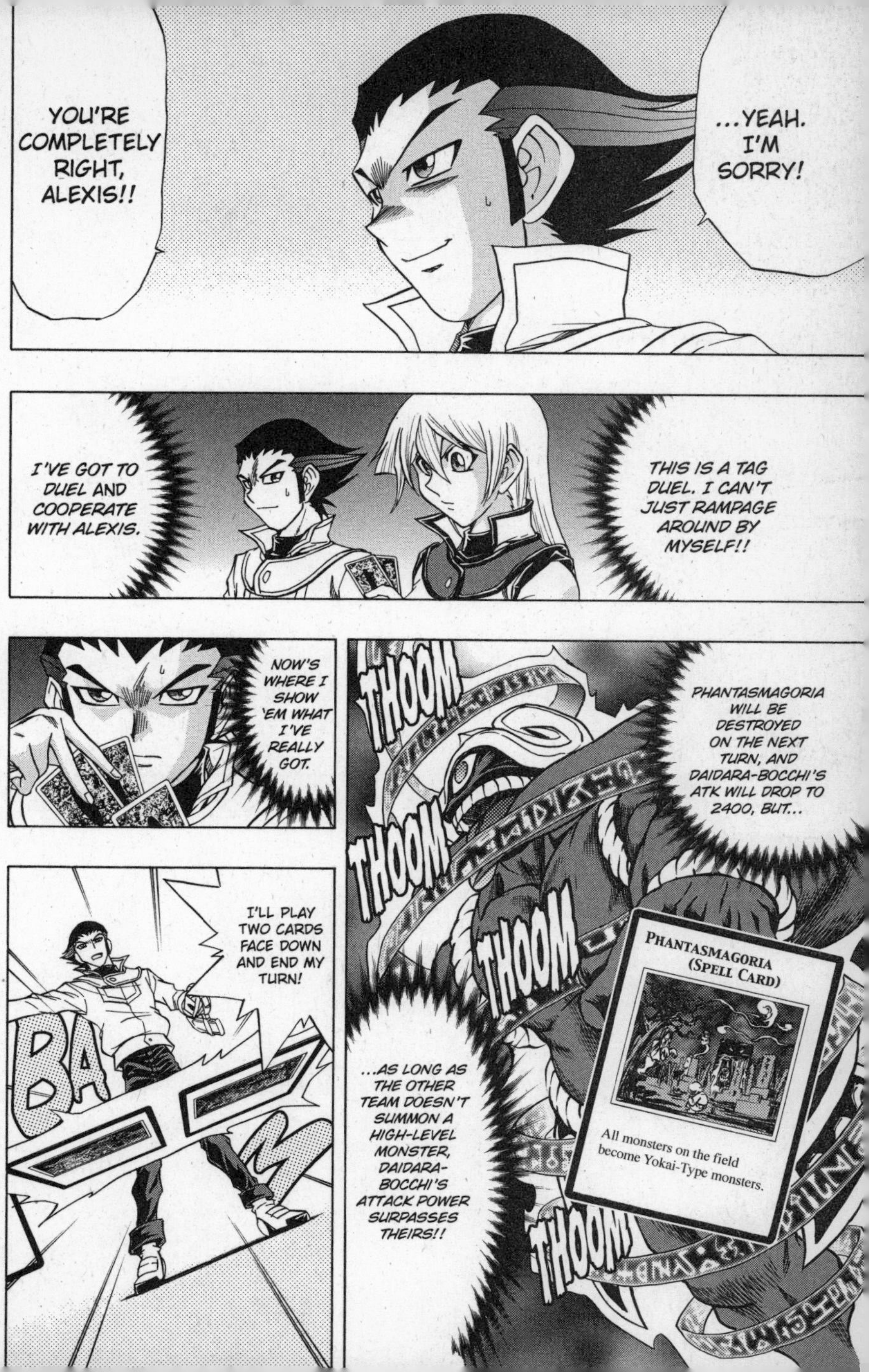
...YEAH. I'M SORRY!
YOU'RE COMPLETELY RIGHT, ALEXIS!!
THIS IS A TAG DUEL. I CAN'T JUST RAMPAGE AROUND BY MYSELF!!
I'VE GOT TO DUEL AND COOPERATE WITH ALEXIS.
THOOM
PHANTASMAGORIA WILL BE DESTROYED ON THE NEXT TURN, AND DAIDARA-BOCCHI'S ATK WILL DROP TO 2400, BUT...
THOOM
THOOM
PHANTASMAGORIA (SPELL CARD)
All monsters on the field become Yokai-Type monsters.
...AS LONG AS THE OTHER TEAM DOESN'T SUMMON A HIGH-LEVEL MONSTER, DAIDARA-BOCCHI'S ATTACK POWER SURPASSES THEIRS!!
THOOM
NOW'S WHERE I SHOW 'EM WHAT I'VE REALLY GOT.
I'LL PLAY TWO CARDS FACE DOWN AND END MY TURN!
BAM

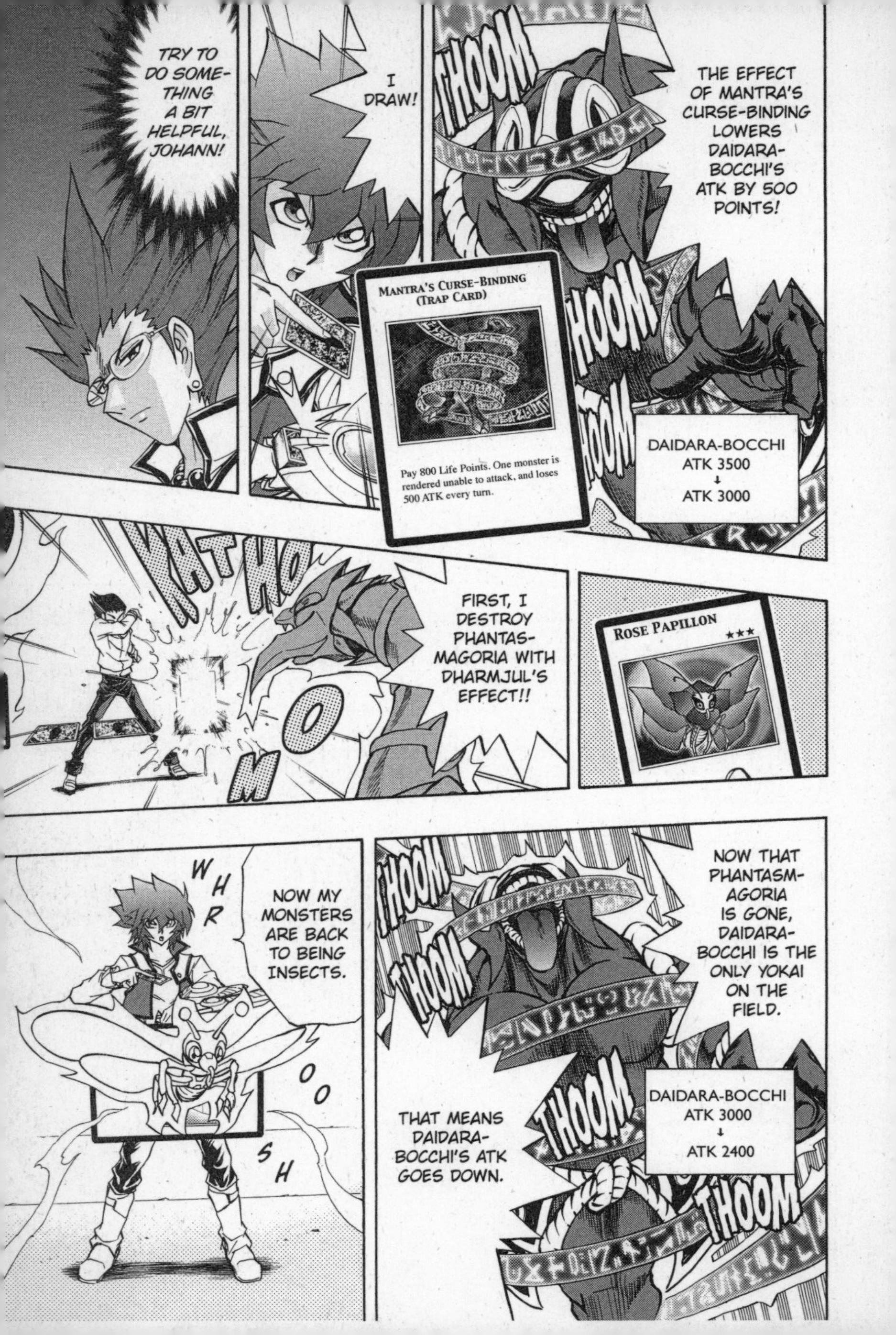
THOOM
THE EFFECT OF MANTRA'S CURSE-BINDING LOWERS DAIDARA-BOCCHI'S ATK BY 500 POINTS!
MANTRA'S CURSE-BINDING (TRAP CARD)
Pay 800 Life Points. One monster is rendered unable to attack, and loses 500 ATK every turn.
THOOM
THOOM
DAIDARA-BOCCHI ATK 3500 ↓ ATK 3000
I DRAW!
TRY TO DO SOMETHING A BIT HELPFUL, JOHANN!
ROSE PAPILLON ★★★
FIRST, I DESTROY PHANTASMAGORIA WITH DHARMJUL'S EFFECT!!
KATHOOM
NOW THAT PHANTASMAGORIA IS GONE, DAIDARA-BOCCHI IS THE ONLY YOKAI ON THE FIELD.
THOOM
THOOM
THOOM
DAIDARA-BOCCHI ATK 3000 ↓ ATK 2400
THAT MEANS DAIDARA-BOCCHI'S ATK GOES DOWN.
THOOM
NOW MY MONSTERS ARE BACK TO BEING INSECTS.
WHR
OOSH

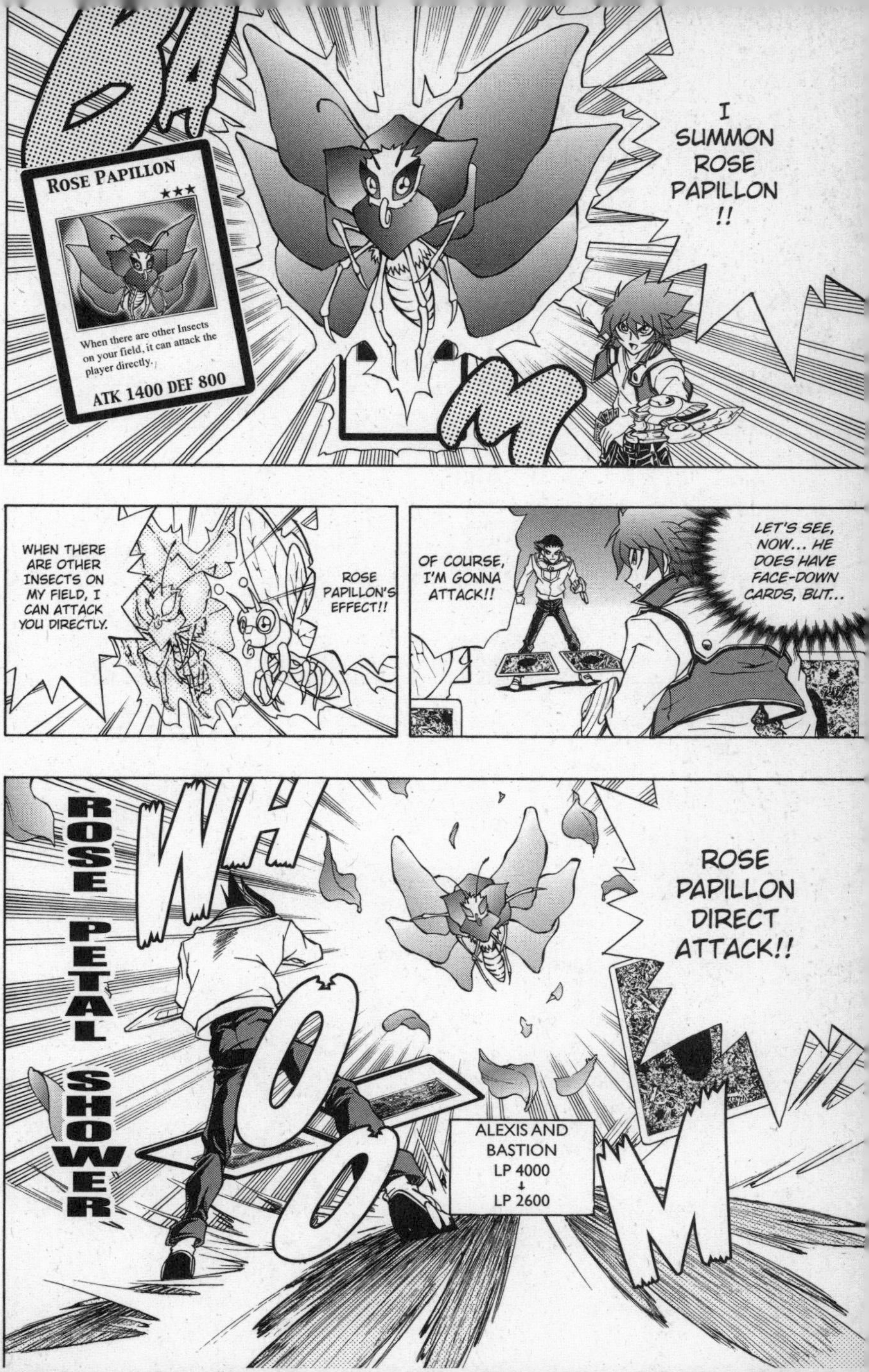
I SUMMON ROSE PAPILLON!!
ROSE PAPILLON ★★★
When there are other Insects on your field, it can attack the player directly.
ATK 1400 DEF 800
LET'S SEE, NOW... HE DOES HAVE FACE-DOWN CARDS, BUT...
OF COURSE, I'M GONNA ATTACK!!
ROSE PAPILLON'S EFFECT!!
WHEN THERE ARE OTHER INSECTS ON MY FIELD, I CAN ATTACK YOU DIRECTLY.
ROSE PAPILLON DIRECT ATTACK!!
ROSE PETAL SHOWER
ALEXIS AND BASTION LP 4000 ↓ LP 2600

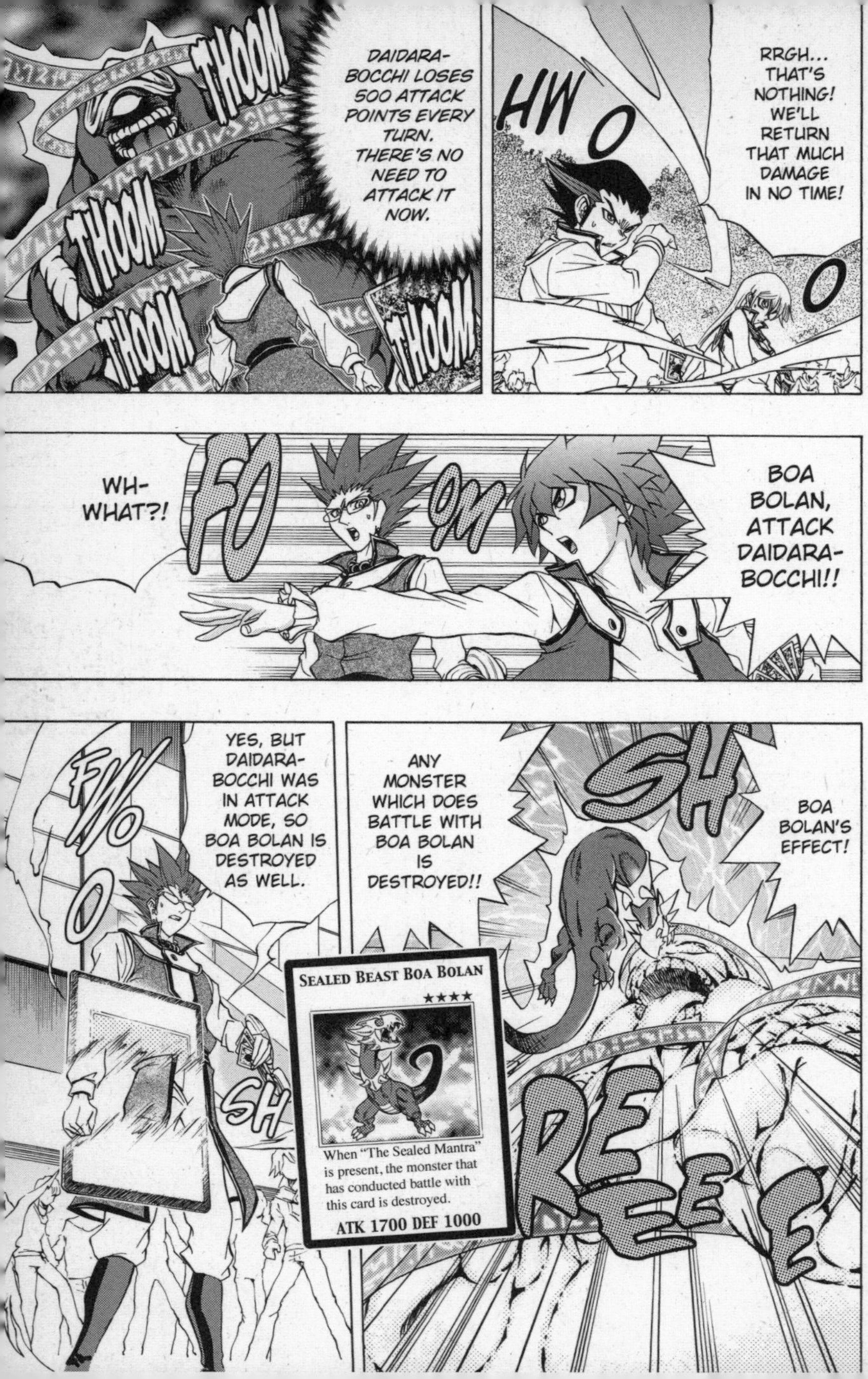
HWOO
RRGH... THAT'S NOTHING! WE'LL RETURN THAT MUCH DAMAGE IN NO TIME!
THOOM
THOOM
THOOM
THOOM
DAIDARA-BOCCHI LOSES 500 ATTACK POINTS EVERY TURN. THERE'S NO NEED TO ATTACK IT NOW.
BOA BOLAN, ATTACK DAIDARA-BOCCHI!!
FOOM
WH-WHAT?!
BOA BOLAN'S EFFECT!
SH
ANY MONSTER WHICH DOES BATTLE WITH BOA BOLAN IS DESTROYED!!
SEALED BEAST BOA BOLAN
When "The Sealed Mantra" is present, the monster that has conducted battle with this card is destroyed.
ATK 1700 DEF 1000
REEEE
YES, BUT DAIDARA-BOCCHI WAS IN ATTACK MODE, SO BOA BOLAN IS DESTROYED AS WELL.
FWOO
SH

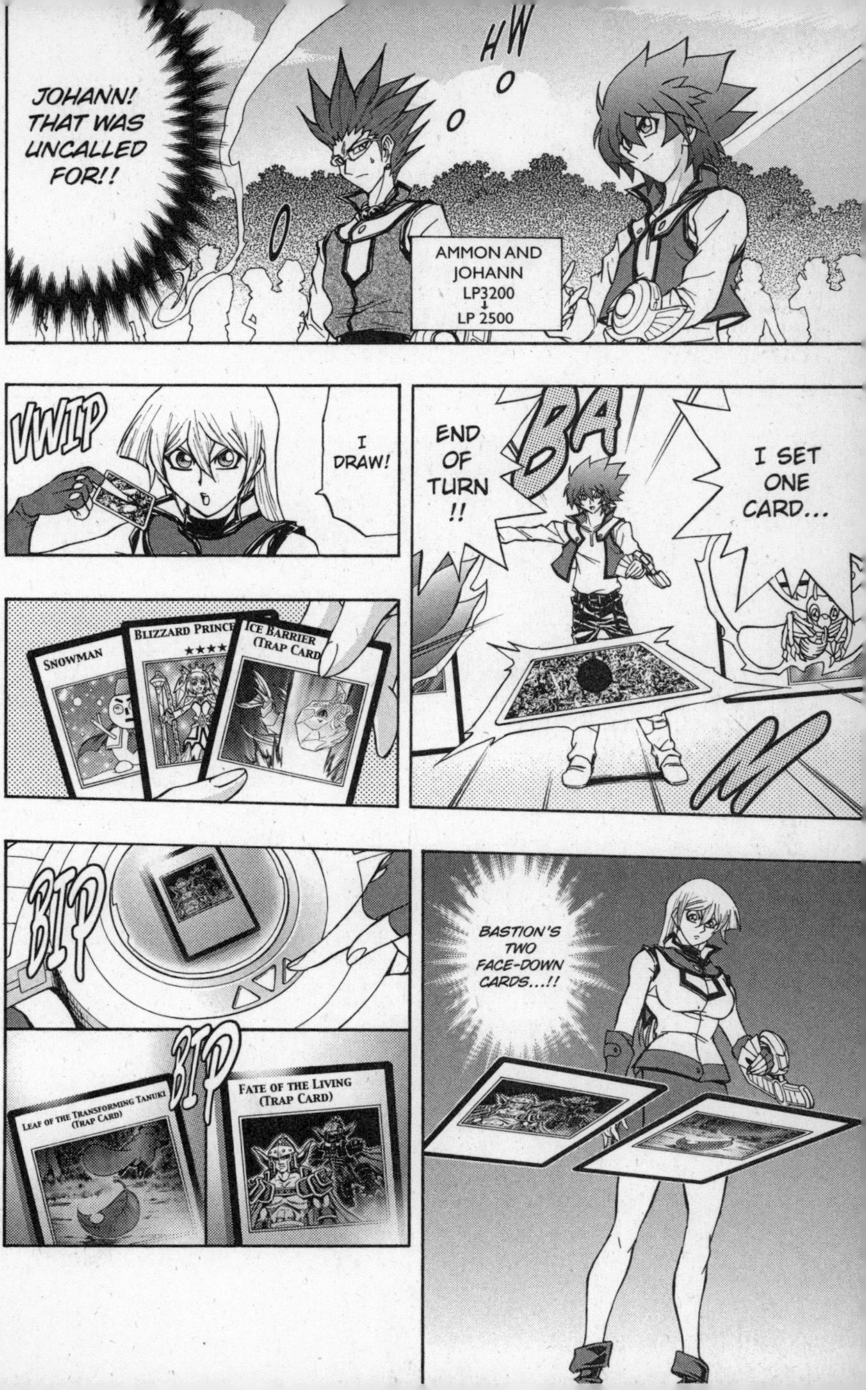
WHOOO
JOHANN! THAT WAS UNCALLED FOR!!
AMMON AND JOHANN LP3200 ↓ LP 2500
I SET ONE CARD...
BA
END OF TURN !!
VWIP
I DRAW!
ICE BARRIER (TRAP CARD)
BLIZZARD PRINCE
SNOWMAN
BASTION'S TWO FACE-DOWN CARDS...!!
BIP
BIP
FATE OF THE LIVING (TRAP CARD)
LEAF OF THE TRANSFORMING TANUKI (TRAP CARD)

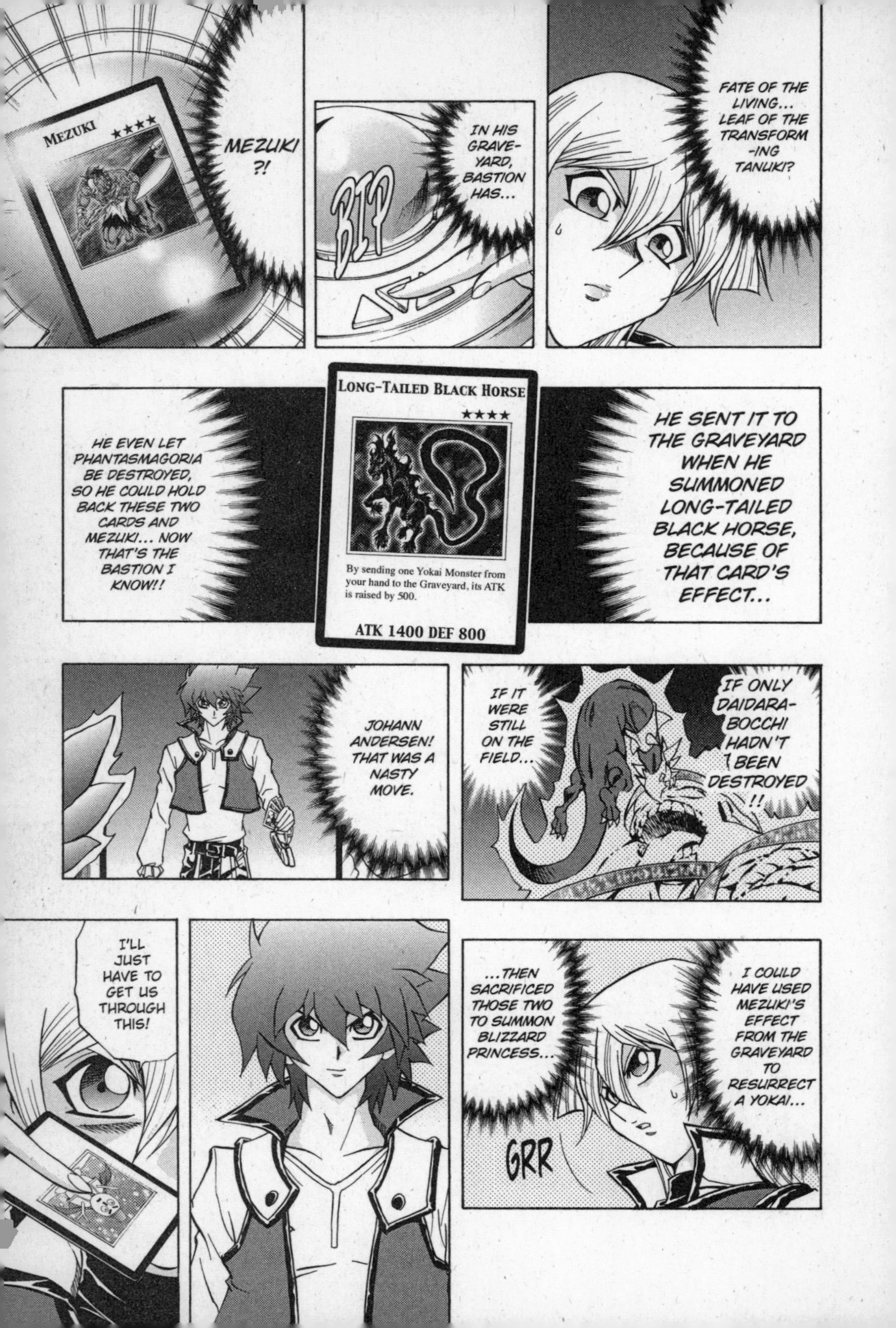
FATE OF THE LIVING... LEAF OF THE TRANSFORM-ING TANUKI?
IN HIS GRAVEYARD, BASTION HAS...
BIP
MEZUKI
MEZUKI ?!
HE SENT IT TO THE GRAVEYARD WHEN HE SUMMONED LONG-TAILED BLACK HORSE, BECAUSE OF THAT CARD'S EFFECT...
LONG-TAILED BLACK HORSE
By sending one Yokai Monster from your hand to the Graveyard, its ATK is raised by 500.
ATK 1400 DEF 800
HE EVEN LET PHANTASMAGORIA BE DESTROYED, SO HE COULD HOLD BACK THESE TWO CARDS AND MEZUKI... NOW THAT'S THE BASTION I KNOW!!
IF ONLY DAIDARA-BOCCHI HADN'T BEEN DESTROYED!!
IF IT WERE STILL ON THE FIELD...
JOHANN ANDERSEN! THAT WAS A NASTY MOVE.
I COULD HAVE USED MEZUKI'S EFFECT FROM THE GRAVEYARD TO RESURRECT A YOKAI...
...THEN SACRIFICED THOSE TWO TO SUMMON BLIZZARD PRINCESS...
GRR
I'LL JUST HAVE TO GET US THROUGH THIS!

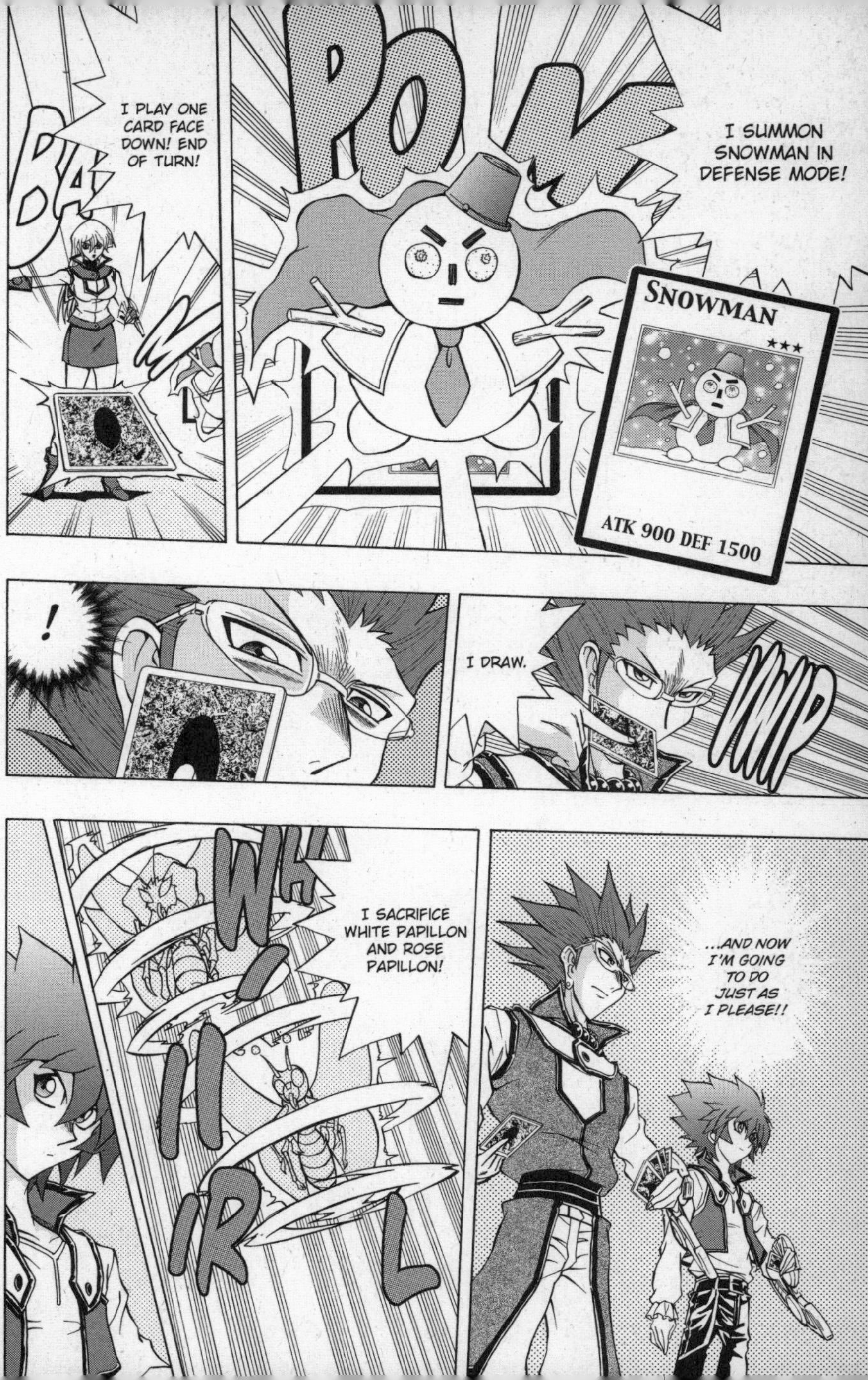
POM
I SUMMON SNOWMAN IN DEFENSE MODE!
SNOWMAN
ATK 900 DEF 1500
I PLAY ONE CARD FACE DOWN! END OF TURN!
I DRAW.
WHIP
!
...AND NOW I'M GOING TO DO JUST AS I PLEASE!!
I SACRIFICE WHITE PAPILLON AND ROSE PAPILLON!
WHIRL

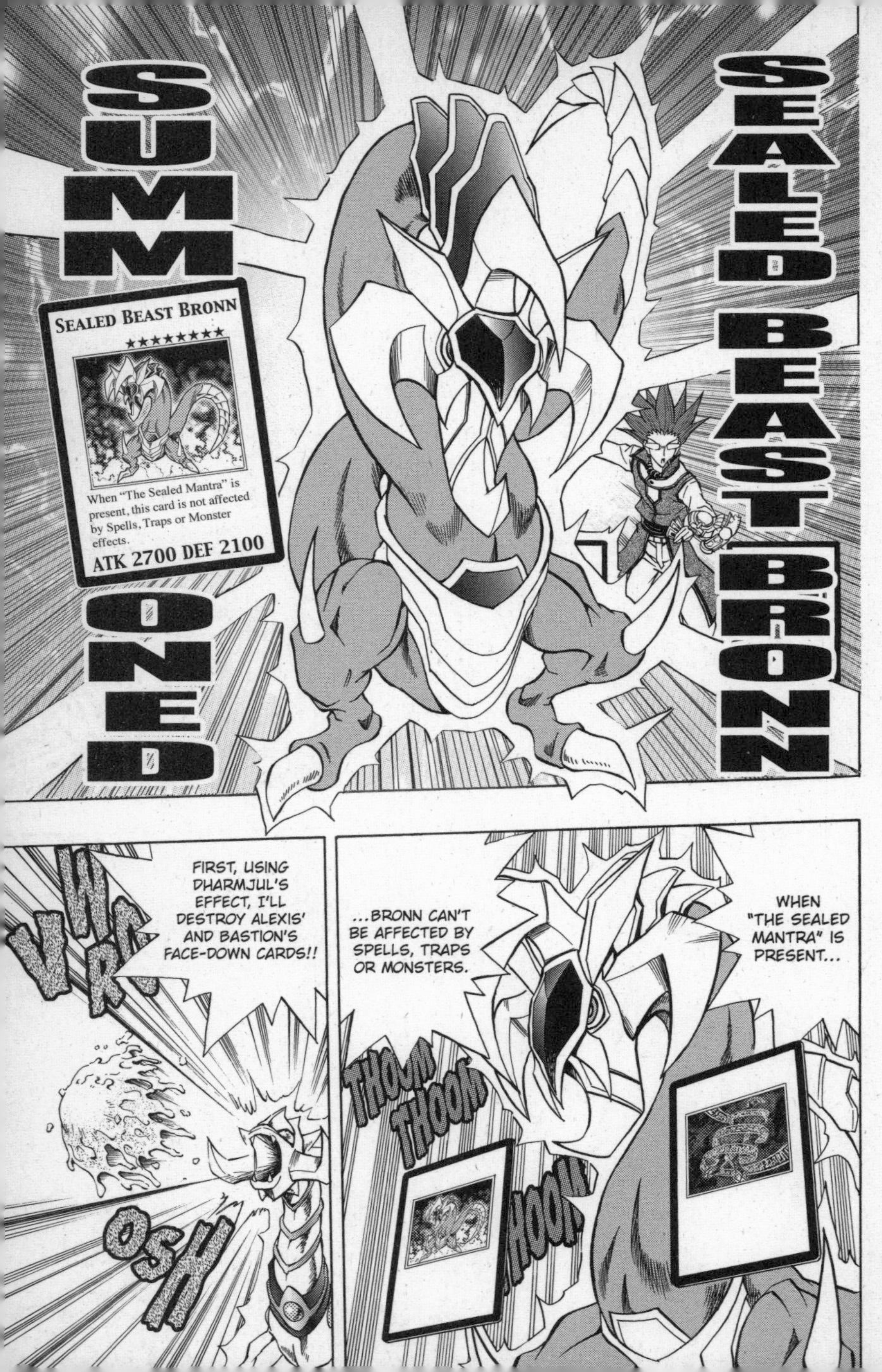
SEALED BEAST BRONN
SUMMONED
Sealed Beast Bronn
★★★★★★★★★
When "The Sealed Mantra" is present, this card is not affected by Spells, Traps or Monster effects.
ATK 2700 DEF 2100
WHEN "THE SEALED MANTRA" IS PRESENT...
...BRONN CAN'T BE AFFECTED BY SPELLS, TRAPS OR MONSTERS.
THOOM
THOOM
THOOM
FIRST, USING DHARMJUL'S EFFECT, I'LL DESTROY ALEXIS' AND BASTION'S FACE-DOWN CARDS!!
OSH

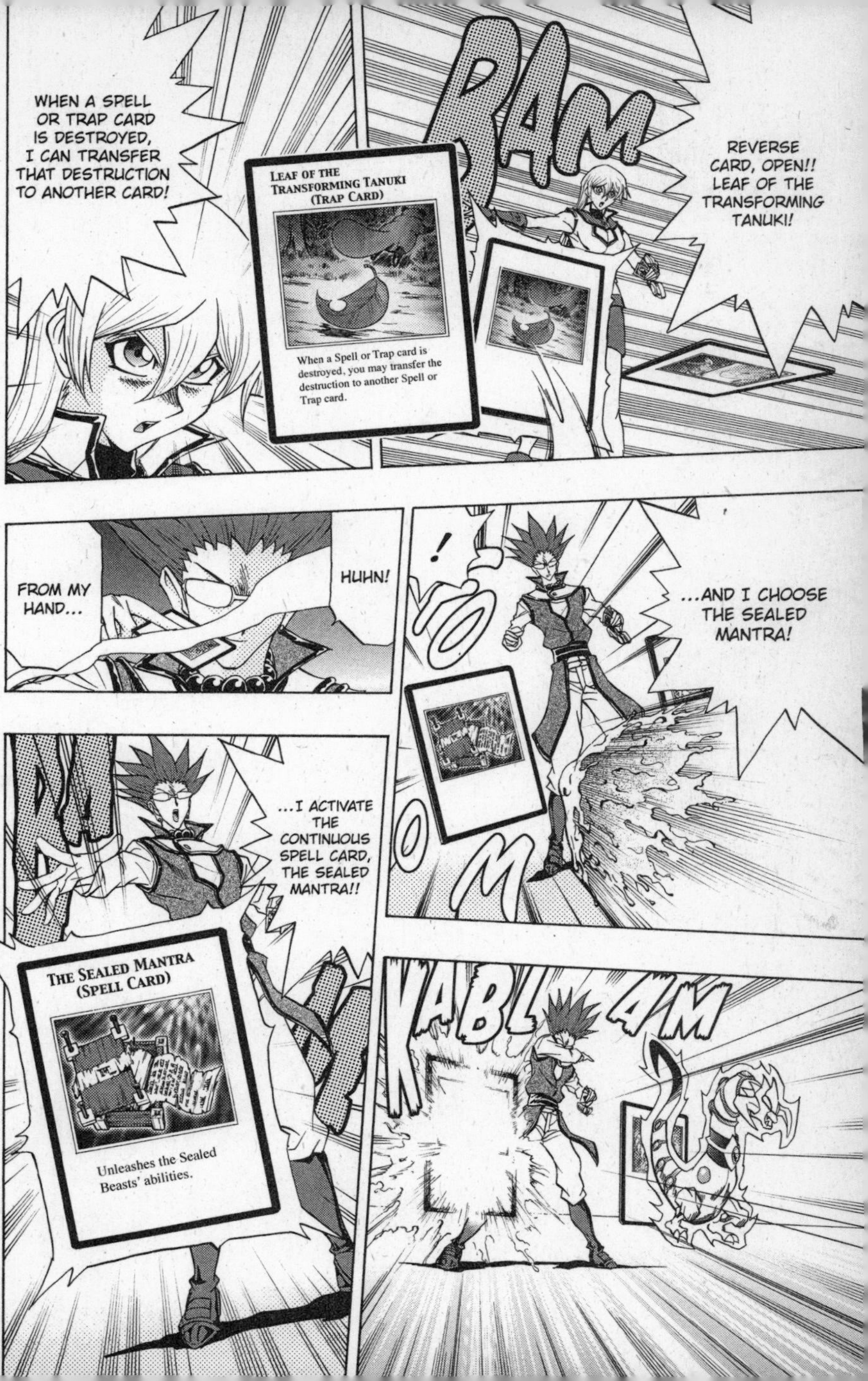

RAM
REVERSE CARD, OPEN!! LEAF OF THE TRANSFORMING TANUKI!
WHEN A SPELL OR TRAP CARD IS DESTROYED, I CAN TRANSFER THAT DESTRUCTION TO ANOTHER CARD!
LEAF OF THE TRANSFORMING TANUKI (TRAP CARD)
When a Spell or Trap card is destroyed, you may transfer the destruction to another Spell or Trap card.
!
VROOM
...AND I CHOOSE THE SEALED MANTRA!
HUHN!
FROM MY HAND...
...I ACTIVATE THE CONTINUOUS SPELL CARD, THE SEALED MANTRA!!
KABLAM
THE SEALED MANTRA (SPELL CARD)
Unleashes the Sealed Beasts' abilities.

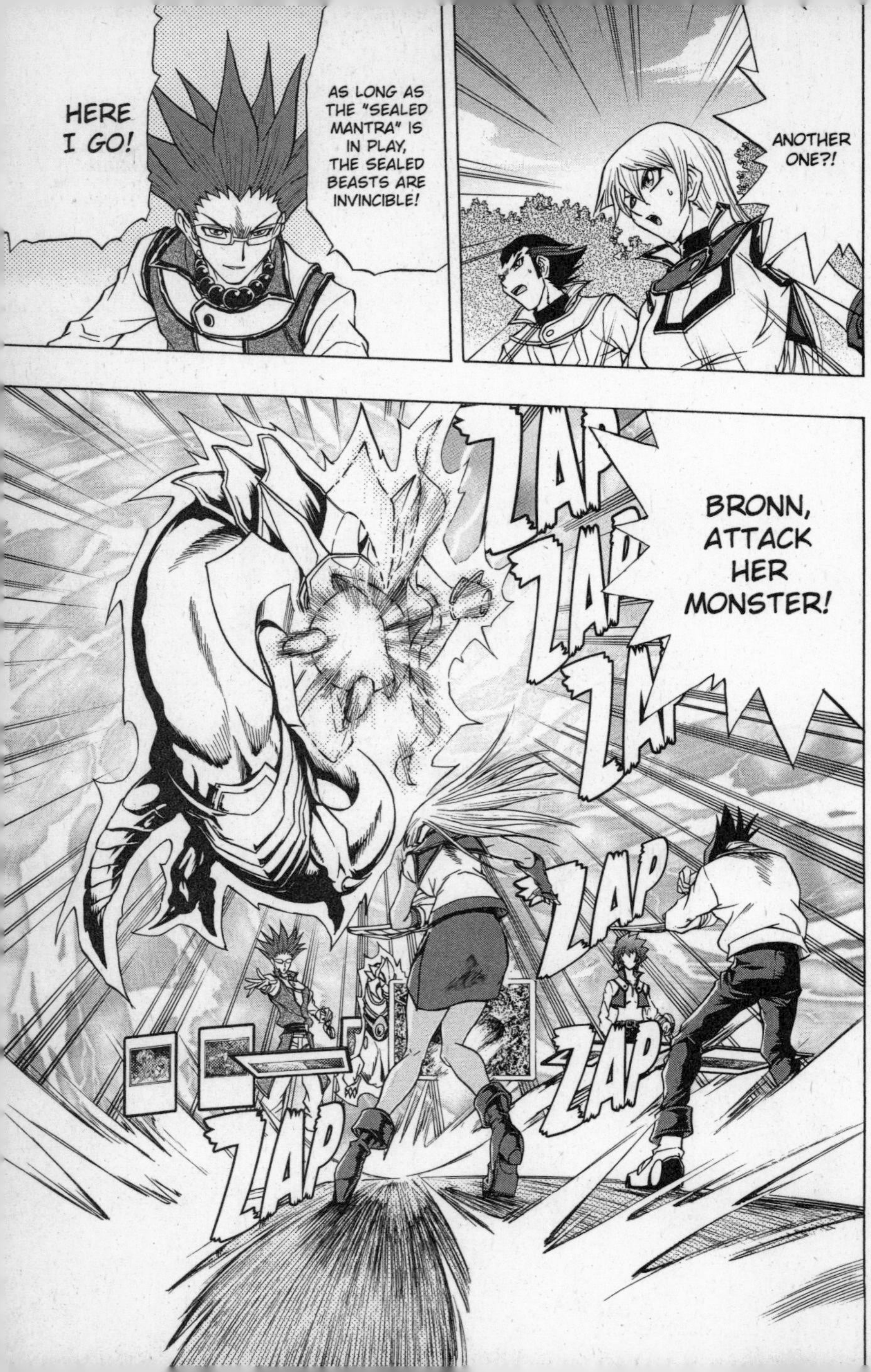
ANOTHER ONE?!
AS LONG AS THE "SEALED MANTRA" IS IN PLAY, THE SEALED BEASTS ARE INVINCIBLE!
HERE I GO!
BRONN, ATTACK HER MONSTER!
ZAP
ZAP
ZAP
ZAP
ZAP
ZAP

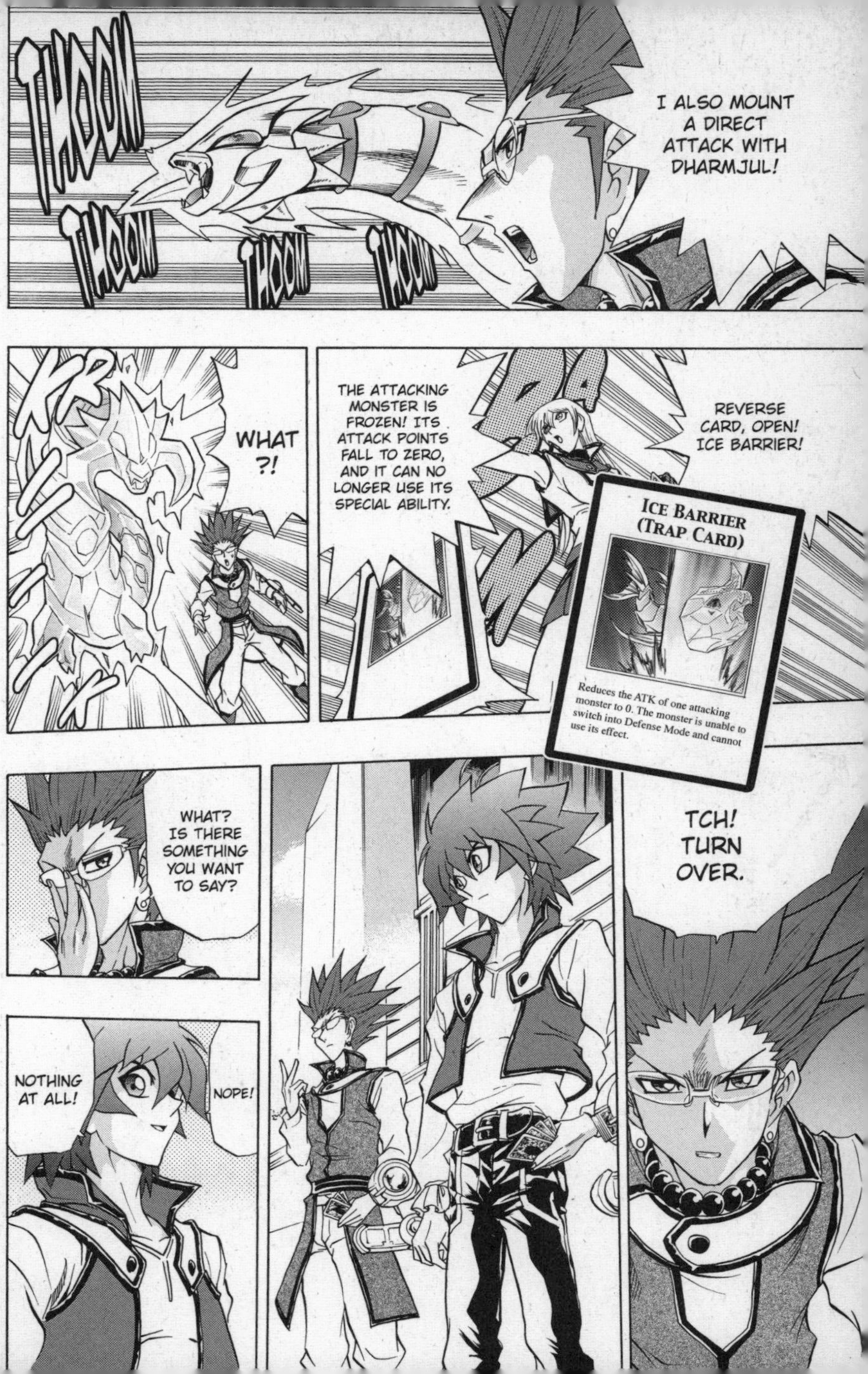
THOOM
THOOM
THOOM
THOOM
I ALSO MOUNT A DIRECT ATTACK WITH DHARMJUL!
REVERSE CARD, OPEN! ICE BARRIER!
THE ATTACKING MONSTER IS FROZEN! ITS ATTACK POINTS FALL TO ZERO, AND IT CAN NO LONGER USE ITS SPECIAL ABILITY.
ICE BARRIER (TRAP CARD)
Reduces the ATK of one attacking monster to 0. The monster is unable to switch into Defense Mode and cannot use its effect.
WHAT ?!
TCH! TURN OVER.
WHAT? IS THERE SOMETHING YOU WANT TO SAY?
NOPE!
NOTHING AT ALL!

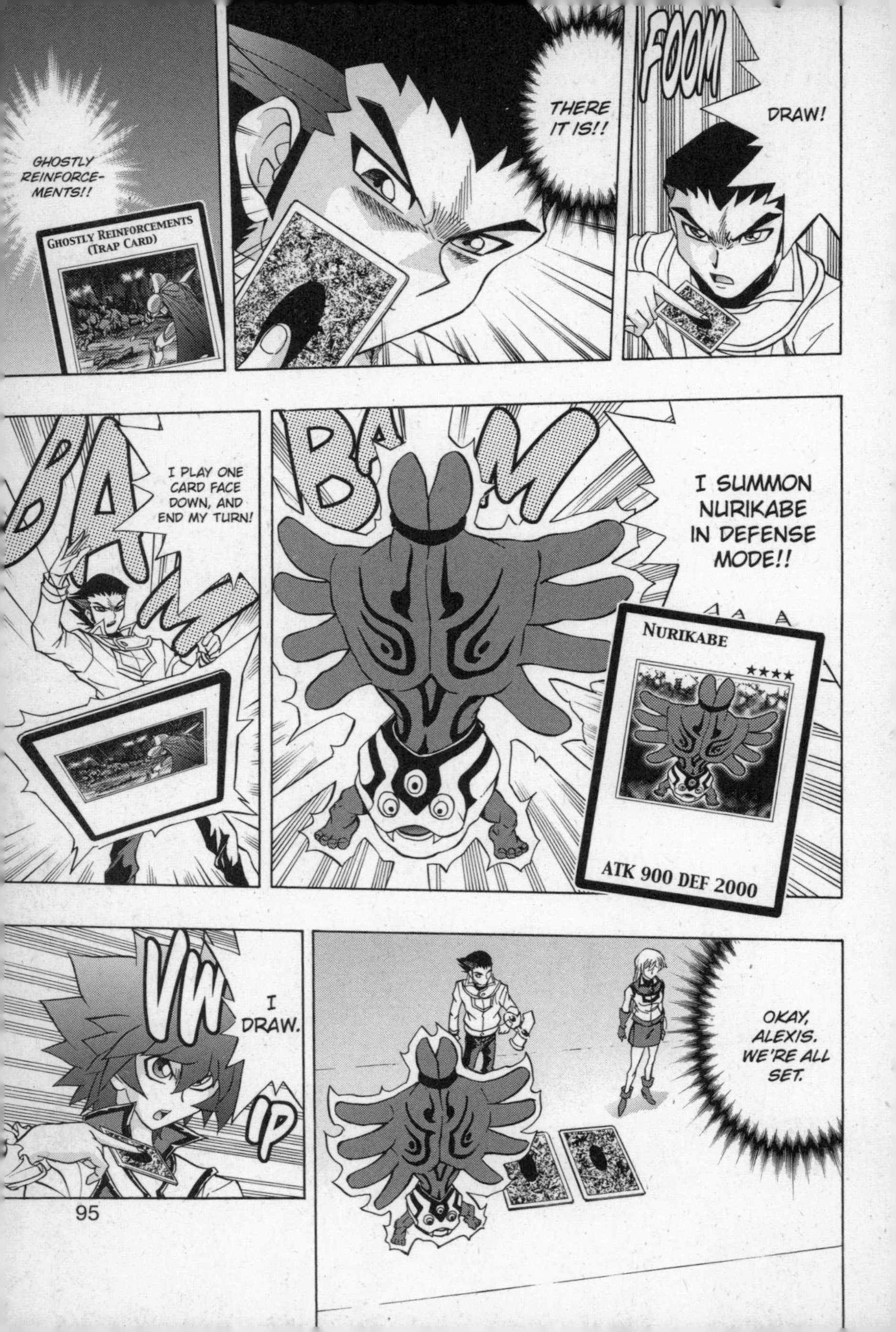
FOOM
DRAW!
THERE IT IS!!
GHOSTLY REINFORCEMENTS!!
GHOSTLY REINFORCEMENTS (TRAP CARD)
BAM
I SUMMON NURIKABE IN DEFENSE MODE!!
NURIKABE
ATK 900 DEF 2000
BAM
I PLAY ONE CARD FACE DOWN, AND END MY TURN!
OKAY, ALEXIS. WE'RE ALL SET.
VWIP
I DRAW.

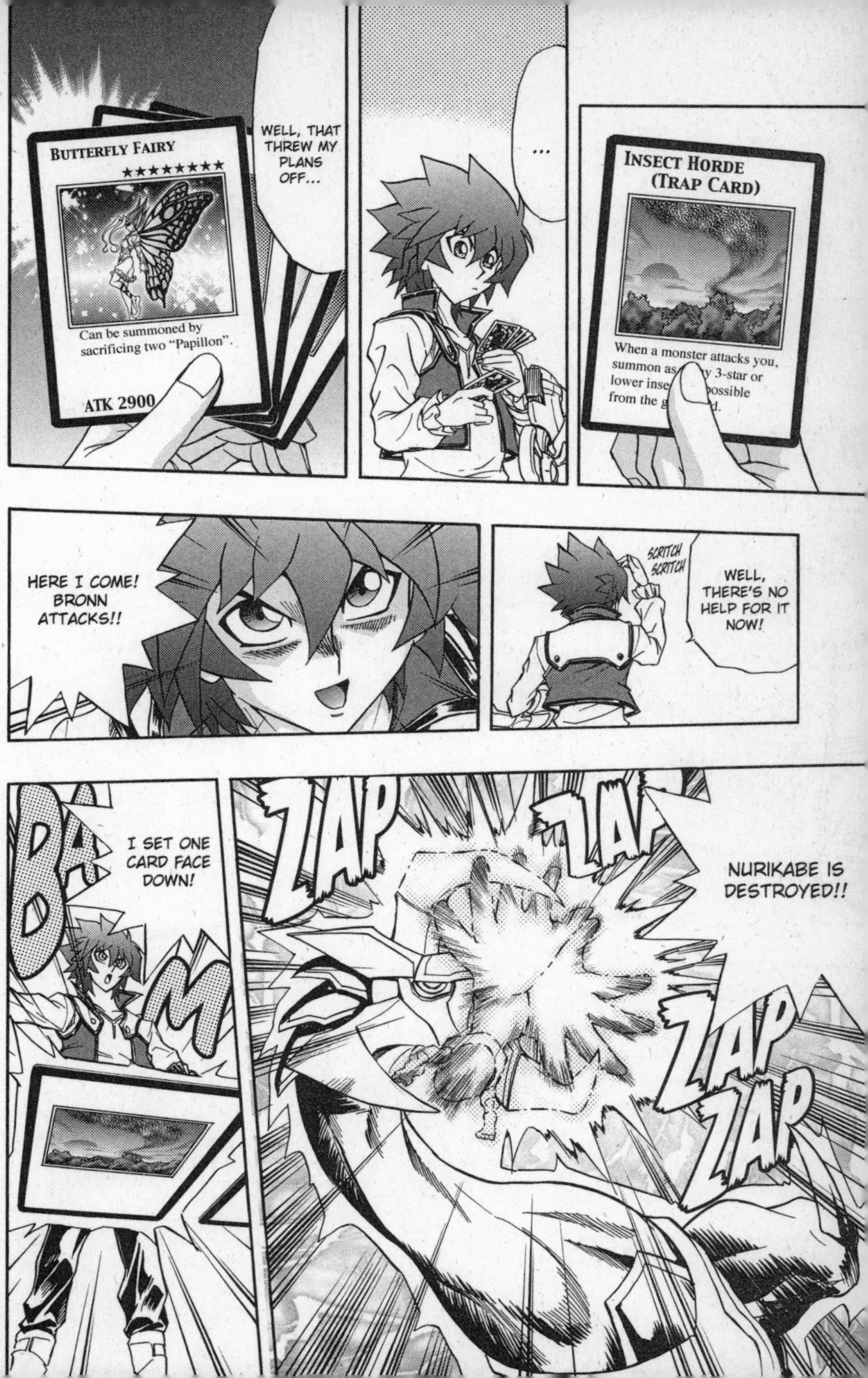

INSECT HORDE (TRAP CARD)
When a monster attacks you,
summon as
y 3-star or
lower inse
possible
from the g
d.
...
WELL, THAT THREW MY PLANS OFF...
BUTTERFLY FAIRY
★★★★★★★★
Can be summoned by sacrificing two "Papillon".
ATK 2900
SCRITCH SCRITCH
WELL, THERE'S NO HELP FOR IT NOW!
HERE I COME! BRONN ATTACKS!!
ZAP
ZAP
NURIKABE IS DESTROYED!!
ZAP
ZAP
BAM
I SET ONE CARD FACE DOWN!

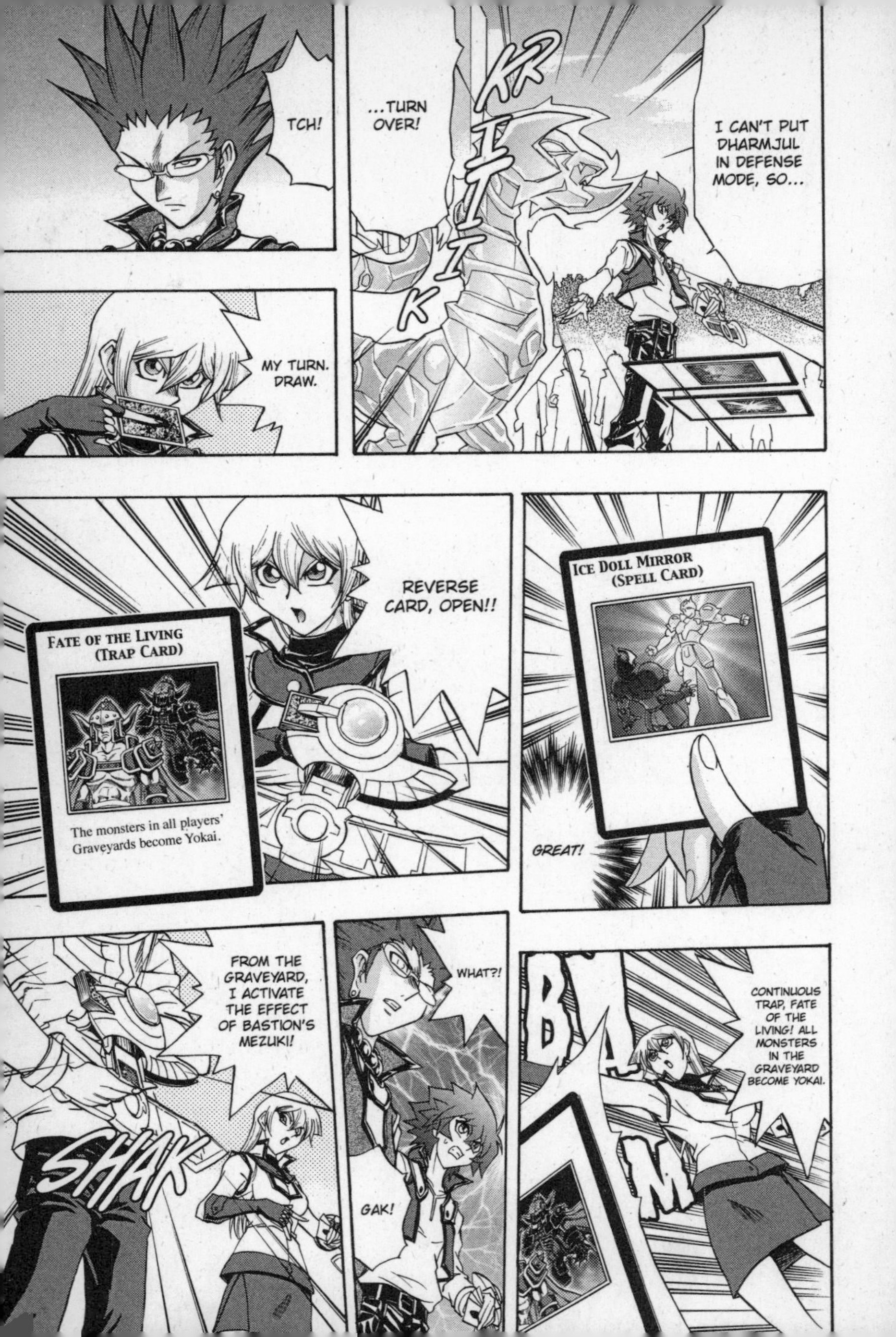
I CAN'T PUT DHARMJUL IN DEFENSE MODE, SO...
KRIIIIK
...TURN OVER!
TCH!
MY TURN. DRAW.
Ice Doll Mirror (Spell Card)
GREAT!
REVERSE CARD, OPEN!!
Fate of the Living (Trap Card)
The monsters in all players' Graveyards become Yokai.
BAM
CONTINUOUS TRAP, FATE OF THE LIVING! ALL MONSTERS IN THE GRAVEYARD BECOME YOKAI.
WHAT?!
GAK!
FROM THE GRAVEYARD, I ACTIVATE THE EFFECT OF BASTION'S MEZUKI!
SHAK

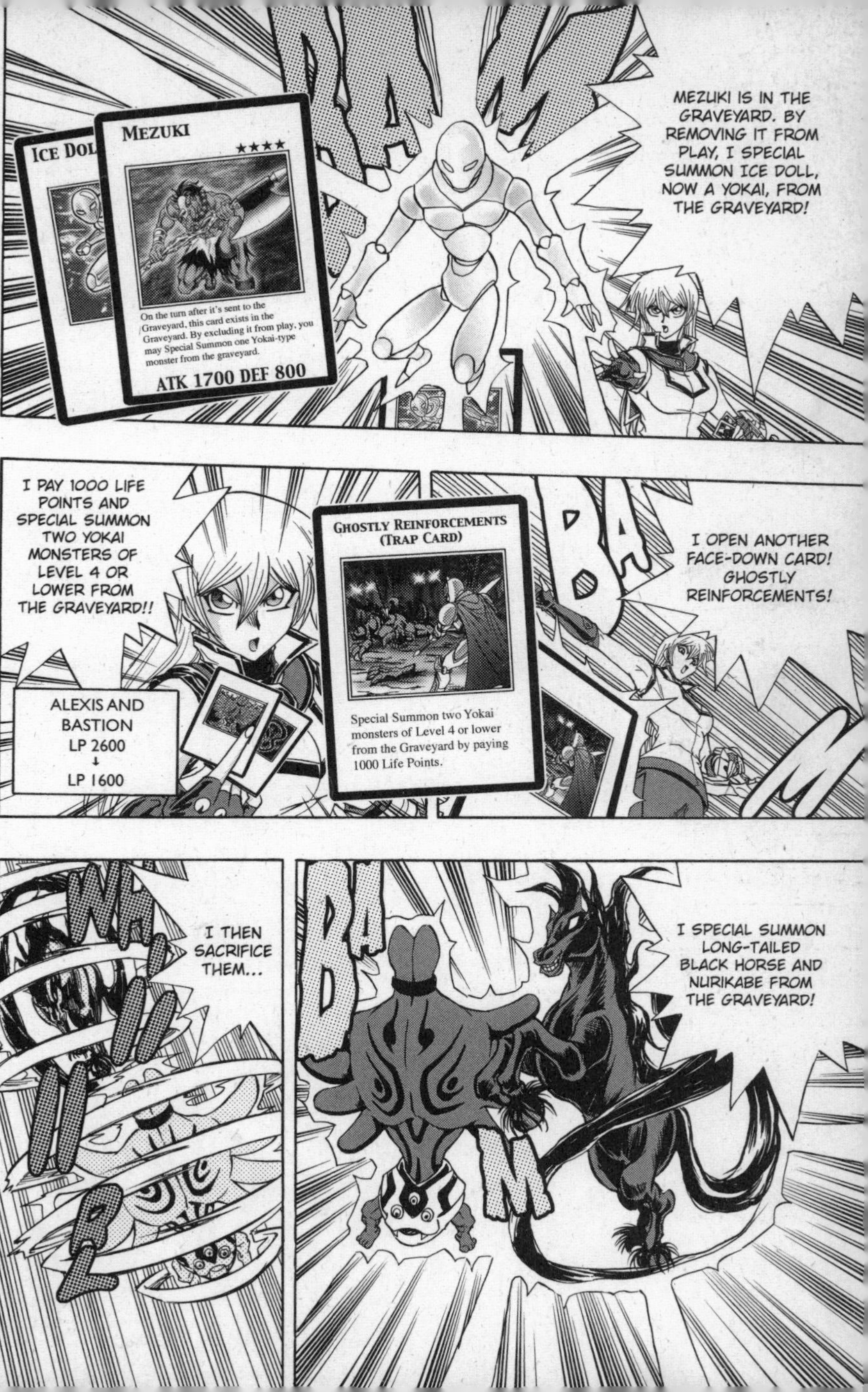
MEZUKI IS IN THE GRAVEYARD. BY REMOVING IT FROM PLAY, I SPECIAL SUMMON ICE DOLL, NOW A YOKAI, FROM THE GRAVEYARD!
ICE DOL
MEZUKI
★★★★
On the turn after it's sent to the Graveyard, this card exists in the Graveyard. By excluding it from play, you may Special Summon one Yokai-type monster from the graveyard.
ATK 1700 DEF 800
I OPEN ANOTHER FACE-DOWN CARD! GHOSTLY REINFORCEMENTS!
GHOSTLY REINFORCEMENTS (TRAP CARD)
Special Summon two Yokai monsters of Level 4 or lower from the Graveyard by paying 1000 Life Points.
I PAY 1000 LIFE POINTS AND SPECIAL SUMMON TWO YOKAI MONSTERS OF LEVEL 4 OR LOWER FROM THE GRAVEYARD!!
ALEXIS AND BASTION LP 2600 ↓ LP 1600
I SPECIAL SUMMON LONG-TAILED BLACK HORSE AND NURIKABE FROM THE GRAVEYARD!
I THEN SACRIFICE THEM...

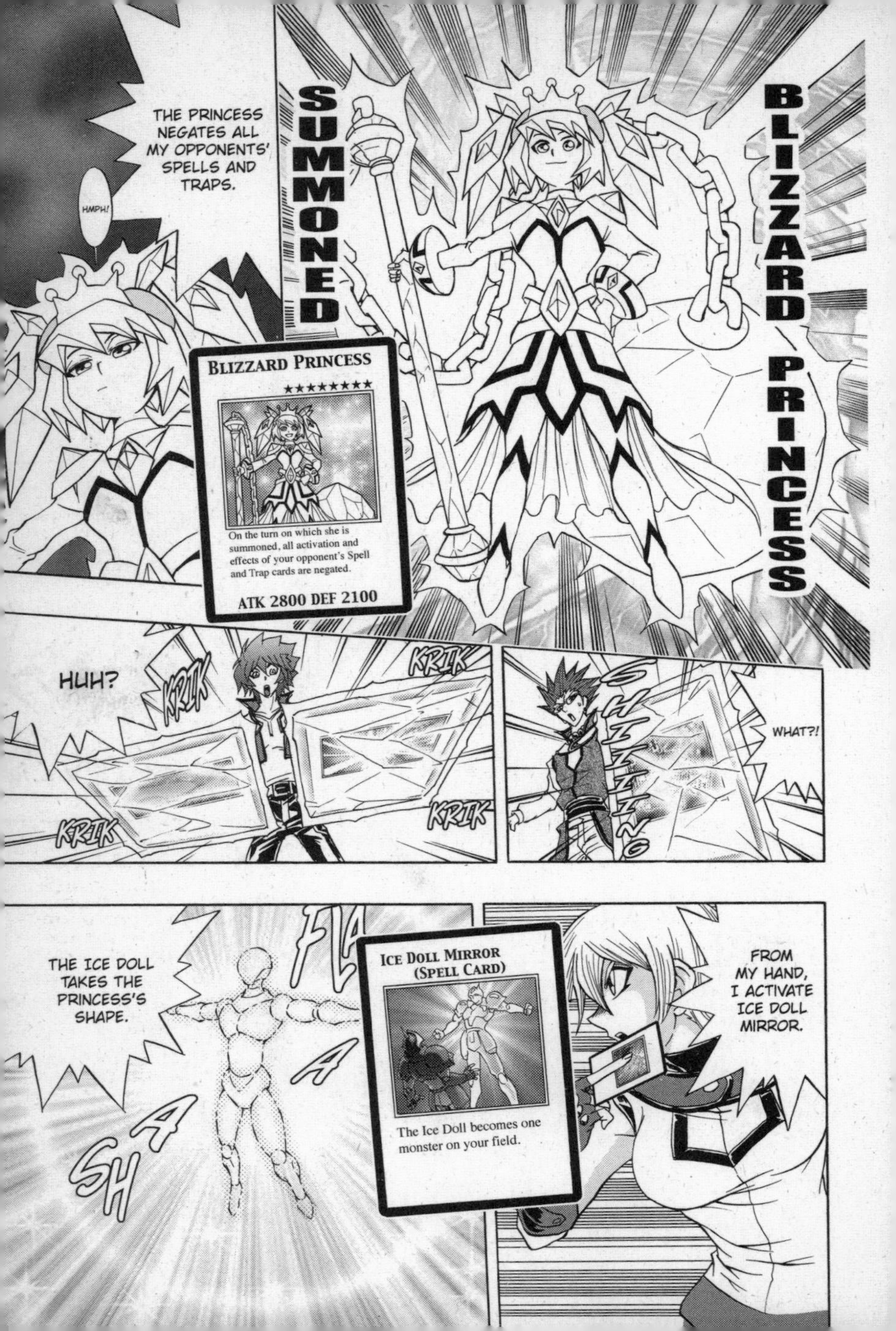
BLIZZARD PRINCESS
SUMMONED
BLIZZARD PRINCESS
★★★★★★★★
On the turn on which she is summoned, all activation and effects of your opponent's Spell and Trap cards are negated.
ATK 2800 DEF 2100
THE PRINCESS NEGATES ALL MY OPPONENTS' SPELLS AND TRAPS.
HMPH!
WHAT?!
SHIIIING
KRIK
HUH?
KRIK
KRIK
KRIK
FROM MY HAND, I ACTIVATE ICE DOLL MIRROR.
ICE DOLL MIRROR (SPELL CARD)
The Ice Doll becomes one monster on your field.
THE ICE DOLL TAKES THE PRINCESS'S SHAPE.
FLA
A
A
SH

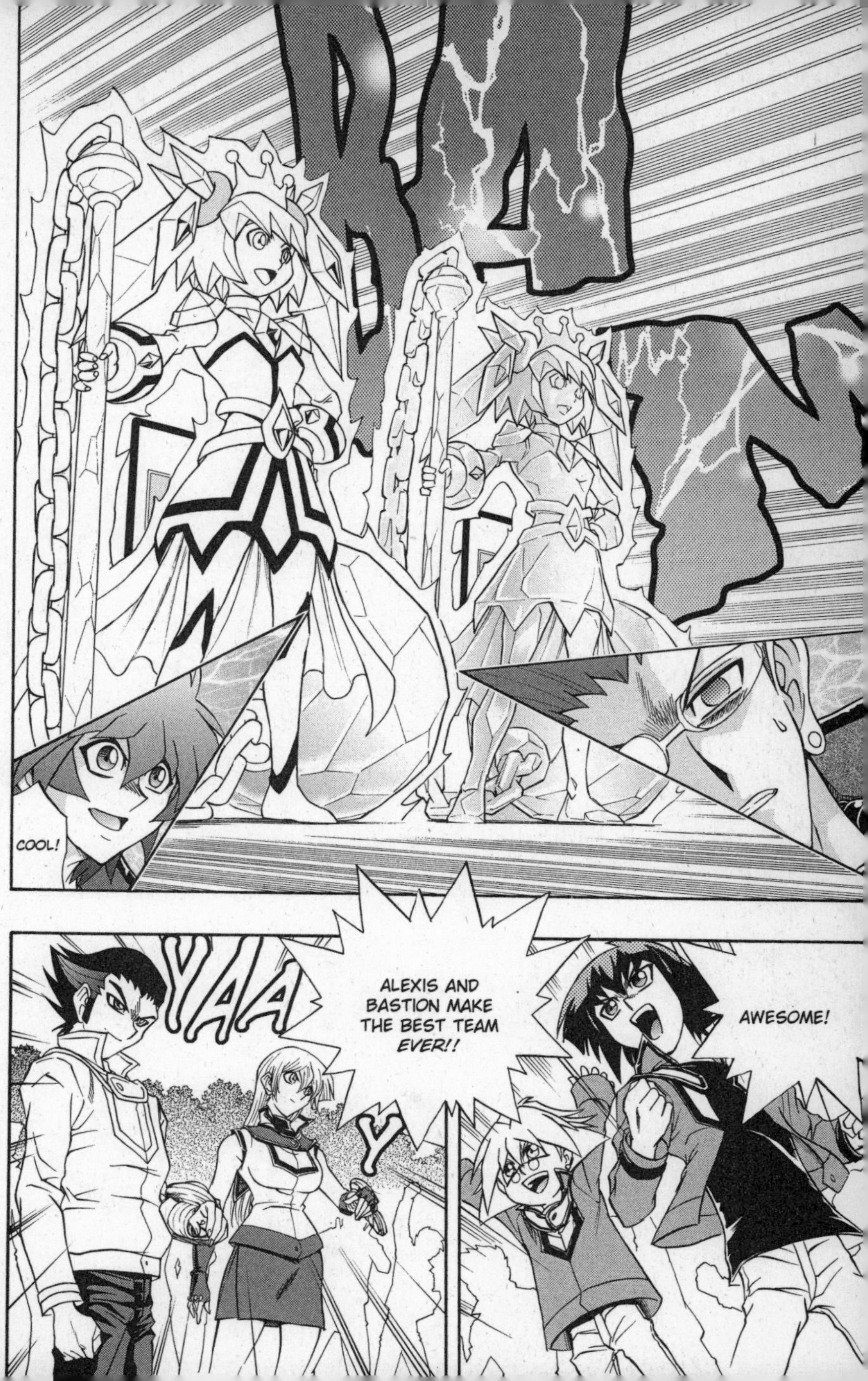
COOL!
AWESOME!
ALEXIS AND BASTION MAKE THE BEST TEAM EVER!!
YAA
Y

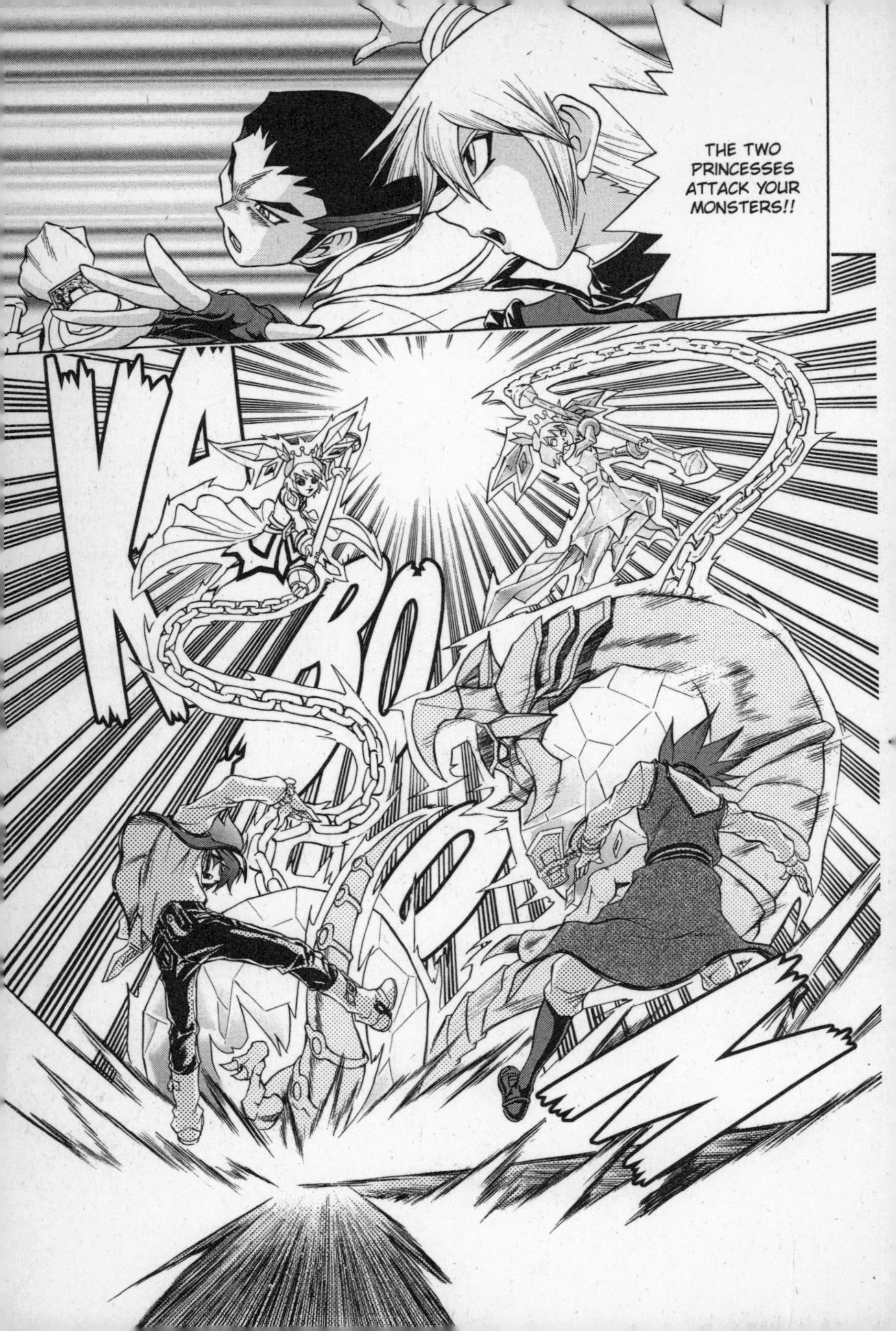
THE TWO PRINCESSES ATTACK YOUR MONSTERS!!
KA-BOOM

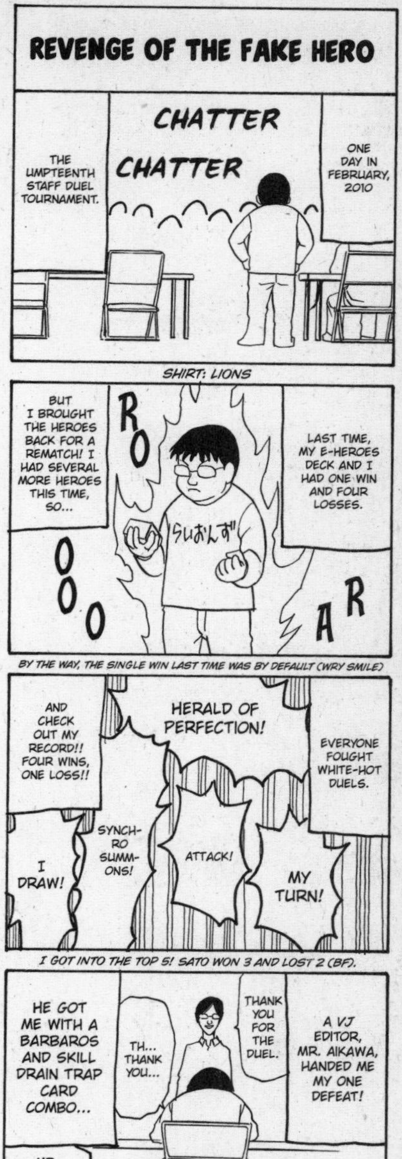
REVENGE OF THE FAKE HERO
ONE DAY IN FEBRUARY, 2010
THE UMPTEENTH STAFF DUEL TOURNAMENT.
CHATTER
CHATTER
SHIRT: LIONS
LAST TIME, MY E-HEROES DECK AND I HAD ONE WIN AND FOUR LOSSES.
BUT I BROUGHT THE HEROES BACK FOR A REMATCH! I HAD SEVERAL MORE HEROES THIS TIME, SO...
ROOOOAR
らいおんず
BY THE WAY, THE SINGLE WIN LAST TIME WAS BY DEFAULT (WRY SMILE)
EVERYONE FOUGHT WHITE-HOT DUELS.
HERALD OF PERFECTION!
AND CHECK OUT MY RECORD!! FOUR WINS, ONE LOSS!!
MY TURN!
ATTACK!
SYNCHRO SUMMONS!
I DRAW!
I GOT INTO THE TOP 5! SATO WON 3 AND LOST 2 (BF).
A VJ EDITOR, MR. AIKAWA, HANDED ME MY ONE DEFEAT!
THANK YOU FOR THE DUEL.
TH... THANK YOU...
HE GOT ME WITH A BARBAROS AND SKILL DRAIN TRAP CARD COMBO...
MR. AIKAWA WON ALL HIS DUELS!
SKILL DRAIN (ALL MONSTER EFFECTS ARE NEGATED!)

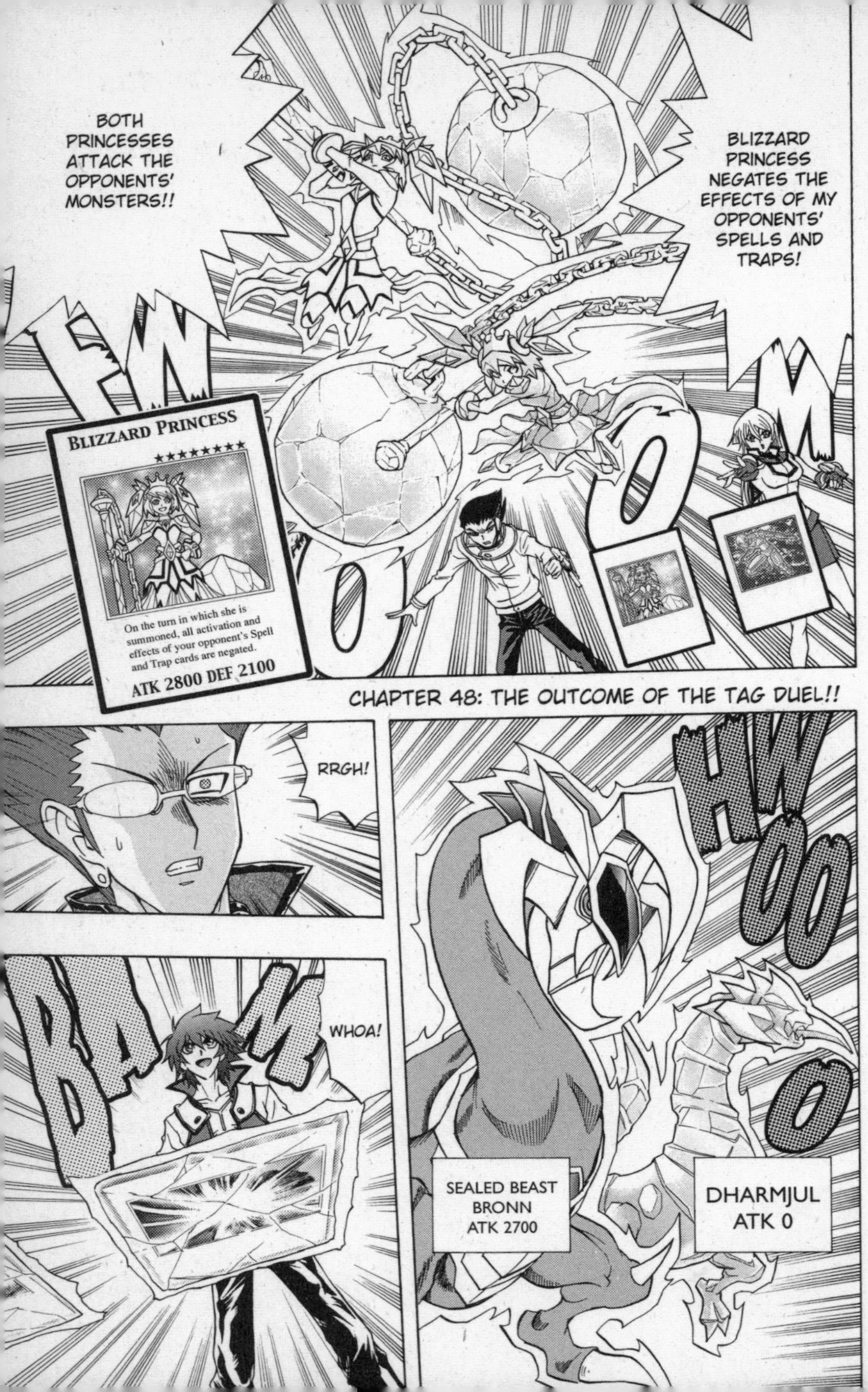
BLIZZARD PRINCESS NEGATES THE EFFECTS OF MY OPPONENTS' SPELLS AND TRAPS!
BOTH PRINCESSES ATTACK THE OPPONENTS' MONSTERS!!
FWOOOM
BLIZZARD PRINCESS
On the turn in which she is summoned, all activation and effects of your opponent's Spell and Trap cards are negated.
ATK 2800 DEF 2100
CHAPTER 48: THE OUTCOME OF THE TAG DUEL!!
HWOOO
SEALED BEAST BRONN ATK 2700
DHARMJUL ATK 0
RRGH!
BAM
WHOA!

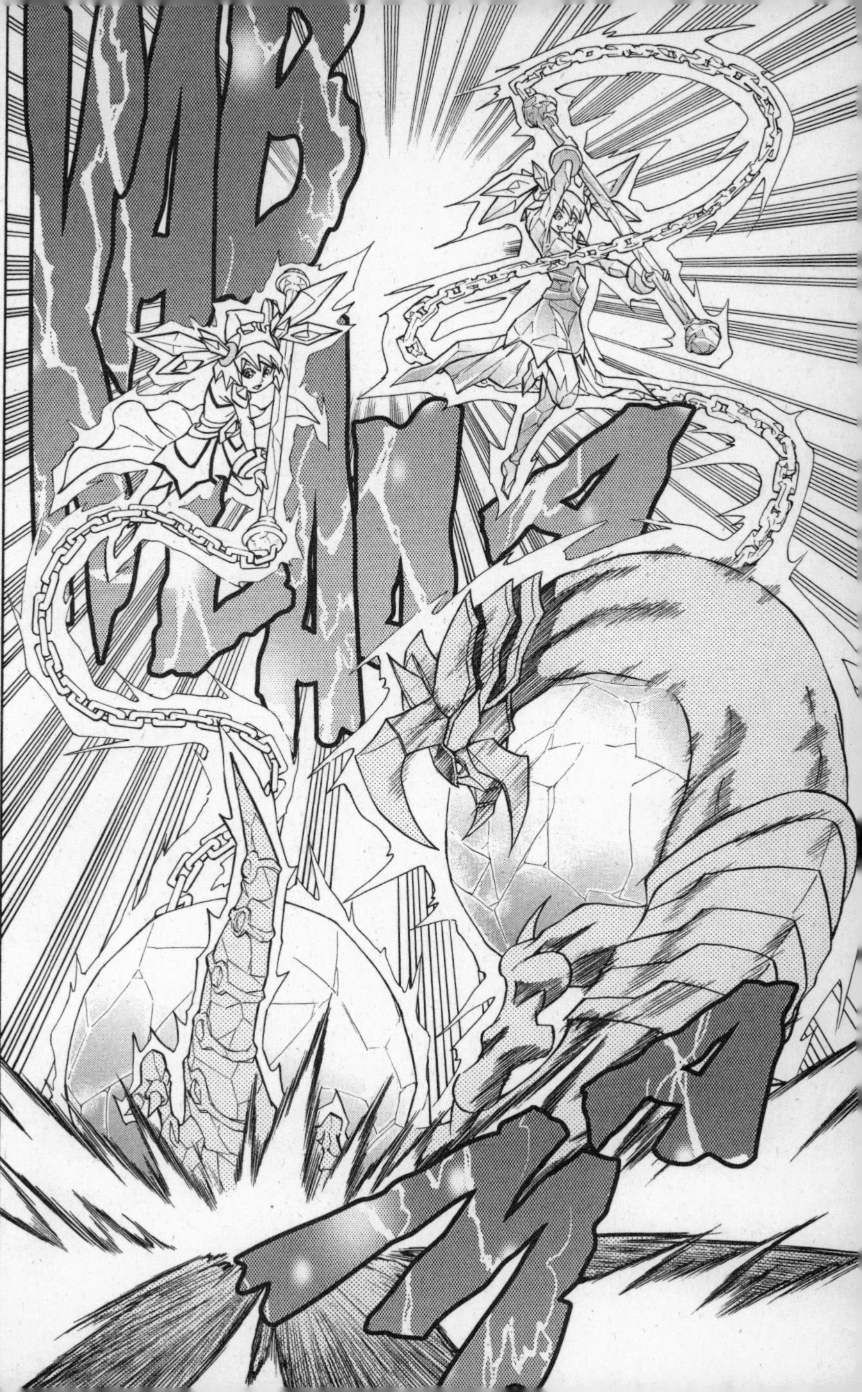

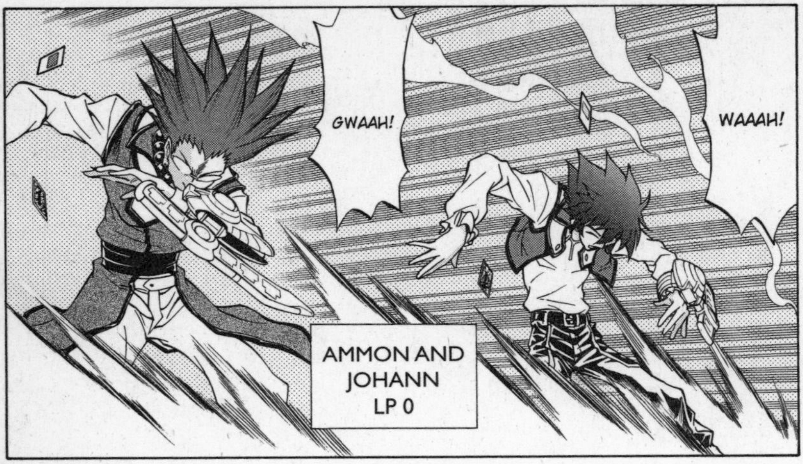
WAAAH!
GWAAH!
AMMON AND JOHANN LP 0

CHAPTER 48: THE OUTCOME OF THE TAG DUEL!!

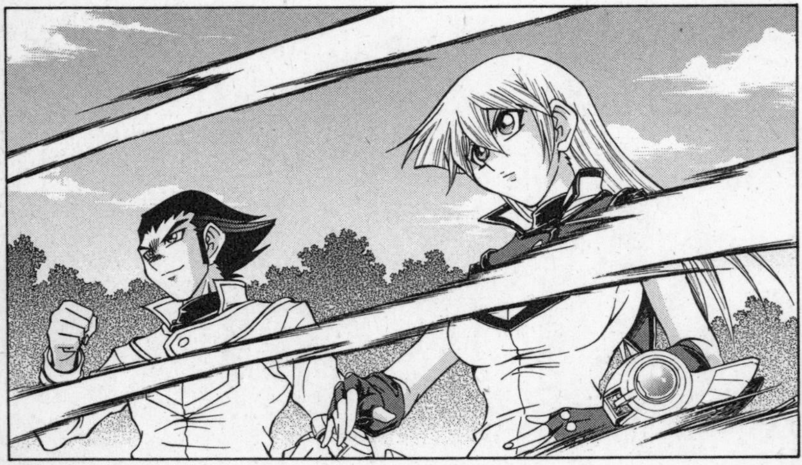

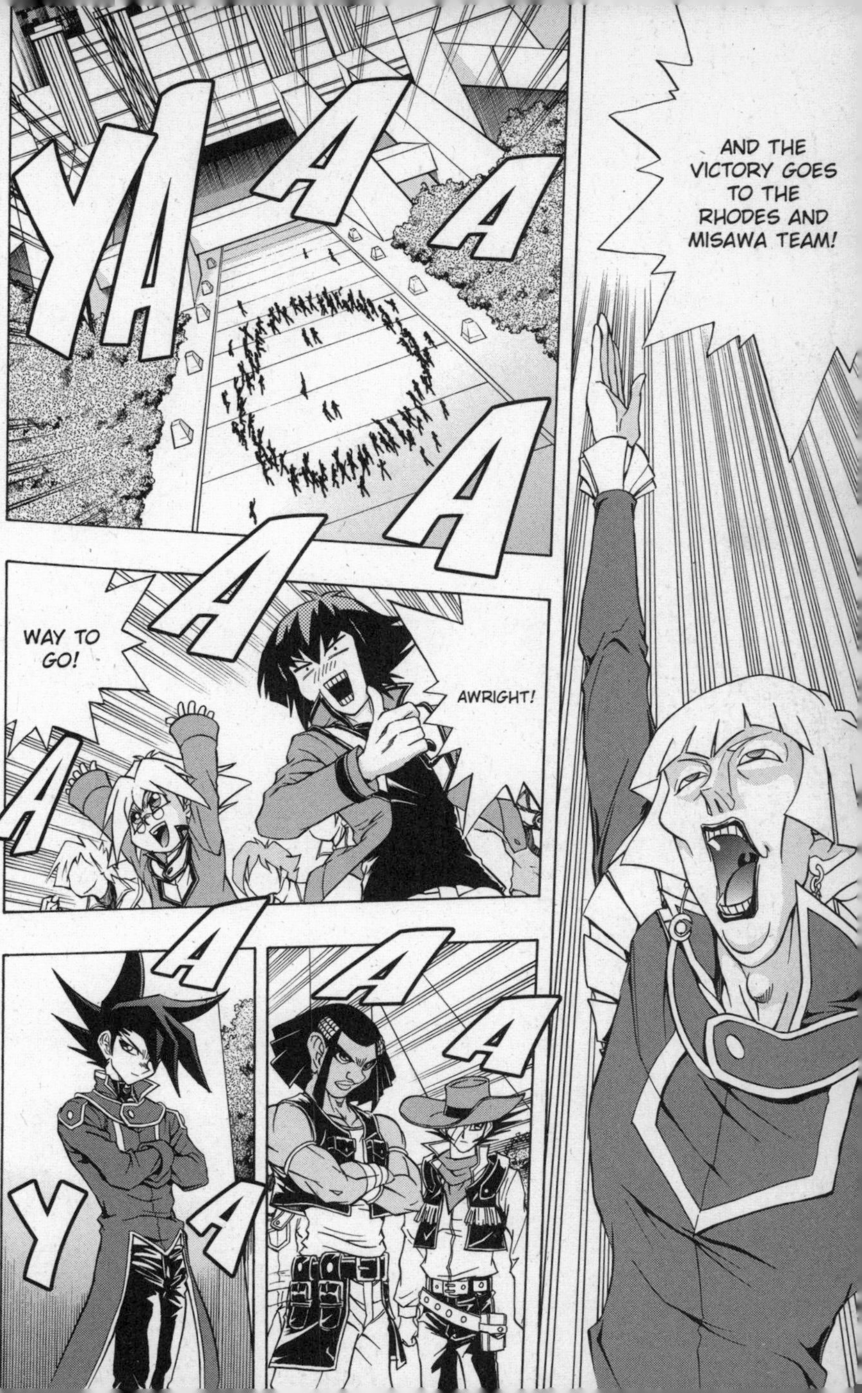
AND THE VICTORY GOES TO THE RHODES AND MISAWA TEAM!
YAAAAAAAAAAAA
AWRIGHT!
WAY TO GO!
YA

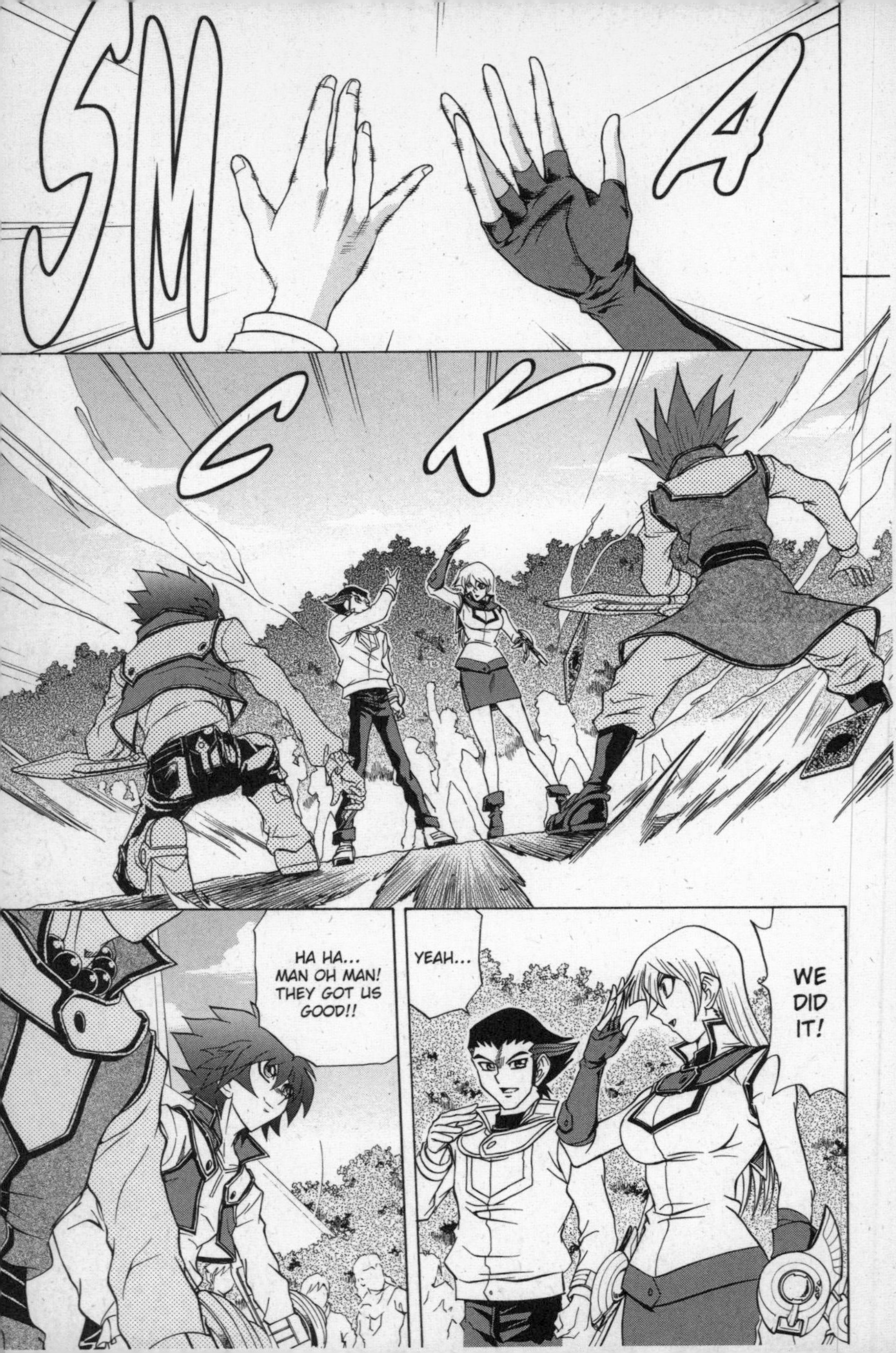
SMACK
WE DID IT!
YEAH...
HA HA... MAN OH MAN! THEY GOT US GOOD!!

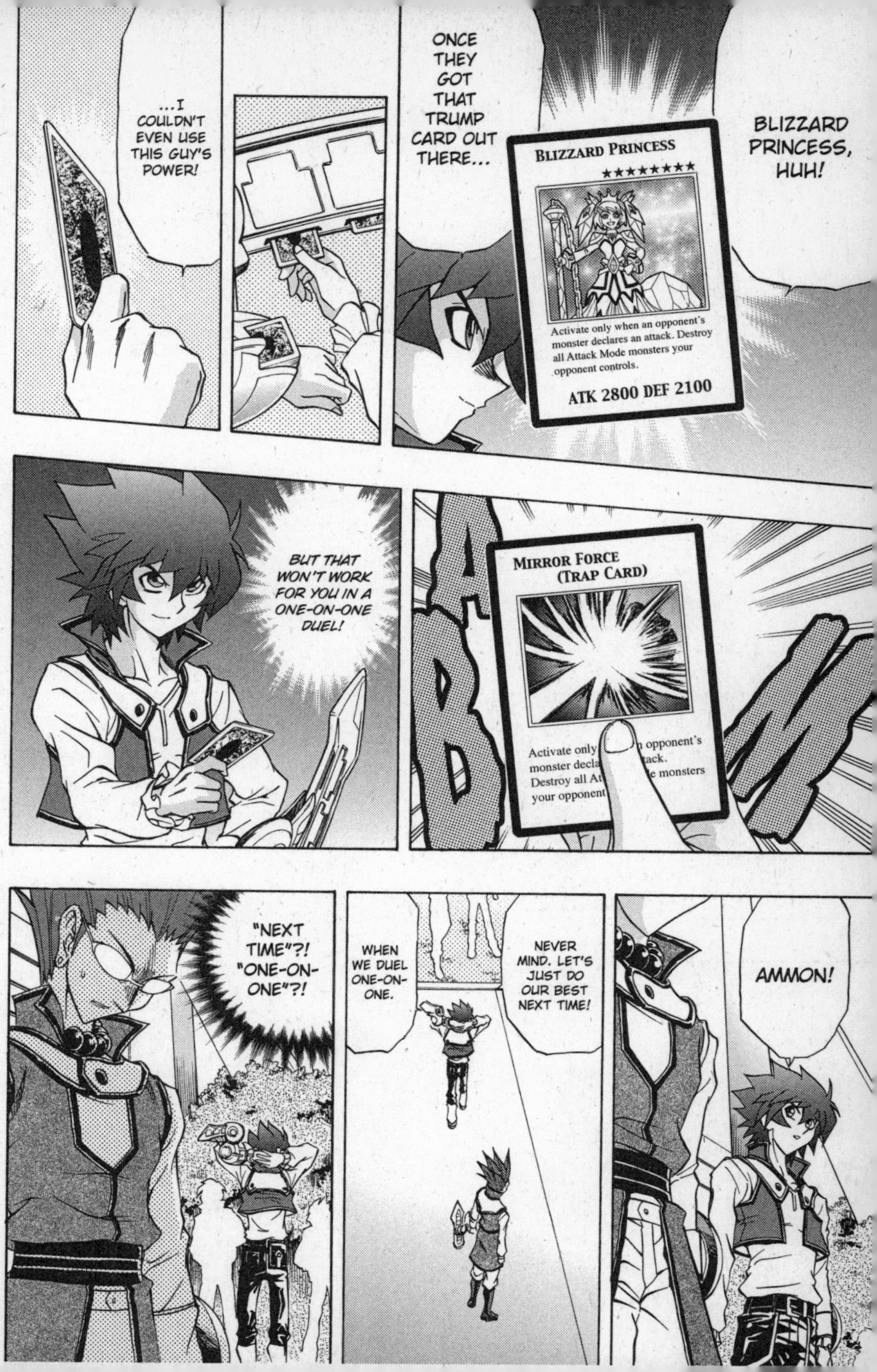

BLIZZARD PRINCESS, HUH!
ONCE THEY GOT THAT TRUMP CARD OUT THERE...
BLIZZARD PRINCESS
Activate only when an opponent's monster declares an attack. Destroy all Attack Mode monsters your opponent controls.
ATK 2800 DEF 2100
...I COULDN'T EVEN USE THIS GUY'S POWER!
MIRROR FORCE (TRAP CARD)
Activate only n opponent's monster decla tack. Destroy all At e monsters your opponent
BUT THAT WON'T WORK FOR YOU IN A ONE-ON-ONE DUEL!
AMMON!
NEVER MIND. LET'S JUST DO OUR BEST NEXT TIME!
WHEN WE DUEL ONE-ON-ONE.
"NEXT TIME"?! "ONE-ON-ONE"?!

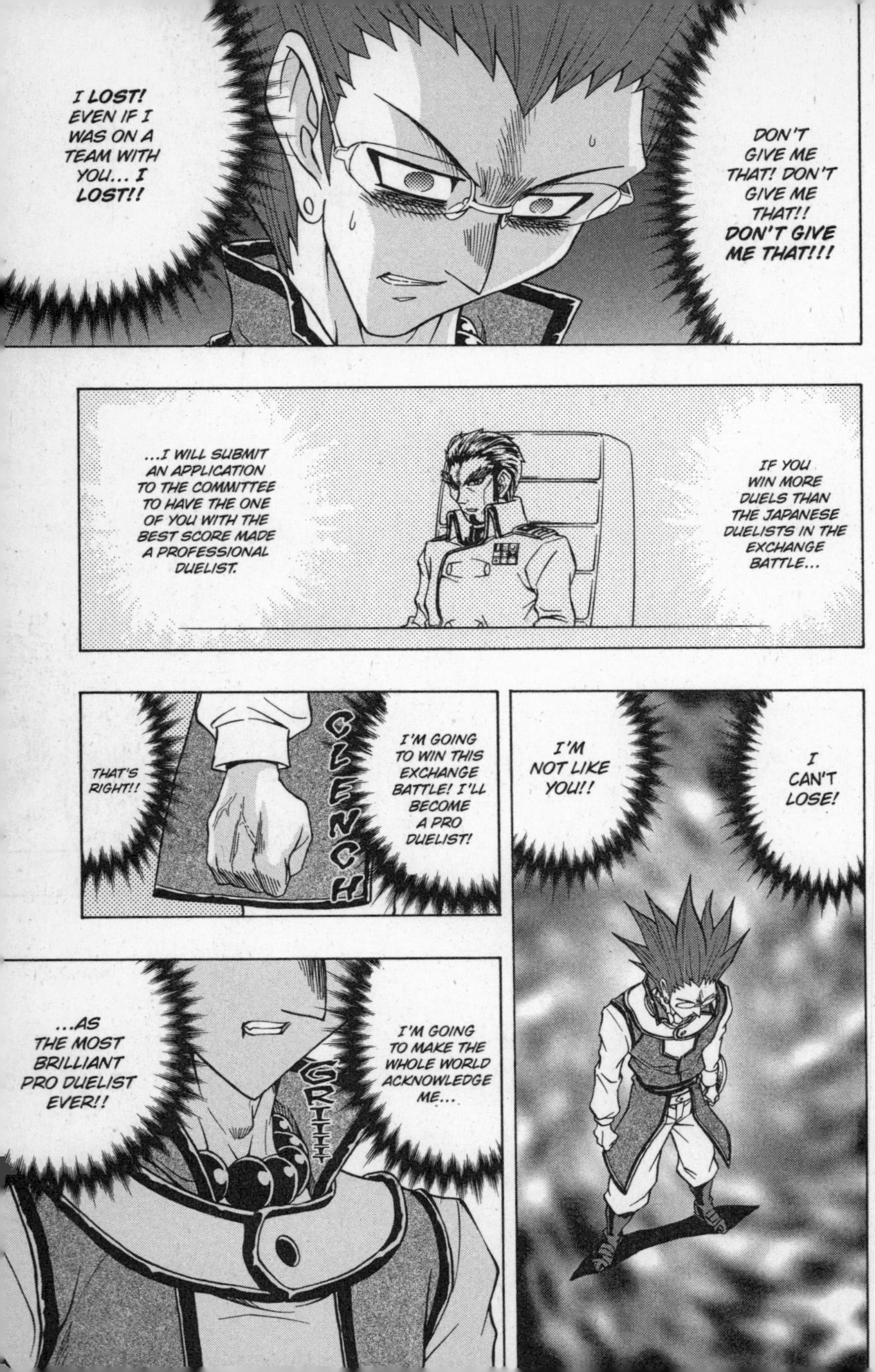
DON'T GIVE ME THAT! DON'T GIVE ME THAT!! DON'T GIVE ME THAT!!!
I LOST! EVEN IF I WAS ON A TEAM WITH YOU... I LOST!!
IF YOU WIN MORE DUELS THAN THE JAPANESE DUELISTS IN THE EXCHANGE BATTLE...
...I WILL SUBMIT AN APPLICATION TO THE COMMITTEE TO HAVE THE ONE OF YOU WITH THE BEST SCORE MADE A PROFESSIONAL DUELIST.
I CAN'T LOSE!
I'M NOT LIKE YOU!!
I'M GOING TO WIN THIS EXCHANGE BATTLE! I'LL BECOME A PRO DUELIST!
CLENCH
THAT'S RIGHT!!
I'M GOING TO MAKE THE WHOLE WORLD ACKNOWLEDGE ME...
GRIIIT
...AS THE MOST BRILLIANT PRO DUELIST EVER!!

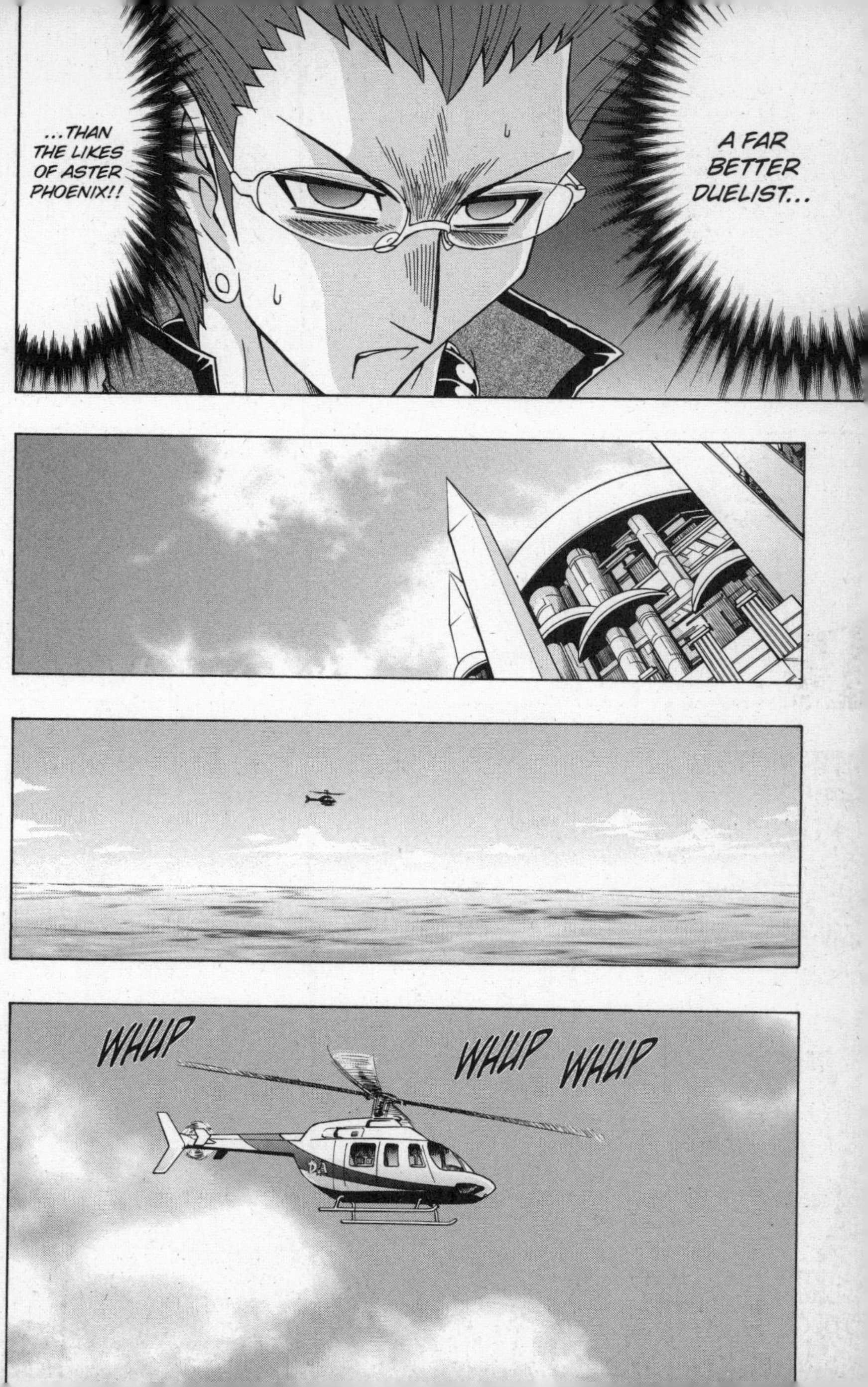
A FAR BETTER DUELIST...
...THAN THE LIKES OF ASTER PHOENIX!!
WHUP
WHUP
WHUP

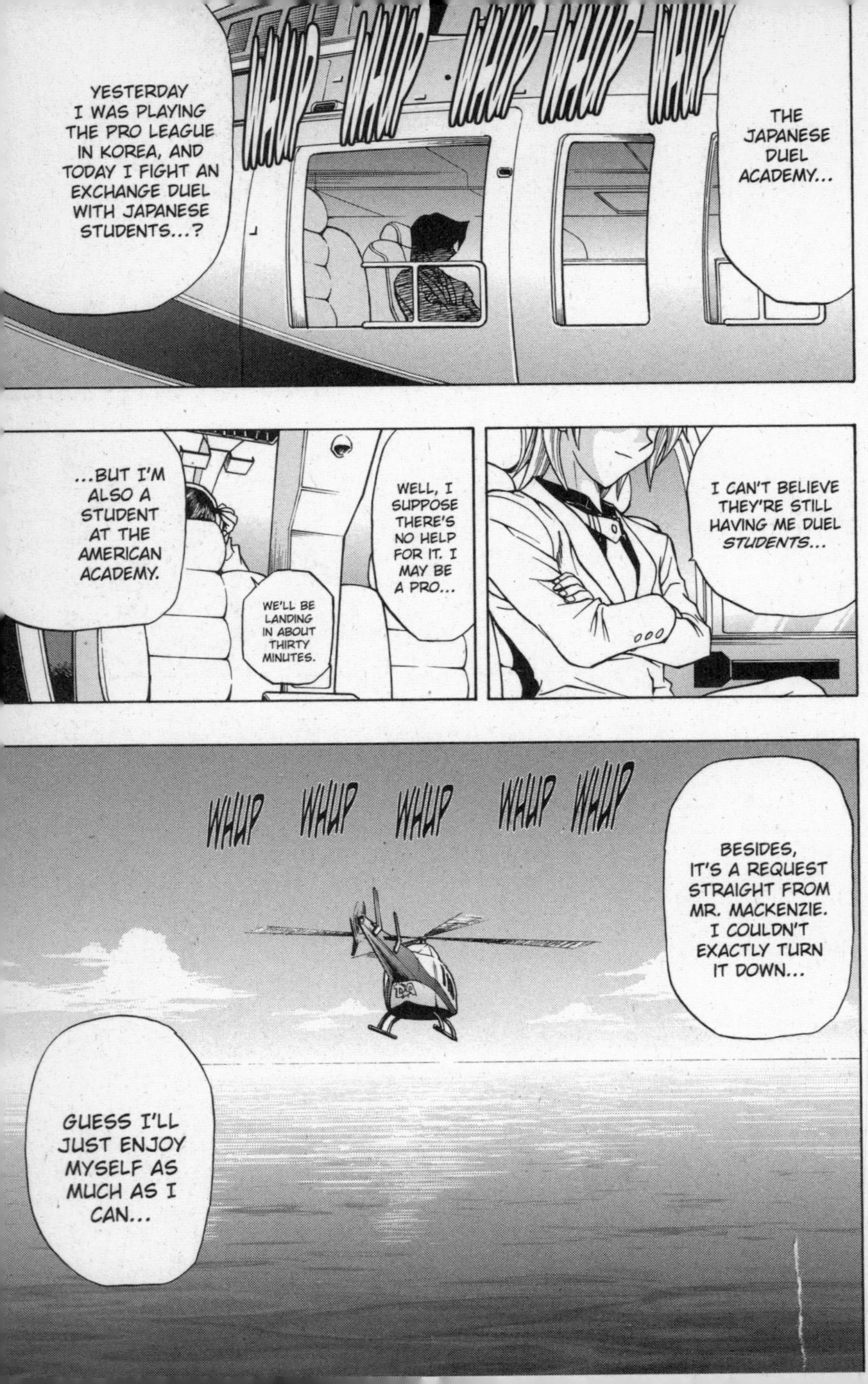
WHUP WHUP WHUP WHUP WHUP
THE JAPANESE DUEL ACADEMY...
YESTERDAY I WAS PLAYING THE PRO LEAGUE IN KOREA, AND TODAY I FIGHT AN EXCHANGE DUEL WITH JAPANESE STUDENTS...?
I CAN'T BELIEVE THEY'RE STILL HAVING ME DUEL *STUDENTS*...
WELL, I SUPPOSE THERE'S NO HELP FOR IT. I MAY BE A PRO...
...BUT I'M ALSO A STUDENT AT THE AMERICAN ACADEMY.
WE'LL BE LANDING IN ABOUT THIRTY MINUTES.
WHUP WHUP WHUP WHUP WHUP
BESIDES, IT'S A REQUEST STRAIGHT FROM MR. MACKENZIE. I COULDN'T EXACTLY TURN IT DOWN...
GUESS I'LL JUST ENJOY MYSELF AS MUCH AS I CAN...

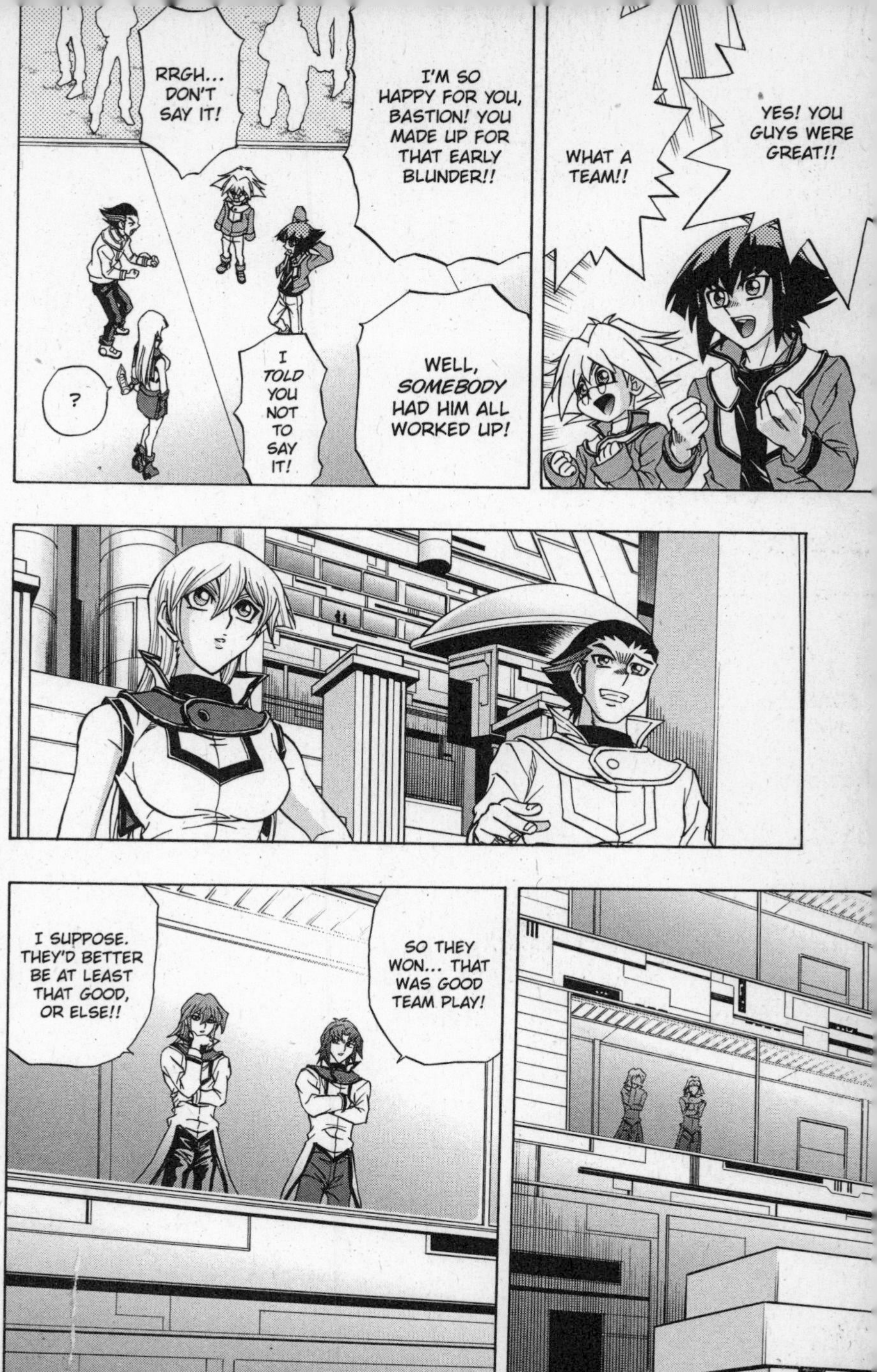
YES! YOU GUYS WERE GREAT!!
WHAT A TEAM!!
I'M SO HAPPY FOR YOU, BASTION! YOU MADE UP FOR THAT EARLY BLUNDER!!
RRGH... DON'T SAY IT!
WELL, *SOMEBODY* HAD HIM ALL WORKED UP!
I *TOLD* YOU NOT TO SAY IT!
?
SO THEY WON... THAT WAS GOOD TEAM PLAY!
I SUPPOSE. THEY'D BETTER BE AT LEAST THAT GOOD, OR ELSE!!

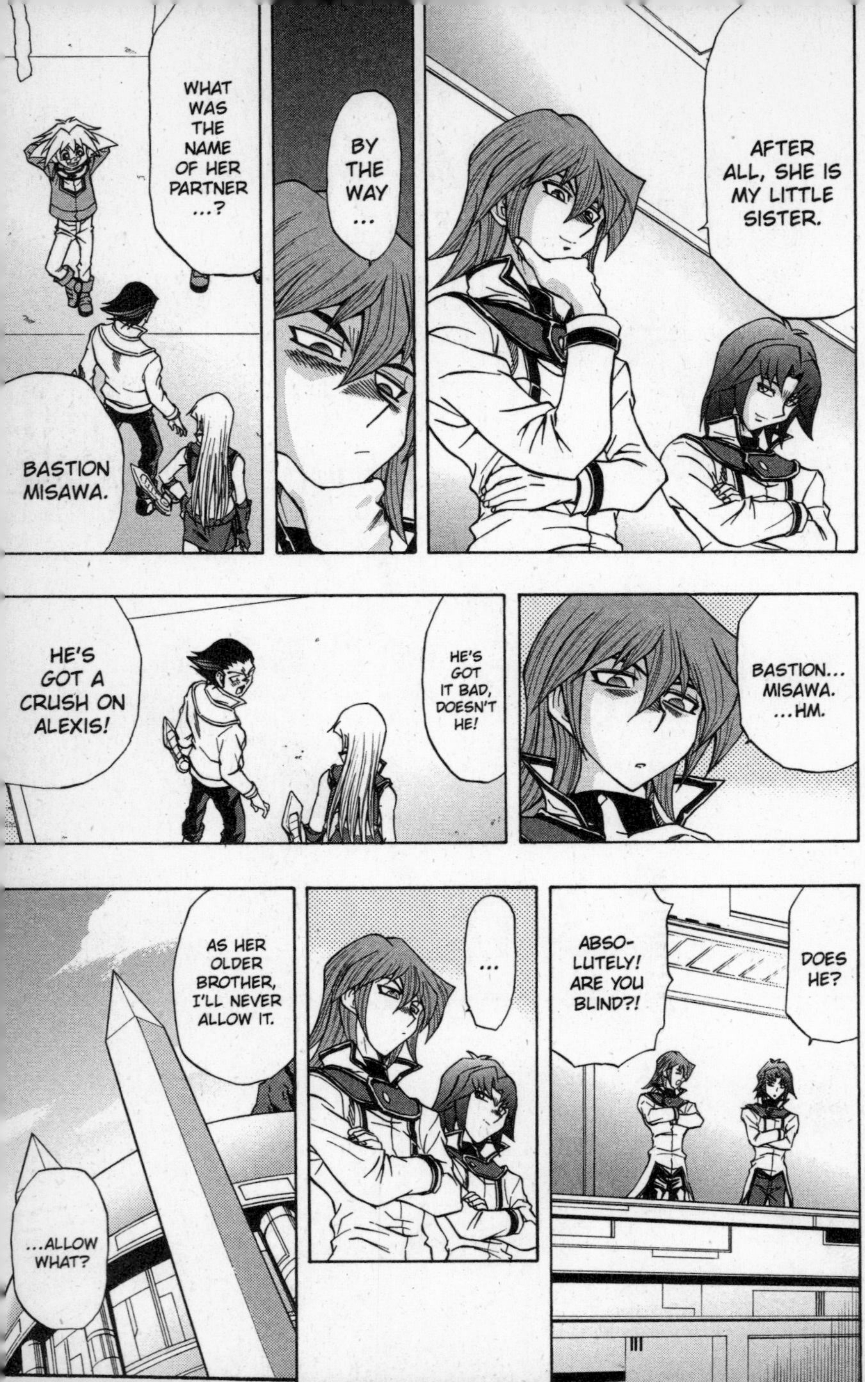
AFTER ALL, SHE IS MY LITTLE SISTER.
BY THE WAY...
WHAT WAS THE NAME OF HER PARTNER...?
BASTION MISAWA.
BASTION... MISAWA. ...HM.
HE'S GOT IT BAD, DOESN'T HE!
HE'S GOT A CRUSH ON ALEXIS!
DOES HE?
ABSO-LUTELY! ARE YOU BLIND?!
...
AS HER OLDER BROTHER, I'LL NEVER ALLOW IT.
...ALLOW WHAT?

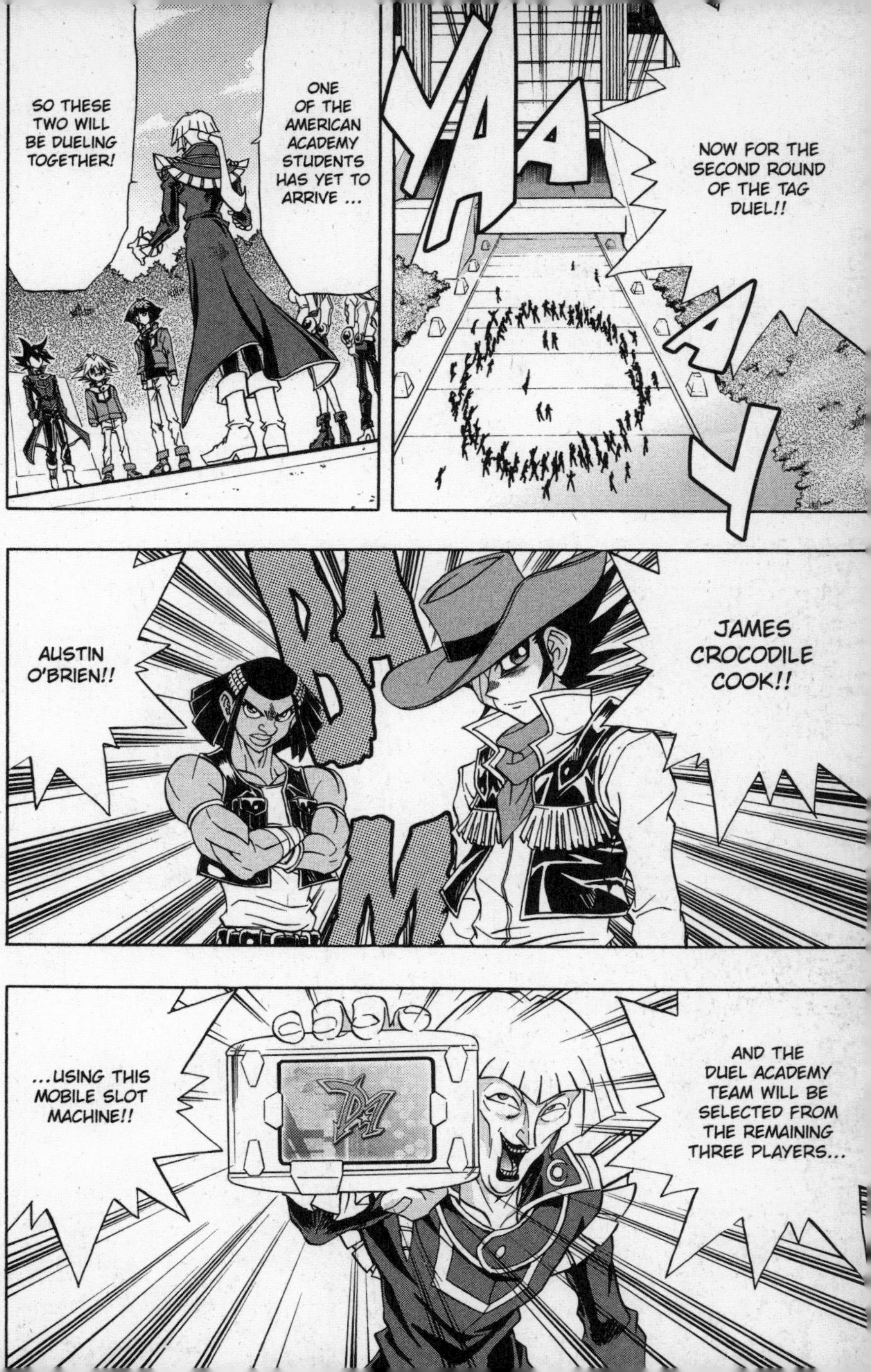
NOW FOR THE SECOND ROUND OF THE TAG DUEL!!
YAAAAY
ONE OF THE AMERICAN ACADEMY STUDENTS HAS YET TO ARRIVE ...
SO THESE TWO WILL BE DUELING TOGETHER!
JAMES CROCODILE COOK!!
BAM
AUSTIN O'BRIEN!!
AND THE DUEL ACADEMY TEAM WILL BE SELECTED FROM THE REMAINING THREE PLAYERS...
...USING THIS MOBILE SLOT MACHINE!!

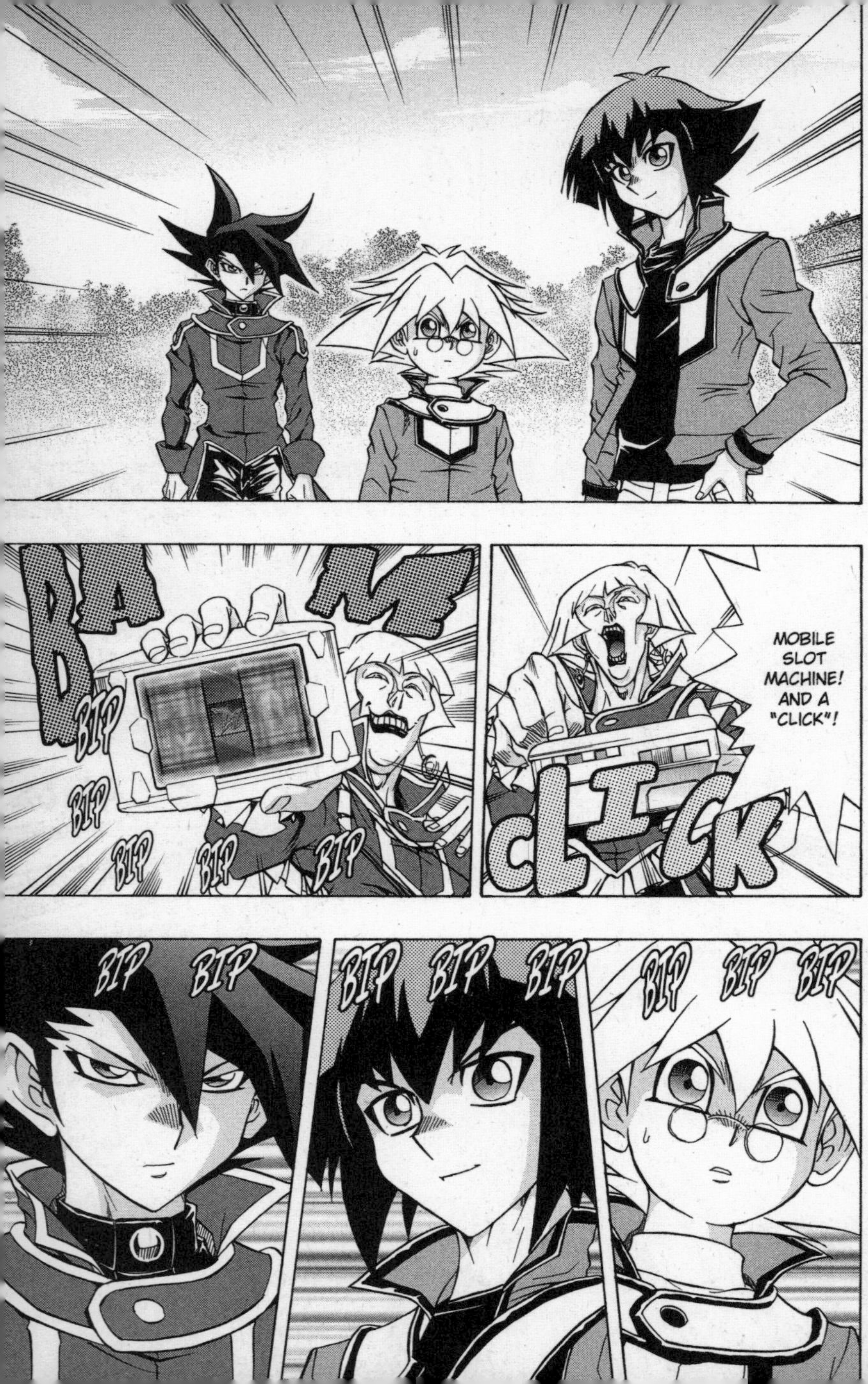
MOBILE SLOT MACHINE! AND A "CLICK"!
CLICK
BAM
BIP BIP BIP BIP BIP
BIP BIP BIP
BIP BIP BIP
BIP BIP

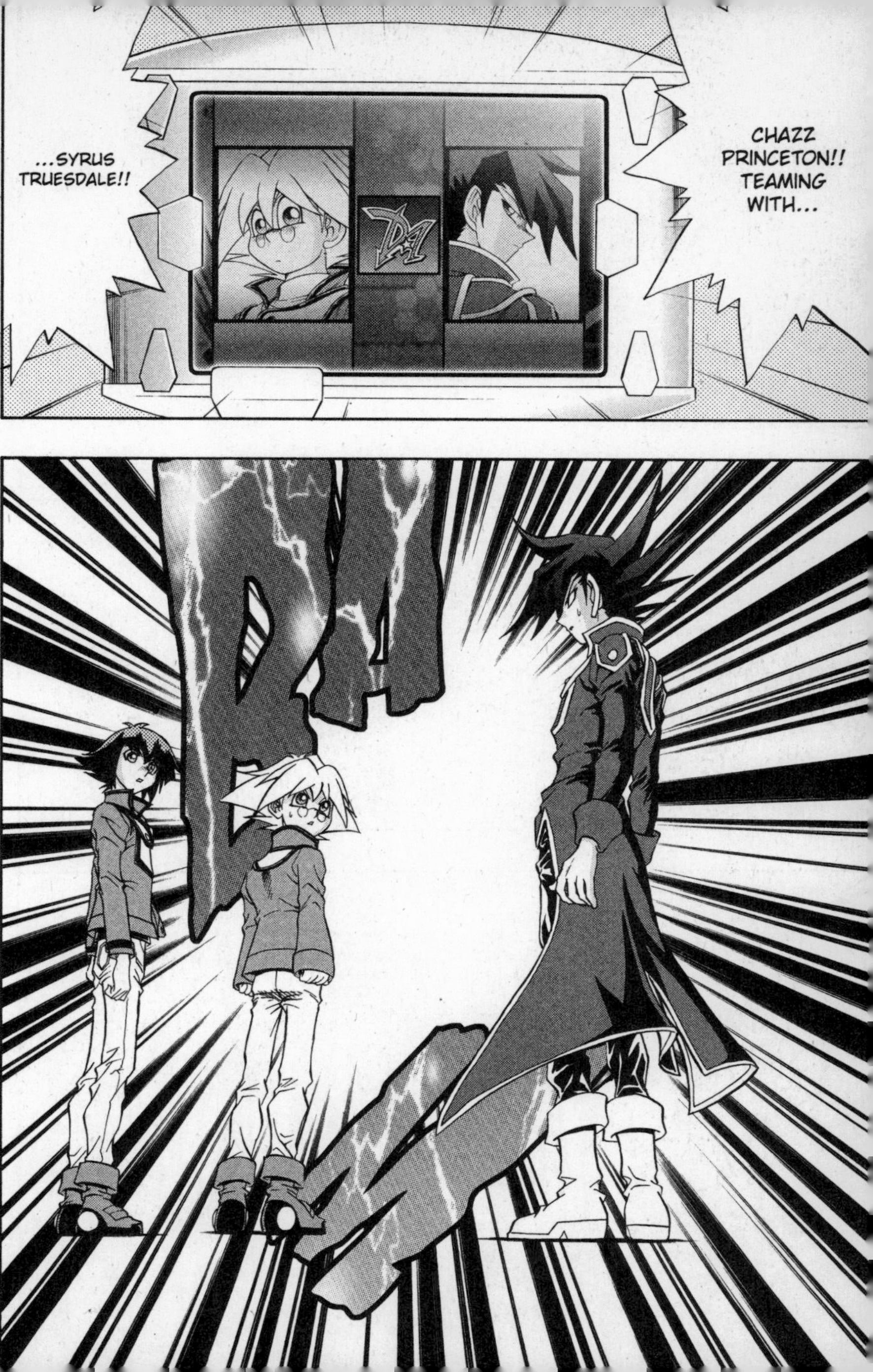
CHAZZ PRINCETON!! TEAMING WITH...
...SYRUS TRUESDALE!!

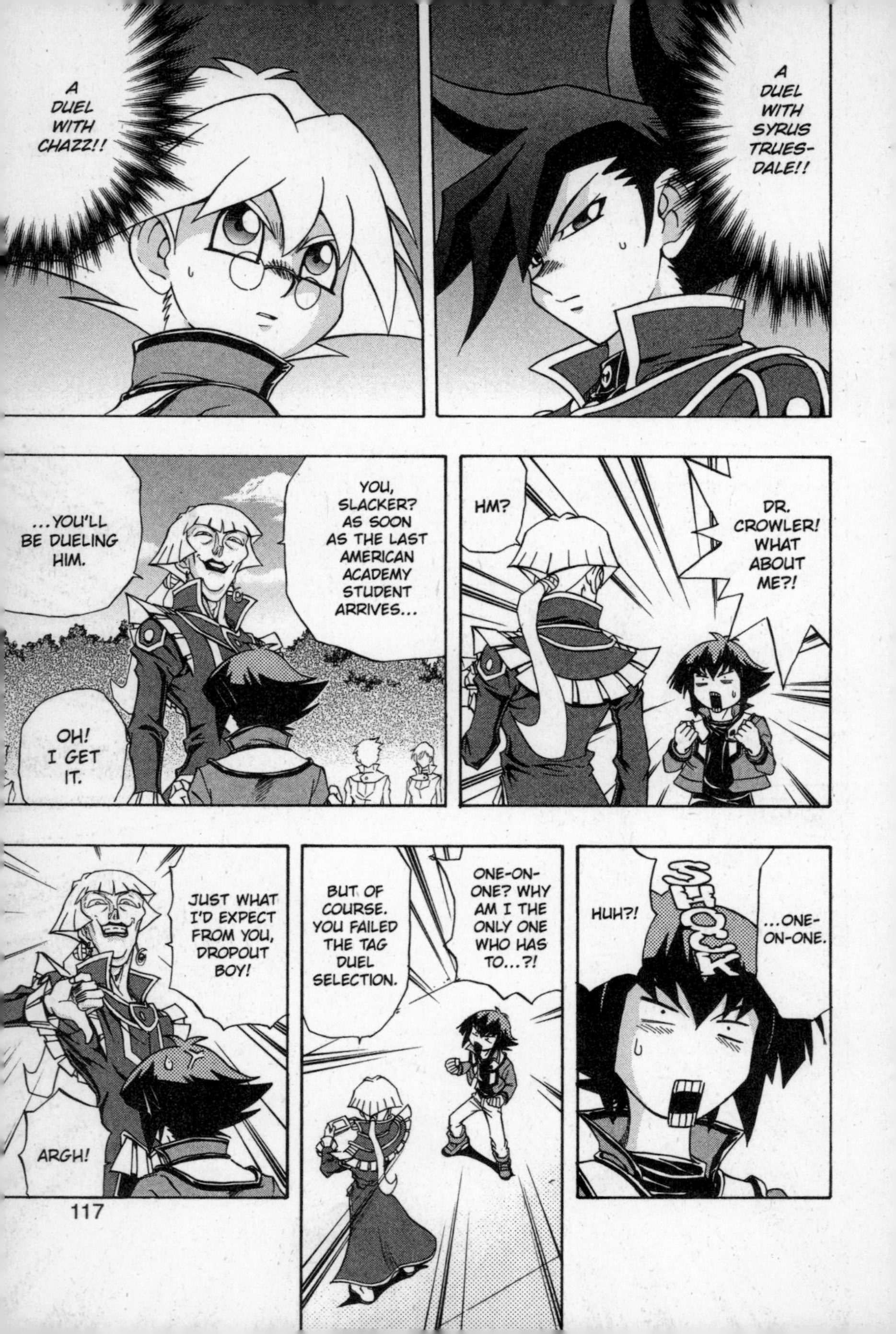
A DUEL WITH SYRUS TRUES-DALE!!
A DUEL WITH CHAZZ!!
DR. CROWLER! WHAT ABOUT ME?!
HM?
YOU, SLACKER? AS SOON AS THE LAST AMERICAN ACADEMY STUDENT ARRIVES...
...YOU'LL BE DUELING HIM.
OH! I GET IT.
...ONE-ON-ONE.
SHOCK
HUH?!
ONE-ON-ONE? WHY AM I THE ONLY ONE WHO HAS TO...?!
BUT OF COURSE. YOU FAILED THE TAG DUEL SELECTION.
JUST WHAT I'D EXPECT FROM YOU, DROPOUT BOY!
ARGH!

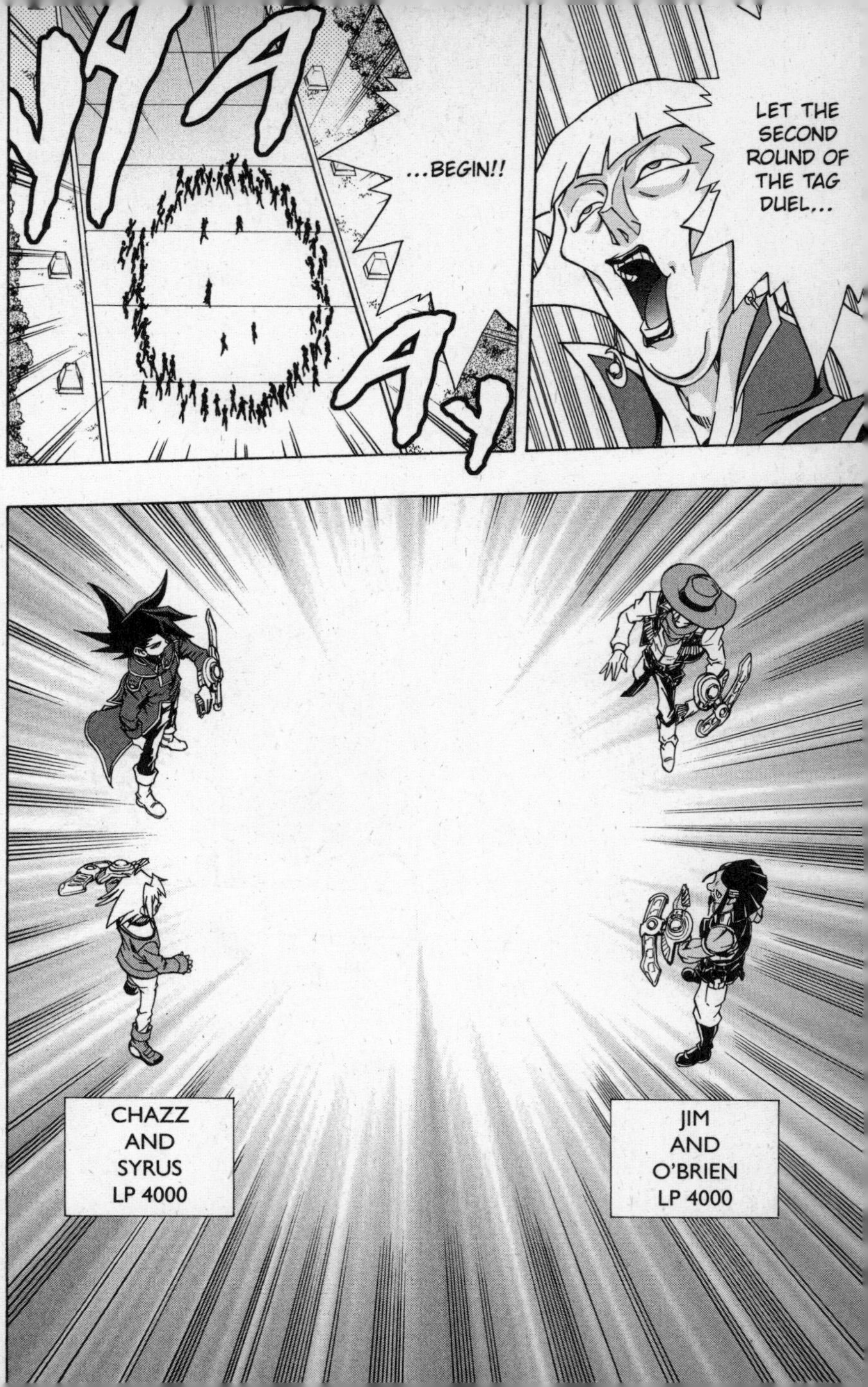
LET THE SECOND ROUND OF THE TAG DUEL...
...BEGIN!!
JIM AND O'BRIEN LP 4000
CHAZZ AND SYRUS LP 4000

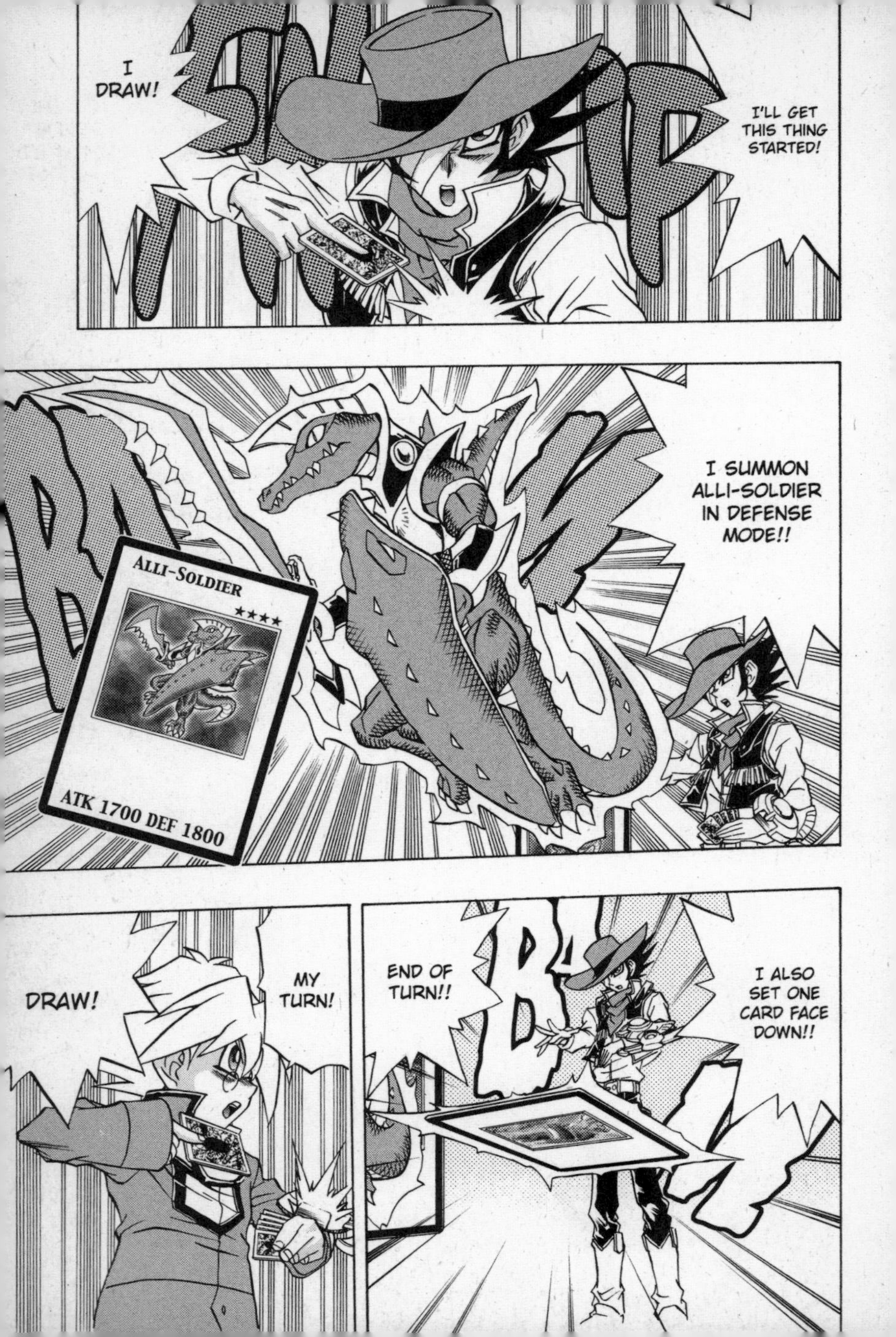
I'LL GET THIS THING STARTED!
I DRAW!
I SUMMON ALLI-SOLDIER IN DEFENSE MODE!!
ALLI-SOLDIER
ATK 1700 DEF 1800
I ALSO SET ONE CARD FACE DOWN!!
END OF TURN!!
MY TURN!
DRAW!

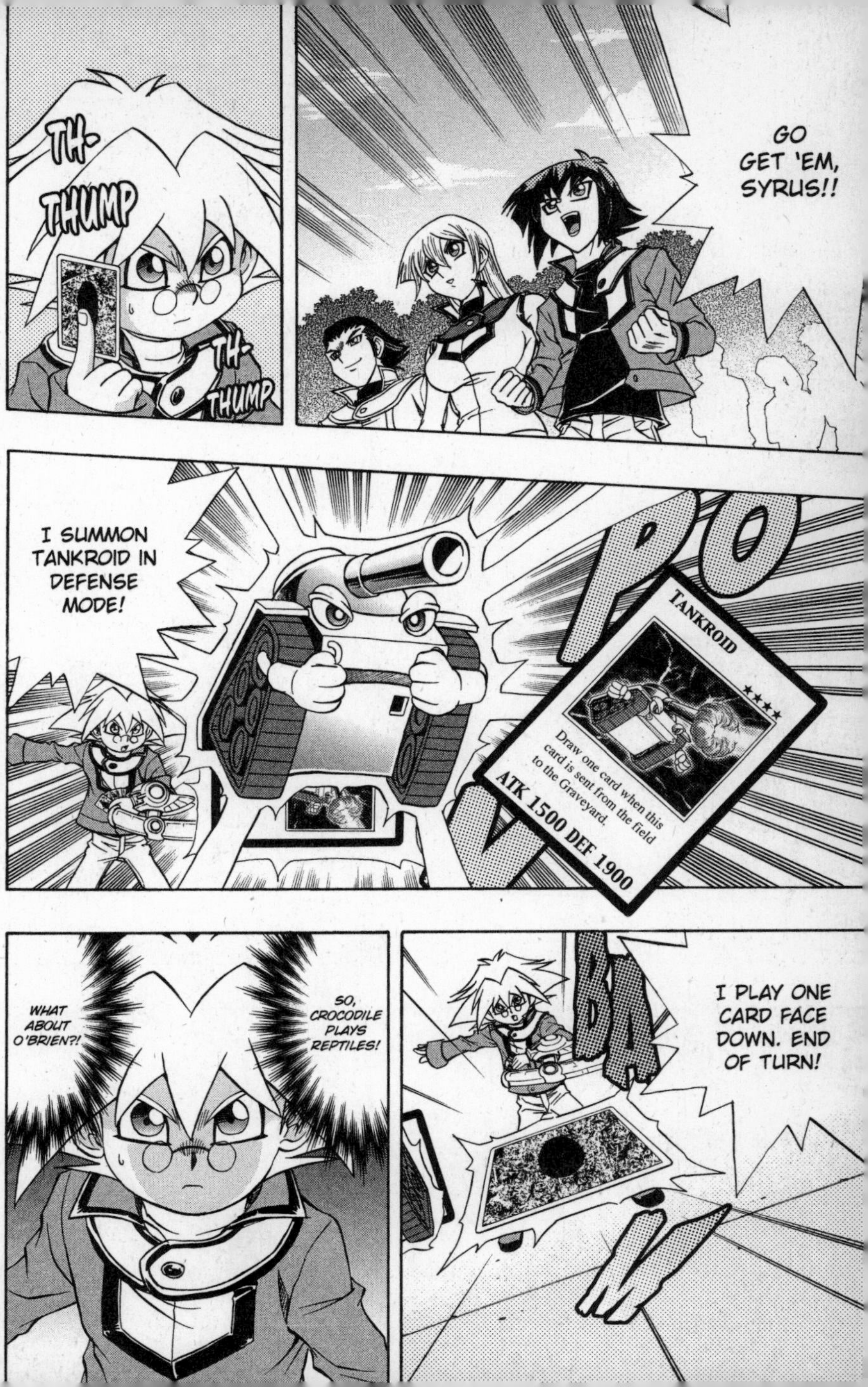
GO GET 'EM, SYRUS!!
TH-THUMP
TH-THUMP
I SUMMON TANKROID IN DEFENSE MODE!
PO
TANKROID
Draw one card when this card is sent from the field to the Graveyard.
ATK 1500 DEF 1900
I PLAY ONE CARD FACE DOWN. END OF TURN!
BA
SO, CROCODILE PLAYS REPTILES!
WHAT ABOUT O'BRIEN?!

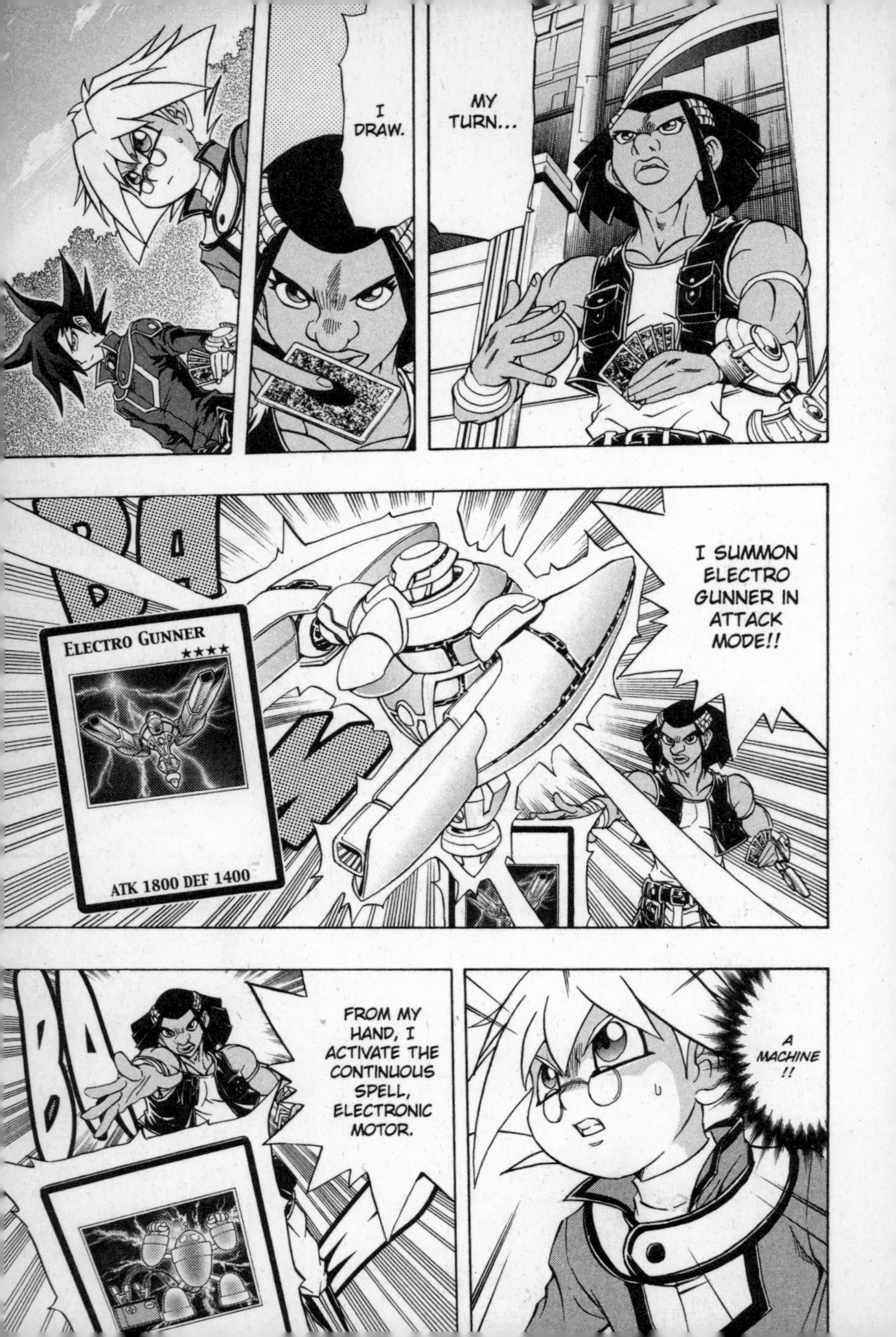
MY TURN...
I DRAW.
I SUMMON ELECTRO GUNNER IN ATTACK MODE!!
ELECTRO GUNNER
ATK 1800 DEF 1400
A MACHINE!!
FROM MY HAND, I ACTIVATE THE CONTINUOUS SPELL, ELECTRONIC MOTOR.

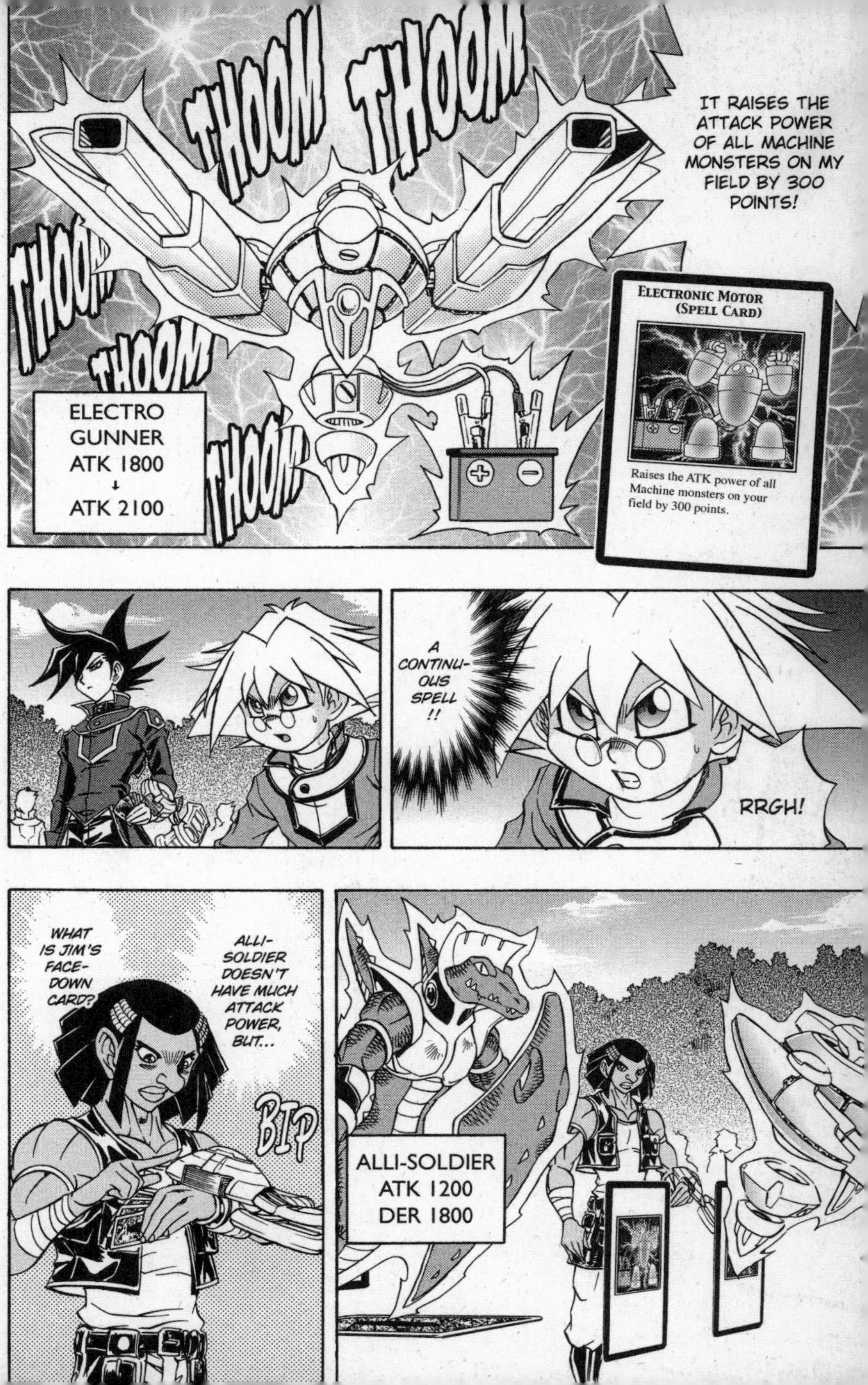
IT RAISES THE ATTACK POWER OF ALL MACHINE MONSTERS ON MY FIELD BY 300 POINTS!
ELECTRONIC MOTOR (SPELL CARD)
Raises the ATK power of all Machine monsters on your field by 300 points.
THOOM THOOM
THOOM
THOOM
THOOM
ELECTRO GUNNER ATK 1800 ↓ ATK 2100
A CONTINU-OUS SPELL!!
RRGH!
ALLI-SOLDIER ATK 1200 DEF 1800
ALLI-SOLDIER DOESN'T HAVE MUCH ATTACK POWER, BUT...
WHAT IS JIM'S FACE-DOWN CARD?
BIP

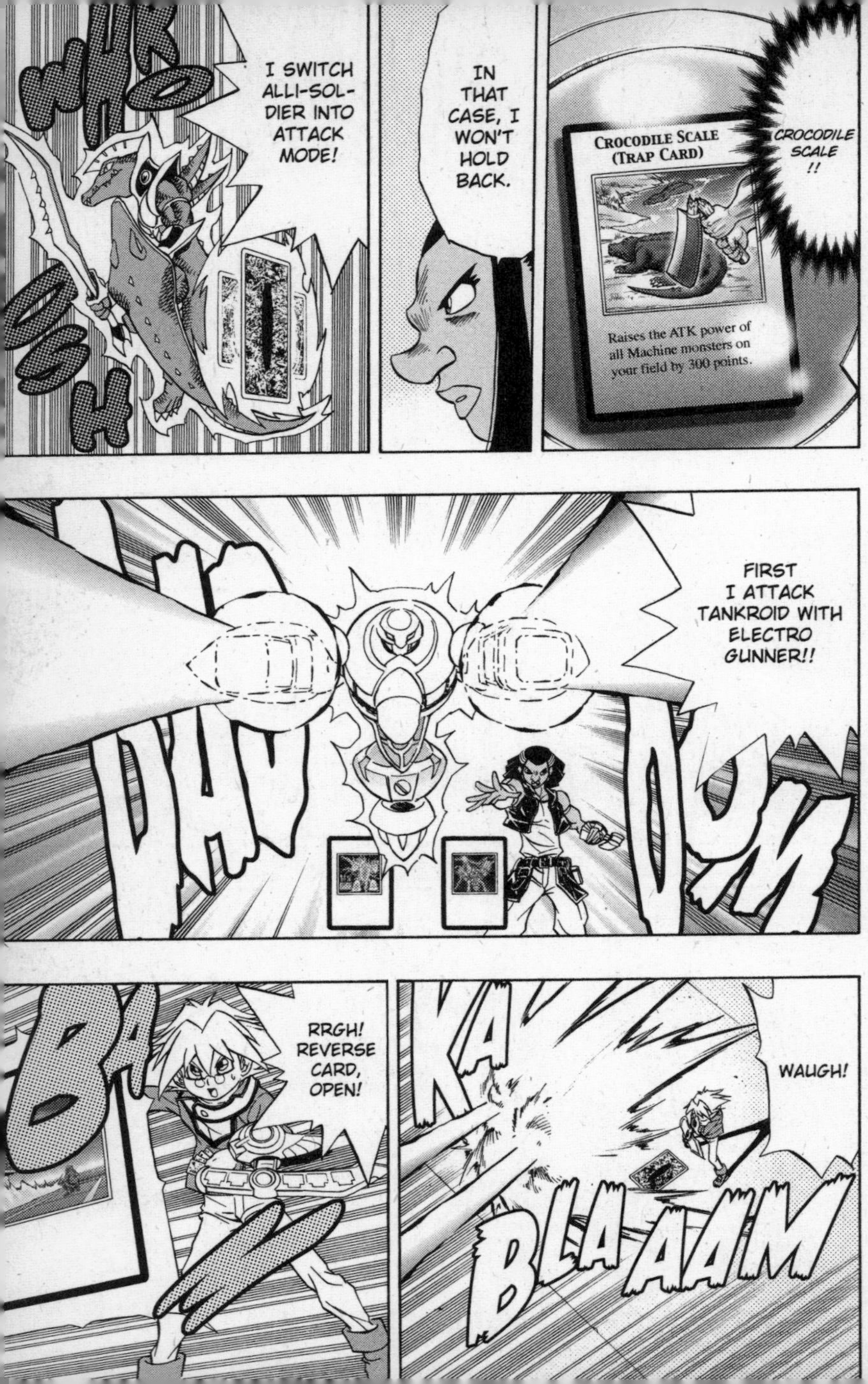
CROCODILE SCALE
(TRAP CARD)
Raises the ATK power of all Machine monsters on your field by 300 points.
CROCODILE SCALE !!
IN THAT CASE, I WON'T HOLD BACK.
I SWITCH ALLI-SOL-DIER INTO ATTACK MODE!
WHOOSH
FIRST I ATTACK TANKROID WITH ELECTRO GUNNER!!
WAUGH!
KA
BLAAAM
RRGH! REVERSE CARD, OPEN!
BA

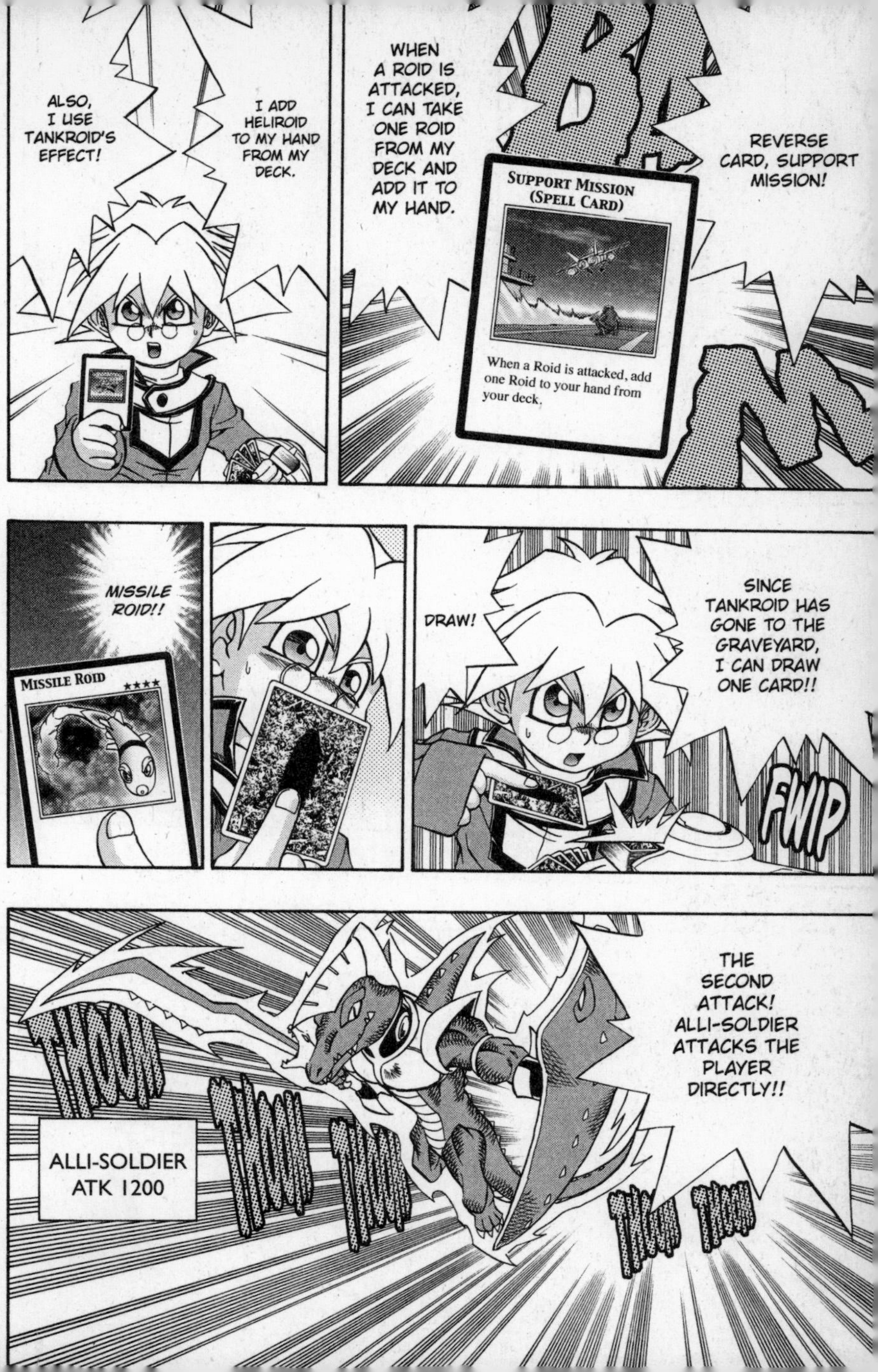

REVERSE CARD, SUPPORT MISSION!
SUPPORT MISSION (SPELL CARD)
When a Roid is attacked, add one Roid to your hand from your deck.
WHEN A ROID IS ATTACKED, I CAN TAKE ONE ROID FROM MY DECK AND ADD IT TO MY HAND.
ALSO, I USE TANKROID'S EFFECT!
I ADD HELIROID TO MY HAND FROM MY DECK.
SINCE TANKROID HAS GONE TO THE GRAVEYARD, I CAN DRAW ONE CARD!!
DRAW!
FWIP
MISSILE ROID!!
MISSILE ROID
THE SECOND ATTACK! ALLI-SOLDIER ATTACKS THE PLAYER DIRECTLY!!
ALLI-SOLDIER ATK 1200

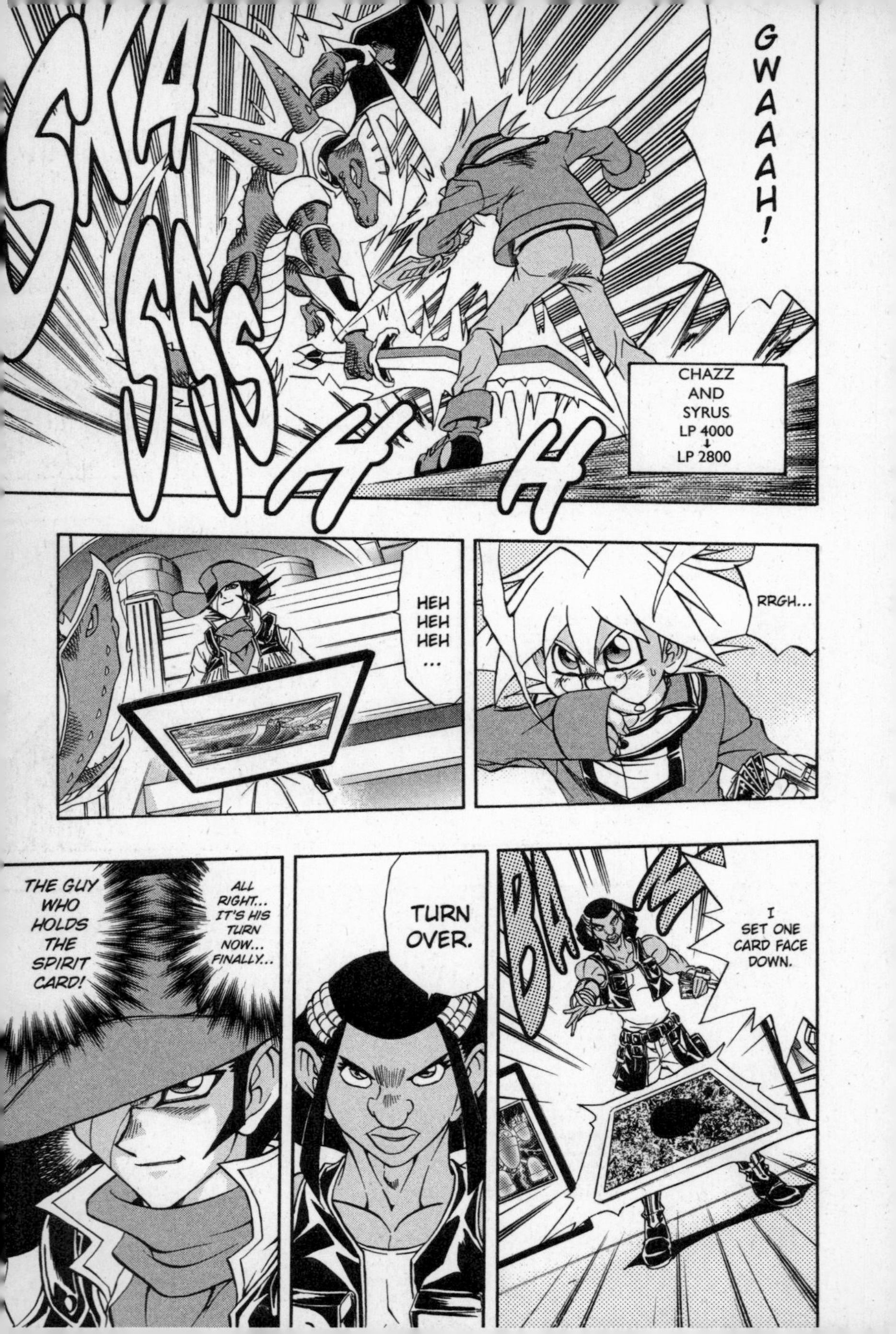
GWAAAAH!
SKASSSHH
CHAZZ AND SYRUS LP 4000 ↓ LP 2800
RRGH...
HEH HEH HEH ...
BAM
I SET ONE CARD FACE DOWN.
TURN OVER.
ALL RIGHT... IT'S HIS TURN NOW... FINALLY...
THE GUY WHO HOLDS THE SPIRIT CARD!

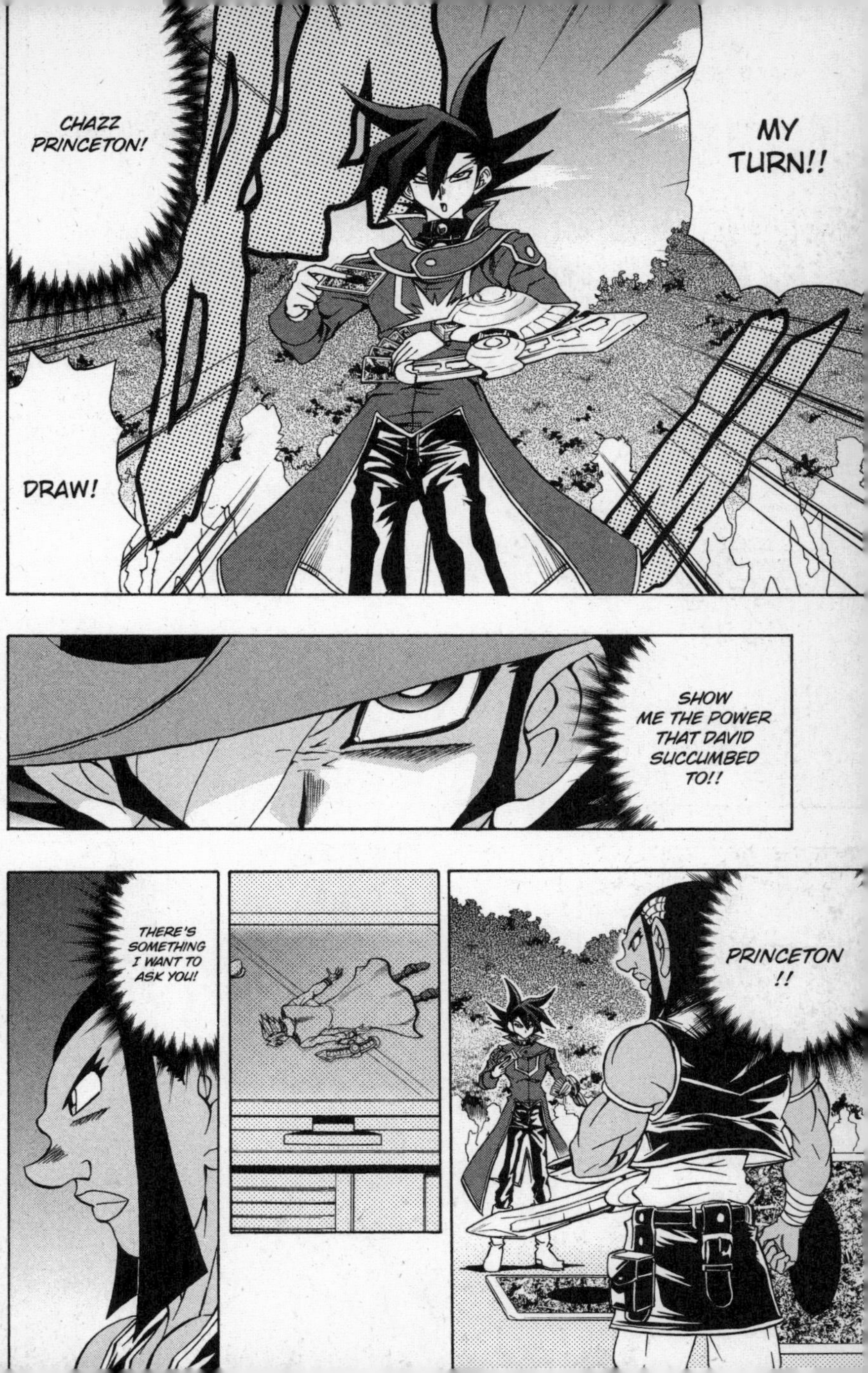
MY TURN!!
CHAZZ PRINCETON!
DRAW!
SHOW ME THE POWER THAT DAVID SUCCUMBED TO!!
PRINCETON !!
THERE'S SOMETHING I WANT TO ASK YOU!

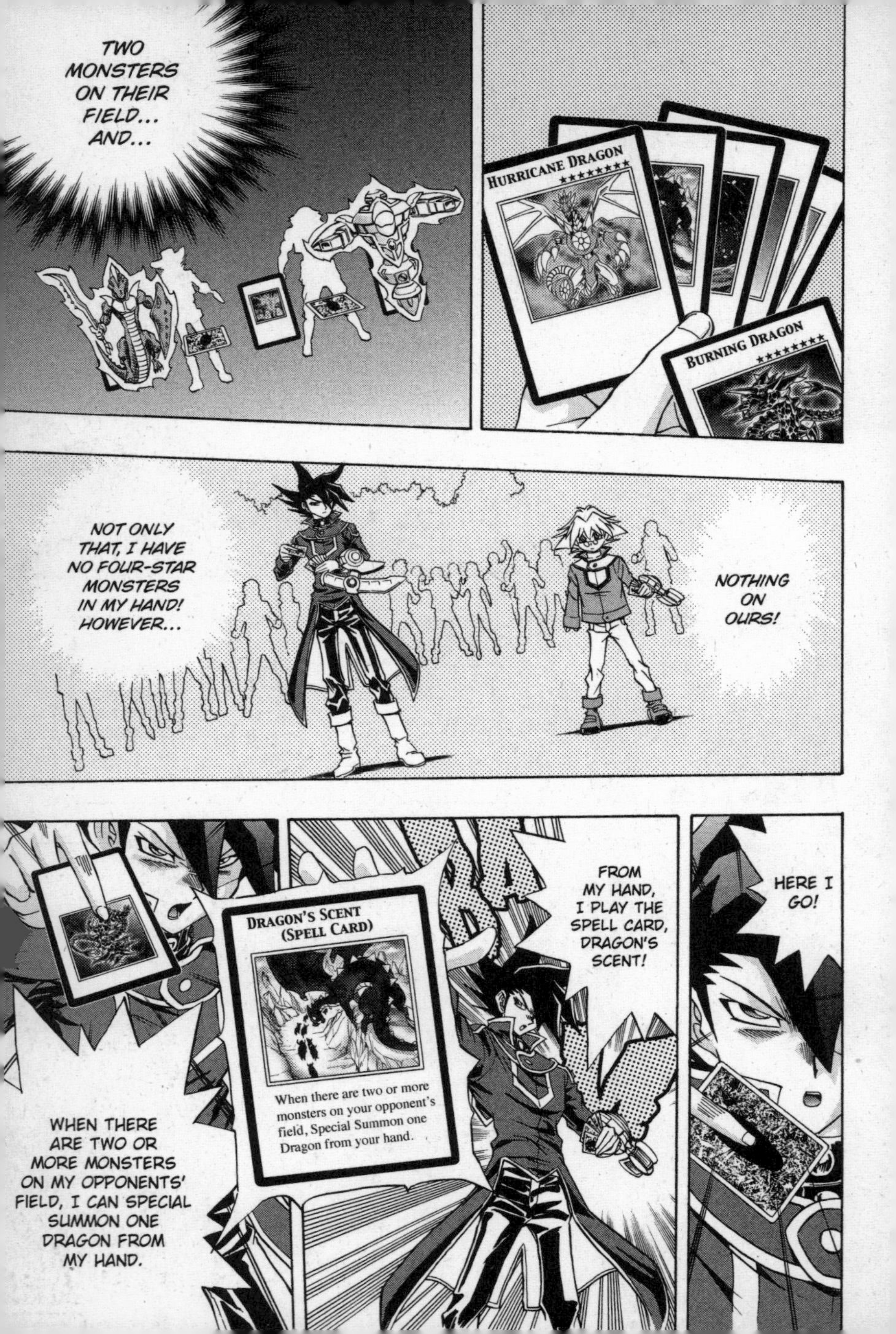
HURRICANE DRAGON
BURNING DRAGON
TWO MONSTERS ON THEIR FIELD... AND...
NOTHING ON OURS!
NOT ONLY THAT, I HAVE NO FOUR-STAR MONSTERS IN MY HAND! HOWEVER...
HERE I GO!
FROM MY HAND, I PLAY THE SPELL CARD, DRAGON'S SCENT!
DRAGON'S SCENT (SPELL CARD)
When there are two or more monsters on your opponent's field, Special Summon one Dragon from your hand.
WHEN THERE ARE TWO OR MORE MONSTERS ON MY OPPONENTS' FIELD, I CAN SPECIAL SUMMON ONE DRAGON FROM MY HAND.

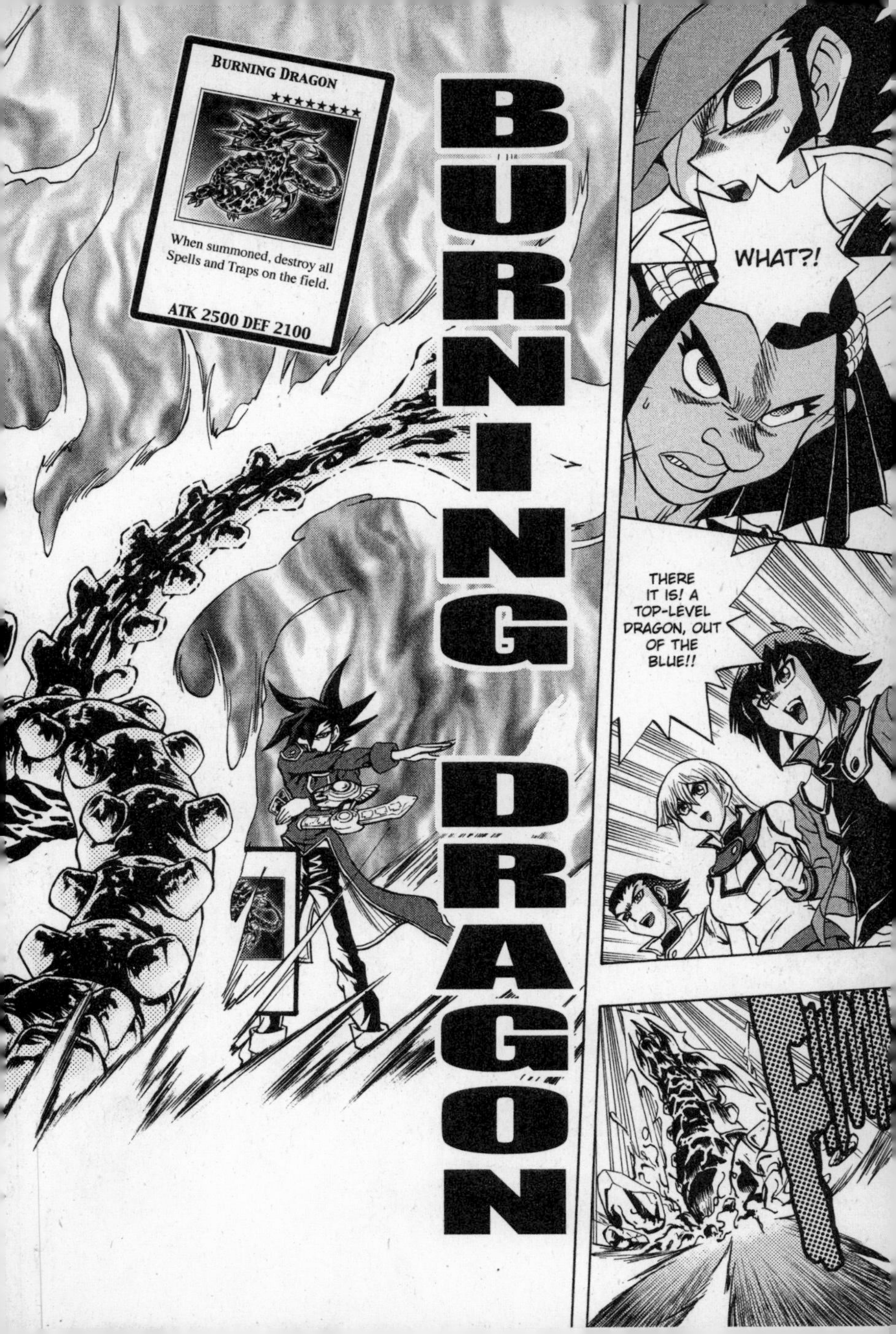
WHAT?!
THERE IT IS! A TOP-LEVEL DRAGON, OUT OF THE BLUE!!
BURNING DRAGON
When summoned, destroy all Spells and Traps on the field.
ATK 2500 DEF 2100
BURNING DRAGON

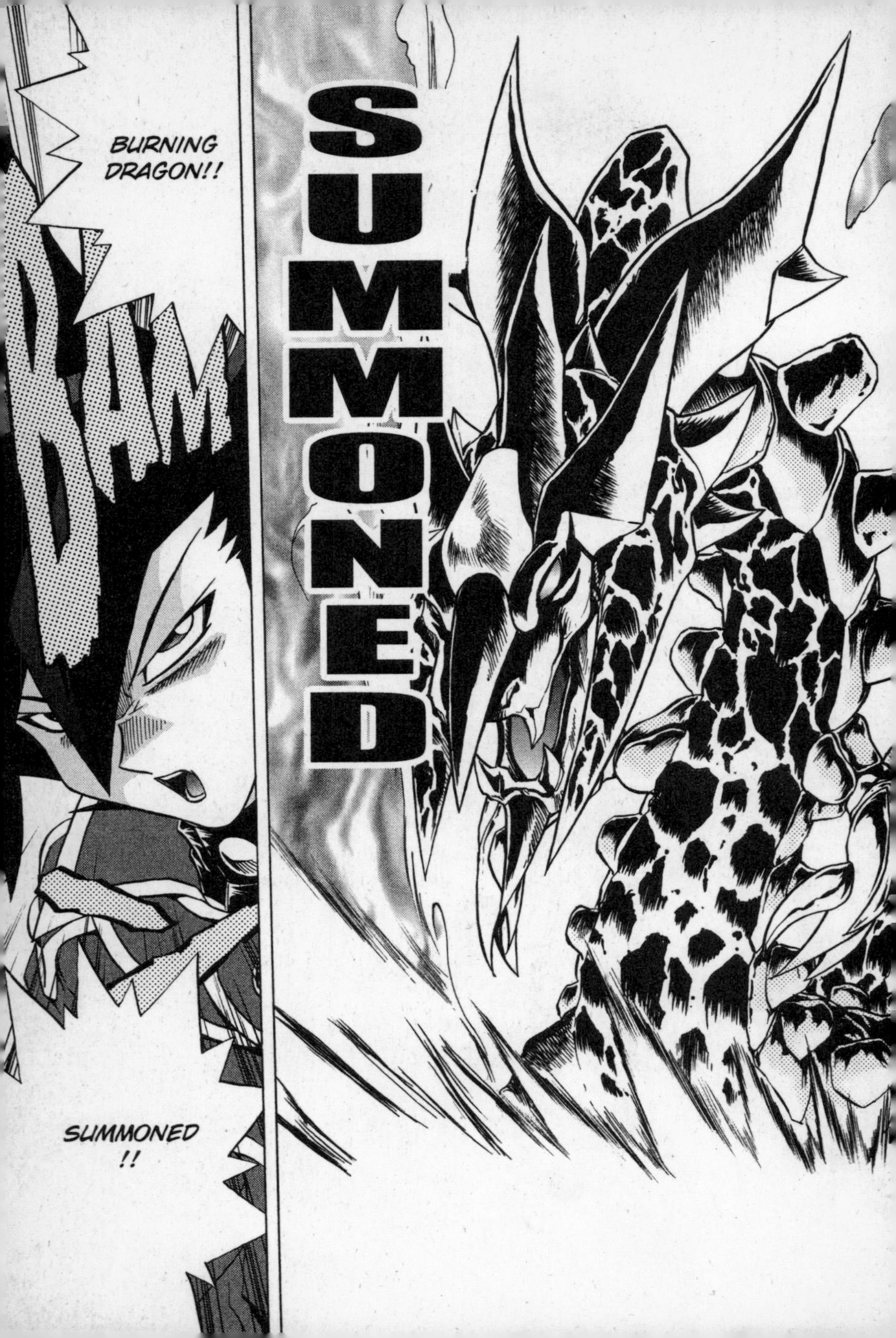
SUMMONED
BURNING DRAGON!!
BAM
SUMMONED !!

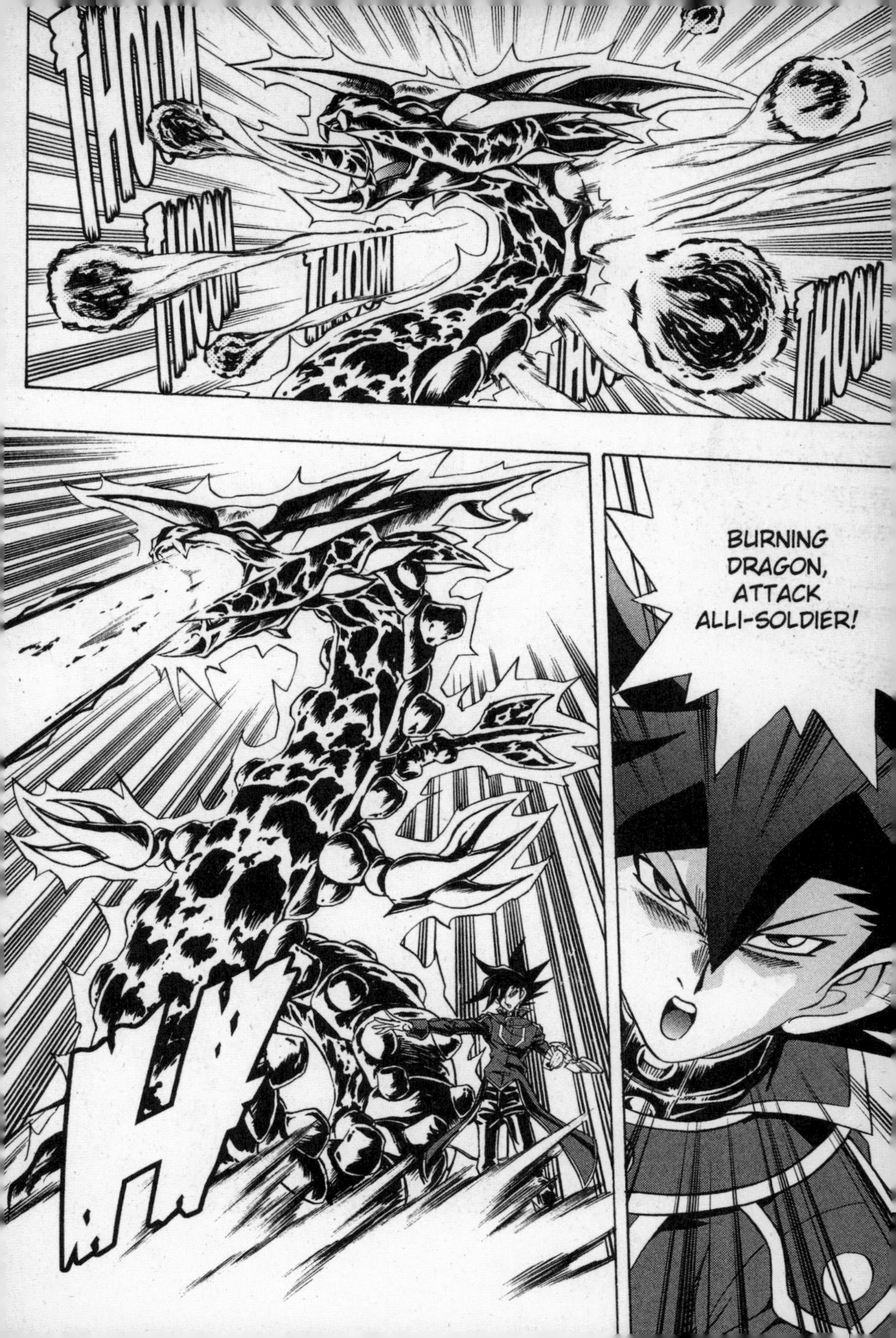
THOOM
THOOM
THOOM
THOOM
BURNING DRAGON, ATTACK ALLI-SOLDIER!

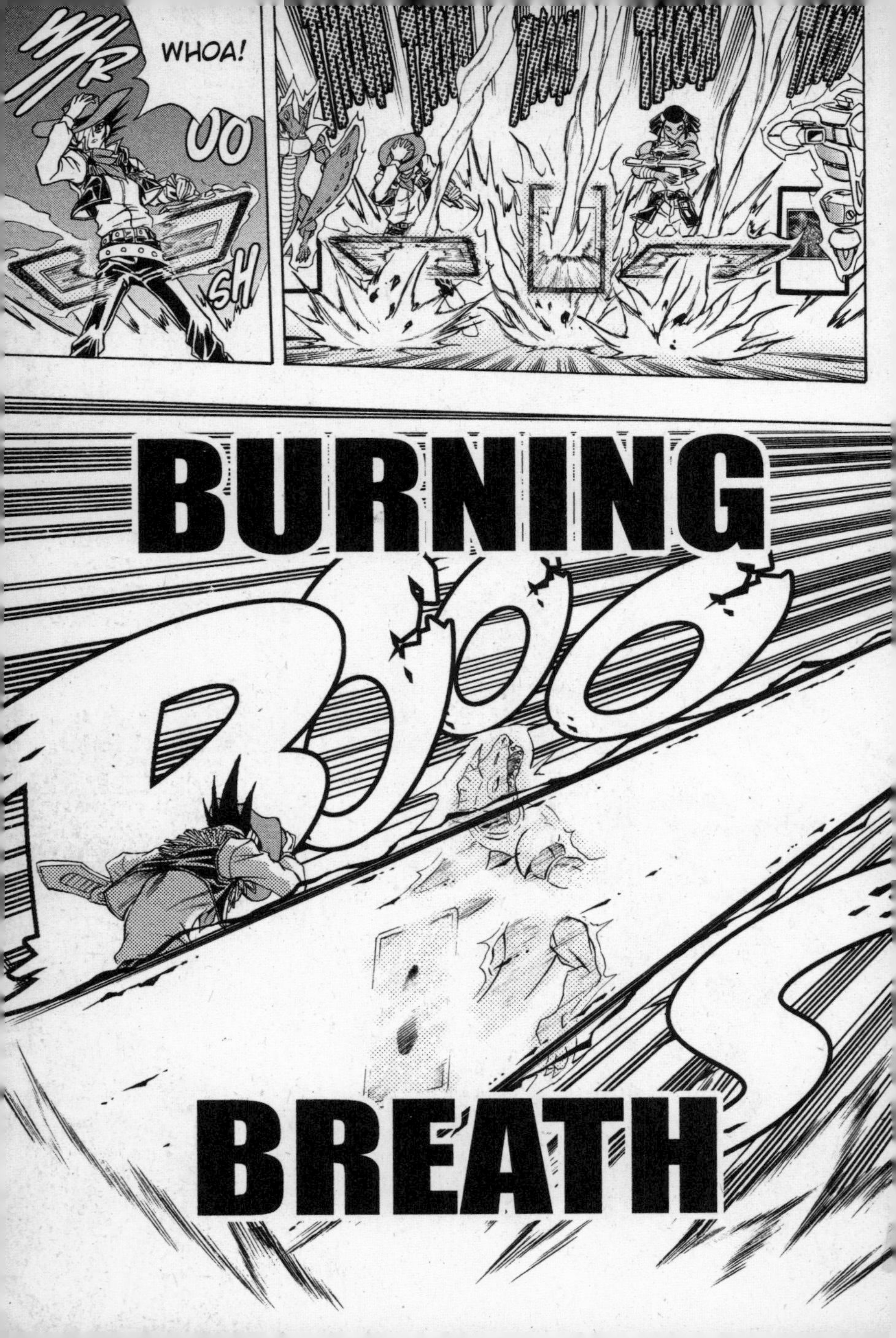
WHR
WHOA!
OO
SH
BURNING
BOOOS
BREATH

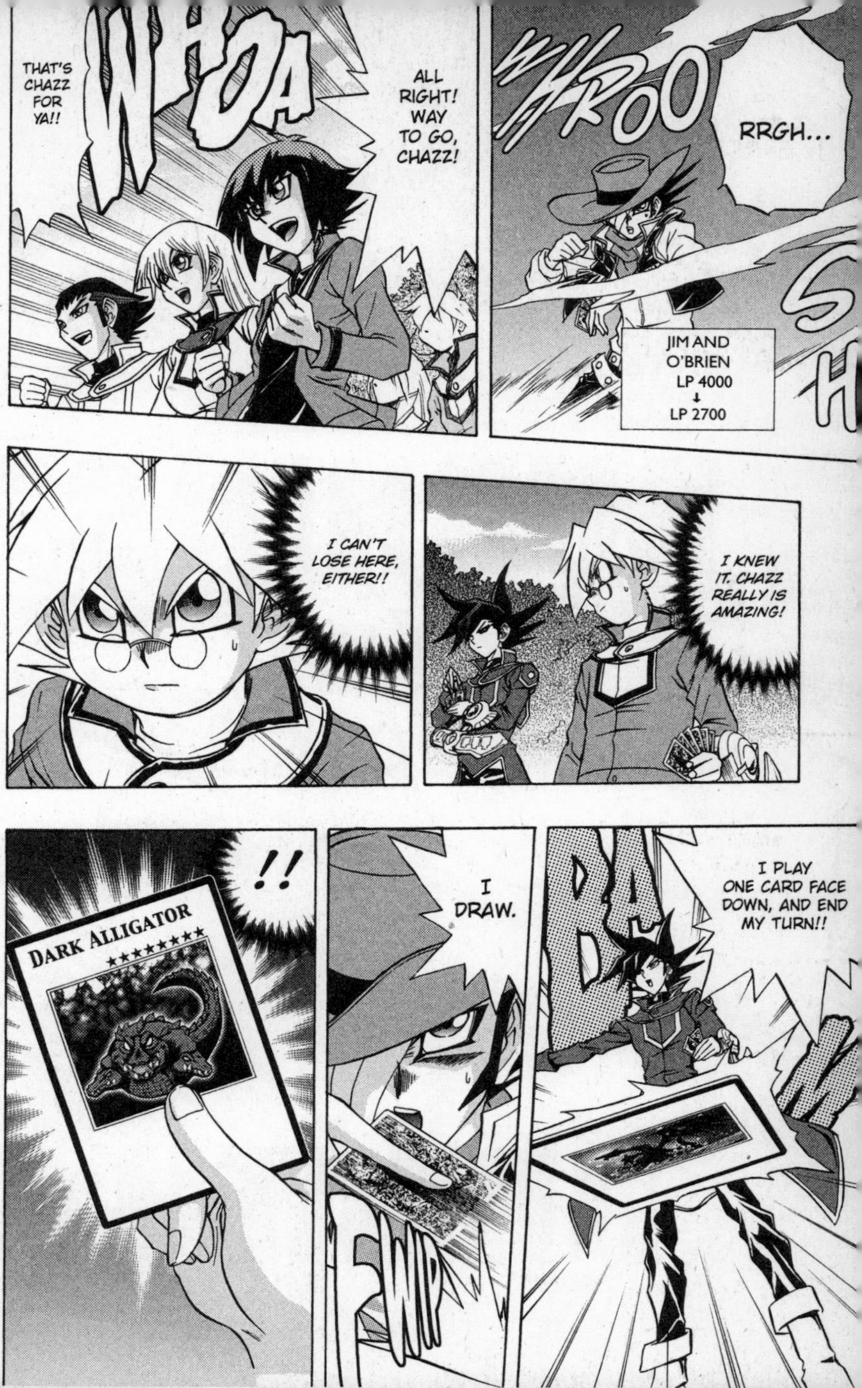
RRGH...
WHROO
SH
JIM AND O'BRIEN LP 4000 ↓ LP 2700
ALL RIGHT! WAY TO GO, CHAZZ!
WHOA
THAT'S CHAZZ FOR YA!!
I KNEW IT. CHAZZ REALLY IS AMAZING!
I CAN'T LOSE HERE, EITHER!!
I PLAY ONE CARD FACE DOWN, AND END MY TURN!!
BA
I DRAW.
FWIP
!!
DARK ALLIGATOR

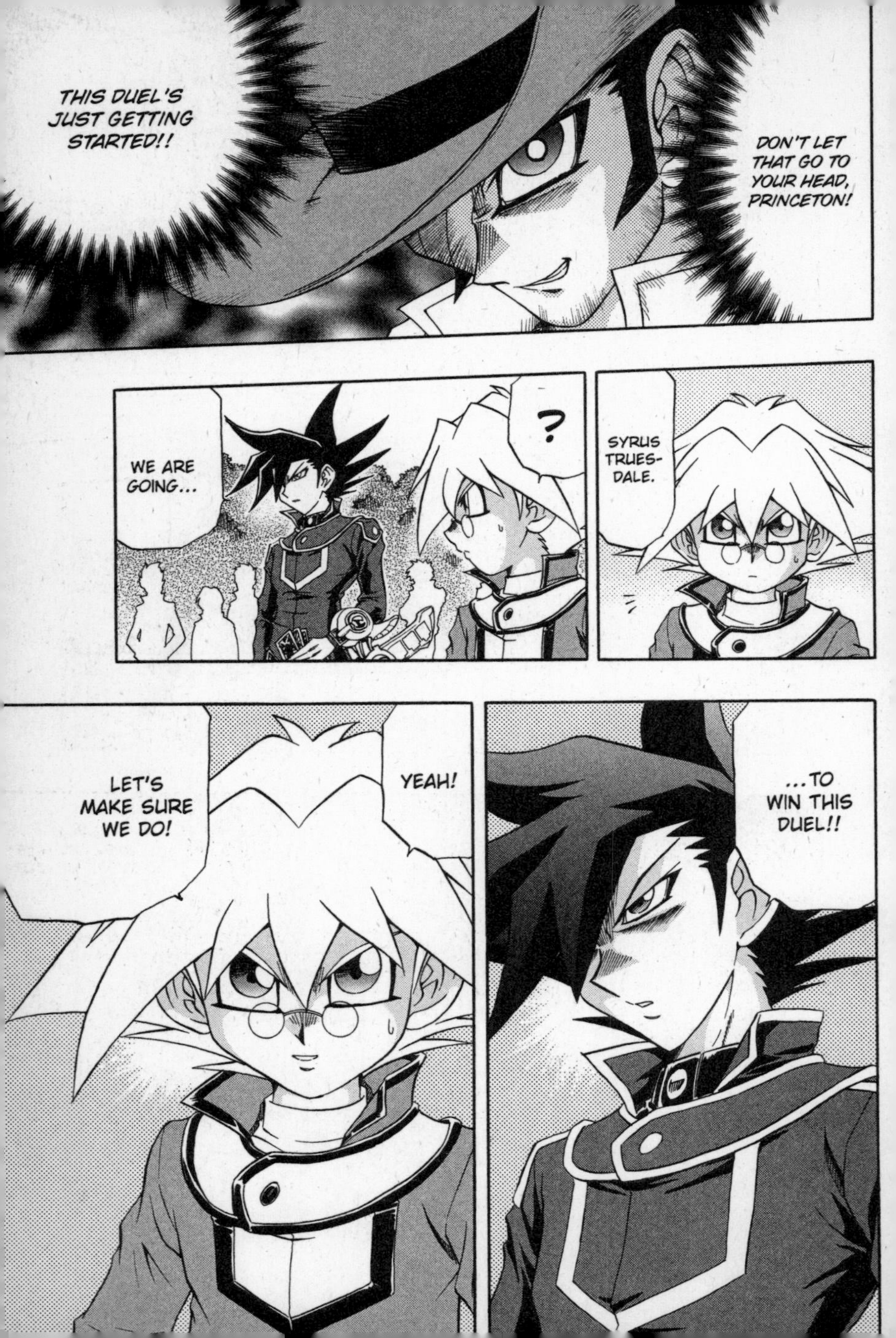
DON'T LET THAT GO TO YOUR HEAD, PRINCETON!
THIS DUEL'S JUST GETTING STARTED!!
SYRUS TRUES-DALE.
?
WE ARE GOING...
...TO WIN THIS DUEL!!
YEAH!
LET'S MAKE SURE WE DO!

WE LIKE DUELS!

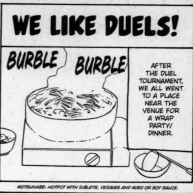

AFTER THE DUEL TOURNAMENT, WE ALL WENT TO A PLACE NEAR THE VENUE FOR A WRAP PARTY/ DINNER.
BURBLE
BURBLE
MOTSUNABE: HOTPOT WITH GIBLETS, VEGGIES AND MISO OR SOY SAUCE.
BUT AFTER A LITTLE WHILE, DUELS STARTED BREAKING OUT ALL OVER THE PLACE.
MY TURN.
THERE WERE OTHER CUSTOMERS, BUT WE JUST DUELED LIKE CRAZY.
I SUMMON...!
FACE: JITSUMATSU
MR. JITSUMATSU, THE PRODUCER, HAD HAD OTHER BUSINESS AND COULDN'T MAKE IT TO THE TOURNAMENT.
SORRY I COULDN'T BE THERE.
HE DID MANAGE TO MAKE IT TO THE WRAP PARTY, BUT...
IT'S OKAY, WE KNOW YOU'RE BUSY.
SHIRT: LIONS
HE DIDN'T EVEN EAT. HE JUST STARTED DUELING...
MY TURN, AND I DRAW!
EVERYONE LOVES DUELS SO MUCH IT'S SCARY...
WE KEEP WORKING HARD EVERY DAY SO THAT PEOPLE LIKE THESE GUYS CAN ENJOY THEMSELVES.

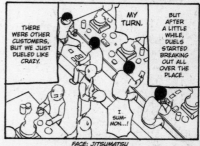

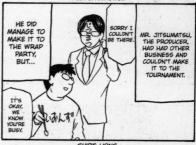

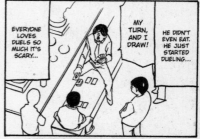

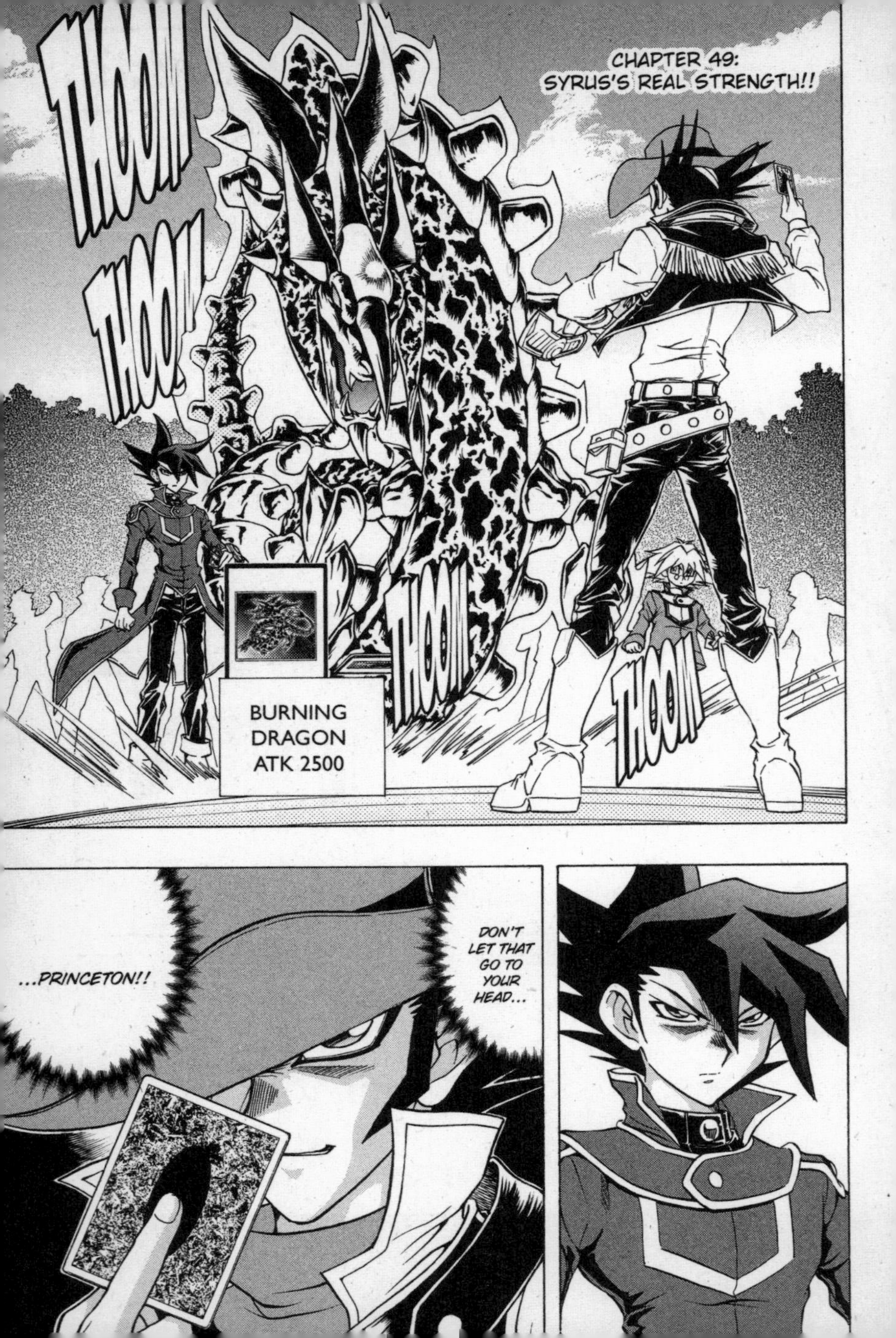
CHAPTER 49:
SYRUS'S REAL STRENGTH!!
THOOM
THOOM
THOOM
THOOM
BURNING DRAGON ATK 2500
DON'T LET THAT GO TO YOUR HEAD...
...PRINCETON!!

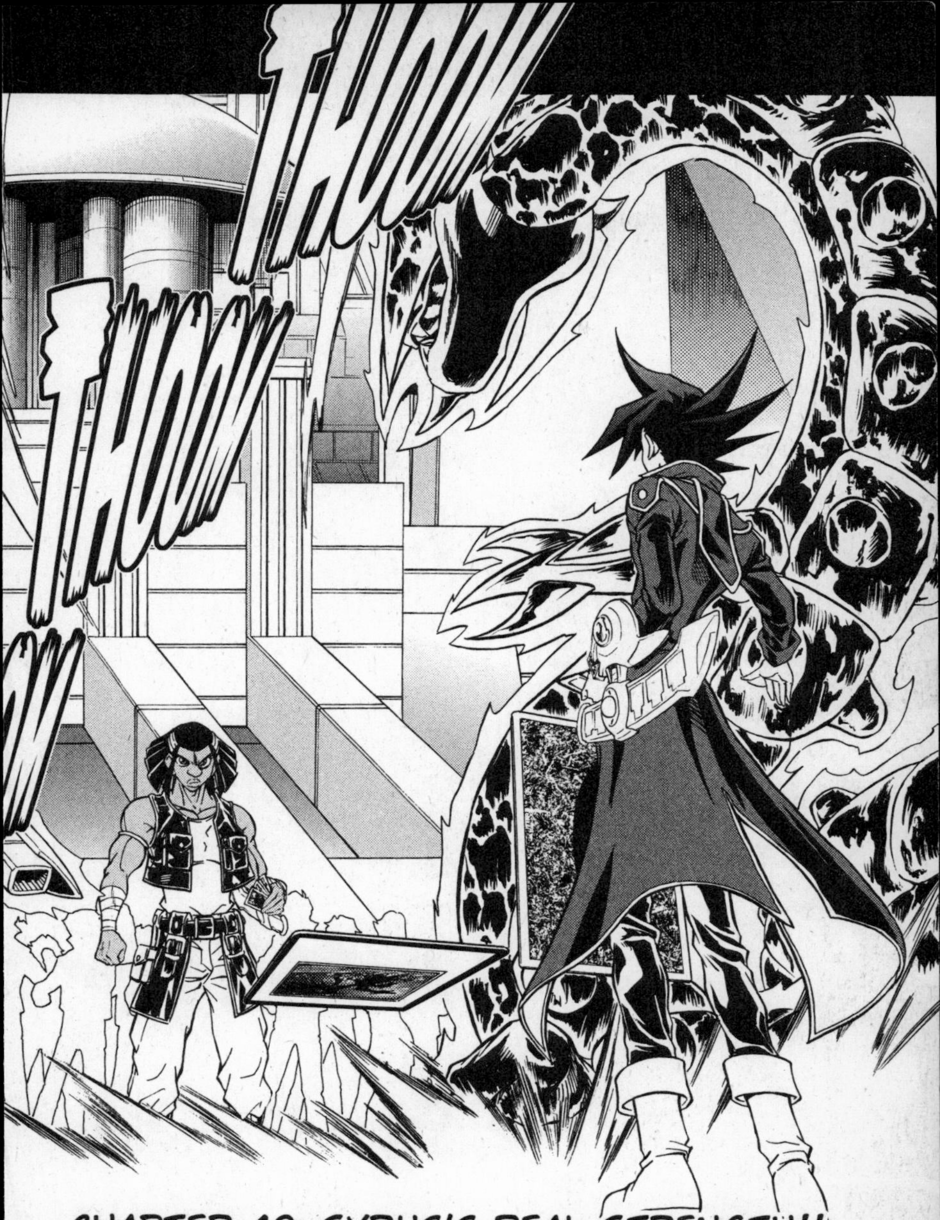
THOOM
THOOM

CHAPTER 49: SYRUS'S REAL STRENGTH!!

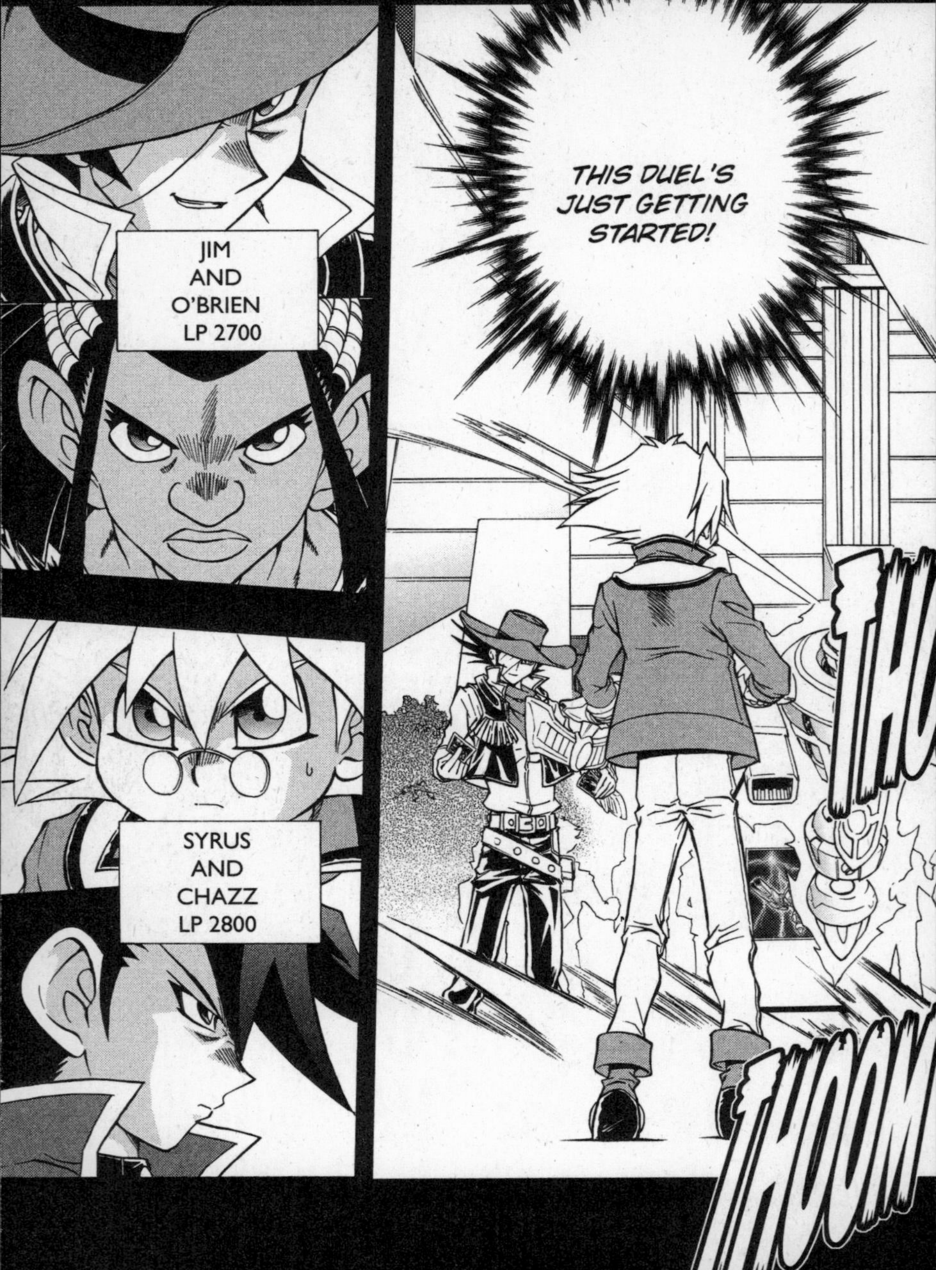
THIS DUEL'S JUST GETTING STARTED!
THOOM
JIM AND O'BRIEN LP 2700
SYRUS AND CHAZZ LP 2800

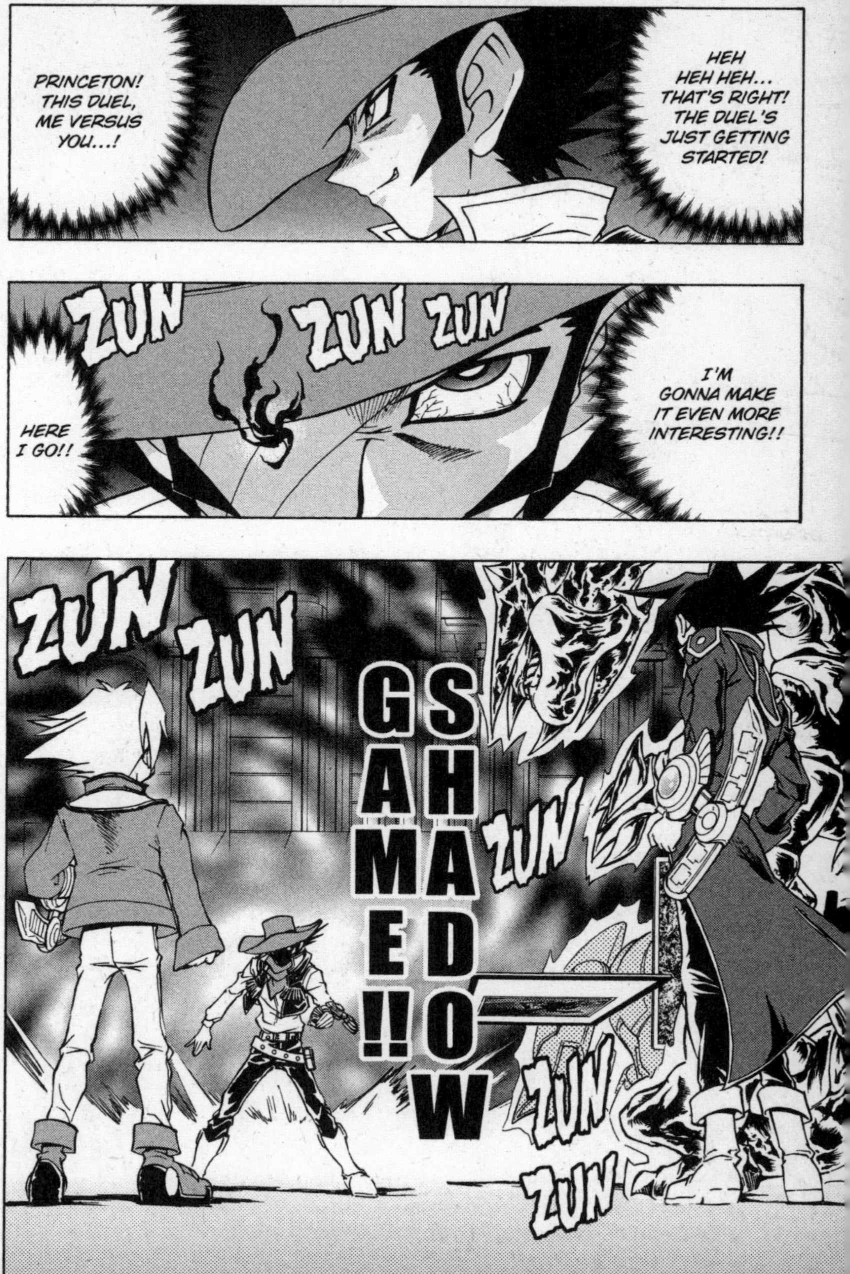
HEH HEH HEH... THAT'S RIGHT! THE DUEL'S JUST GETTING STARTED!
PRINCETON! THIS DUEL, ME VERSUS YOU...!
ZUN
ZUN
ZUN
I'M GONNA MAKE IT EVEN MORE INTERESTING!!
HERE I GO!!
SHADOW
GAME!!
ZUN
ZUN
ZUN
ZUN
ZUN
ZUN

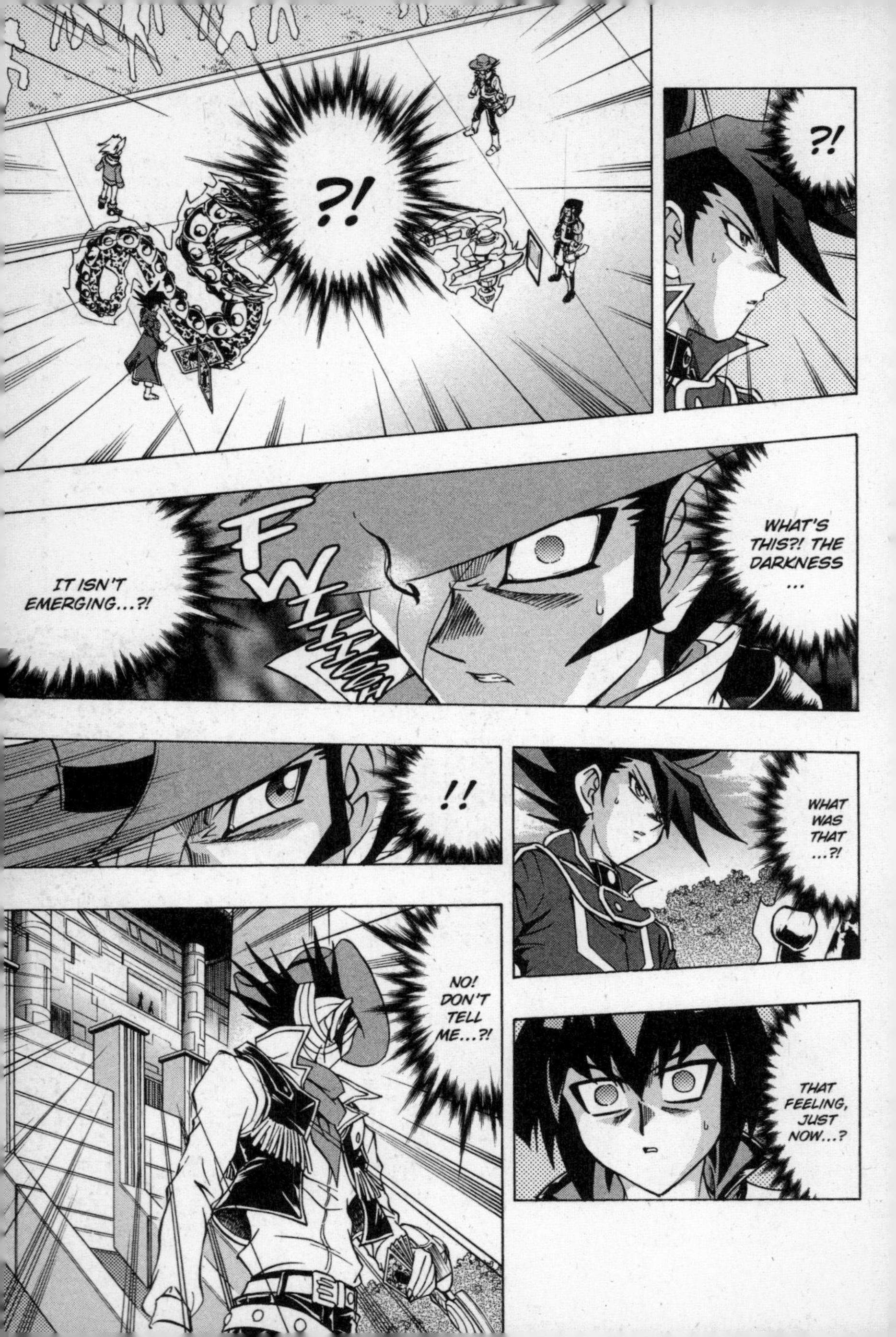
?!
?!
WHAT'S THIS?! THE DARKNESS ...
FWIIIN
IT ISN'T EMERGING...?!
WHAT WAS THAT ...?!
!!
THAT FEELING, JUST NOW...?
NO! DON'T TELL ME...?!

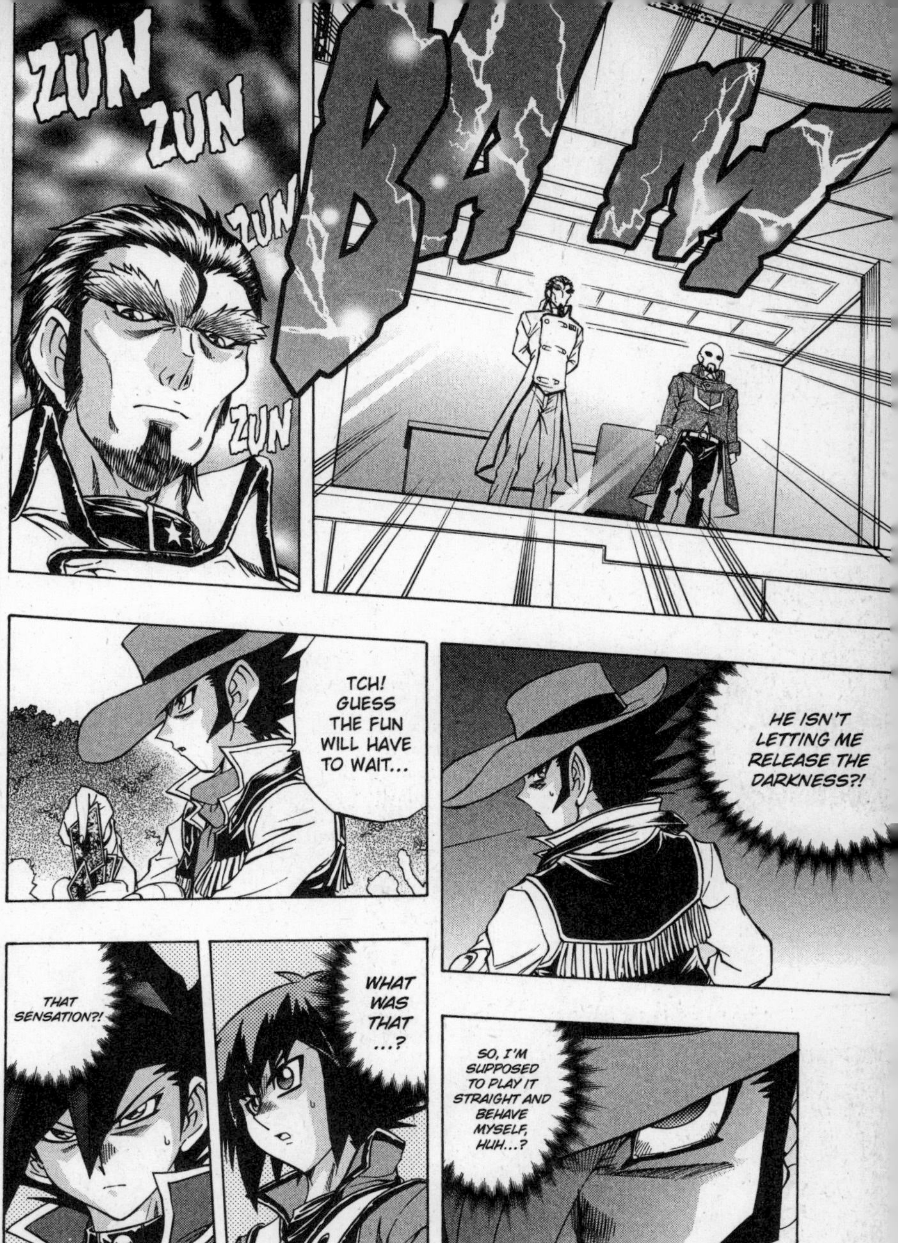
BAM
ZUN
ZUN
ZUN
ZUN
HE ISN'T LETTING ME RELEASE THE DARKNESS?!
TCH! GUESS THE FUN WILL HAVE TO WAIT...
WHAT WAS THAT ...?
THAT SENSATION?!
SO, I'M SUPPOSED TO PLAY IT STRAIGHT AND BEHAVE MYSELF, HUH...?

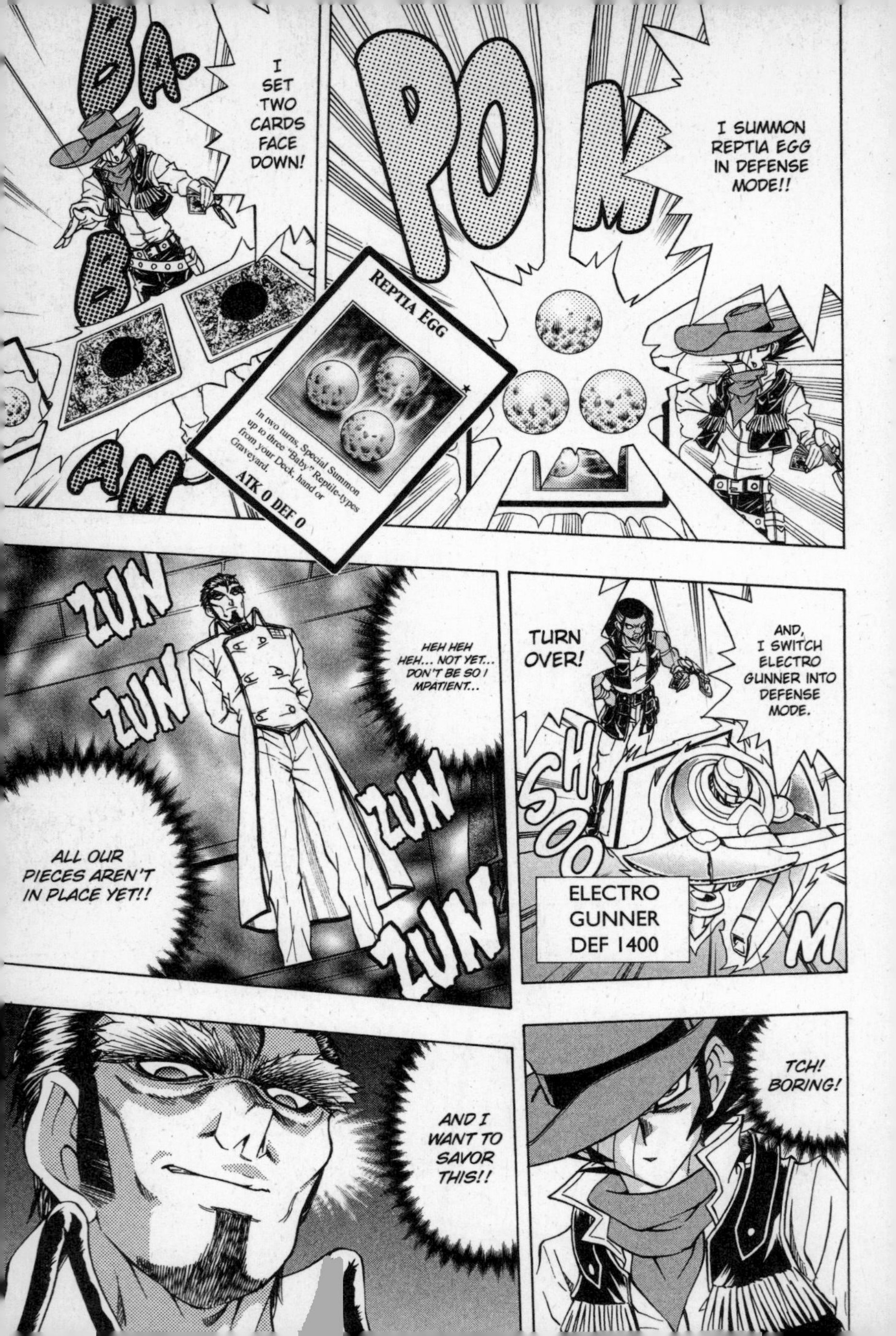

I SUMMON REPTIA EGG IN DEFENSE MODE!!
POM
REPTIA EGG
In two turns, Special Summon up to three "Baby" Reptile-types from your Deck, hand or Graveyard.
ATK 0 DEF 0
I SET TWO CARDS FACE DOWN!
BA-BAM
AND, I SWITCH ELECTRO GUNNER INTO DEFENSE MODE.
TURN OVER!
SHOOM
ELECTRO GUNNER DEF 1400
HEH HEH HEH... NOT YET... DON'T BE SO IMPATIENT...
ZUN
ZUN
ZUN
ZUN
ALL OUR PIECES AREN'T IN PLACE YET!!
TCH! BORING!
AND I WANT TO SAVOR THIS!!

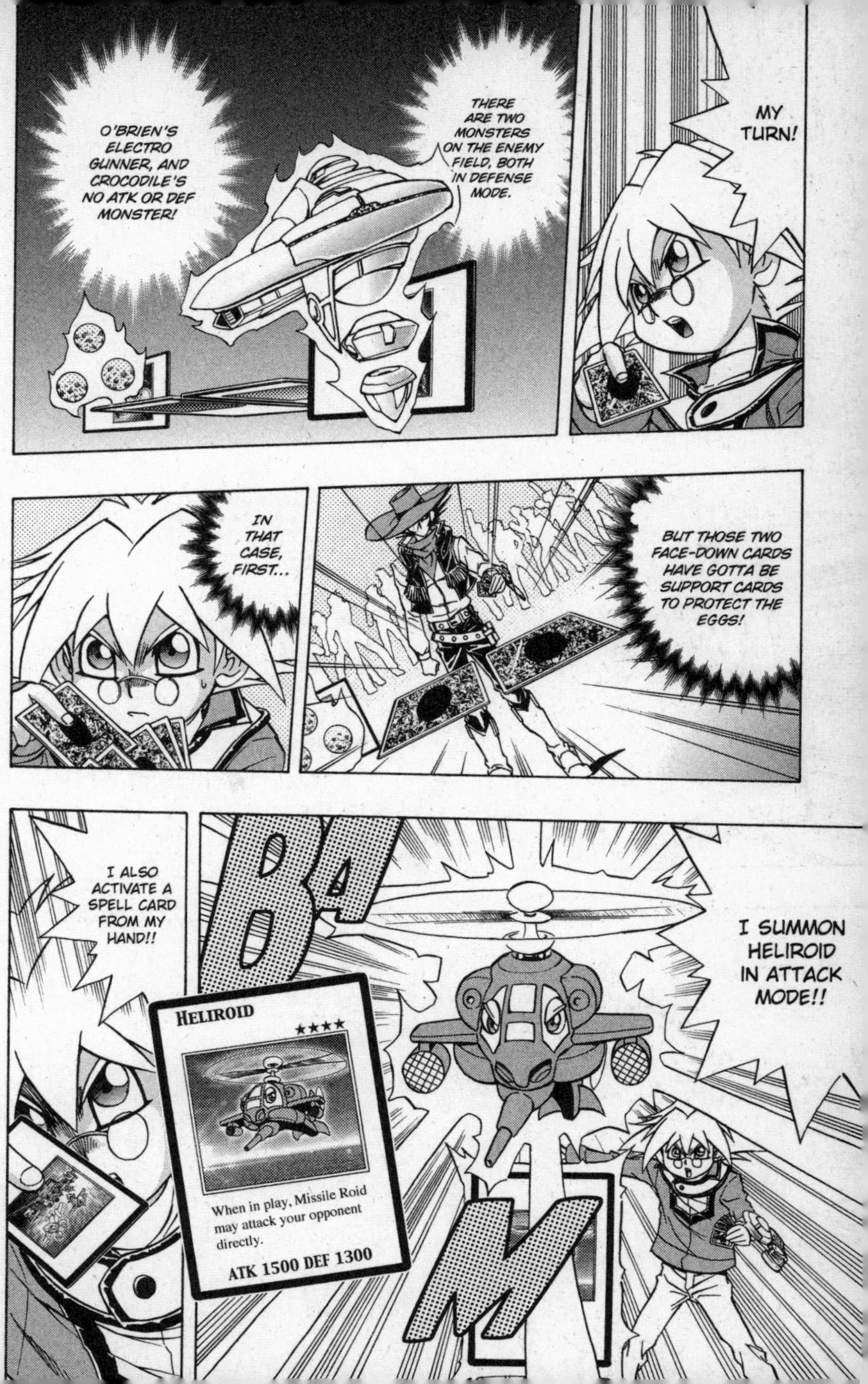
MY TURN!
THERE ARE TWO MONSTERS ON THE ENEMY FIELD, BOTH IN DEFENSE MODE.
O'BRIEN'S ELECTRO GUNNER, AND CROCODILE'S NO ATK OR DEF MONSTER!
BUT THOSE TWO FACE-DOWN CARDS HAVE GOTTA BE SUPPORT CARDS TO PROTECT THE EGGS!
IN THAT CASE, FIRST...
I SUMMON HELIROID IN ATTACK MODE!!
BAM
HELIROID
★★★★
When in play, Missile Roid may attack your opponent directly.
ATK 1500 DEF 1300
I ALSO ACTIVATE A SPELL CARD FROM MY HAND!!

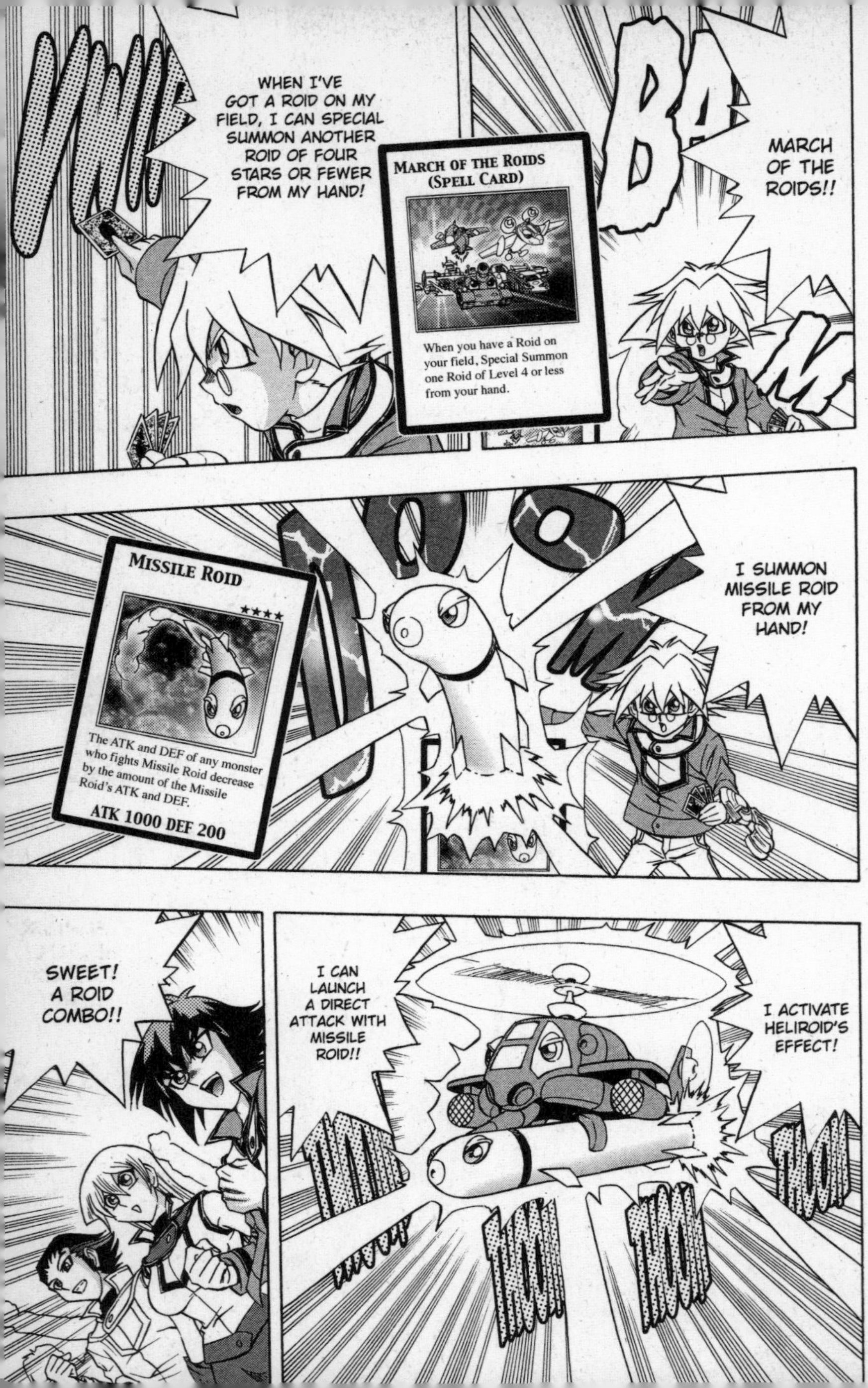
MARCH OF THE ROIDS!!
MARCH OF THE ROIDS (SPELL CARD)
When you have a Roid on your field, Special Summon one Roid of Level 4 or less from your hand.
WHEN I'VE GOT A ROID ON MY FIELD, I CAN SPECIAL SUMMON ANOTHER ROID OF FOUR STARS OR FEWER FROM MY HAND!
I SUMMON MISSILE ROID FROM MY HAND!
MISSILE ROID
The ATK and DEF of any monster who fights Missile Roid decrease by the amount of the Missile Roid's ATK and DEF.
ATK 1000 DEF 200
I ACTIVATE HELIROID'S EFFECT!
I CAN LAUNCH A DIRECT ATTACK WITH MISSILE ROID!!
SWEET! A ROID COMBO!!

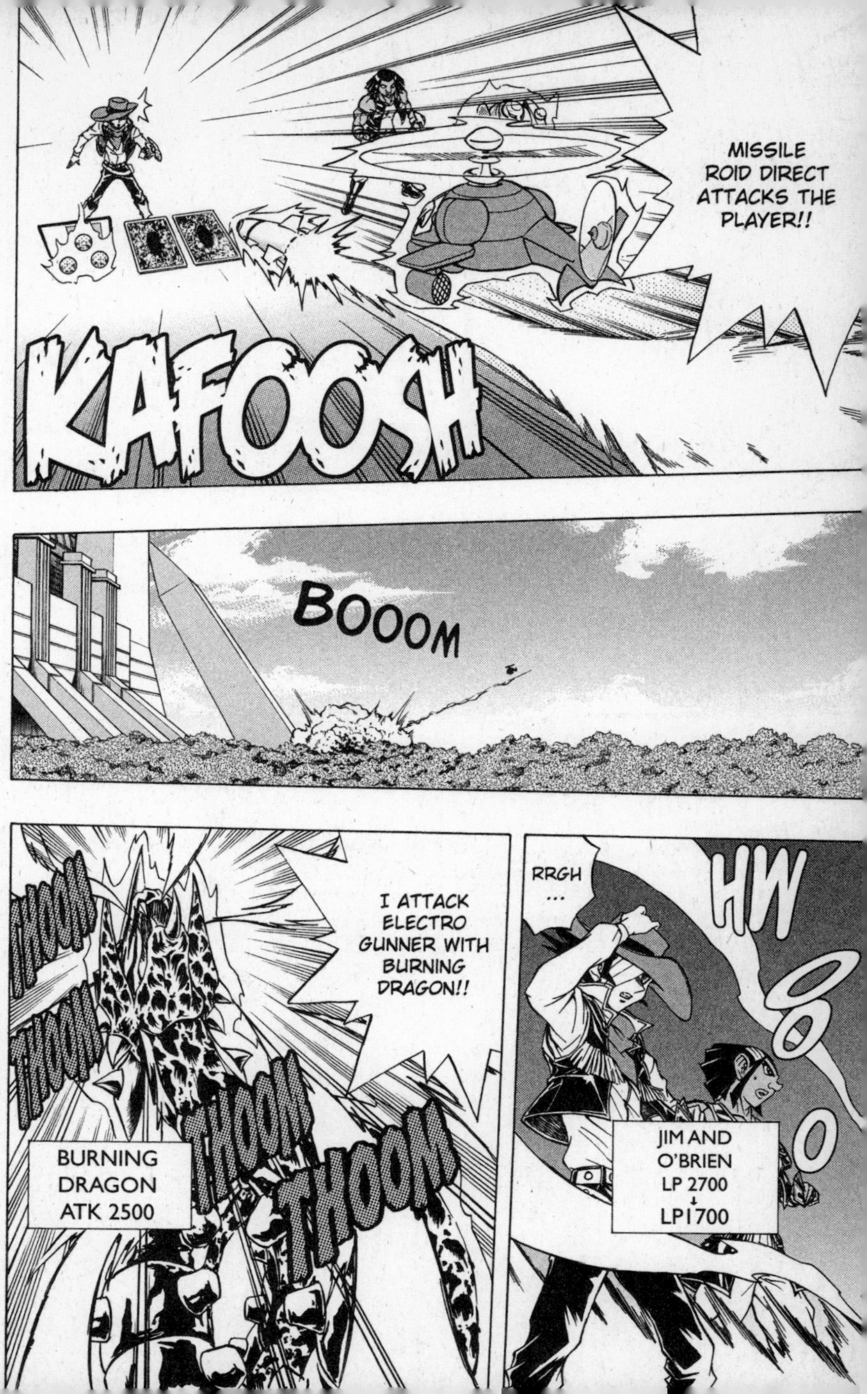
MISSILE ROID DIRECT ATTACKS THE PLAYER!!
KAFOOSH
BOOOM
RRGH ...
HWOOO
JIM AND O'BRIEN LP 2700 ↓ LP1700
I ATTACK ELECTRO GUNNER WITH BURNING DRAGON!!
THOOM
THOOM
THOOM
THOOM
BURNING DRAGON ATK 2500

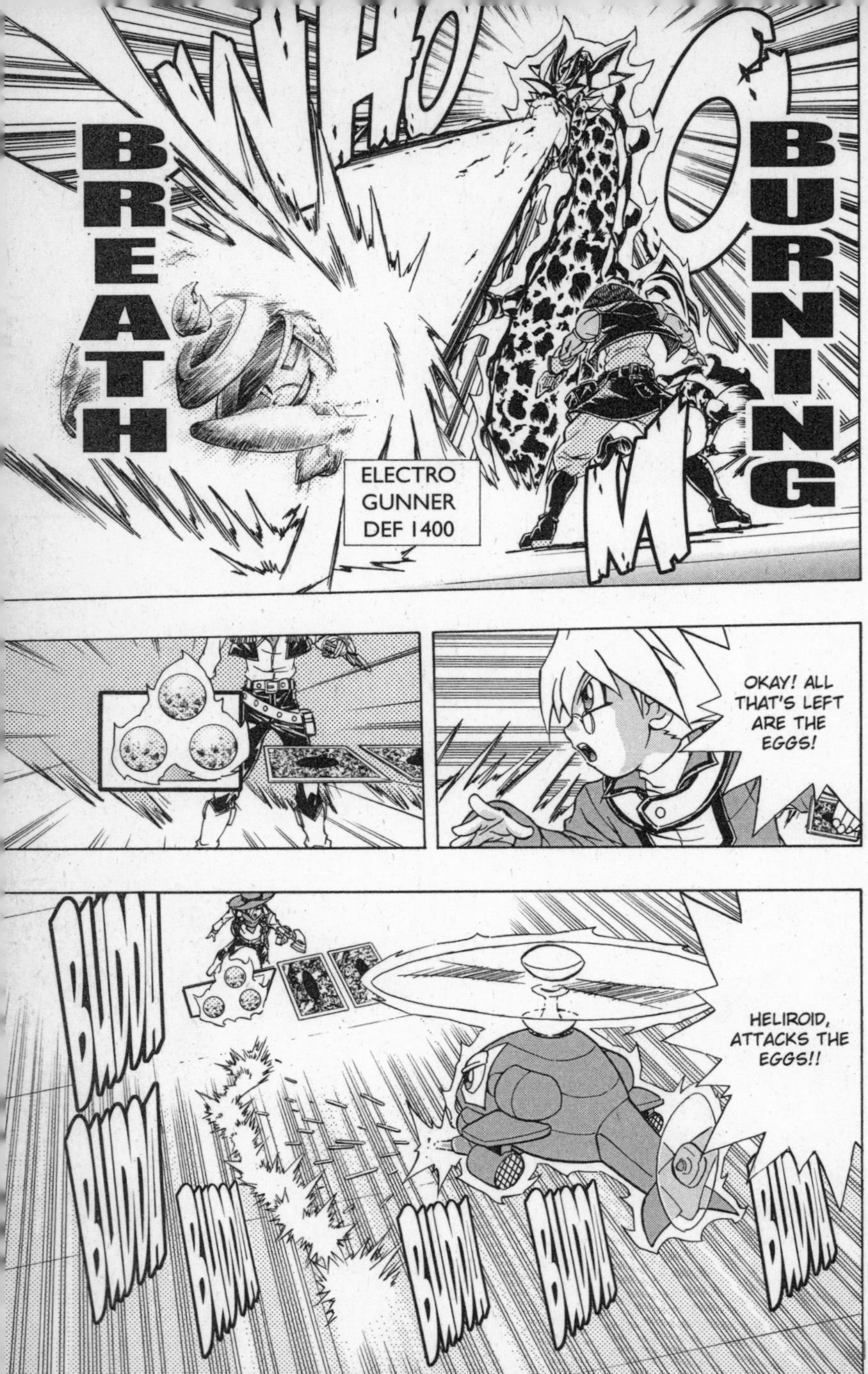
BURNING
BREATH
ELECTRO GUNNER DEF 1400
OKAY! ALL THAT'S LEFT ARE THE EGGS!
HELIROID, ATTACKS THE EGGS!!

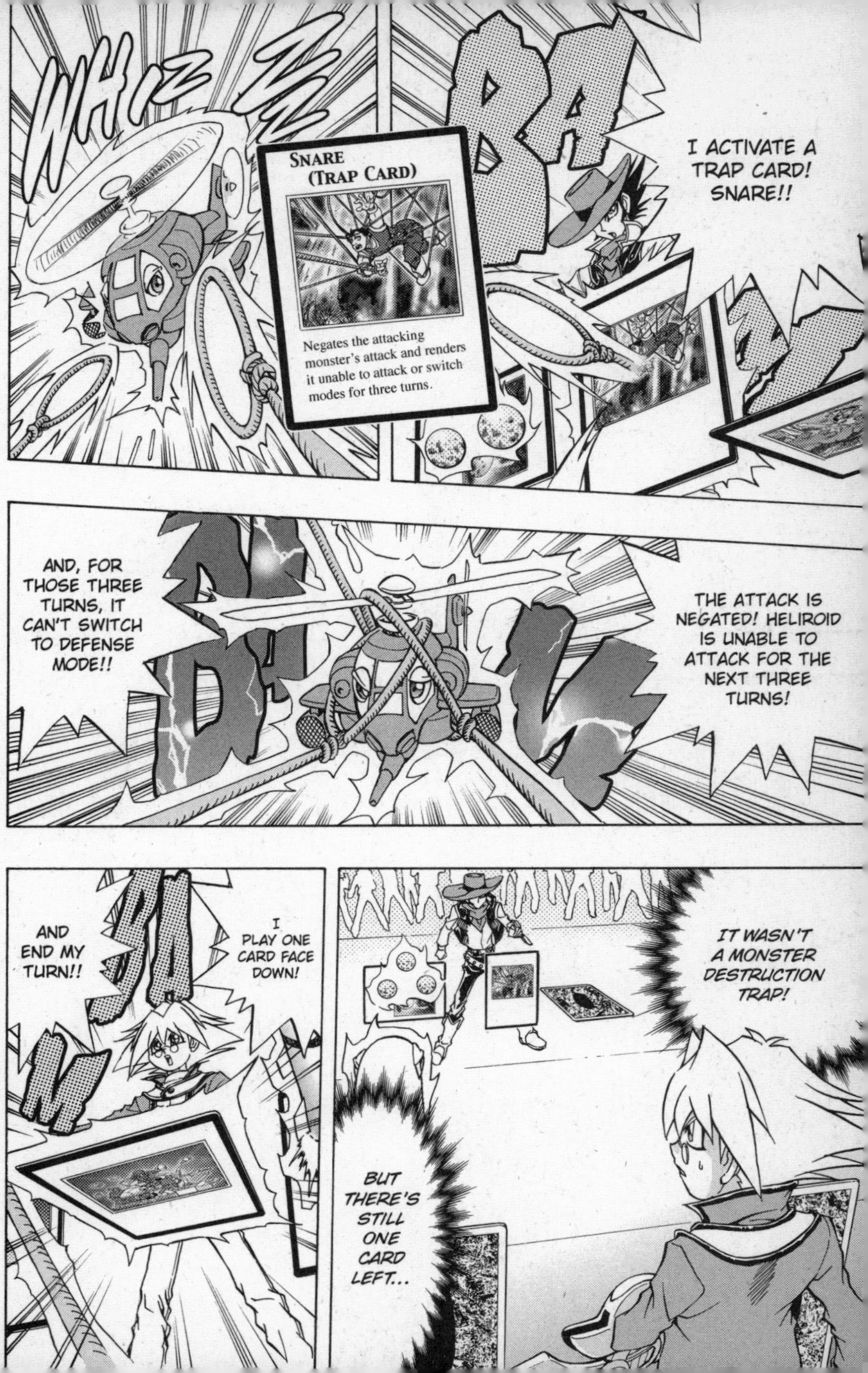
I ACTIVATE A TRAP CARD! SNARE!!
BA
Snare (Trap Card)
Negates the attacking monster's attack and renders it unable to attack or switch modes for three turns.
WHIZ
THE ATTACK IS NEGATED! HELIROID IS UNABLE TO ATTACK FOR THE NEXT THREE TURNS!
AND, FOR THOSE THREE TURNS, IT CAN'T SWITCH TO DEFENSE MODE!!
IT WASN'T A MONSTER DESTRUCTION TRAP!
BUT THERE'S STILL ONE CARD LEFT...
I PLAY ONE CARD FACE DOWN!
AND END MY TURN!!
BA

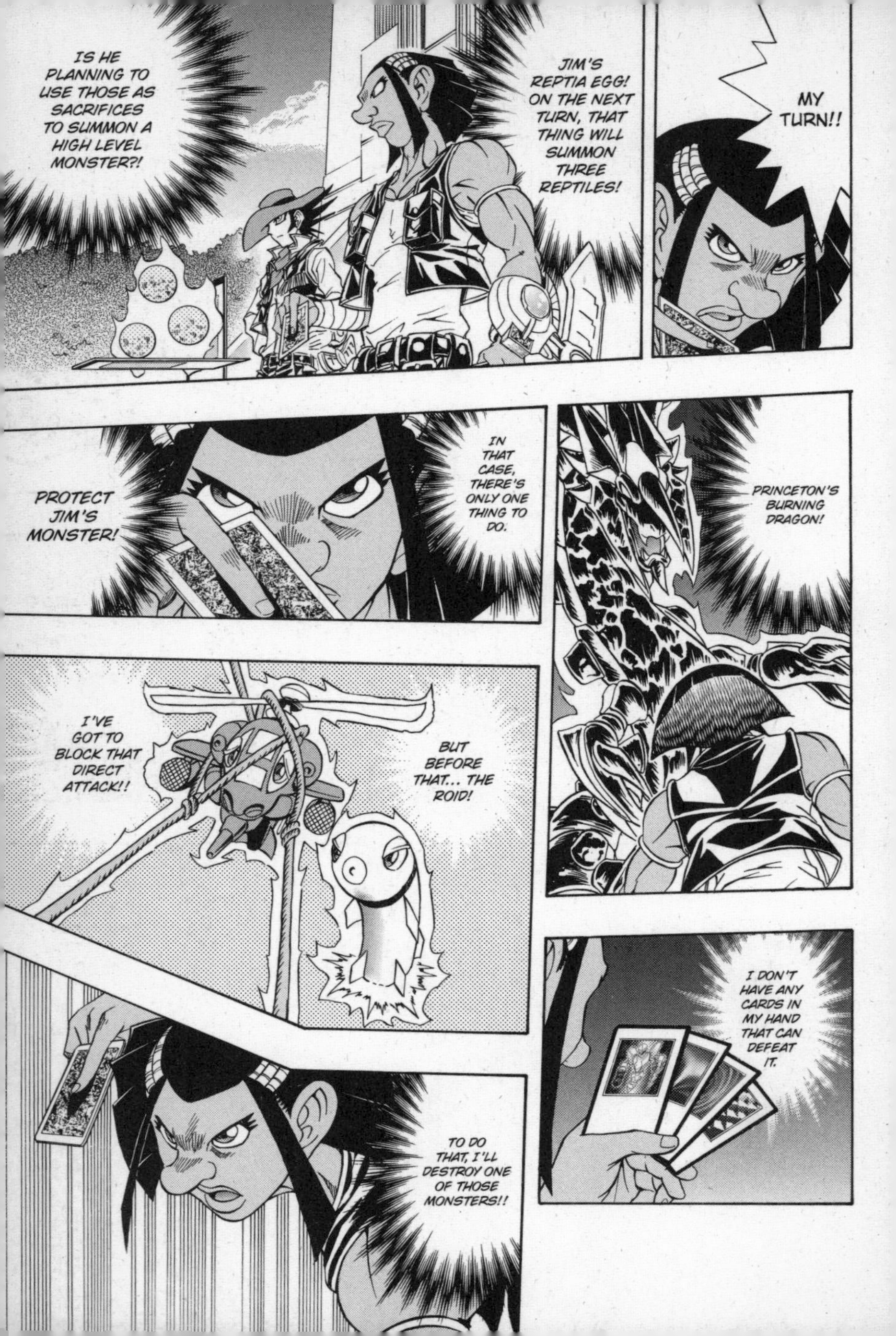
MY TURN!!
JIM'S REPTIA EGG! ON THE NEXT TURN, THAT THING WILL SUMMON THREE REPTILES!
IS HE PLANNING TO USE THOSE AS SACRIFICES TO SUMMON A HIGH LEVEL MONSTER?!
PRINCETON'S BURNING DRAGON!
IN THAT CASE, THERE'S ONLY ONE THING TO DO.
PROTECT JIM'S MONSTER!
BUT BEFORE THAT... THE ROID!
I'VE GOT TO BLOCK THAT DIRECT ATTACK!!
I DON'T HAVE ANY CARDS IN MY HAND THAT CAN DEFEAT IT.
TO DO THAT, I'LL DESTROY ONE OF THOSE MONSTERS!!

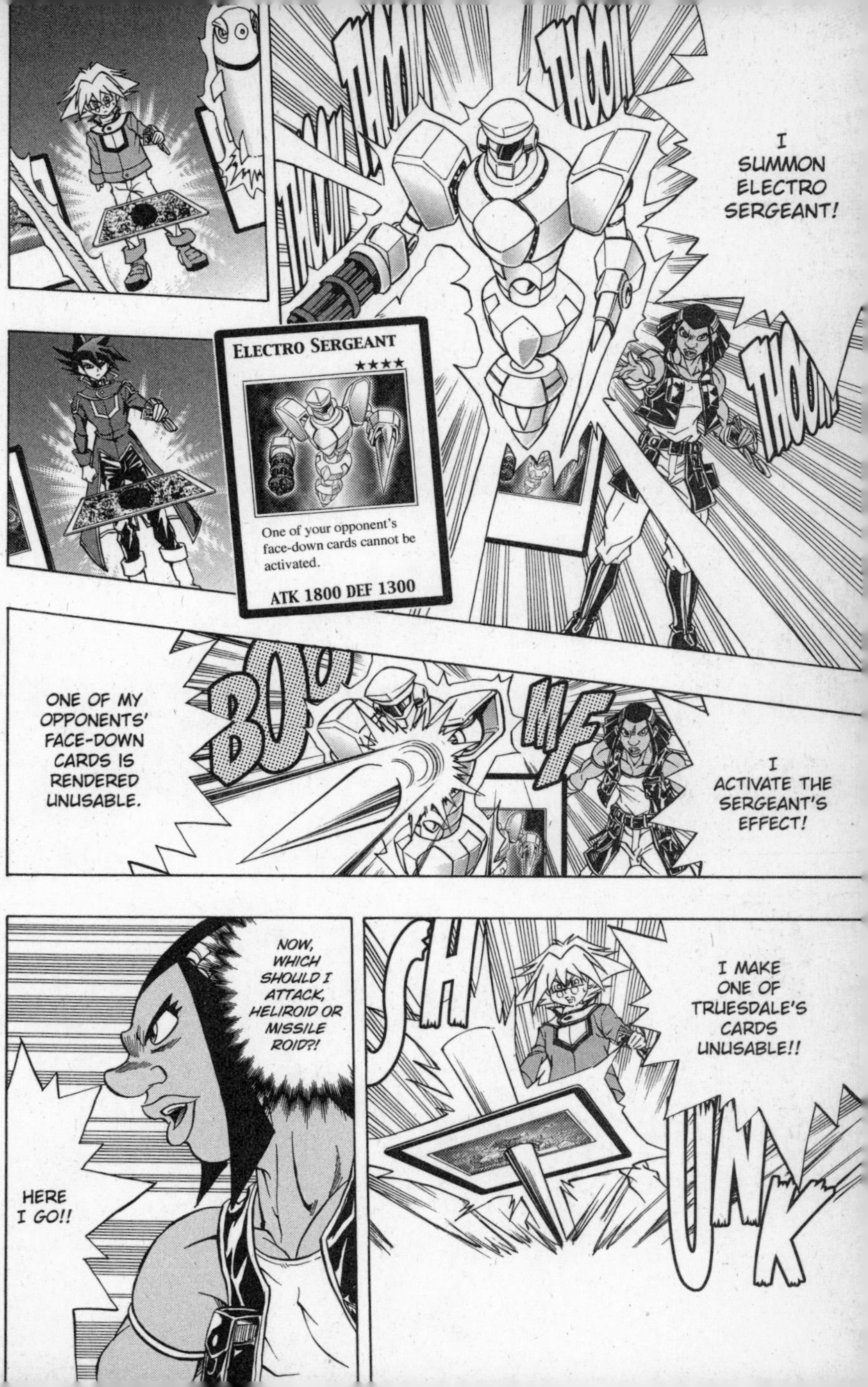
THOOM
THOOM
THOOM
THOOM
I SUMMON ELECTRO SERGEANT!
THOOM
ELECTRO SERGEANT
★★★★
One of your opponent's face-down cards cannot be activated.
ATK 1800 DEF 1300
I ACTIVATE THE SERGEANT'S EFFECT!
MF
BOO
ONE OF MY OPPONENTS' FACE-DOWN CARDS IS RENDERED UNUSABLE.
I MAKE ONE OF TRUESDALE'S CARDS UNUSABLE!!
SCH
UNK
NOW, WHICH SHOULD I ATTACK, HELIROID OR MISSILE ROID?!
HERE I GO!!

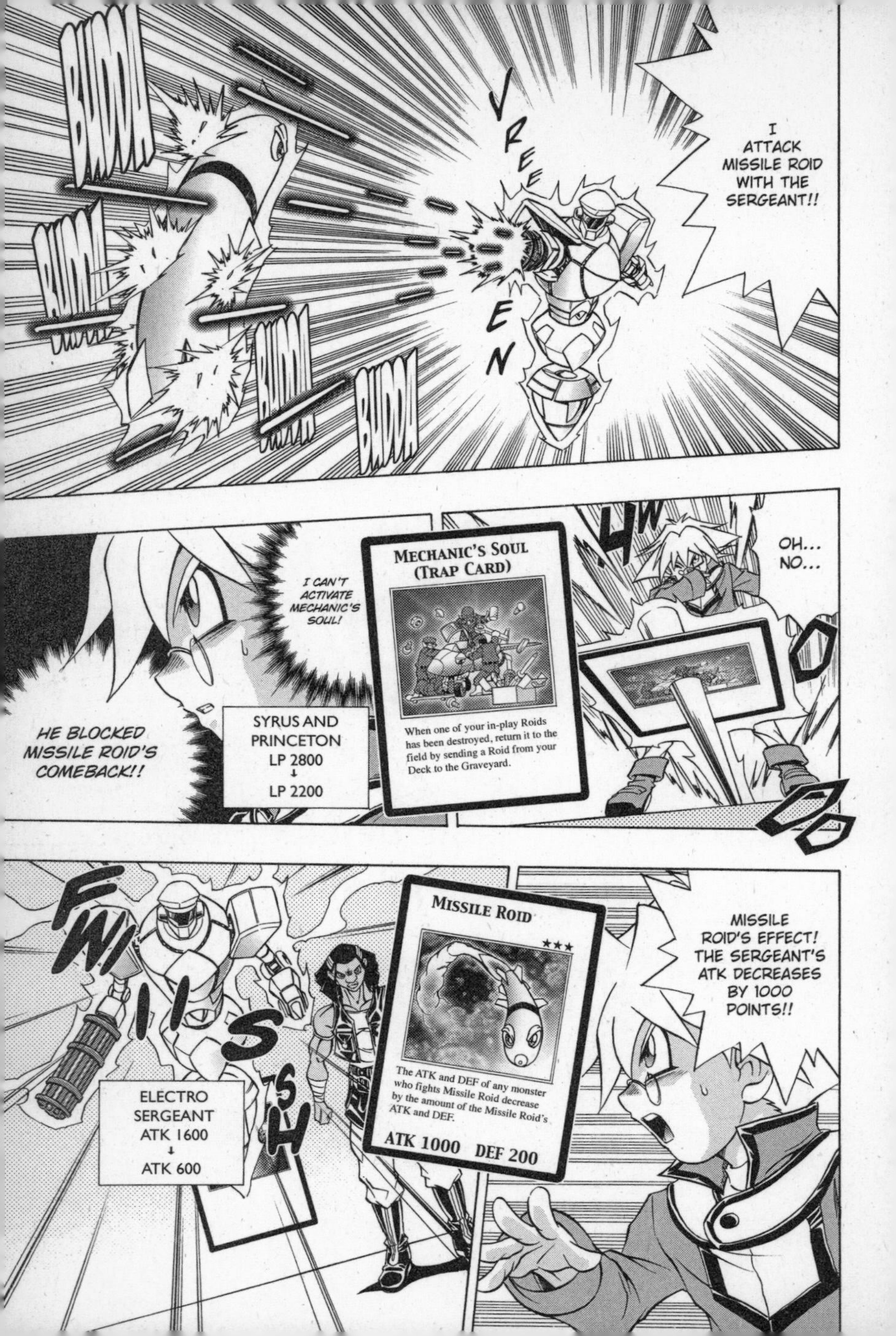
I ATTACK MISSILE ROID WITH THE SERGEANT!!
VREEEN
BUDDA
BUDDA
BUDDA
BUDDA
OH... NO...
MECHANIC'S SOUL (TRAP CARD)
When one of your in-play Roids has been destroyed, return it to the field by sending a Roid from your Deck to the Graveyard.
I CAN'T ACTIVATE MECHANIC'S SOUL!
HE BLOCKED MISSILE ROID'S COMEBACK!!
SYRUS AND PRINCETON LP 2800 ↓ LP 2200
MISSILE ROID'S EFFECT! THE SERGEANT'S ATK DECREASES BY 1000 POINTS!!
MISSILE ROID
The ATK and DEF of any monster who fights Missile Roid decrease by the amount of the Missile Roid's ATK and DEF.
ATK 1000 DEF 200
FWIIISH
ELECTRO SERGEANT ATK 1600 ↓ ATK 600

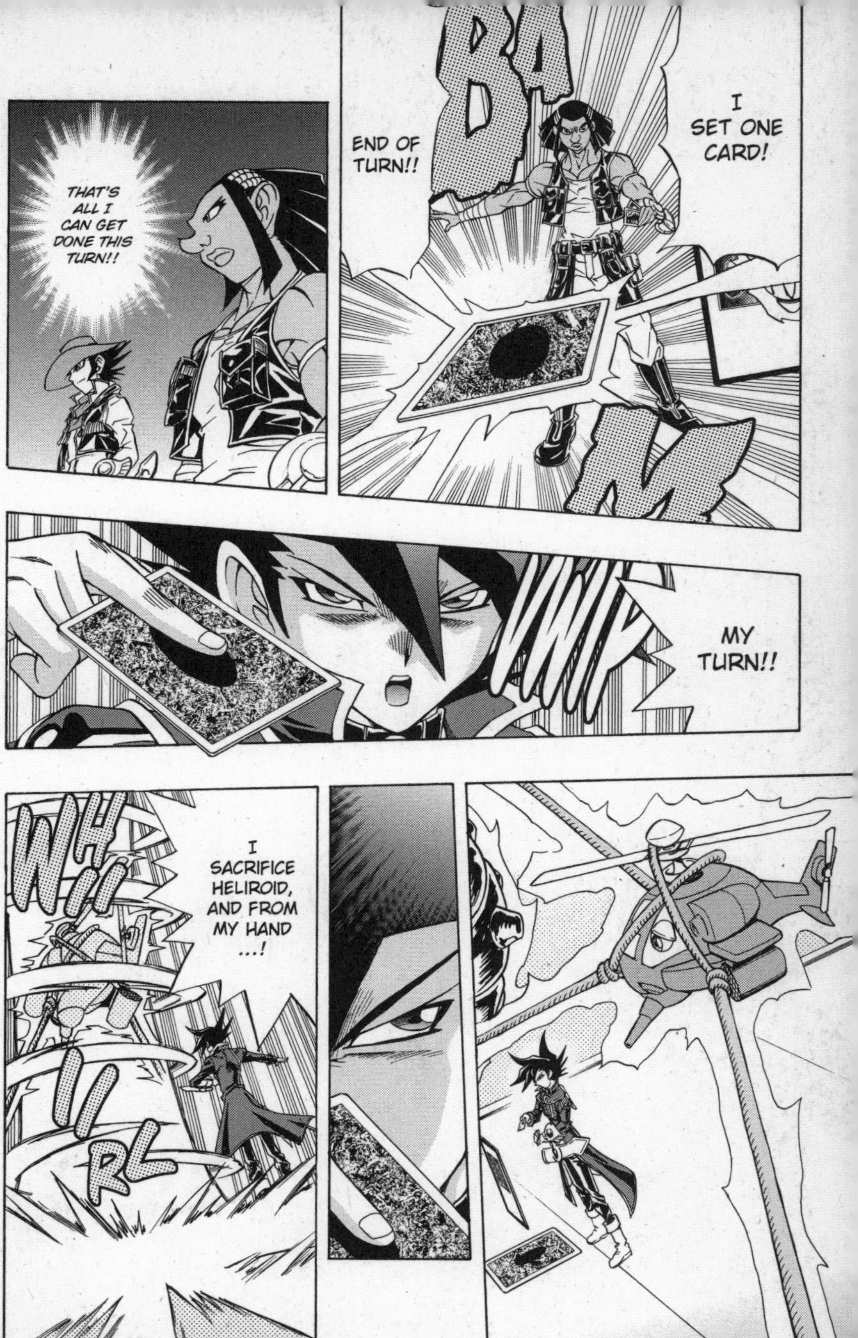
I SET ONE CARD!
BAM
END OF TURN!!
THAT'S ALL I CAN GET DONE THIS TURN!!
MY TURN!!
I SACRIFICE HELIROID, AND FROM MY HAND ...!
WHIRL

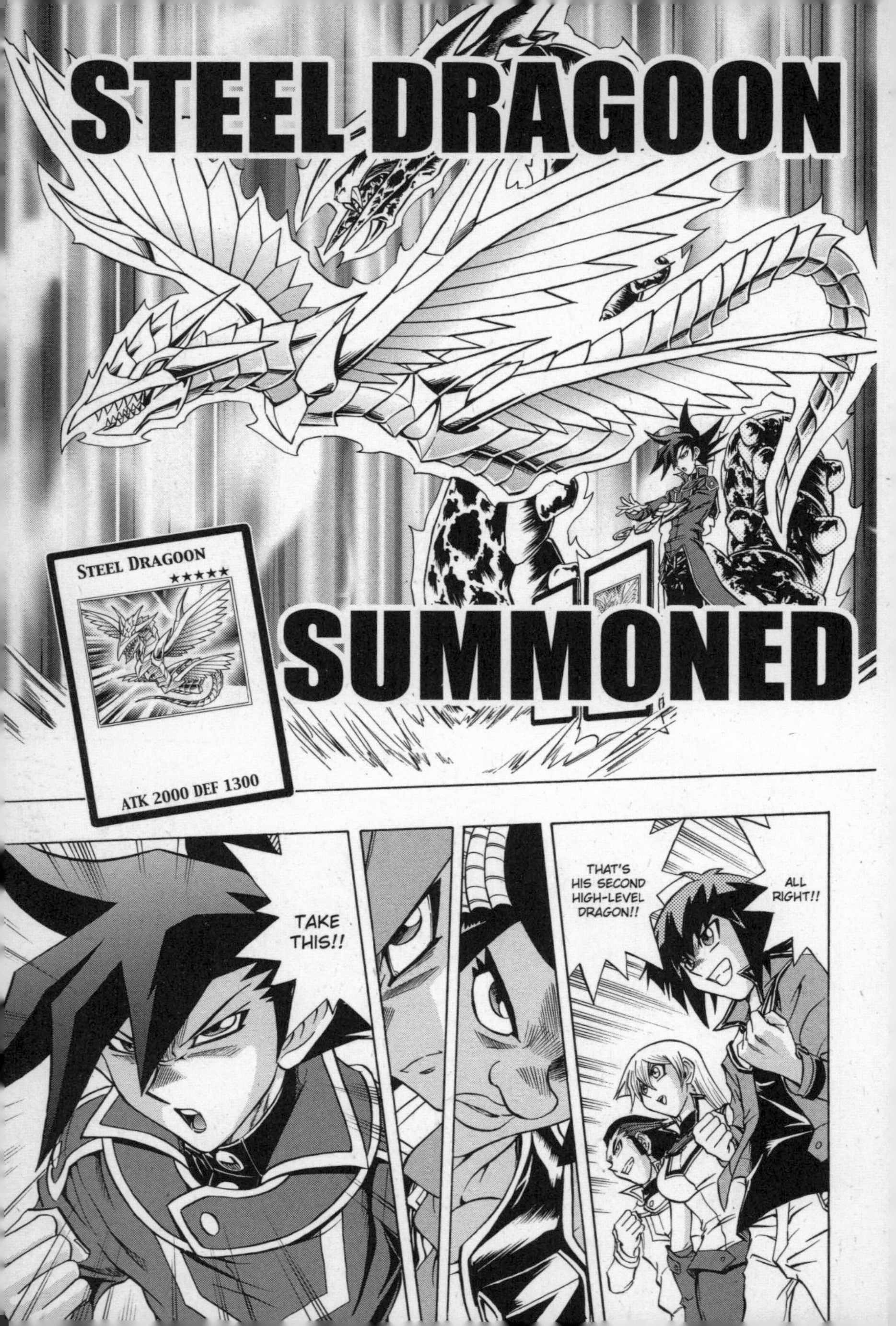
STEEL DRAGOON
SUMMONED
STEEL DRAGOON ★★★★★
ATK 2000 DEF 1300
ALL RIGHT!!
THAT'S HIS SECOND HIGH-LEVEL DRAGON!!
TAKE THIS!!

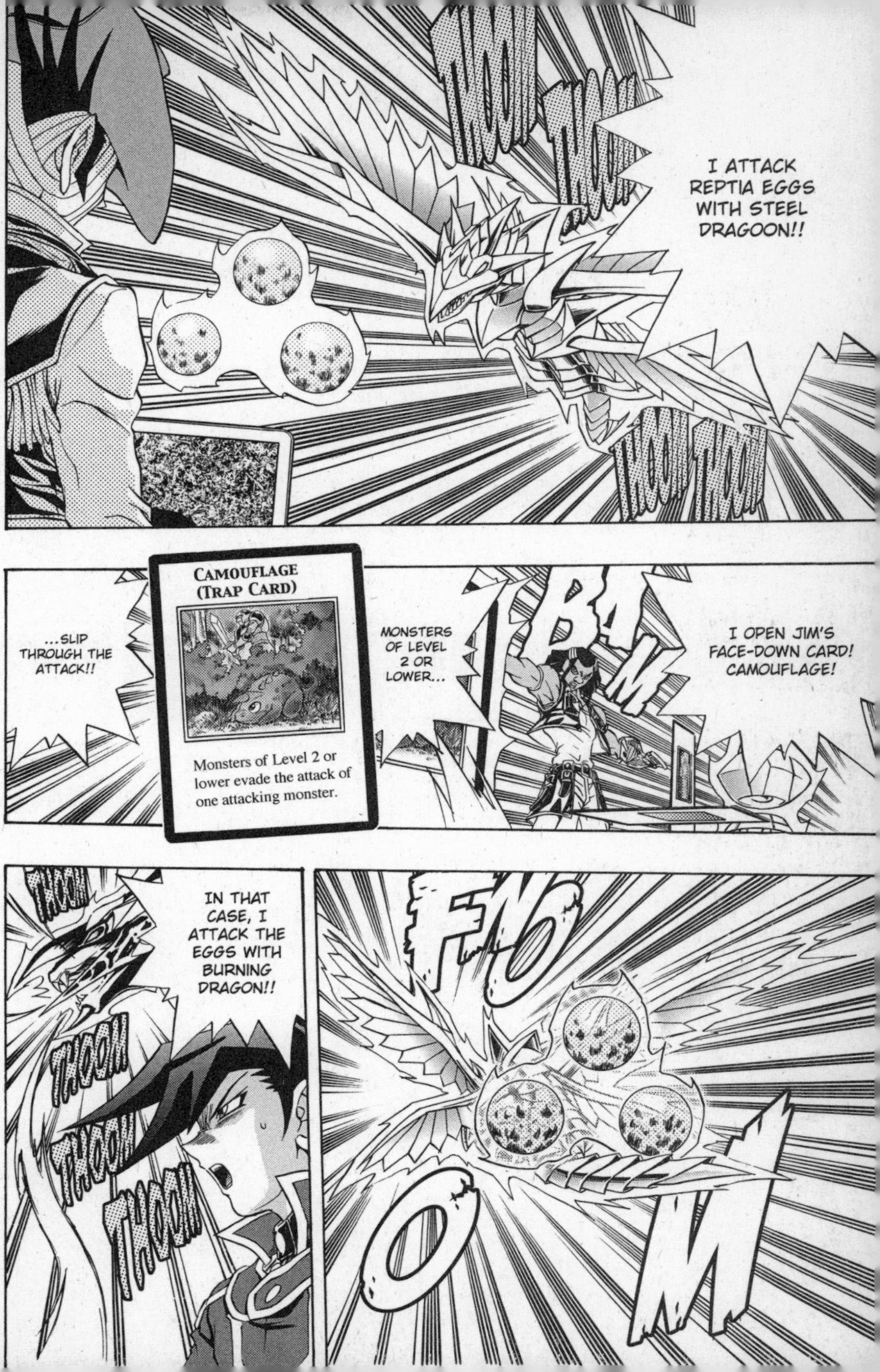
THOOM THOOM
I ATTACK REPTIA EGGS WITH STEEL DRAGOON!!
THOOM THOOM
BAM
I OPEN JIM'S FACE-DOWN CARD! CAMOUFLAGE!
MONSTERS OF LEVEL 2 OR LOWER...
CAMOUFLAGE (TRAP CARD)
Monsters of Level 2 or lower evade the attack of one attacking monster.
...SLIP THROUGH THE ATTACK!!
FWOOM
THOOM
IN THAT CASE, I ATTACK THE EGGS WITH BURNING DRAGON!!
THOOM
THOOM
THOOM

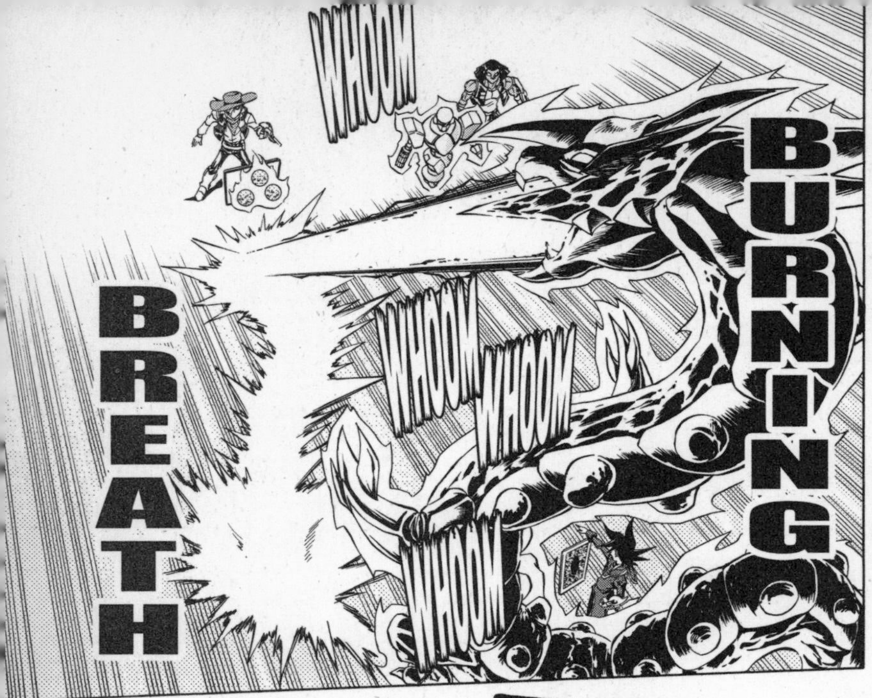
WHOOM
BURNING
WHOOM
WHOOM
WHOOM
BREATH

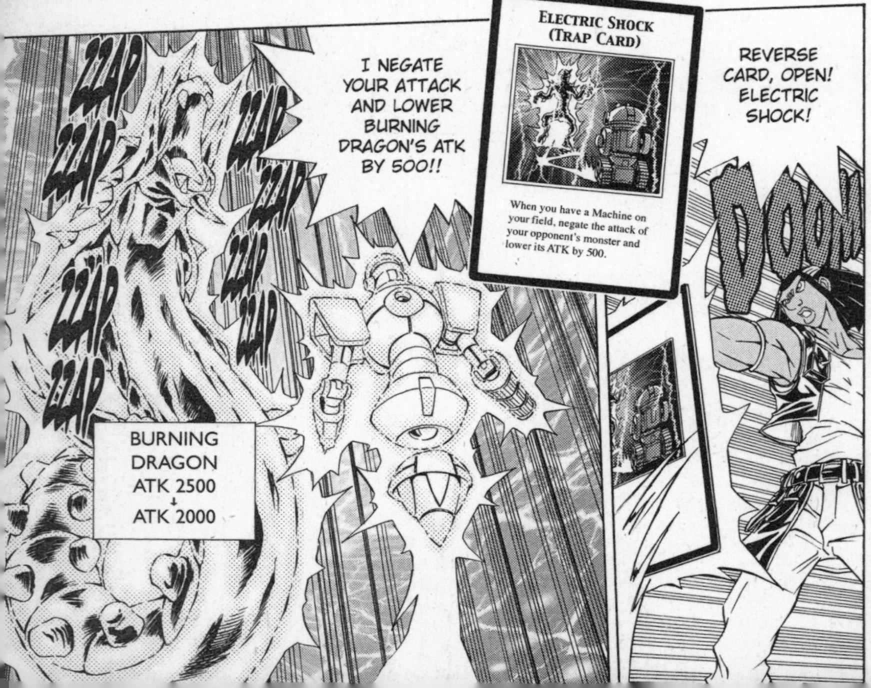
REVERSE CARD, OPEN! ELECTRIC SHOCK!
DOOM
ELECTRIC SHOCK (TRAP CARD)
When you have a Machine on your field, negate the attack of your opponent's monster and lower its ATK by 500.
I NEGATE YOUR ATTACK AND LOWER BURNING DRAGON'S ATK BY 500!!
ZZAP ZZAP ZZAP ZZAP ZZAP ZZAP
ZZAP ZZAP ZZAP ZZAP ZZAP ZZAP
BURNING DRAGON ATK 2500 ↓ ATK 2000

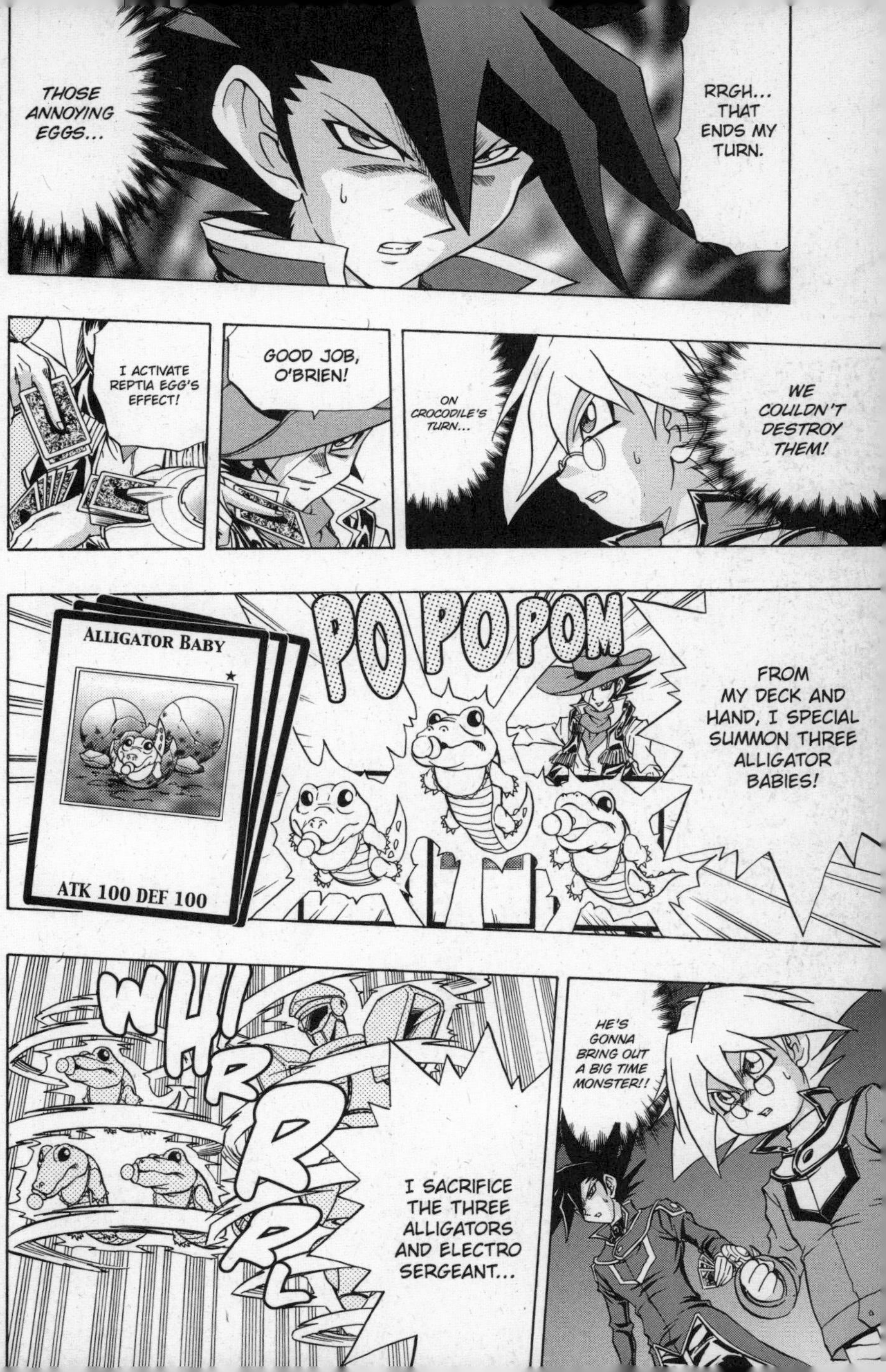
RRGH... THAT ENDS MY TURN.
THOSE ANNOYING EGGS...
ON CROCODILE'S TURN...
WE COULDN'T DESTROY THEM!
GOOD JOB, O'BRIEN!
I ACTIVATE REPTIA EGG'S EFFECT!
FROM MY DECK AND HAND, I SPECIAL SUMMON THREE ALLIGATOR BABIES!
PO PO POM
ALLIGATOR BABY
ATK 100 DEF 100
HE'S GONNA BRING OUT A BIG TIME MONSTER!!
I SACRIFICE THE THREE ALLIGATORS AND ELECTRO SERGEANT...
WHIRRRL

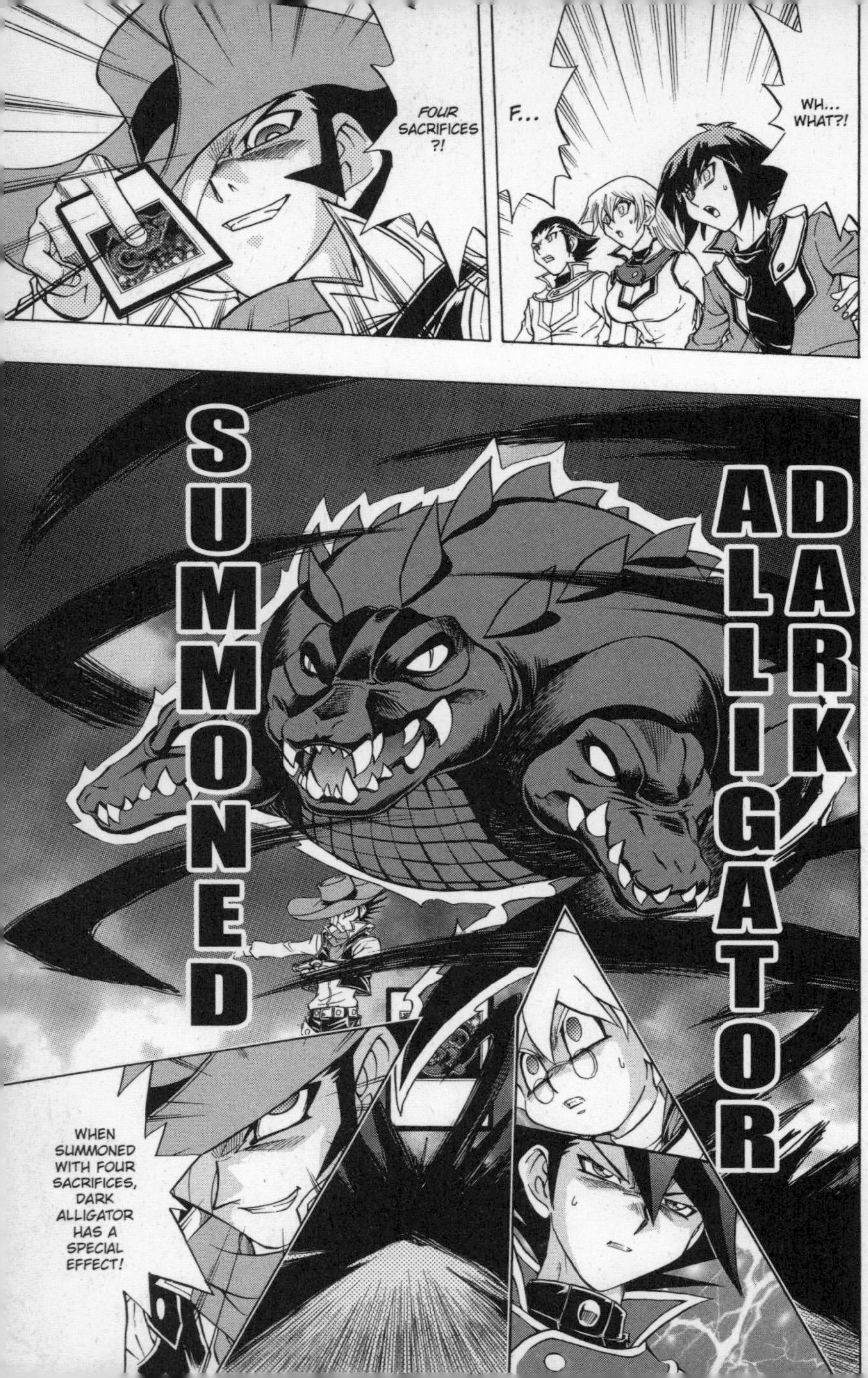
WH... WHAT?!
F...
FOUR SACRIFICES ?!
DARK
ALLIGATOR
SUMMONED
WHEN SUMMONED WITH FOUR SACRIFICES, DARK ALLIGATOR HAS A SPECIAL EFFECT!

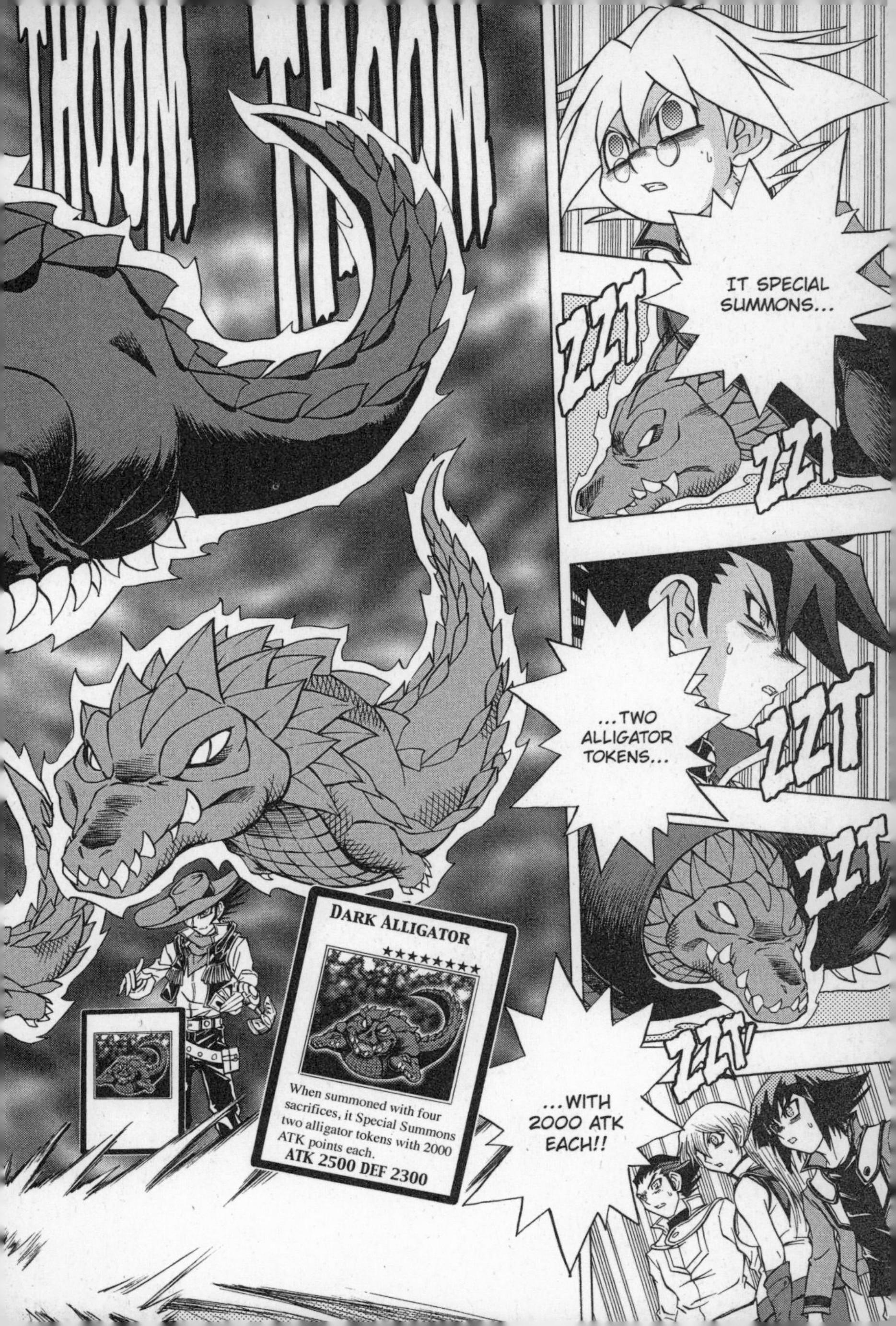
IT SPECIAL SUMMONS...
ZZT
ZZT
...TWO ALLIGATOR TOKENS...
ZZT
ZZT
ZZT
...WITH 2000 ATK EACH!!
THOOM
THOOM
DARK ALLIGATOR
When summoned with four sacrifices, it Special Summons two alligator tokens with 2000 ATK points each.
ATK 2500 DEF 2300

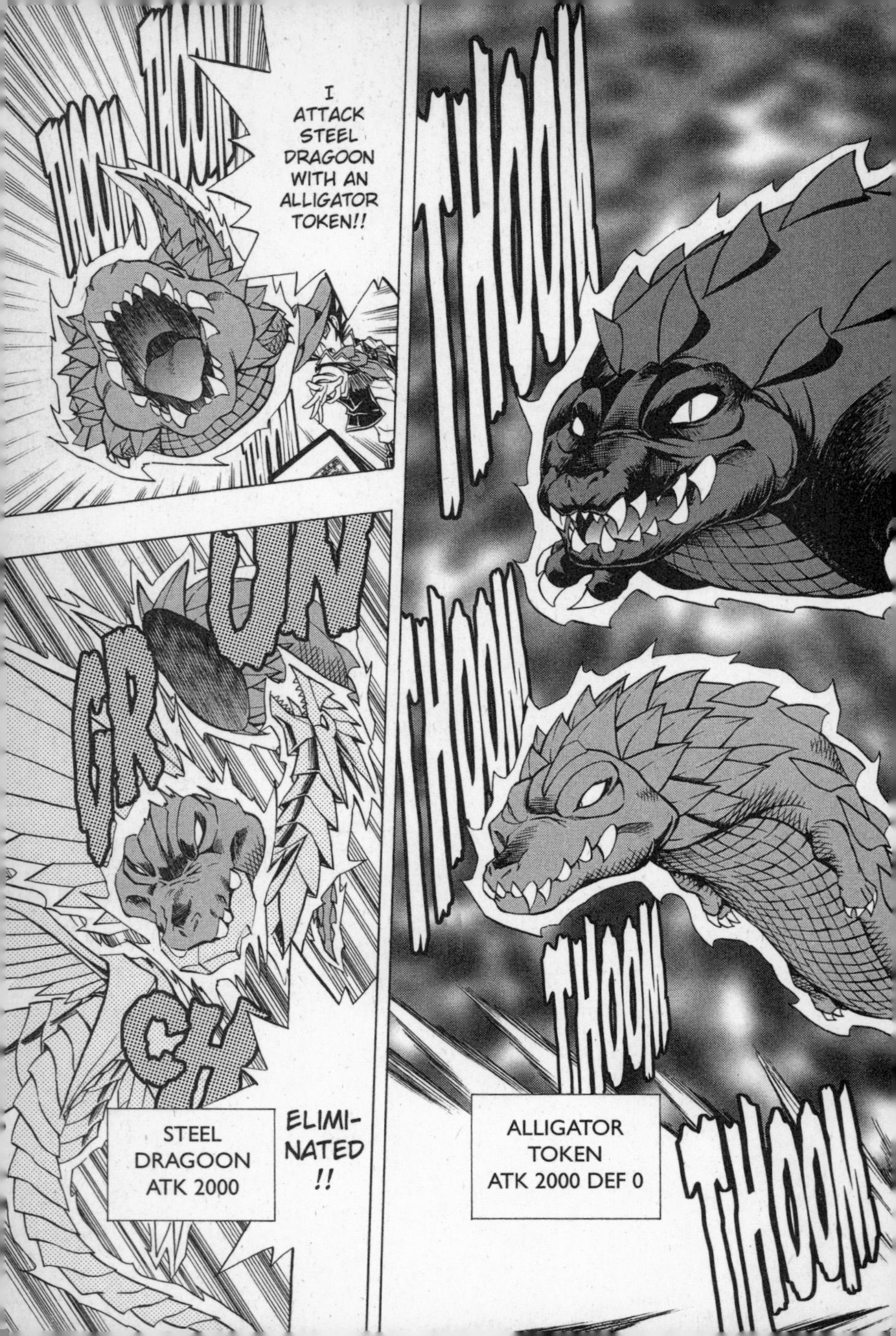
THOOM
THOOM
THOOM
THOOM
ALLIGATOR TOKEN ATK 2000 DEF 0
I ATTACK STEEL DRAGOON WITH AN ALLIGATOR TOKEN!!
THOOM
THOOM
THOOM
CRUNCH
ELIMINATED!!
STEEL DRAGOON ATK 2000

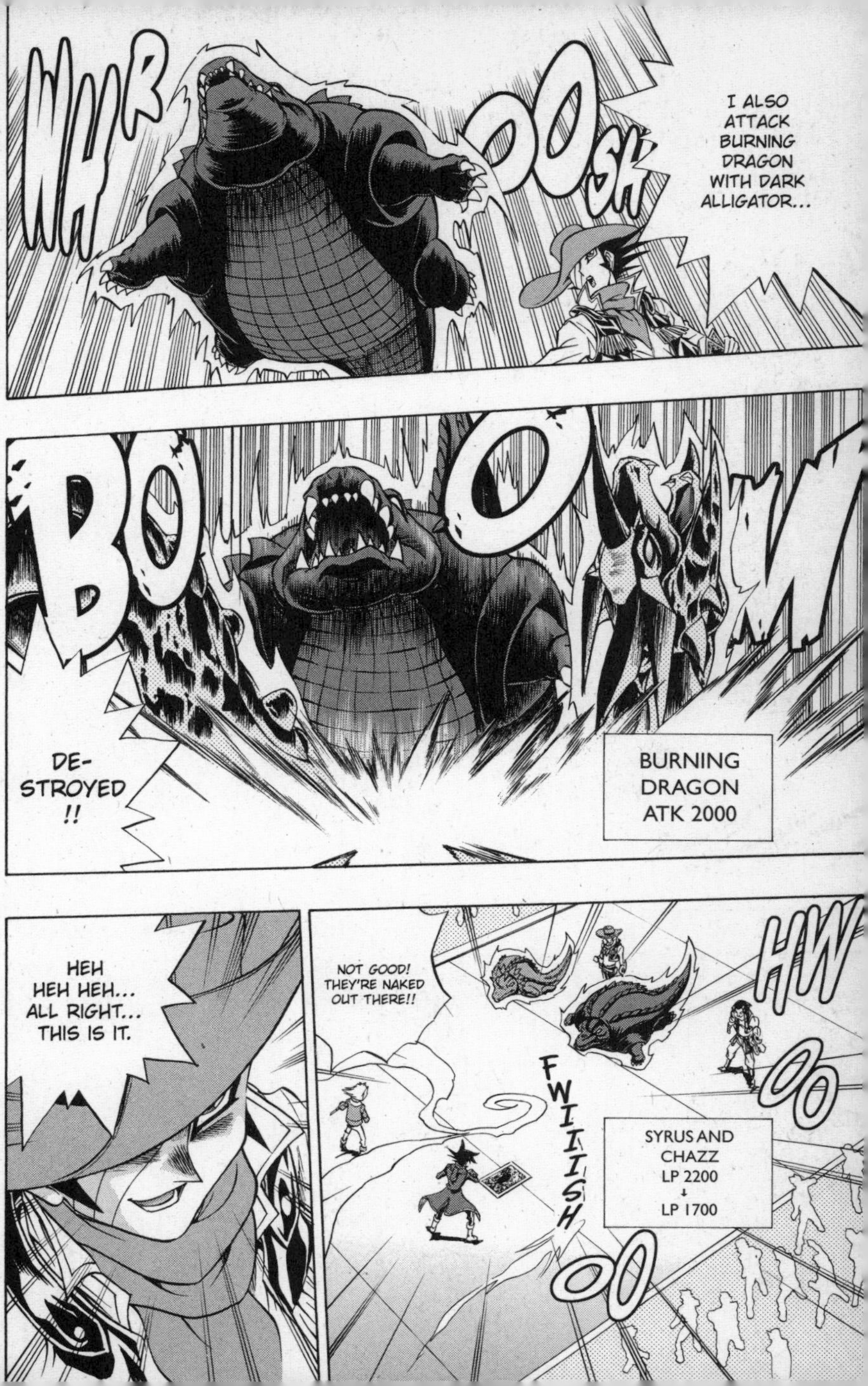
I ALSO ATTACK BURNING DRAGON WITH DARK ALLIGATOR...
WHIR
OOOSH
BOOM
BURNING DRAGON ATK 2000
DE-STROYED !!
HWOO
SYRUS AND CHAZZ LP 2200 ↓ LP 1700
FWIIISH
OO
NOT GOOD! THEY'RE NAKED OUT THERE!!
HEH HEH HEH... ALL RIGHT... THIS IS IT.

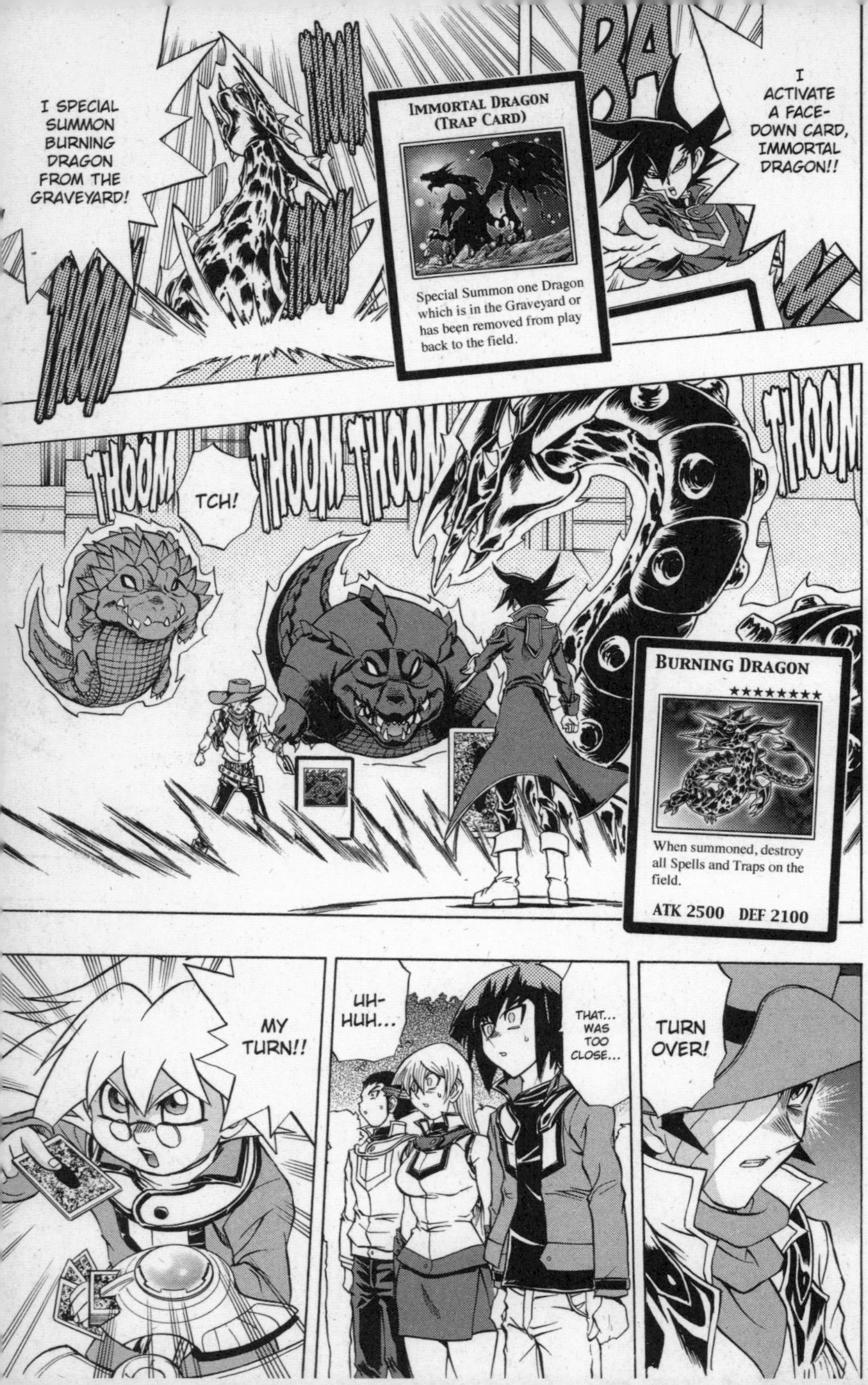
BA
I ACTIVATE A FACE-DOWN CARD, IMMORTAL DRAGON!!
IMMORTAL DRAGON (TRAP CARD)
Special Summon one Dragon which is in the Graveyard or has been removed from play back to the field.
I SPECIAL SUMMON BURNING DRAGON FROM THE GRAVEYARD!
THOOM
BURNING DRAGON
★★★★★★★★
When summoned, destroy all Spells and Traps on the field.
ATK 2500 DEF 2100
THOOM THOOM
TCH!
THOOM
TURN OVER!
THAT... WAS TOO CLOSE...
UH-HUH...
MY TURN!!

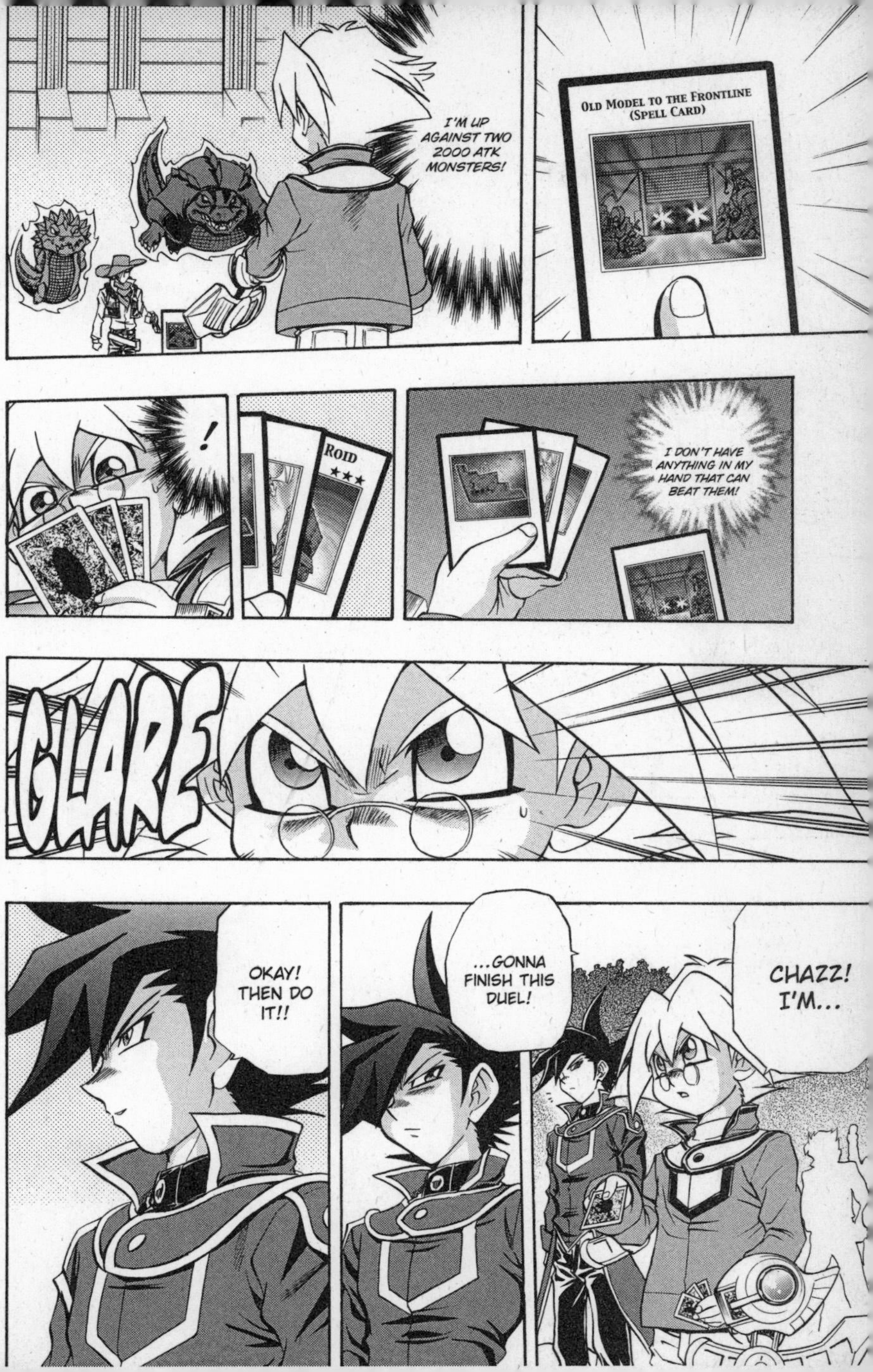
OLD MODEL TO THE FRONTLINE
(SPELL CARD)
I'M UP AGAINST TWO 2000 ATK MONSTERS!
I DON'T HAVE ANYTHING IN MY HAND THAT CAN BEAT THEM!
ROID
!
GLARE
CHAZZ! I'M...
...GONNA FINISH THIS DUEL!
OKAY! THEN DO IT!!

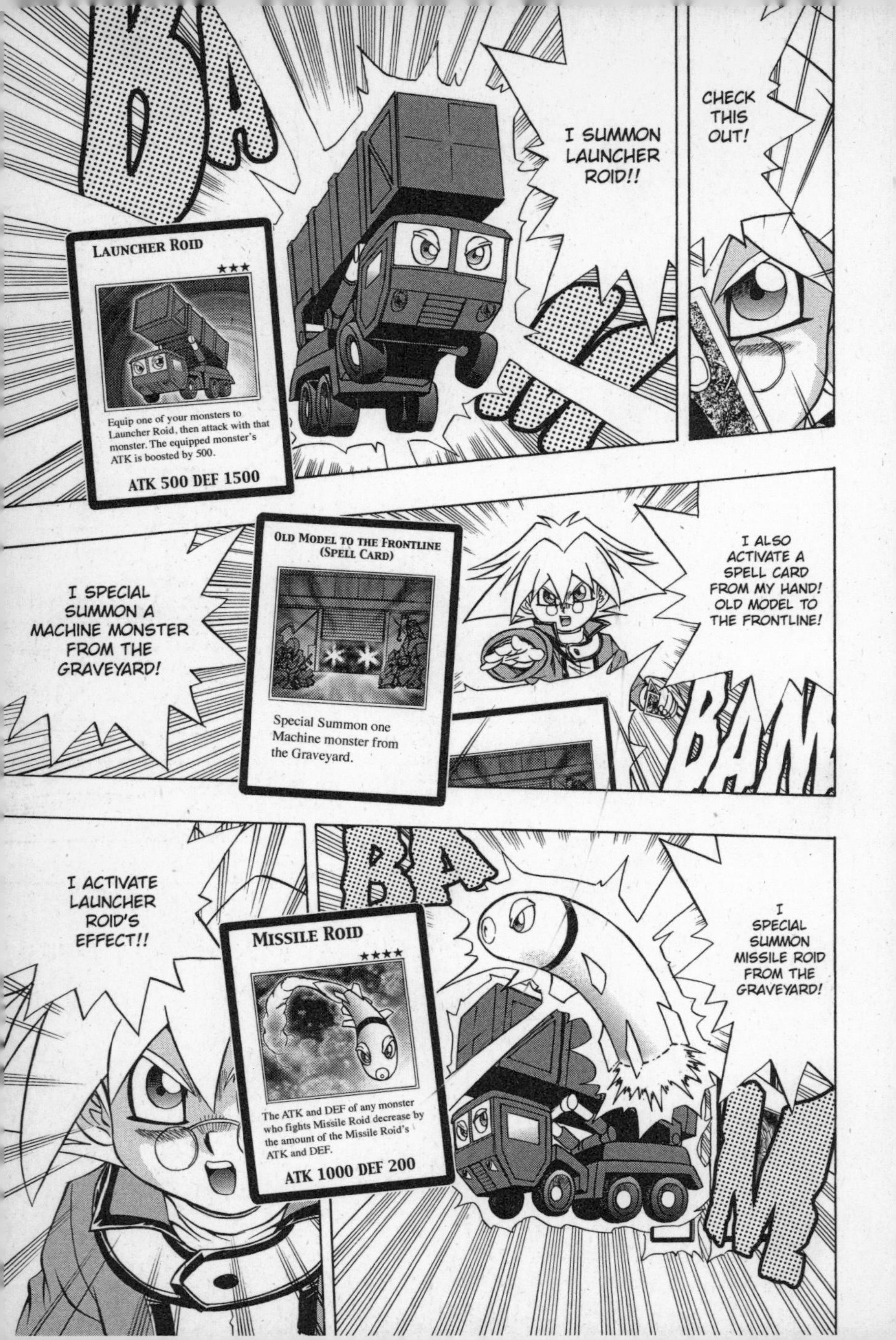
CHECK THIS OUT!
I SUMMON LAUNCHER ROID!!
DA
LAUNCHER ROID
Equip one of your monsters to Launcher Roid, then attack with that monster. The equipped monster's ATK is boosted by 500.
ATK 500 DEF 1500
I ALSO ACTIVATE A SPELL CARD FROM MY HAND! OLD MODEL TO THE FRONTLINE!
BAM
OLD MODEL TO THE FRONTLINE (SPELL CARD)
Special Summon one Machine monster from the Graveyard.
I SPECIAL SUMMON A MACHINE MONSTER FROM THE GRAVEYARD!
I SPECIAL SUMMON MISSILE ROID FROM THE GRAVEYARD!
BA
M!
MISSILE ROID
The ATK and DEF of any monster who fights Missile Roid decrease by the amount of the Missile Roid's ATK and DEF.
ATK 1000 DEF 200
I ACTIVATE LAUNCHER ROID'S EFFECT!!

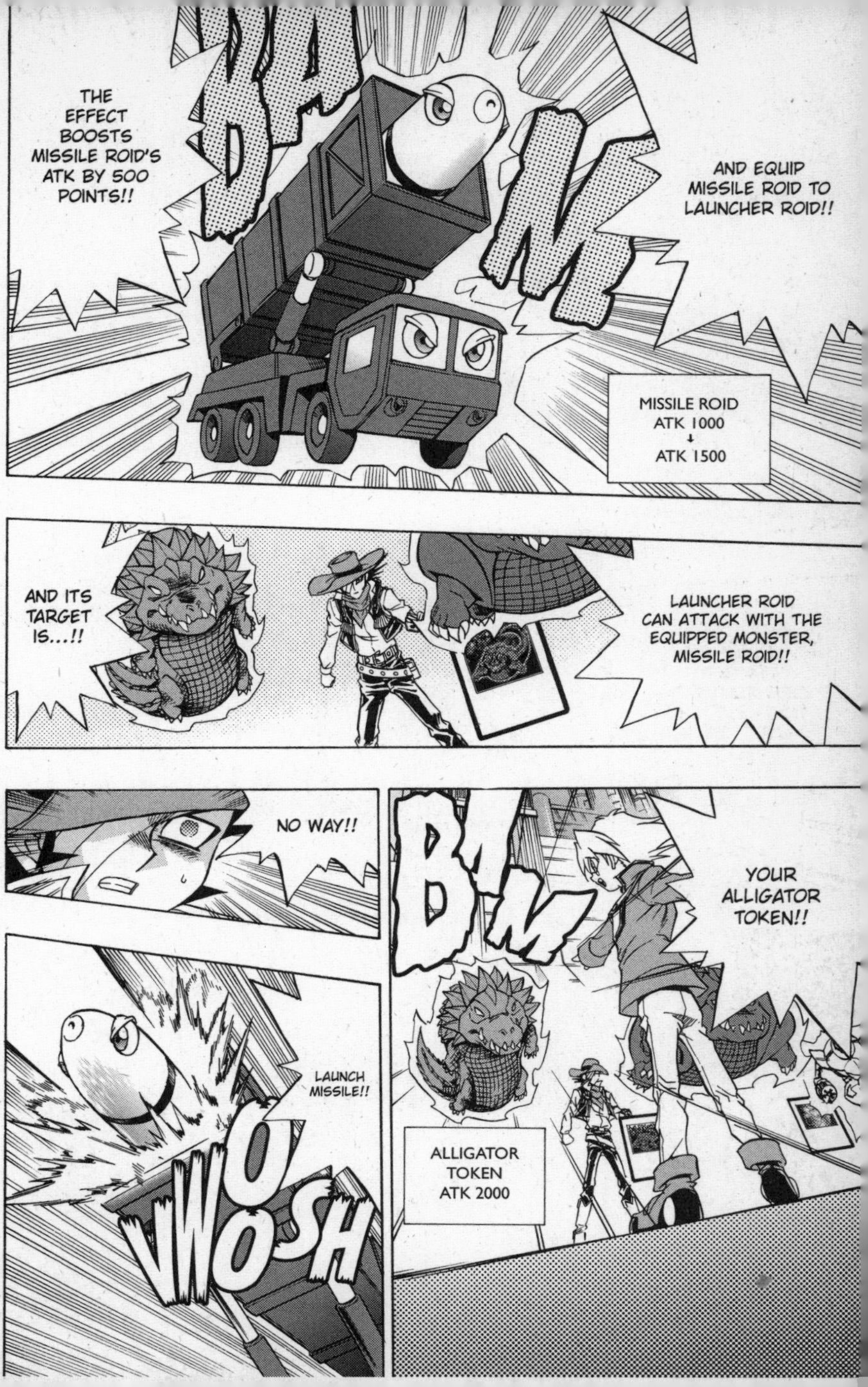
BAM
AND EQUIP MISSILE ROID TO LAUNCHER ROID!!
THE EFFECT BOOSTS MISSILE ROID'S ATK BY 500 POINTS!!
MISSILE ROID
ATK 1000
↓
ATK 1500
LAUNCHER ROID CAN ATTACK WITH THE EQUIPPED MONSTER, MISSILE ROID!!
AND ITS TARGET IS...!!
YOUR ALLIGATOR TOKEN!!
ALLIGATOR TOKEN
ATK 2000
NO WAY!!
LAUNCH MISSILE!!
WOOSH

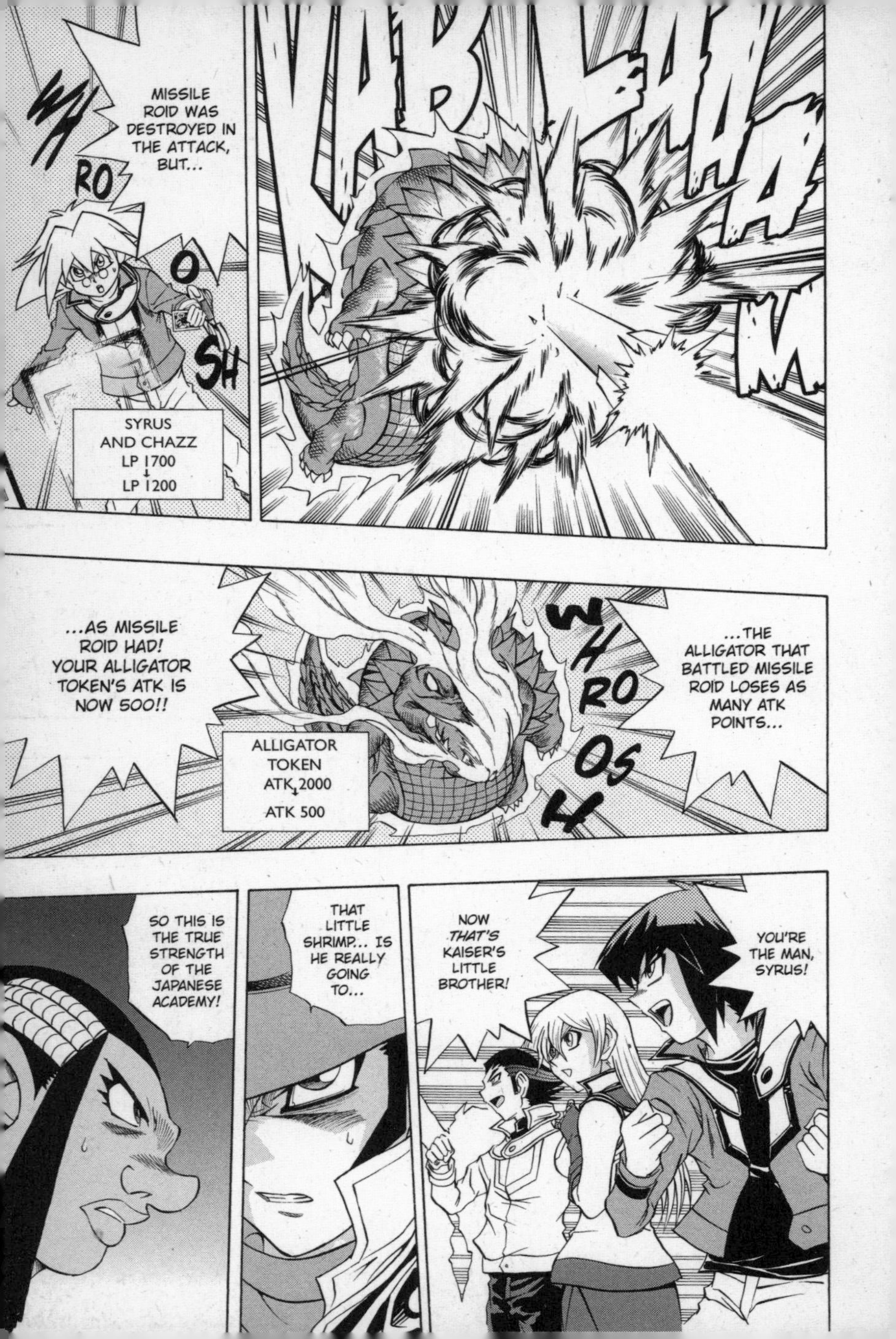
MISSILE ROID WAS DESTROYED IN THE ATTACK, BUT...
WH
RO
O
SH
SYRUS AND CHAZZ
LP 1700
↓
LP 1200
...THE ALLIGATOR THAT BATTLED MISSILE ROID LOSES AS MANY ATK POINTS...
WH
RO
OS
H
ALLIGATOR TOKEN
ATK 2000
↓
ATK 500
...AS MISSILE ROID HAD! YOUR ALLIGATOR TOKEN'S ATK IS NOW 500!!
YOU'RE THE MAN, SYRUS!
NOW *THAT'S* KAISER'S LITTLE BROTHER!
THAT LITTLE SHRIMP... IS HE REALLY GOING TO...
SO THIS IS THE TRUE STRENGTH OF THE JAPANESE ACADEMY!

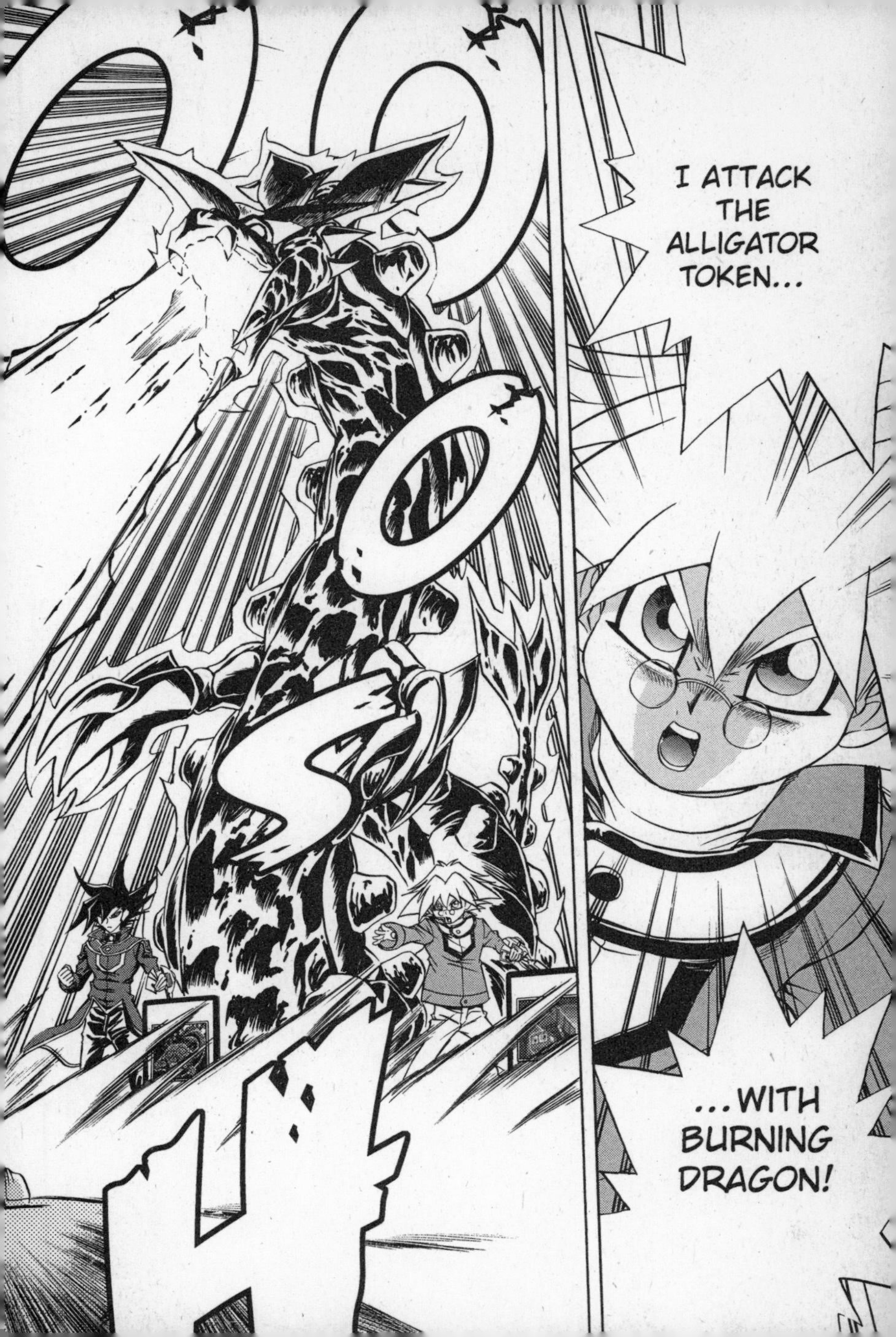
I ATTACK THE ALLIGATOR TOKEN...
...WITH BURNING DRAGON!

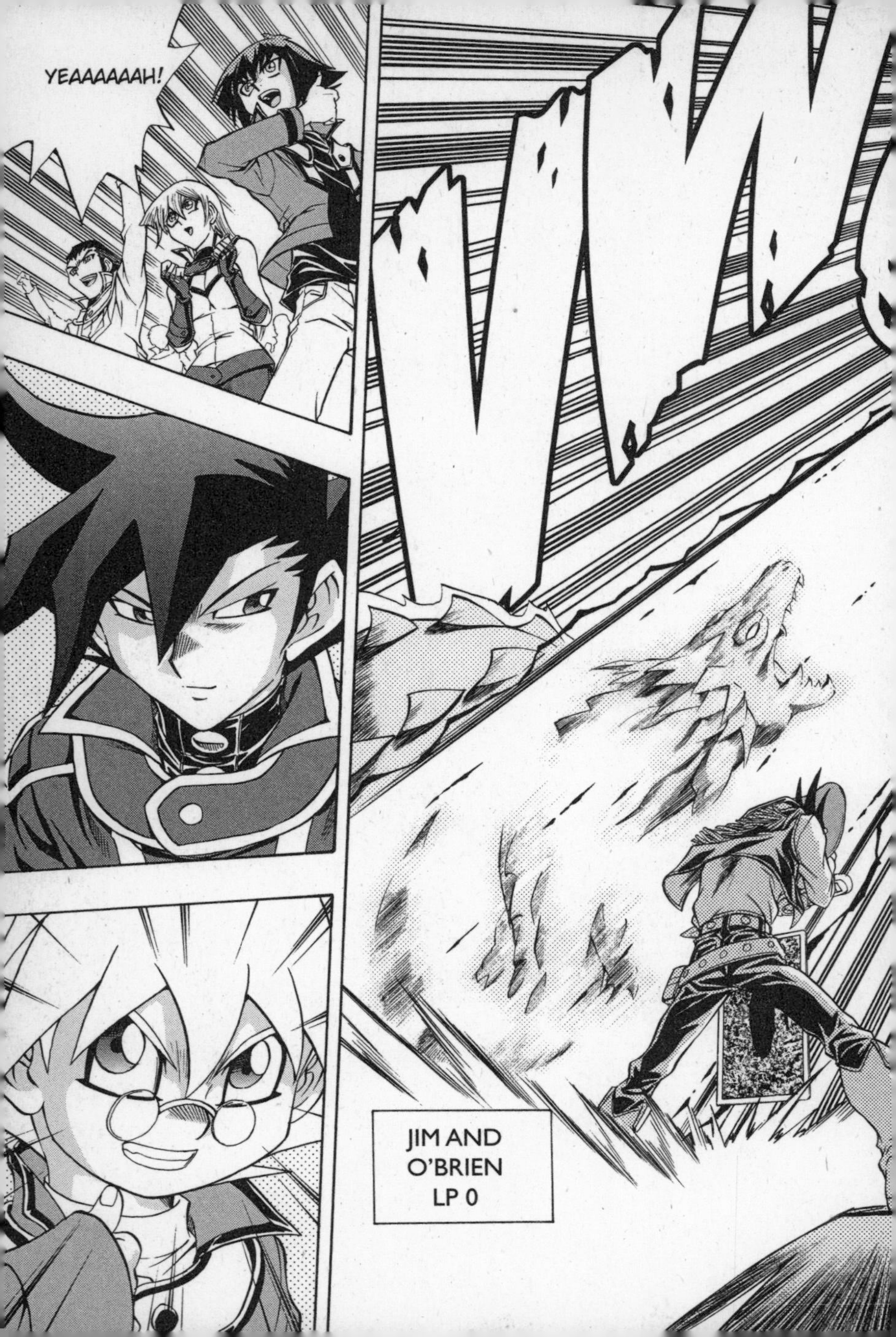
YEAAAAAAH!
JIM AND O'BRIEN LP 0

ELEMENTAL HERO DECK

ELEMENTAL HERO WOODSMAN (X 2)
ELEMENTAL HERO OCEAN (X 3)
ELEMENTAL HERO HEAT
ELEMENTAL HERO STRATOS
ELEMENTAL HERO LADY HEAT
ELEMENTAL HERO KNOSPE
ELEMENTAL HERO ICE EDGE
ELEMENTAL HERO VOLTIC
ELEMENTAL HERO FLASH

SPELL CARDS
POLYMERIZATION (X3)
MIRACLE FUSION (X3)
PARALLEL WORLD FUSION (X2)
SUPER POLYMERIZATION (2)
E-EMERGENCY CALL (3)
REINFORCEMENT OF THE ARMY
THE WARRIOR RETURNING ALIVE
LIGHTNING VORTEX
R-RIGHTEOUS JUSTICE (X2)
DE-FUSION
HERO'S BOND
HEAVY STORM
SKYSCRAPER
MYSTICAL SPACE TYPHOON

TRAP CARDS
COMPULSORY EVACUATION DEVICE (X3)
MIRROR FORCE
HERO SIGNAL

FUSION MONSTERS
ELEMENTAL HERO TERRA FIRMA (X2)
ELEMENTAL HERO THE SHINING (X2)
ELEMENTAL HERO GAIA (X2)
ELEMENTAL HERO GREAT TORNADO (X2)
ELEMENTAL HERO ABSOLUTE ZERO (X3)
ELEMENTAL HERO INFERNO

THIS IS MY HERO DECK RECIPE!

As of May this year! (2010)

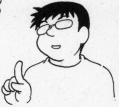

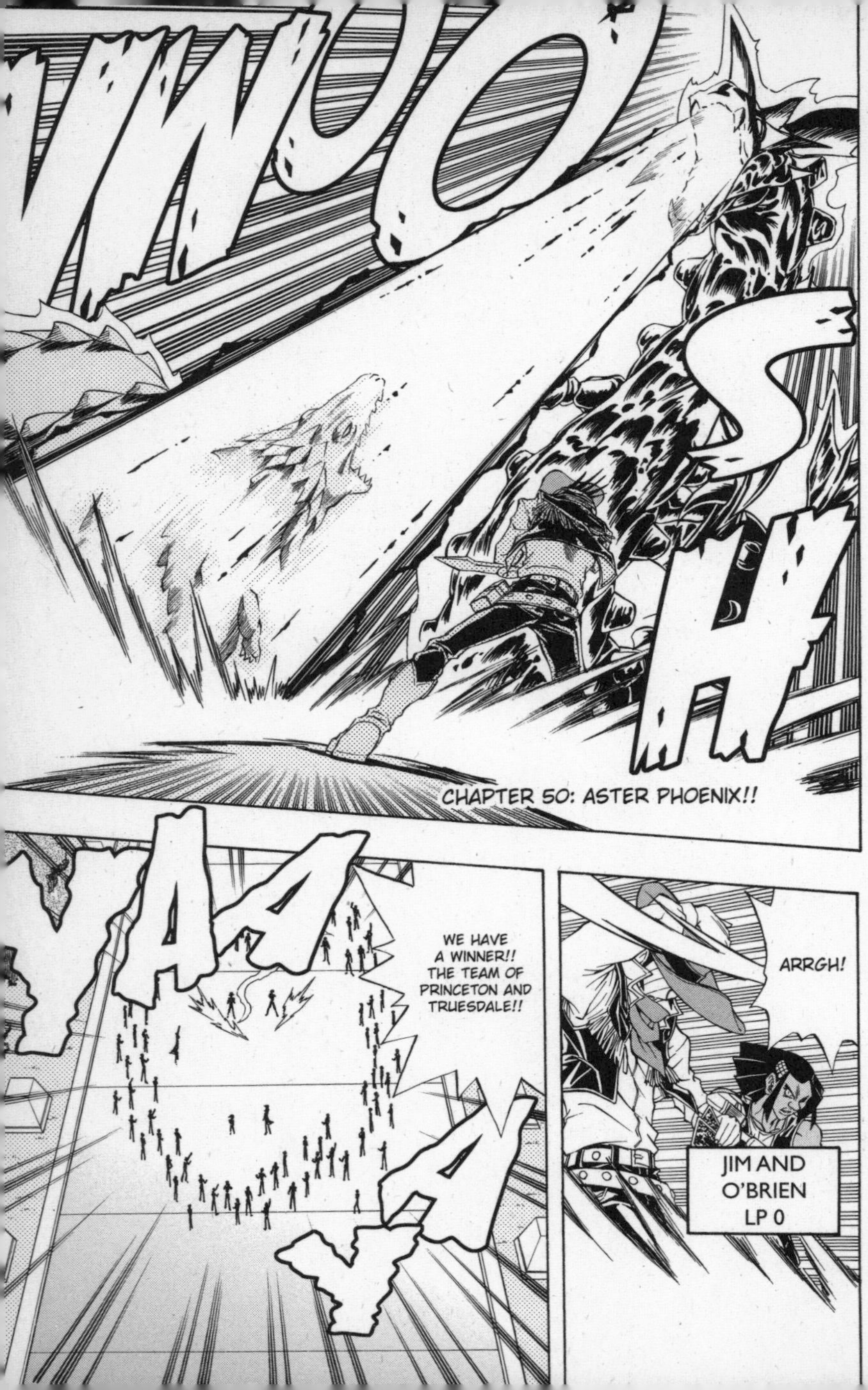
WUOOSH
CHAPTER 50: ASTER PHOENIX!!
ARRGH!
JIM AND O'BRIEN LP 0
YAAA
WE HAVE A WINNER!! THE TEAM OF PRINCETON AND TRUESDALE!!

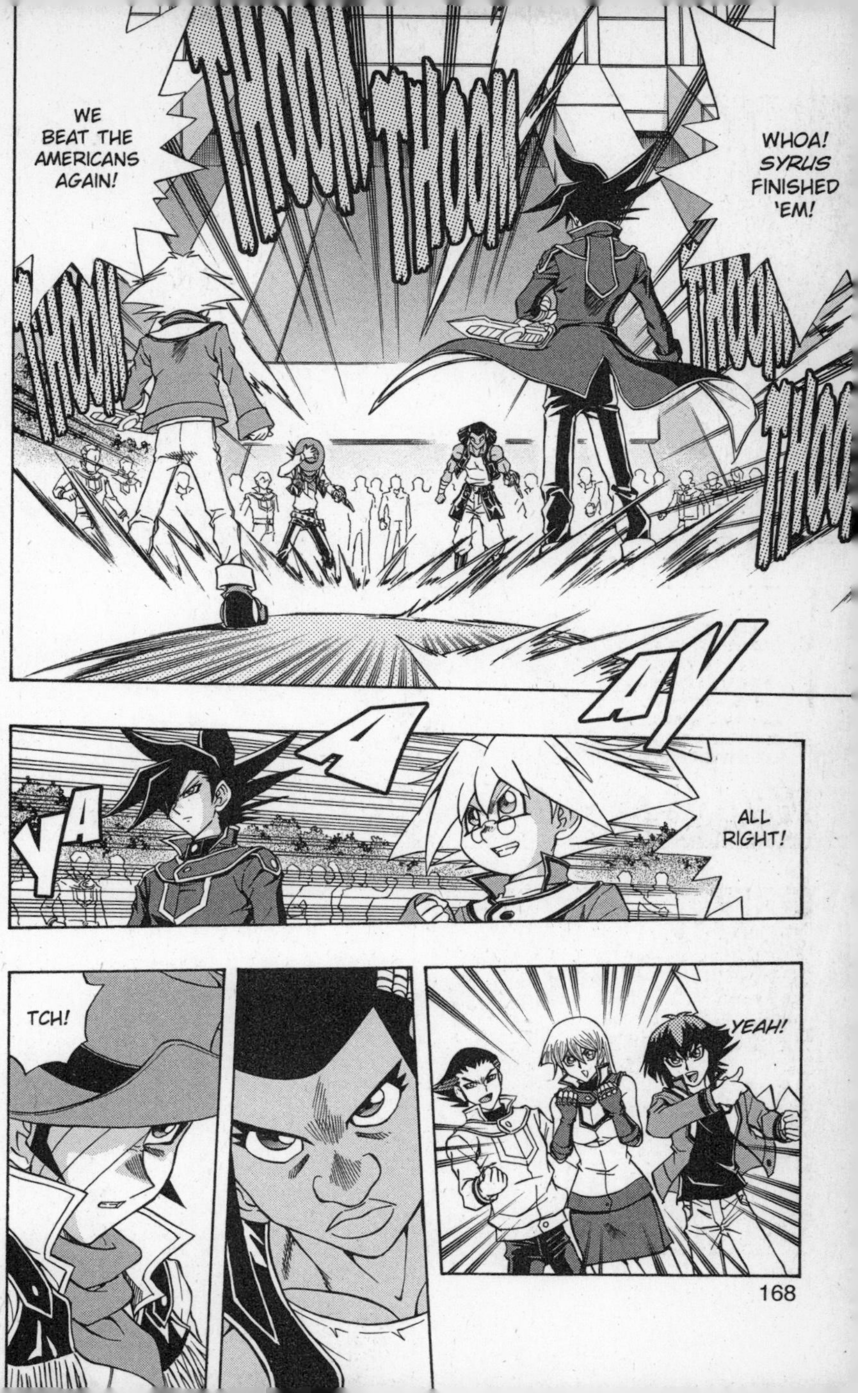
WHOA! SYRUS FINISHED 'EM!
THOOM
THOOM
THOOM
THOOM
WE BEAT THE AMERICANS AGAIN!
YAAAY
ALL RIGHT!
YEAH!
TCH!

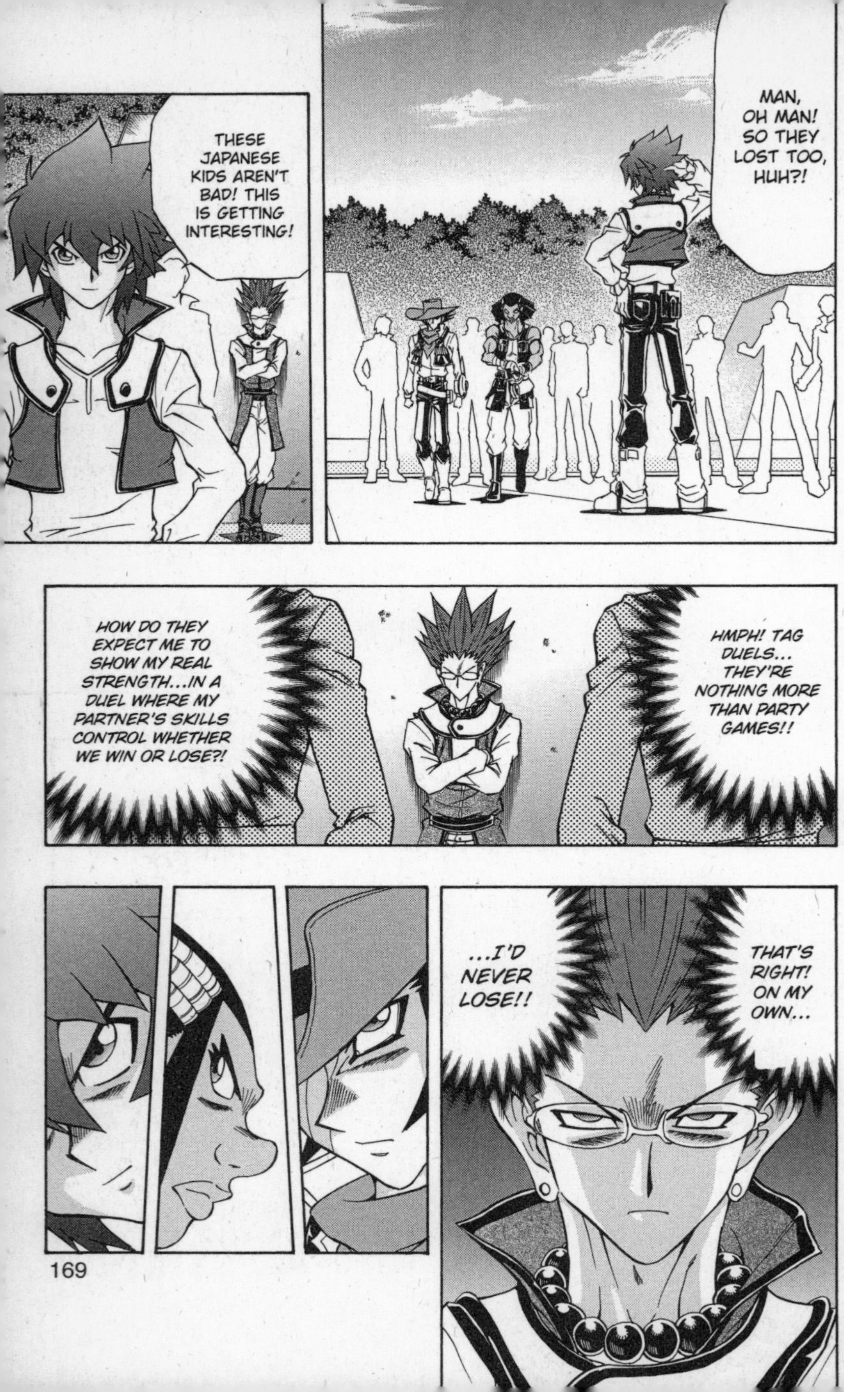
MAN, OH MAN! SO THEY LOST TOO, HUH?!
THESE JAPANESE KIDS AREN'T BAD! THIS IS GETTING INTERESTING!
HMPH! TAG DUELS... THEY'RE NOTHING MORE THAN PARTY GAMES!!
HOW DO THEY EXPECT ME TO SHOW MY REAL STRENGTH...IN A DUEL WHERE MY PARTNER'S SKILLS CONTROL WHETHER WE WIN OR LOSE?!
THAT'S RIGHT! ON MY OWN...
...I'D NEVER LOSE!!

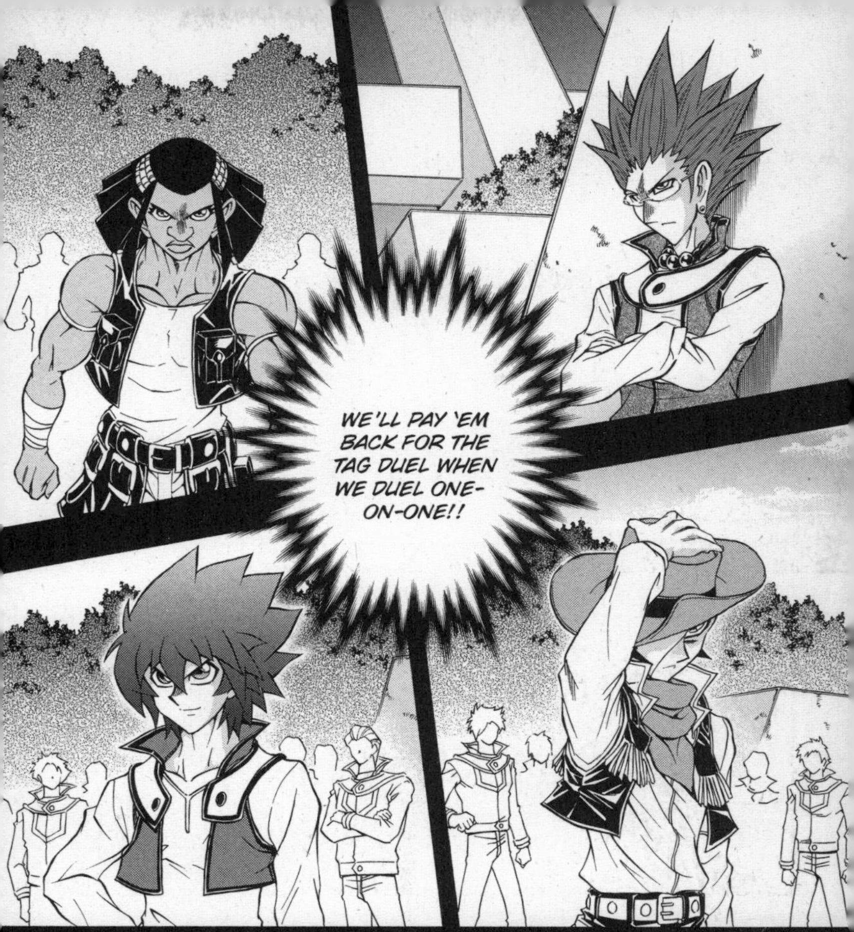
WE'LL PAY 'EM BACK FOR THE TAG DUEL WHEN WE DUEL ONE-ON-ONE!!

CHAPTER 50: ASTER PHOENIX!!

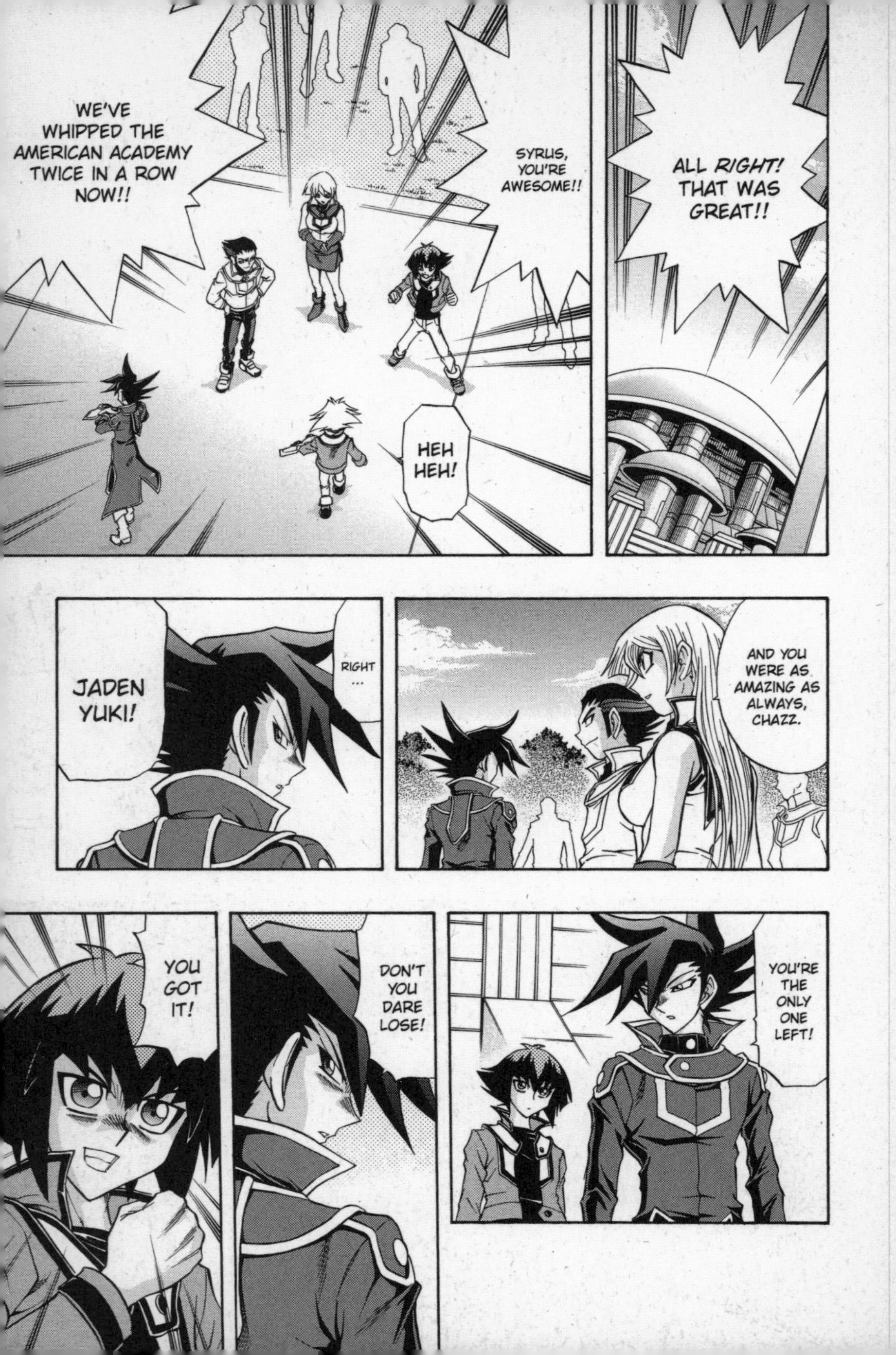
ALL *RIGHT!* THAT WAS GREAT!!
SYRUS, YOU'RE AWESOME!!
WE'VE WHIPPED THE AMERICAN ACADEMY TWICE IN A ROW NOW!!
HEH HEH!
AND YOU WERE AS AMAZING AS ALWAYS, CHAZZ.
RIGHT ...
JADEN YUKI!
YOU'RE THE ONLY ONE LEFT!
DON'T YOU DARE LOSE!
YOU GOT IT!

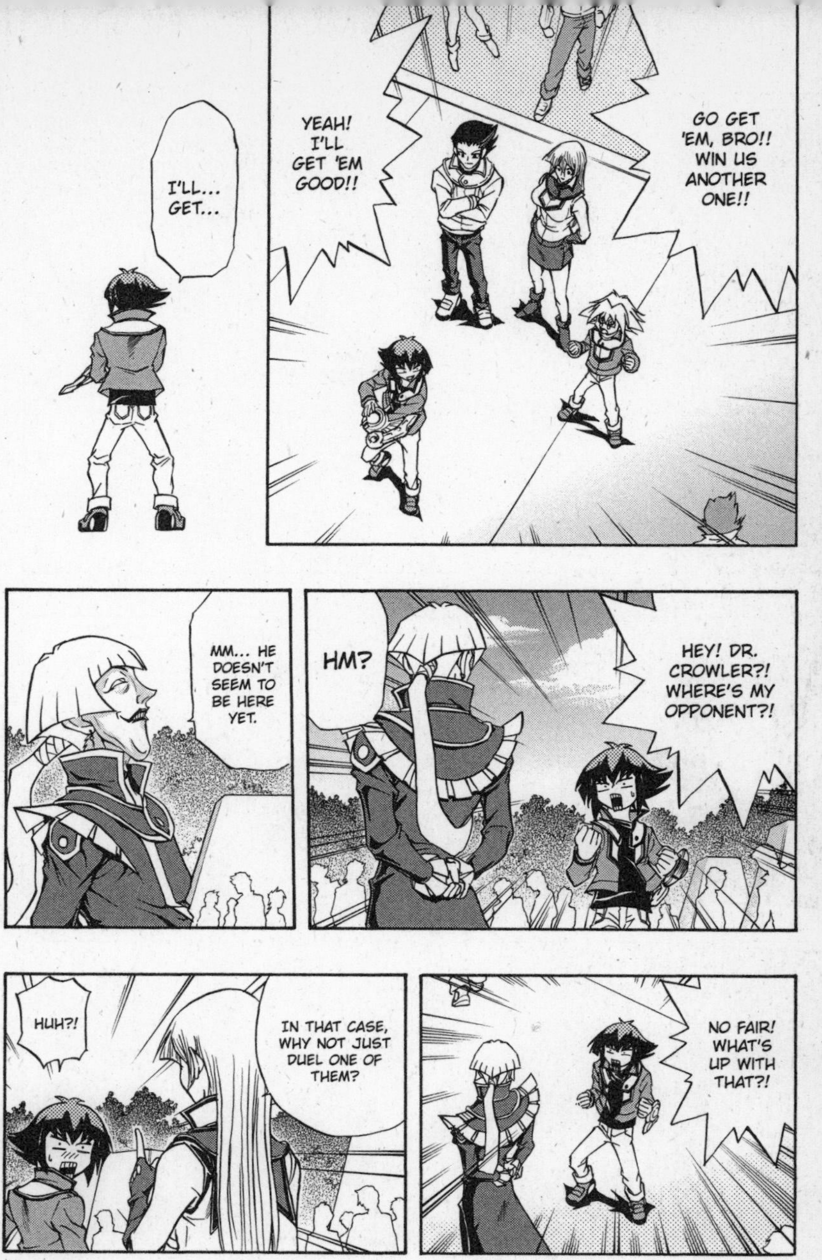
GO GET 'EM, BRO!! WIN US ANOTHER ONE!!
YEAH! I'LL GET 'EM GOOD!!
I'LL... GET...
HEY! DR. CROWLER?! WHERE'S MY OPPONENT?!
HM?
MM... HE DOESN'T SEEM TO BE HERE YET.
NO FAIR! WHAT'S UP WITH THAT?!
IN THAT CASE, WHY NOT JUST DUEL ONE OF THEM?
HUH?!

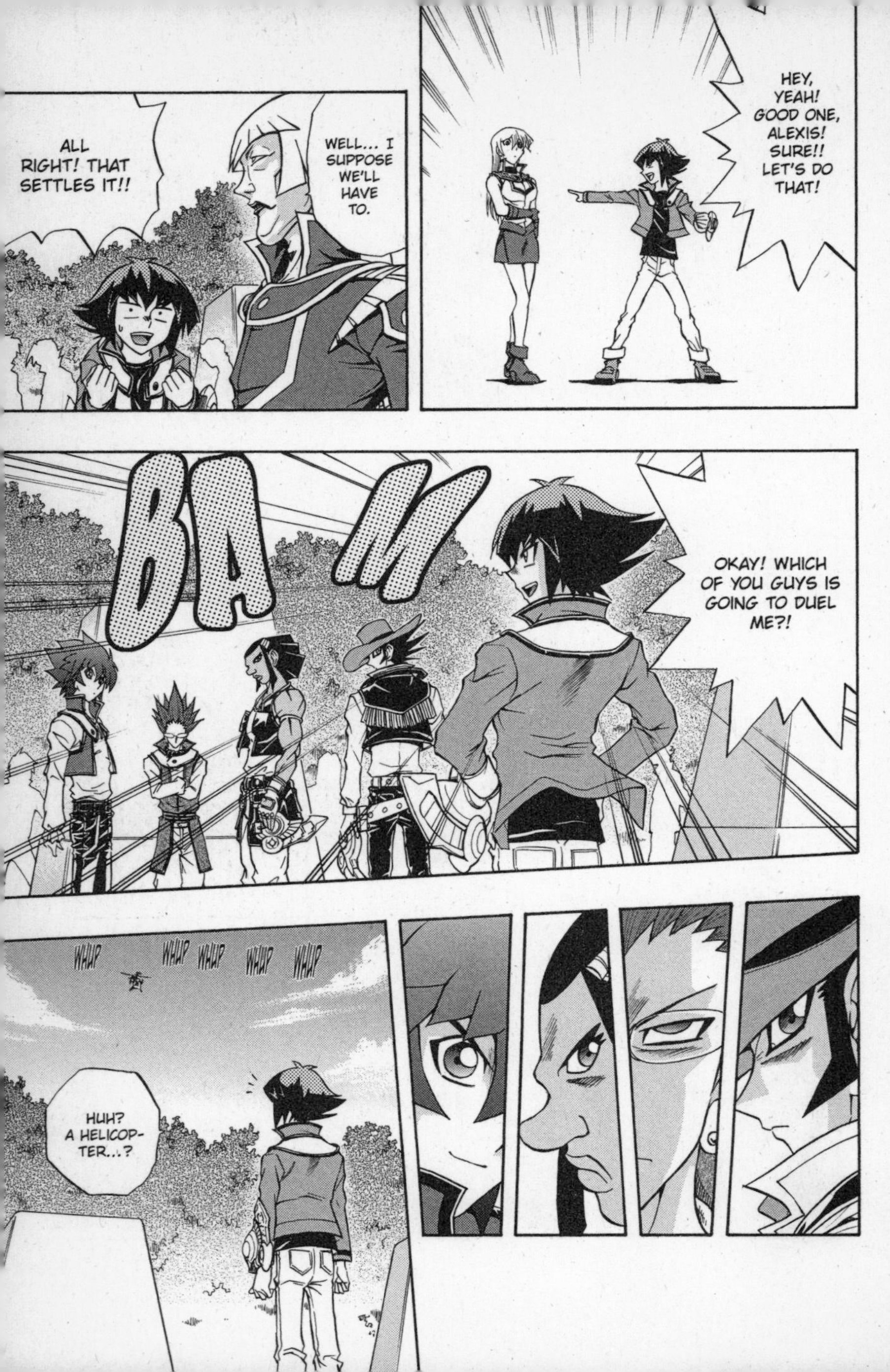
HEY, YEAH! GOOD ONE, ALEXIS! SURE!! LET'S DO THAT!
WELL... I SUPPOSE WE'LL HAVE TO.
ALL RIGHT! THAT SETTLES IT!!
OKAY! WHICH OF YOU GUYS IS GOING TO DUEL ME?!
BAM
WHUP WHUP WHUP WHUP WHUP
HUH? A HELICOPTER...?

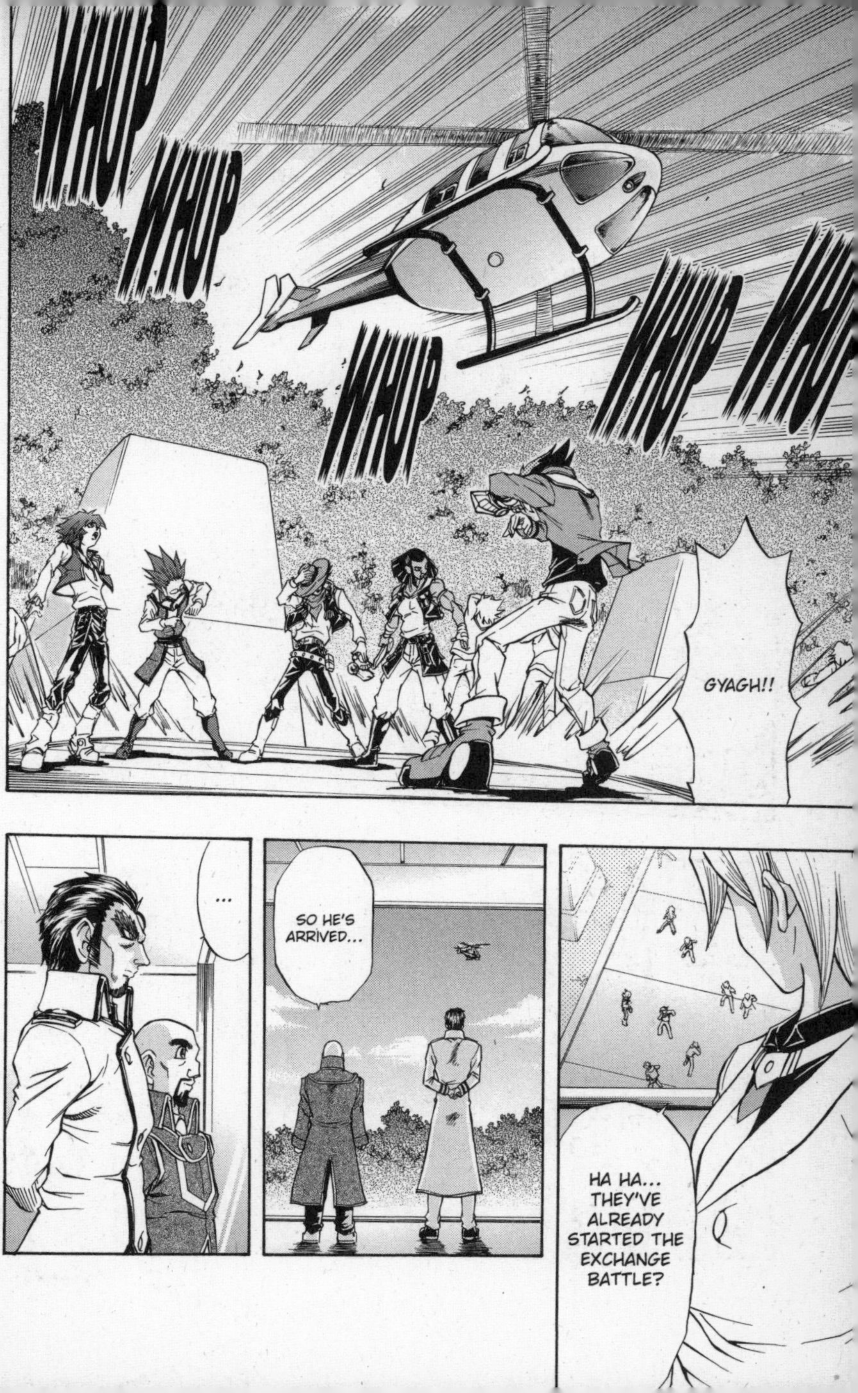
WHUP
WHUP
WHUP
WHUP
GYAGH!!
HA HA... THEY'VE ALREADY STARTED THE EXCHANGE BATTLE?
SO HE'S ARRIVED...
...

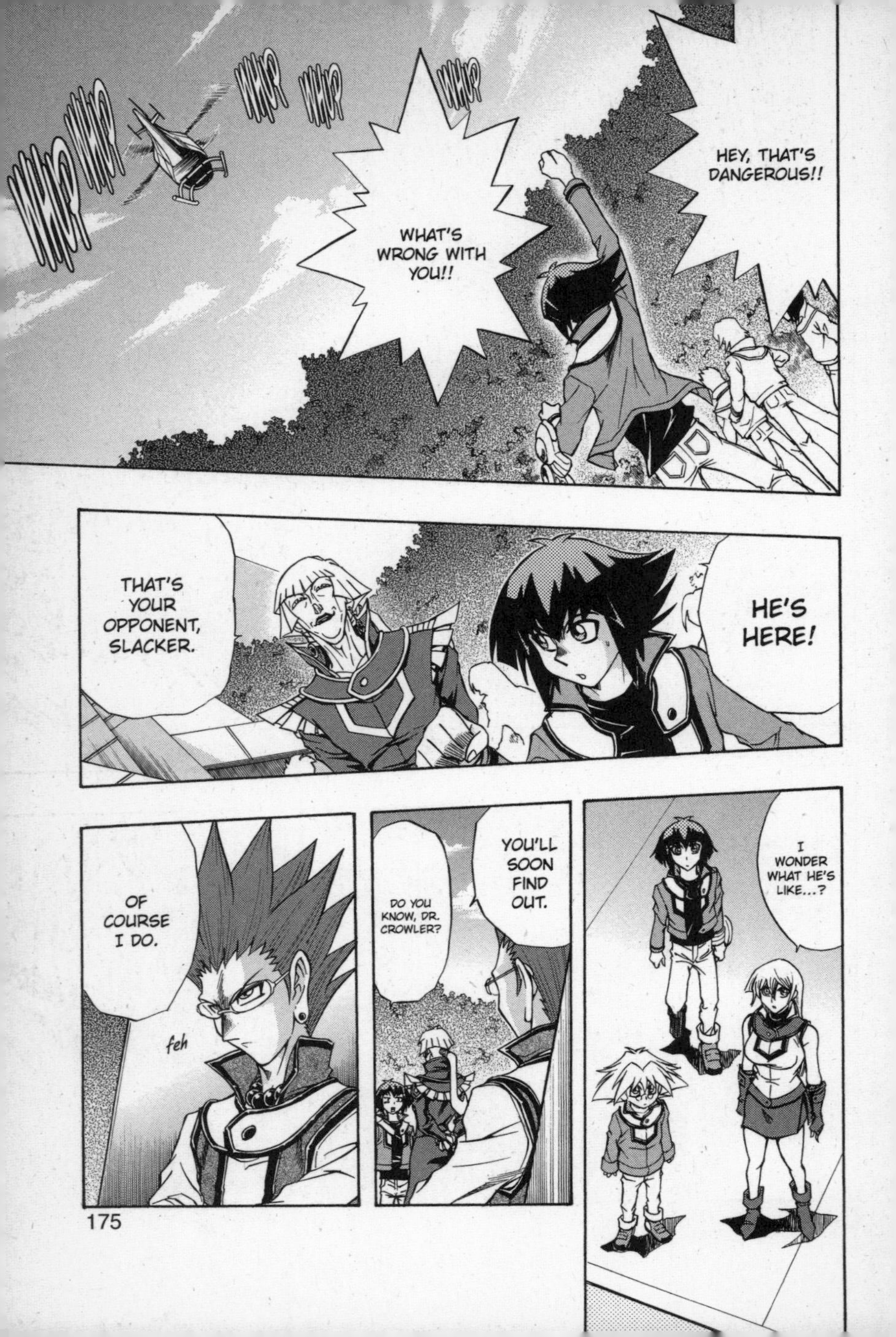
WHIP
WHIP
WHIP
WHIP WHIP
HEY, THAT'S DANGEROUS!!
WHAT'S WRONG WITH YOU!!
HE'S HERE!
THAT'S YOUR OPPONENT, SLACKER.
I WONDER WHAT HE'S LIKE...?
YOU'LL SOON FIND OUT.
DO YOU KNOW, DR. CROWLER?
OF COURSE I DO.
feh

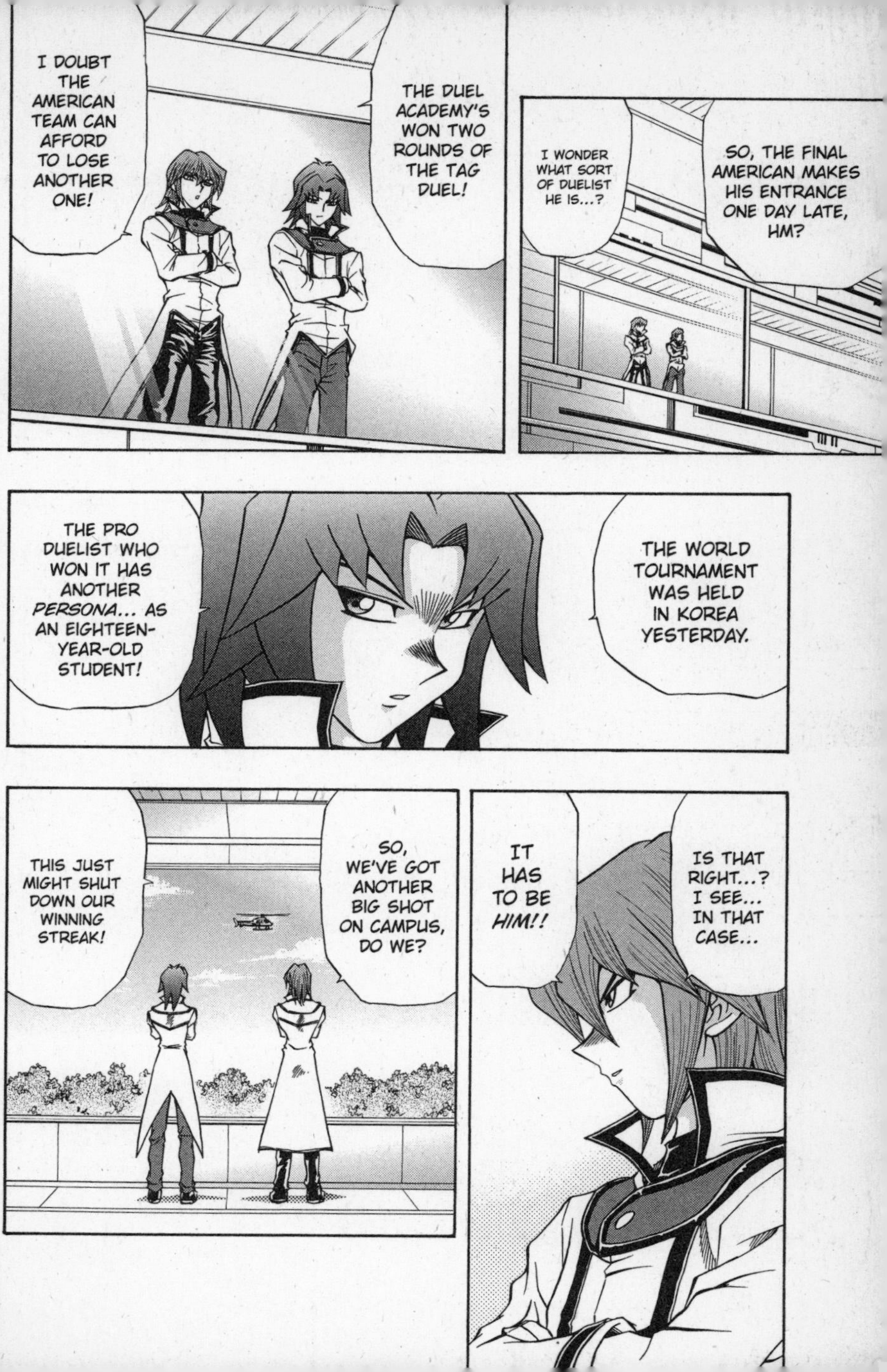
SO, THE FINAL AMERICAN MAKES HIS ENTRANCE ONE DAY LATE, HM?
I WONDER WHAT SORT OF DUELIST HE IS...?
THE DUEL ACADEMY'S WON TWO ROUNDS OF THE TAG DUEL!
I DOUBT THE AMERICAN TEAM CAN AFFORD TO LOSE ANOTHER ONE!
THE WORLD TOURNAMENT WAS HELD IN KOREA YESTERDAY.
THE PRO DUELIST WHO WON IT HAS ANOTHER *PERSONA*... AS AN EIGHTEEN-YEAR-OLD STUDENT!
IS THAT RIGHT...? I SEE... IN THAT CASE...
IT HAS TO BE *HIM!!*
SO, WE'VE GOT ANOTHER BIG SHOT ON CAMPUS, DO WE?
THIS JUST MIGHT SHUT DOWN OUR WINNING STREAK!

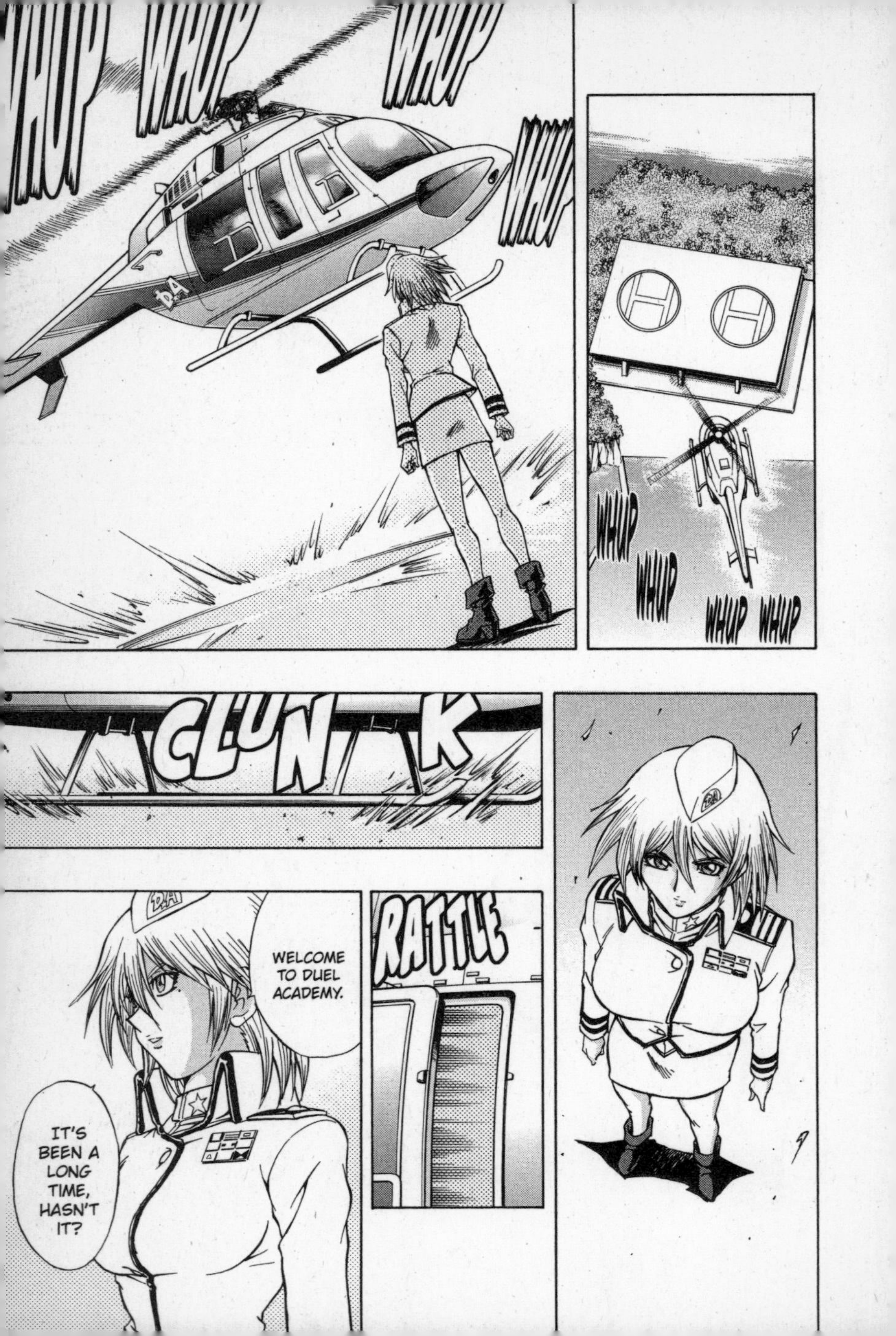
WHUP
WHUP
WHUP
WHUP
WHUP
WHUP
WHUP
WHUP
CLUNK
RATTLE
WELCOME TO DUEL ACADEMY.
IT'S BEEN A LONG TIME, HASN'T IT?

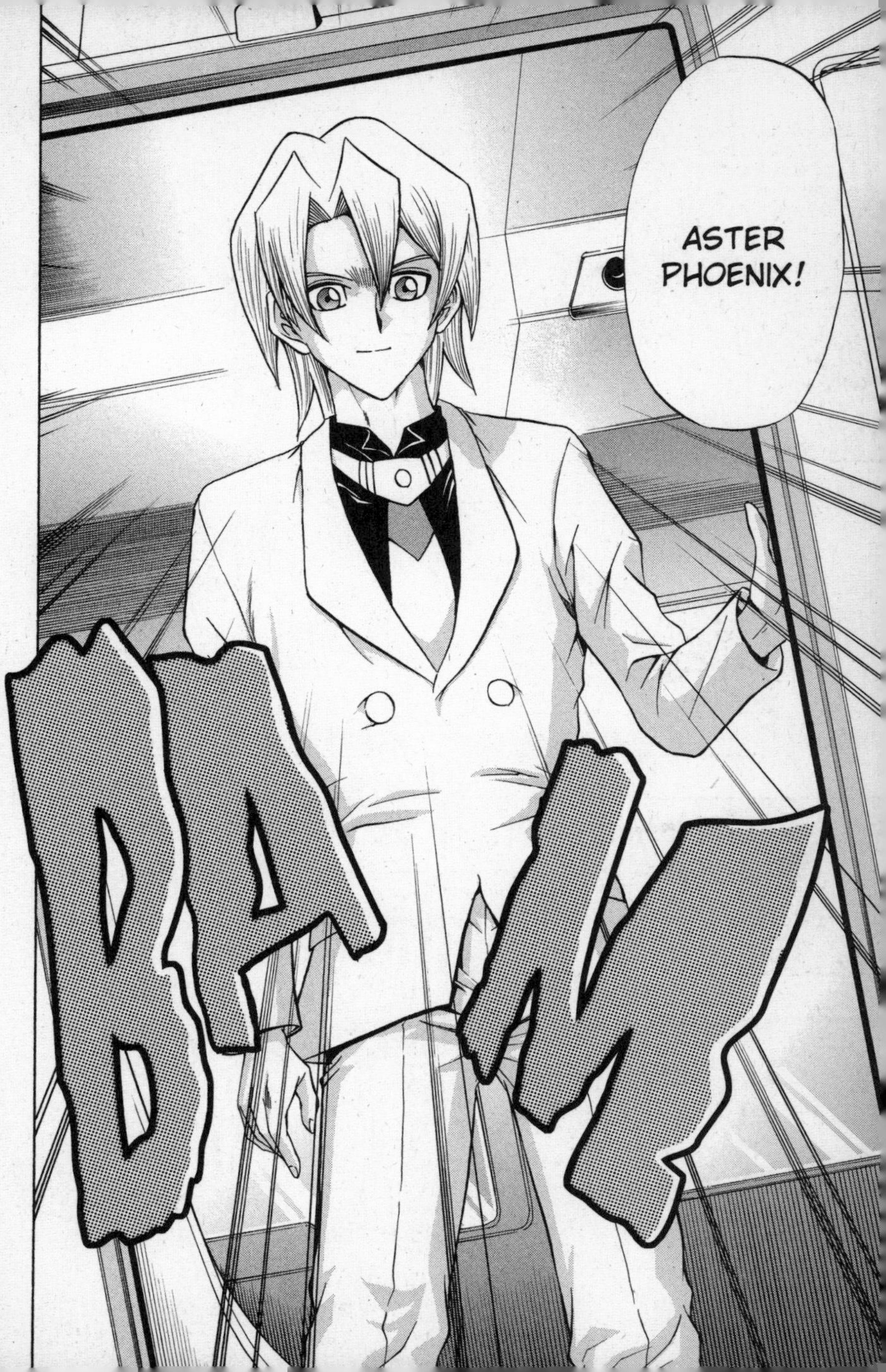
ASTER PHOENIX!
BAM

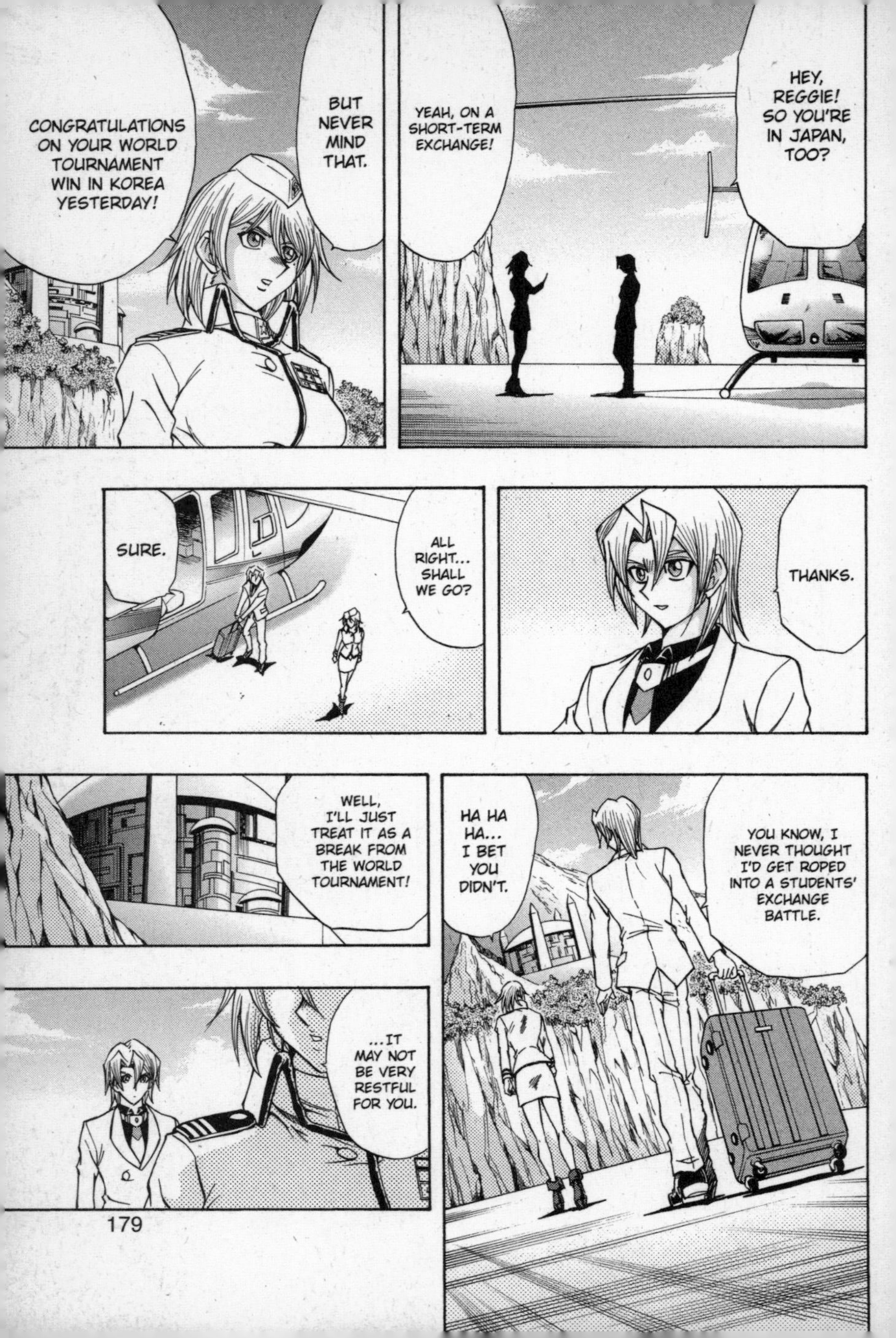
HEY, REGGIE! SO YOU'RE IN JAPAN, TOO?
YEAH, ON A SHORT-TERM EXCHANGE!
BUT NEVER MIND THAT.
CONGRATULATIONS ON YOUR WORLD TOURNAMENT WIN IN KOREA YESTERDAY!
THANKS.
ALL RIGHT... SHALL WE GO?
SURE.
YOU KNOW, I NEVER THOUGHT I'D GET ROPED INTO A STUDENTS' EXCHANGE BATTLE.
HA HA HA... I BET YOU DIDN'T.
WELL, I'LL JUST TREAT IT AS A BREAK FROM THE WORLD TOURNAMENT!
...IT MAY NOT BE VERY RESTFUL FOR YOU.

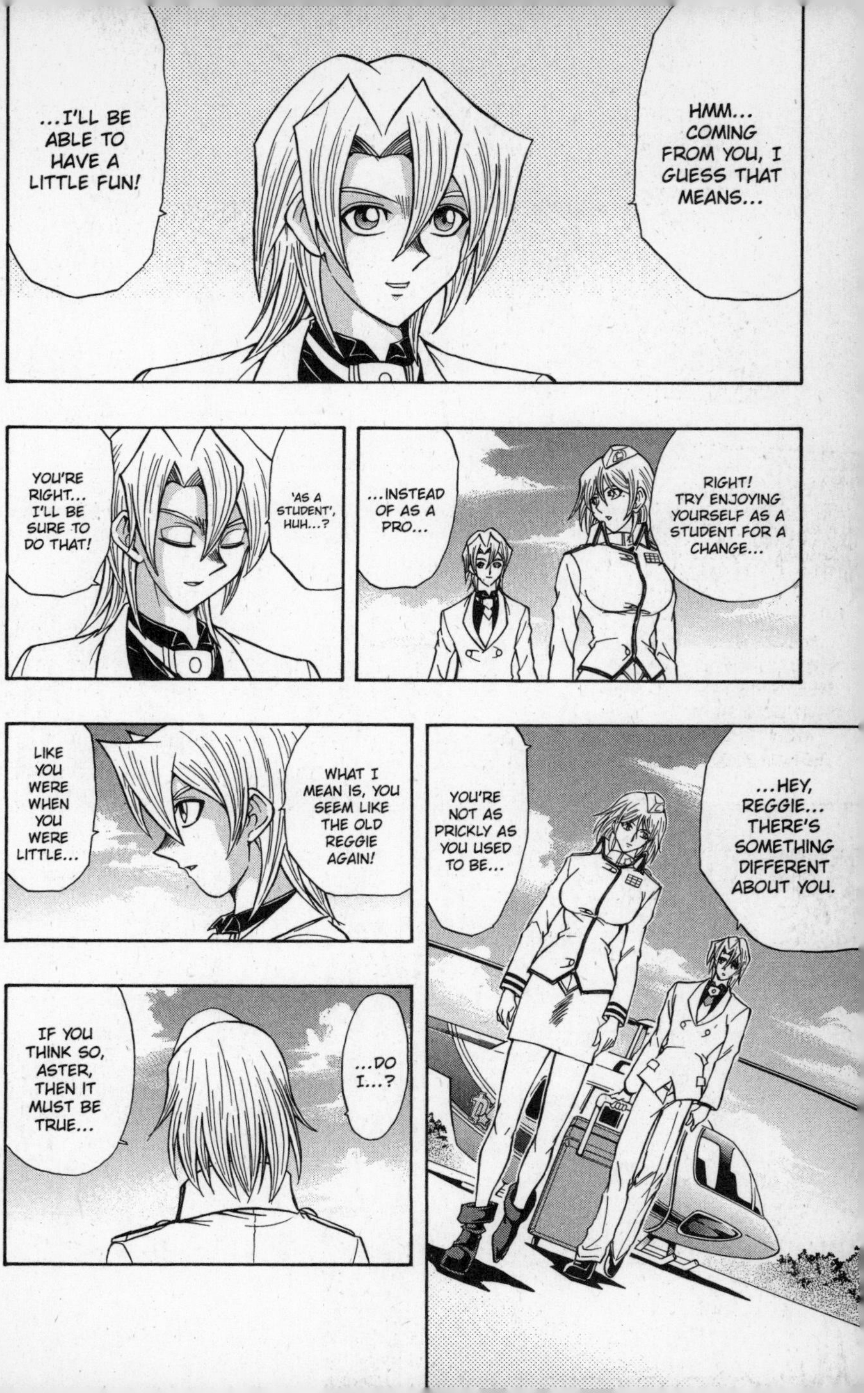
HMM... COMING FROM YOU, I GUESS THAT MEANS...
...I'LL BE ABLE TO HAVE A LITTLE FUN!
RIGHT! TRY ENJOYING YOURSELF AS A STUDENT FOR A CHANGE...
...INSTEAD OF AS A PRO...
'AS A STUDENT', HUH...?
YOU'RE RIGHT... I'LL BE SURE TO DO THAT!
...HEY, REGGIE... THERE'S SOMETHING DIFFERENT ABOUT YOU.
YOU'RE NOT AS PRICKLY AS YOU USED TO BE...
WHAT I MEAN IS, YOU SEEM LIKE THE OLD REGGIE AGAIN!
LIKE YOU WERE WHEN YOU WERE LITTLE...
...DO I...?
IF YOU THINK SO, ASTER, THEN IT MUST BE TRUE...

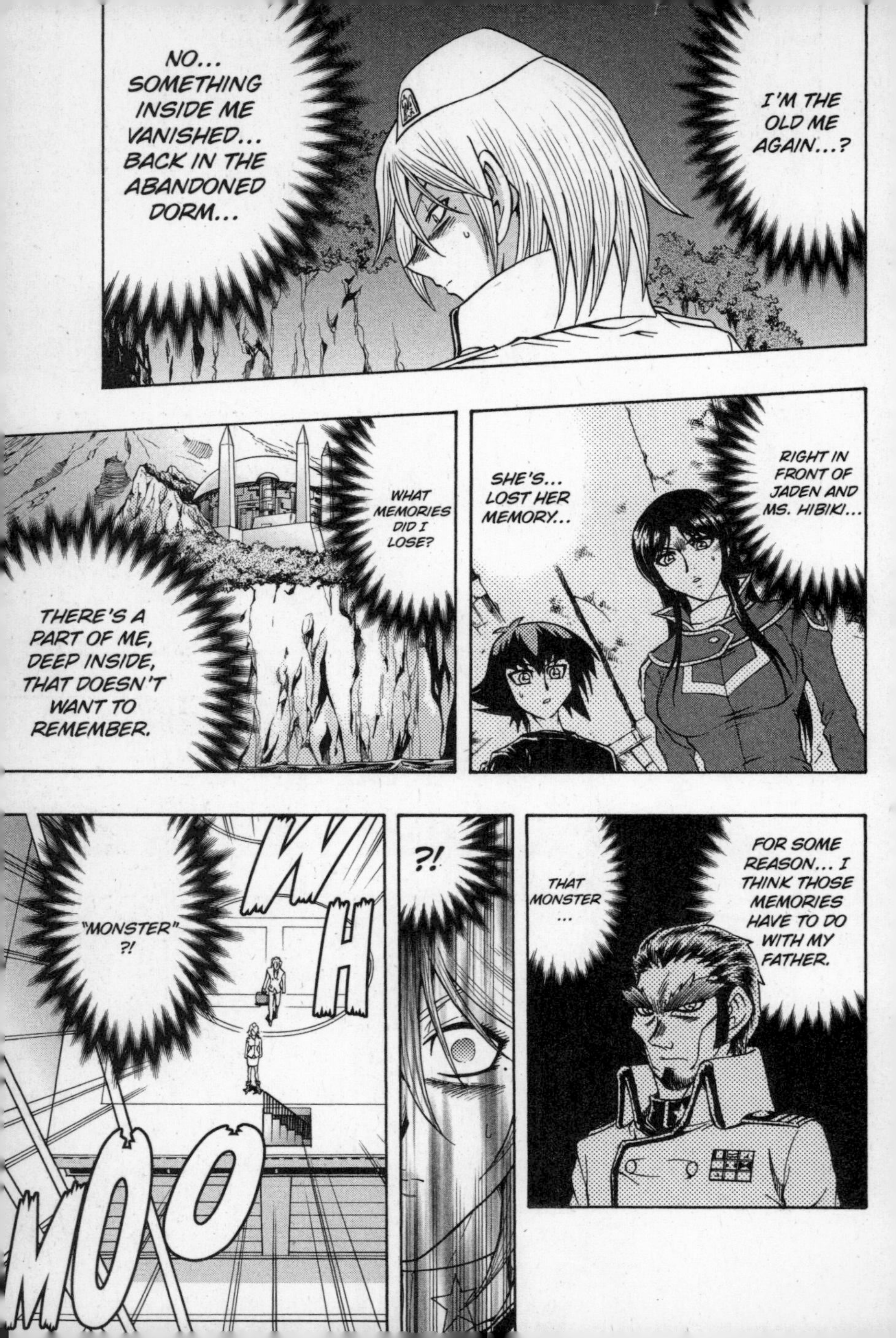
I'M THE OLD ME AGAIN...?
NO... SOMETHING INSIDE ME VANISHED... BACK IN THE ABANDONED DORM...
RIGHT IN FRONT OF JADEN AND MS. HIBIKI...
SHE'S... LOST HER MEMORY...
WHAT MEMORIES DID I LOSE?
THERE'S A PART OF ME, DEEP INSIDE, THAT DOESN'T WANT TO REMEMBER.
FOR SOME REASON... I THINK THOSE MEMORIES HAVE TO DO WITH MY FATHER.
THAT MONSTER ...
?!
WH
"MONSTER" ?!
MOO

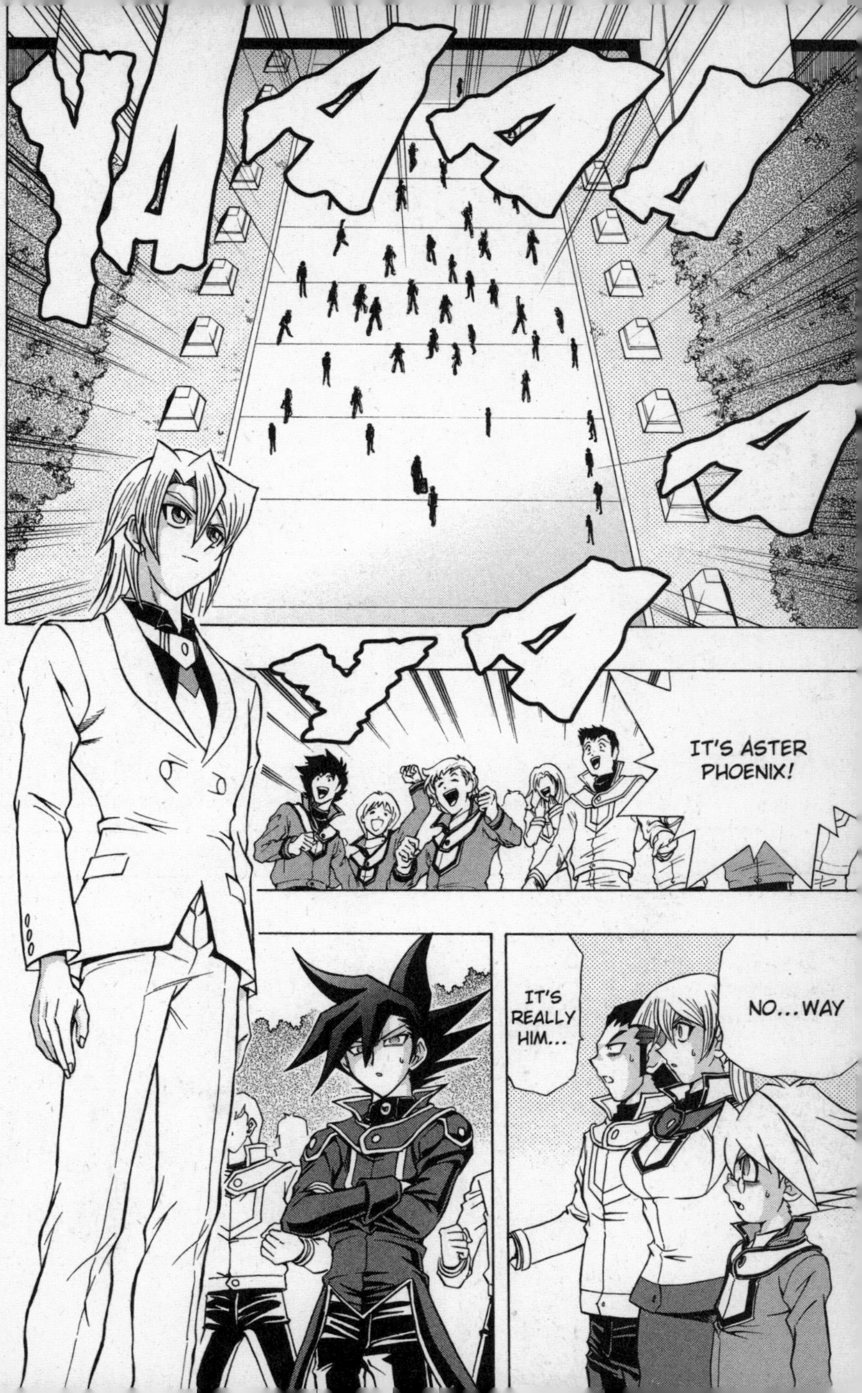
YAAAAAA
YA
IT'S ASTER PHOENIX!
NO...WAY
IT'S REALLY HIM...

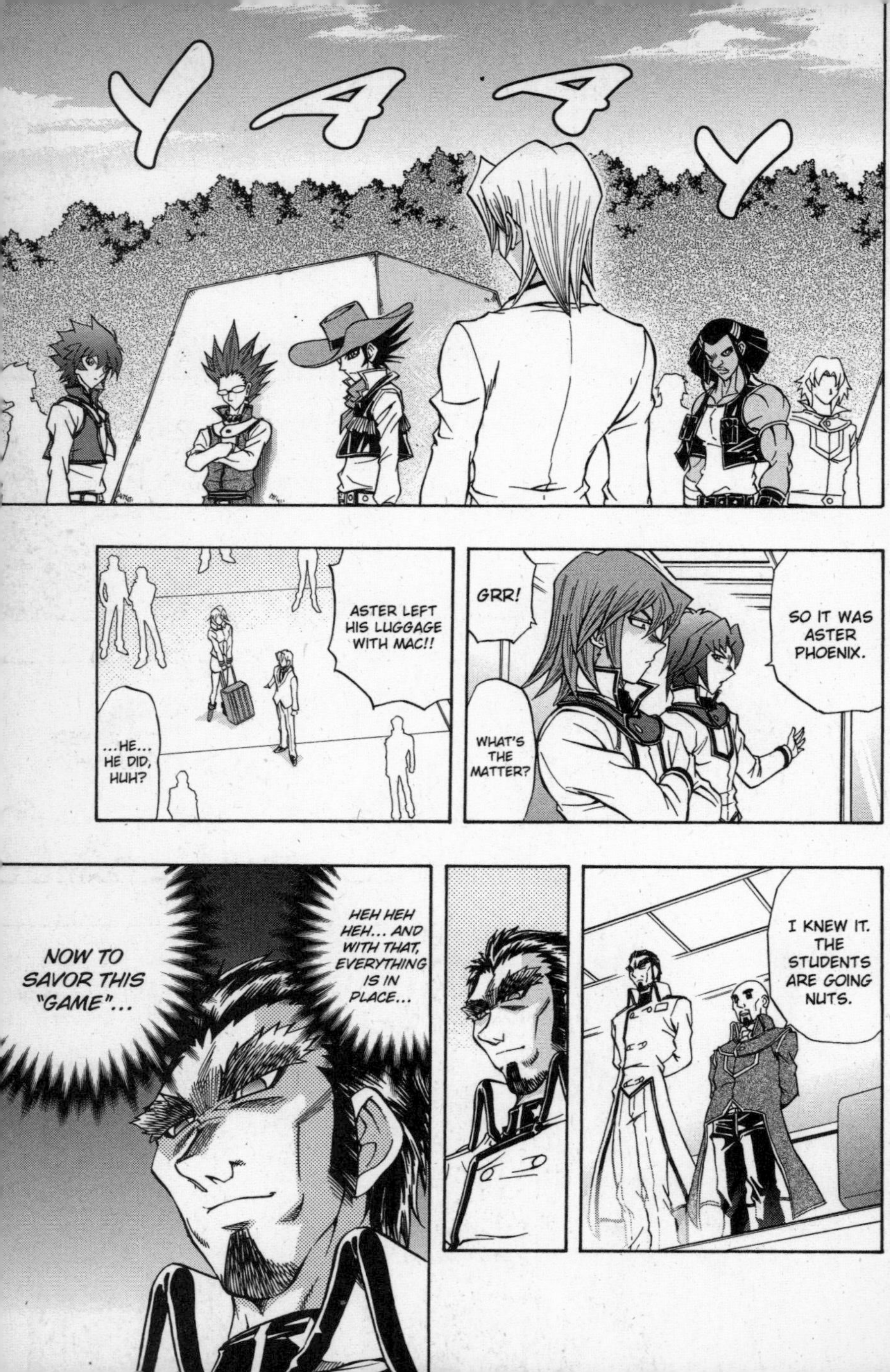
YAAY
SO IT WAS ASTER PHOENIX.
GRR!
WHAT'S THE MATTER?
ASTER LEFT HIS LUGGAGE WITH MAC!!
...HE... HE DID, HUH?
I KNEW IT. THE STUDENTS ARE GOING NUTS.
HEH HEH HEH... AND WITH THAT, EVERYTHING IS IN PLACE...
NOW TO SAVOR THIS "GAME"...

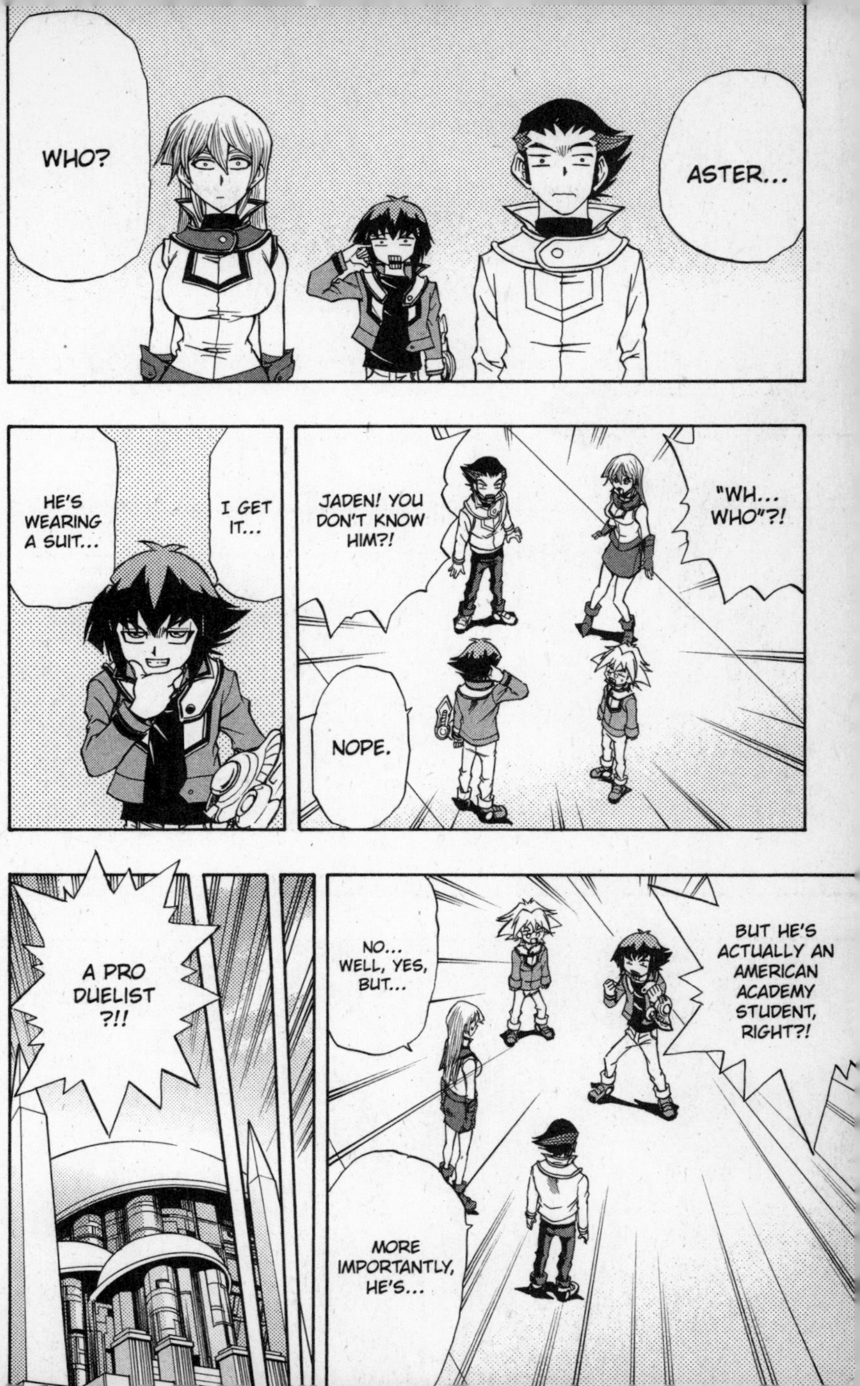
ASTER...
WHO?
"WH... WHO"?!
JADEN! YOU DON'T KNOW HIM?!
NOPE.
I GET IT...
HE'S WEARING A SUIT...
BUT HE'S ACTUALLY AN AMERICAN ACADEMY STUDENT, RIGHT?!
NO... WELL, YES, BUT...
MORE IMPORTANTLY, HE'S...
A PRO DUELIST?!!

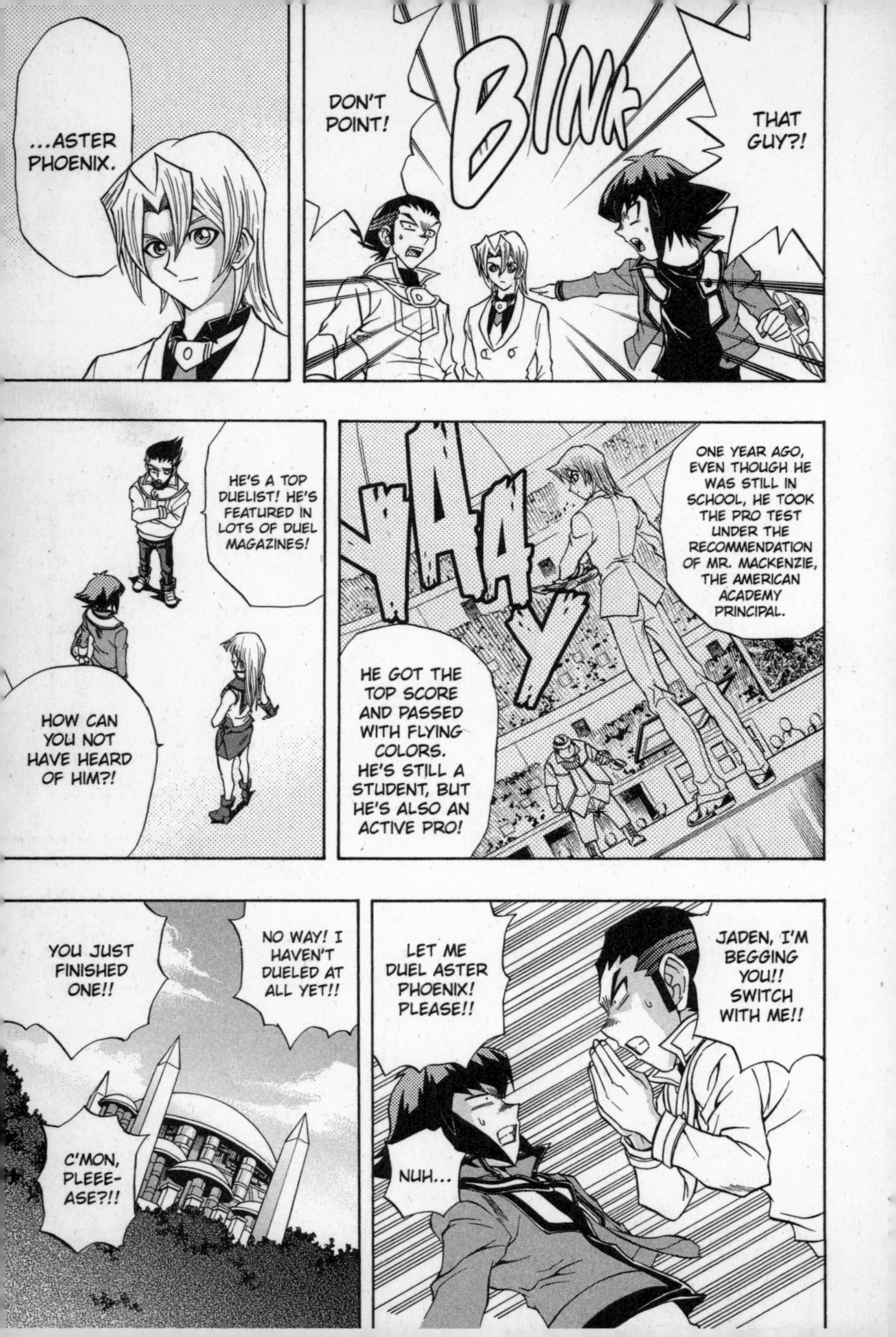
THAT GUY?!
BLINK
DON'T POINT!
...ASTER PHOENIX.
ONE YEAR AGO, EVEN THOUGH HE WAS STILL IN SCHOOL, HE TOOK THE PRO TEST UNDER THE RECOMMENDATION OF MR. MACKENZIE, THE AMERICAN ACADEMY PRINCIPAL.
YAAAY
HE GOT THE TOP SCORE AND PASSED WITH FLYING COLORS. HE'S STILL A STUDENT, BUT HE'S ALSO AN ACTIVE PRO!
HE'S A TOP DUELIST! HE'S FEATURED IN LOTS OF DUEL MAGAZINES!
HOW CAN YOU NOT HAVE HEARD OF HIM?!
JADEN, I'M BEGGING YOU!! SWITCH WITH ME!!
LET ME DUEL ASTER PHOENIX! PLEASE!!
NUH...
NO WAY! I HAVEN'T DUELED AT ALL YET!!
YOU JUST FINISHED ONE!!
C'MON, PLEEE-ASE?!!

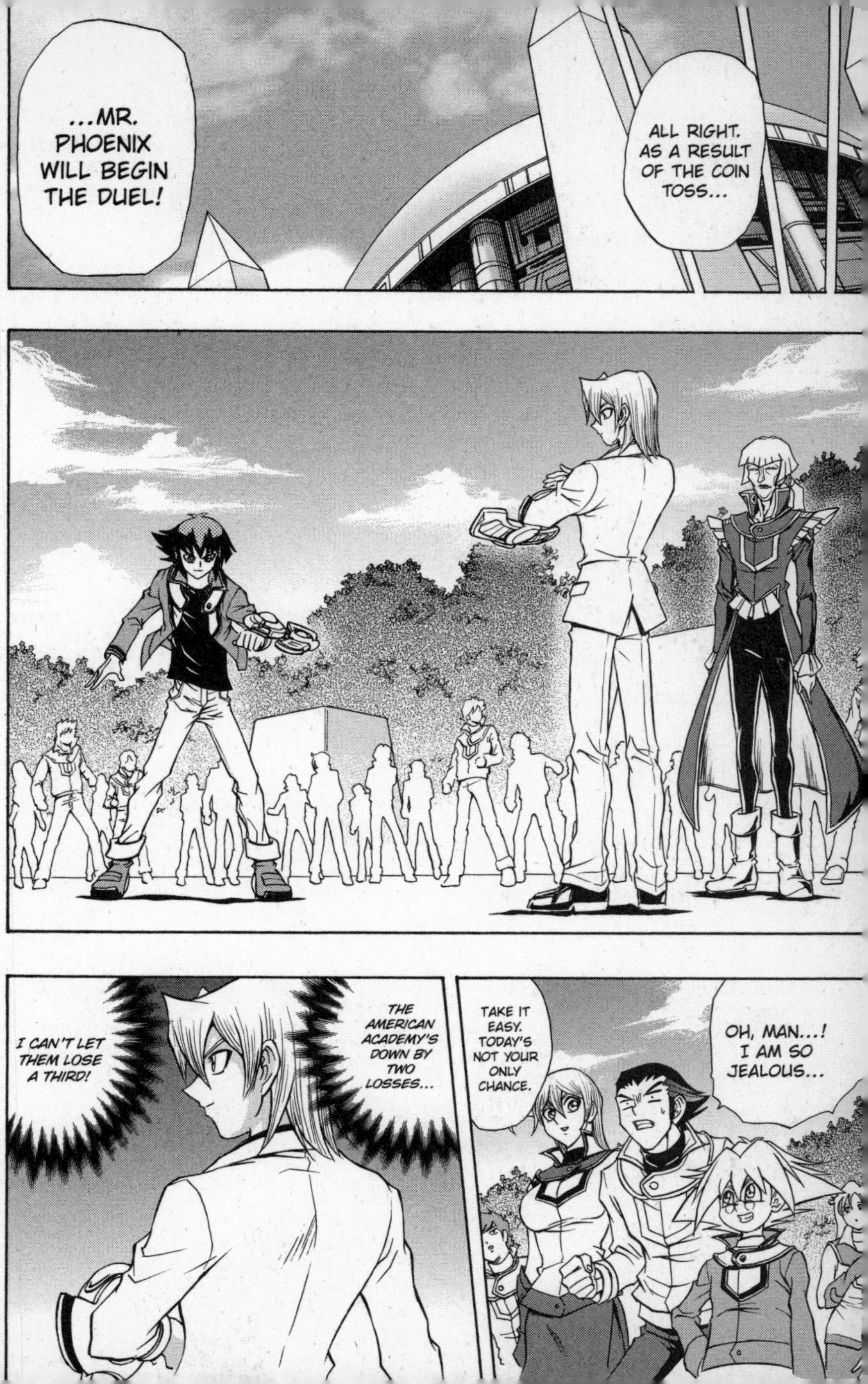
ALL RIGHT. AS A RESULT OF THE COIN TOSS...
...MR. PHOENIX WILL BEGIN THE DUEL!
OH, MAN...! I AM SO JEALOUS...
TAKE IT EASY. TODAY'S NOT YOUR ONLY CHANCE.
THE AMERICAN ACADEMY'S DOWN BY TWO LOSSES...
I CAN'T LET THEM LOSE A THIRD!

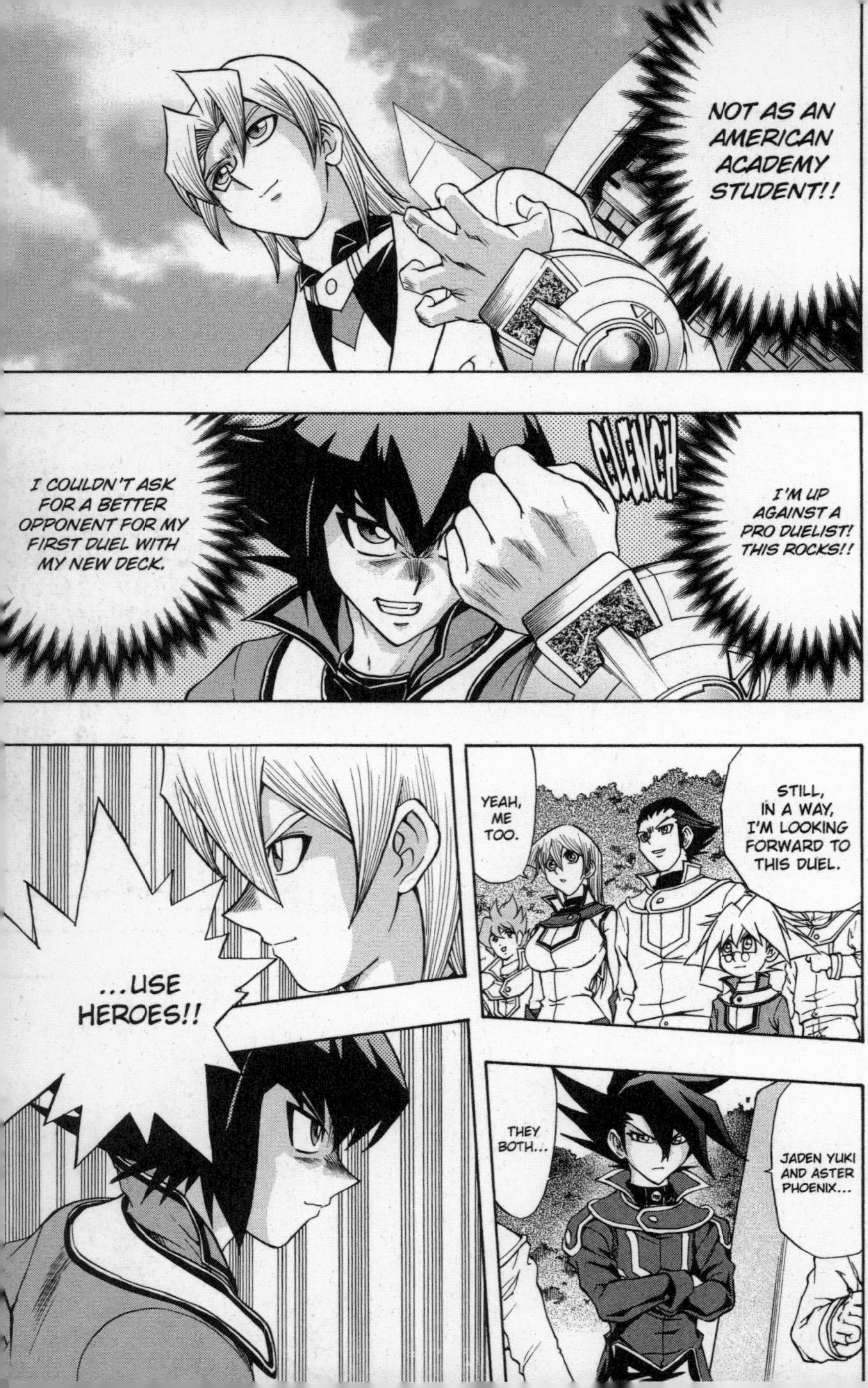
NOT AS AN AMERICAN ACADEMY STUDENT!!
I'M UP AGAINST A PRO DUELIST! THIS ROCKS!!
CLENCH
I COULDN'T ASK FOR A BETTER OPPONENT FOR MY FIRST DUEL WITH MY NEW DECK.
STILL, IN A WAY, I'M LOOKING FORWARD TO THIS DUEL.
YEAH, ME TOO.
JADEN YUKI AND ASTER PHOENIX...
THEY BOTH...
...USE HEROES!!

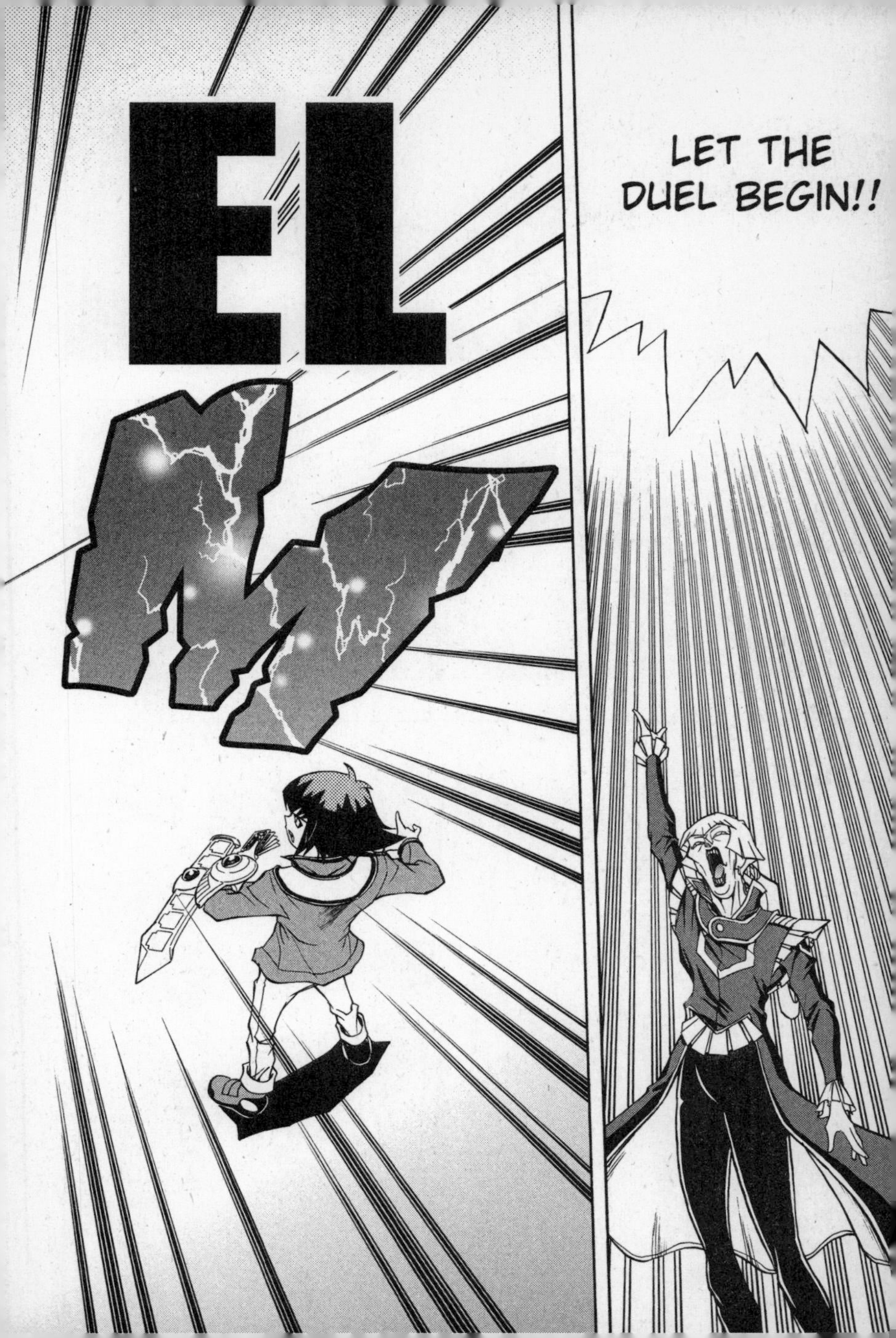
LET THE DUEL BEGIN!!
EL

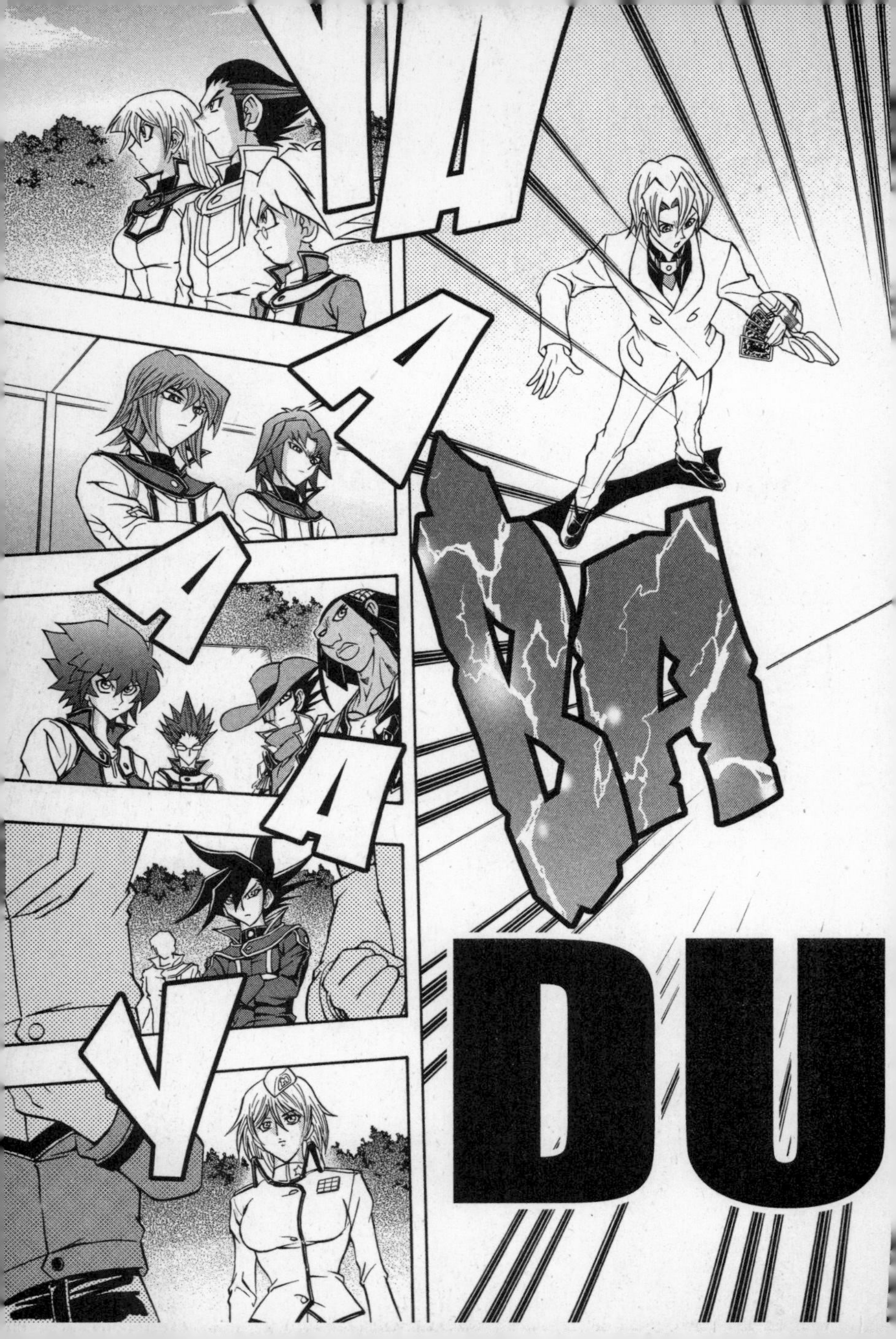
BA
DU

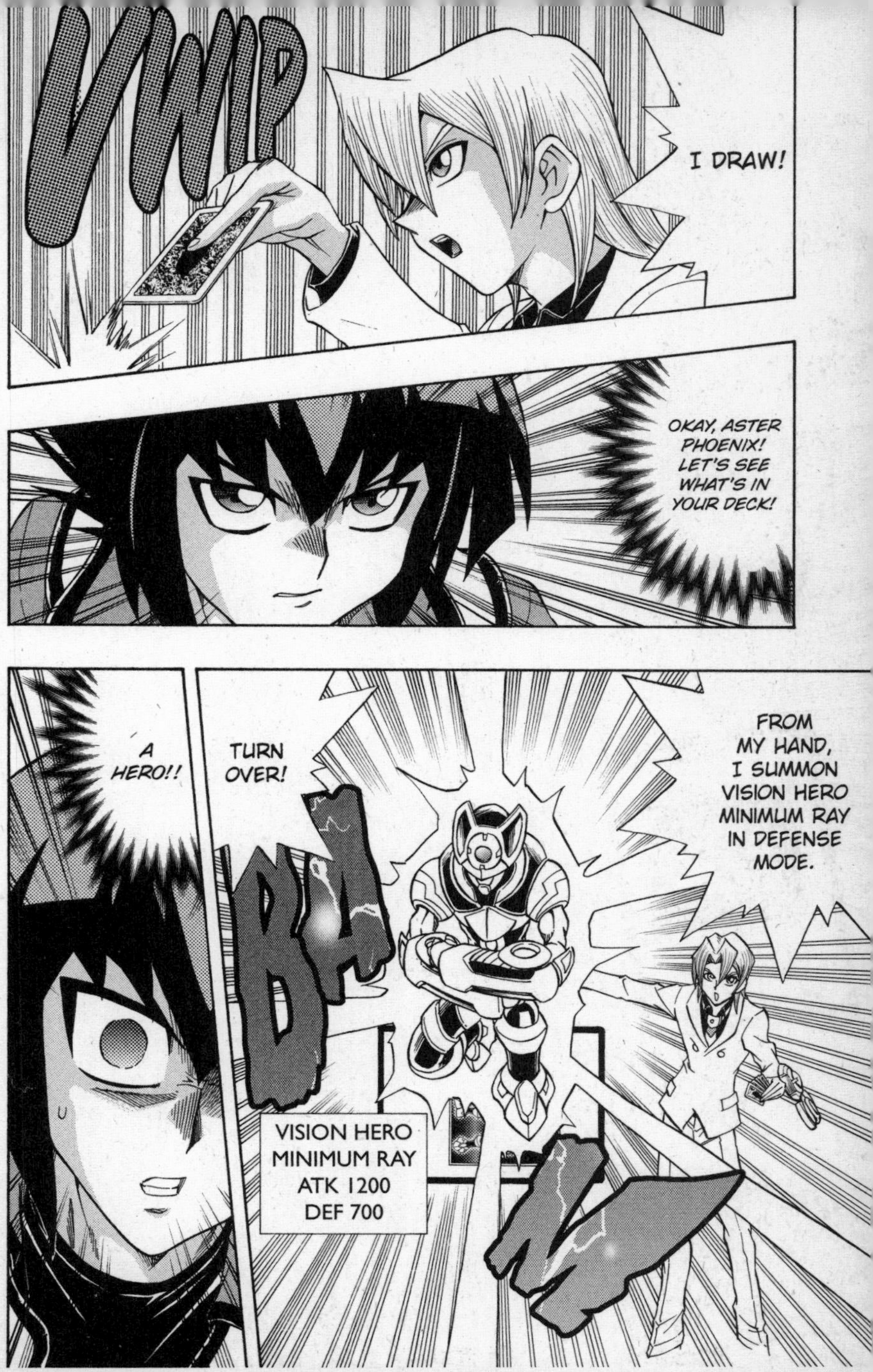
VWIP
I DRAW!
OKAY, ASTER PHOENIX! LET'S SEE WHAT'S IN YOUR DECK!
FROM MY HAND, I SUMMON VISION HERO MINIMUM RAY IN DEFENSE MODE.
TURN OVER!
BAM
VISION HERO MINIMUM RAY ATK 1200 DEF 700
A HERO!!

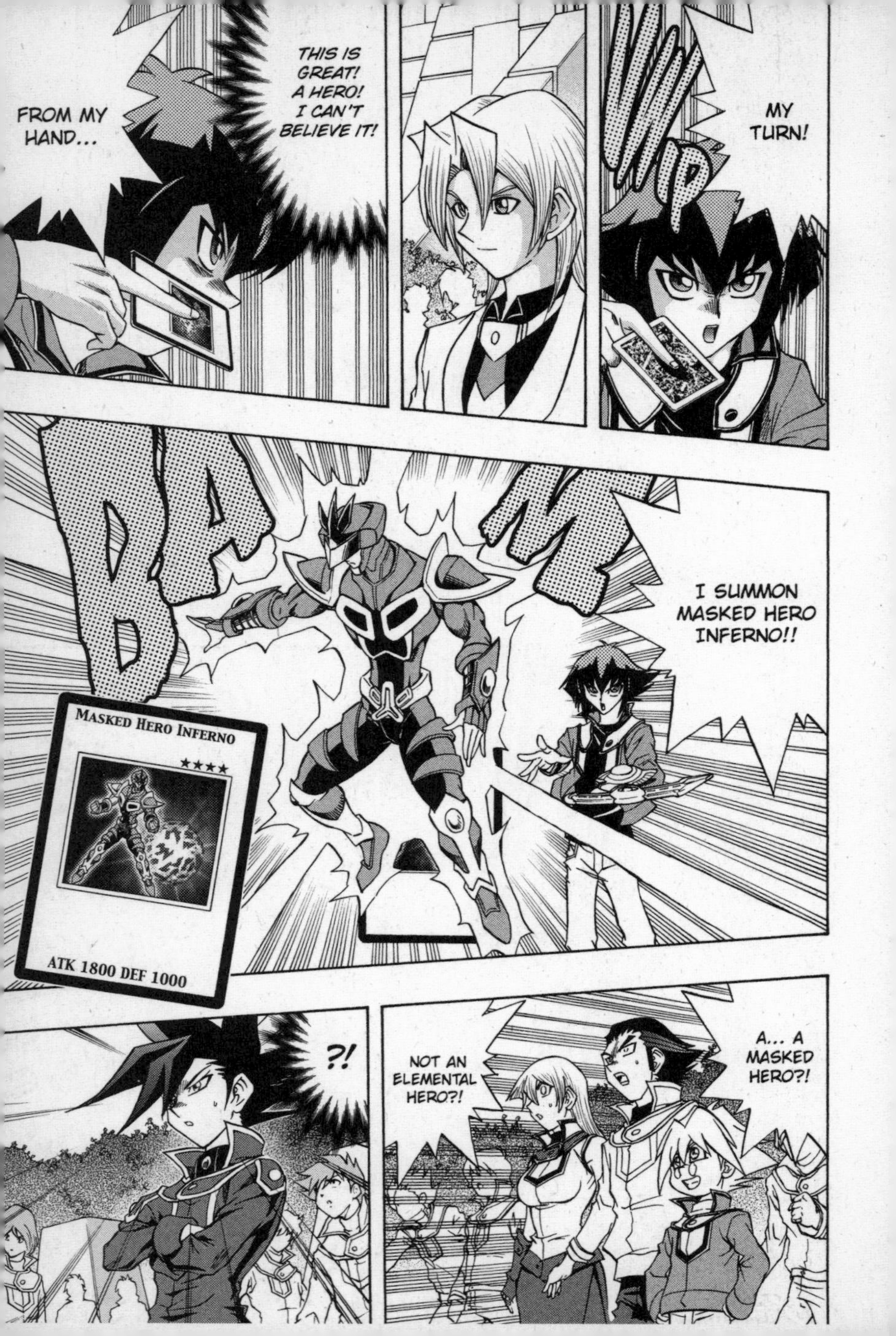

WHIP
MY TURN!
THIS IS GREAT! A HERO! I CAN'T BELIEVE IT!
FROM MY HAND...
I SUMMON MASKED HERO INFERNO!!
BAM
MASKED HERO INFERNO
★★★★
ATK 1800 DEF 1000
A... A MASKED HERO?!
NOT AN ELEMENTAL HERO?!
?!

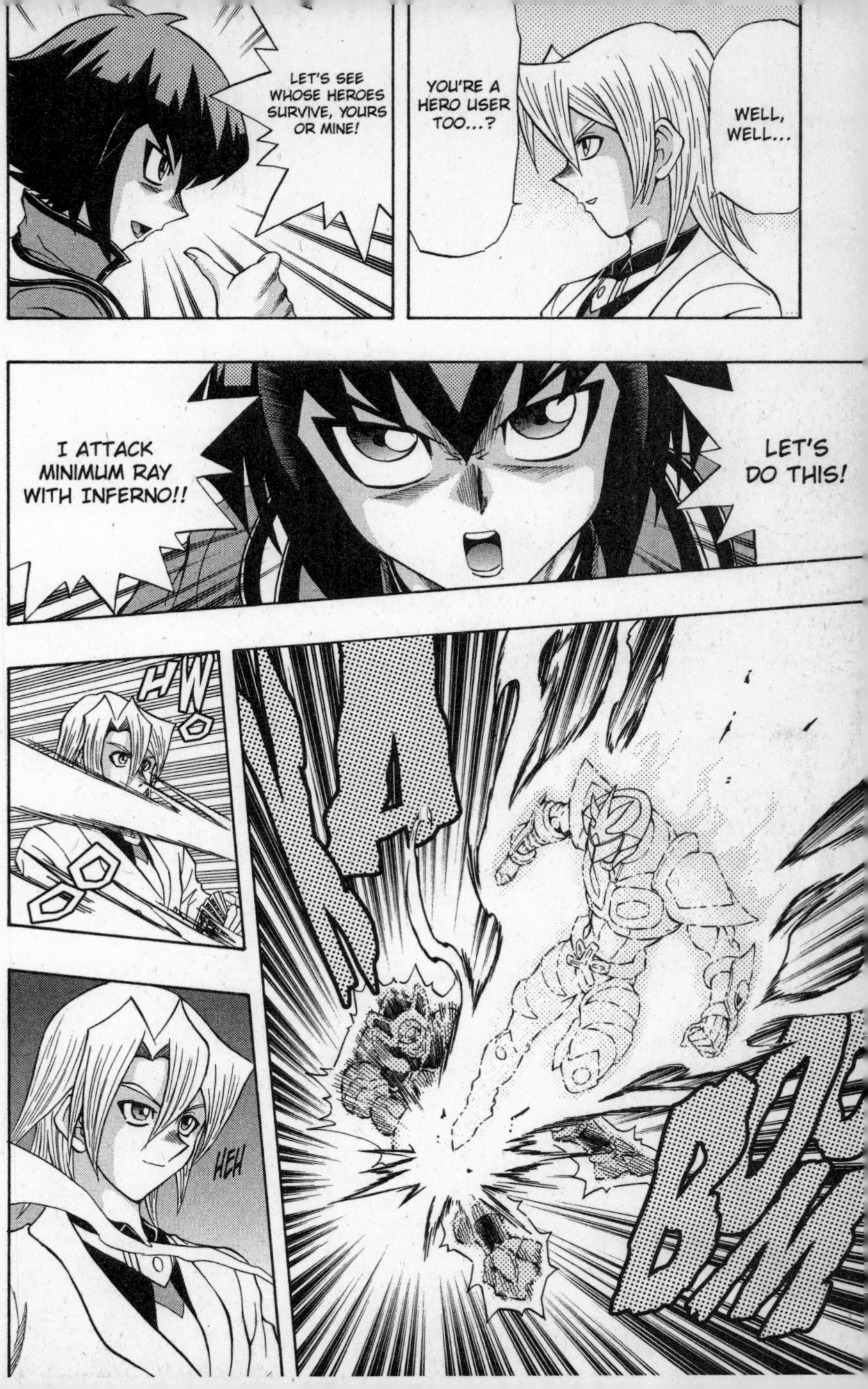
WELL, WELL...
YOU'RE A HERO USER TOO...?
LET'S SEE WHOSE HEROES SURVIVE, YOURS OR MINE!
LET'S DO THIS!
I ATTACK MINIMUM RAY WITH INFERNO!!
HEH

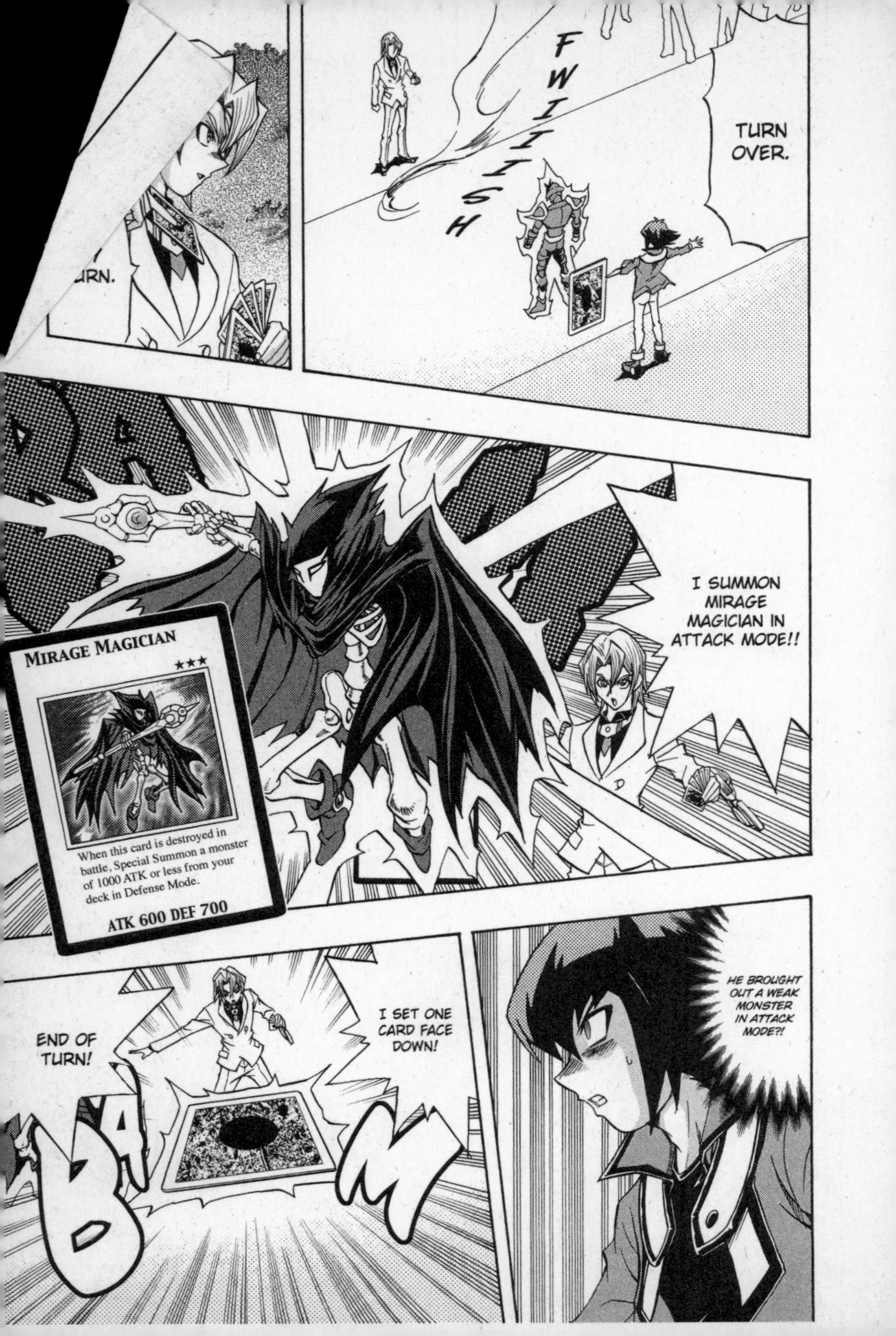
TURN OVER.
FWIIISH
URN.
I SUMMON MIRAGE MAGICIAN IN ATTACK MODE!!
MIRAGE MAGICIAN
★★★
When this card is destroyed in battle, Special Summon a monster of 1000 ATK or less from your deck in Defense Mode.
ATK 600 DEF 700
HE BROUGHT OUT A WEAK MONSTER IN ATTACK MODE?!
I SET ONE CARD FACE DOWN!
END OF TURN!
BAM

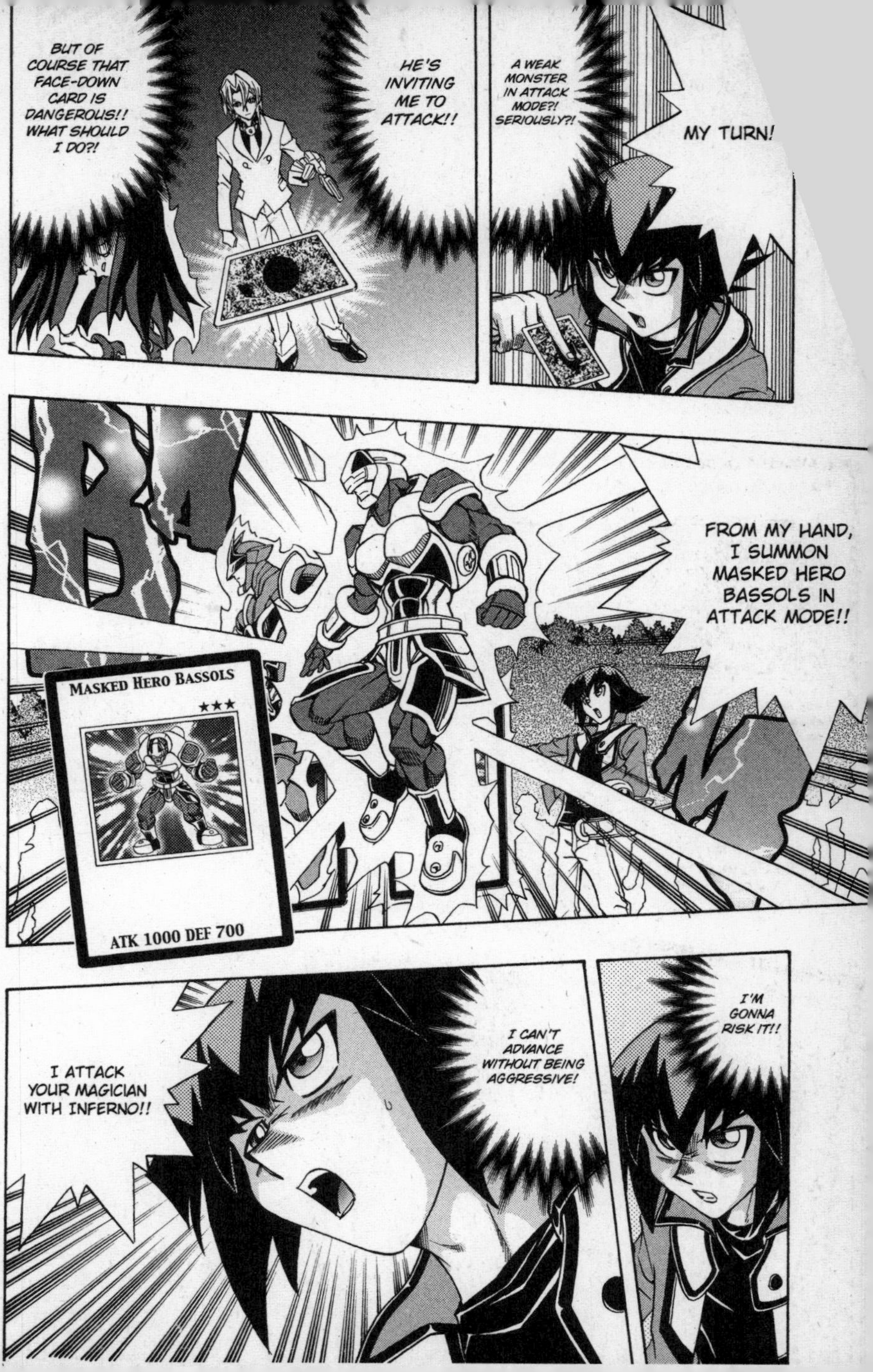
A WEAK MONSTER IN ATTACK MODE?! SERIOUSLY?!
MY TURN!
HE'S INVITING ME TO ATTACK!!
BUT OF COURSE THAT FACE-DOWN CARD IS DANGEROUS!! WHAT SHOULD I DO?!
FROM MY HAND, I SUMMON MASKED HERO BASSOLS IN ATTACK MODE!!
MASKED HERO BASSOLS
ATK 1000 DEF 700
I'M GONNA RISK IT!!
I CAN'T ADVANCE WITHOUT BEING AGGRESSIVE!
I ATTACK YOUR MAGICIAN WITH INFERNO!!

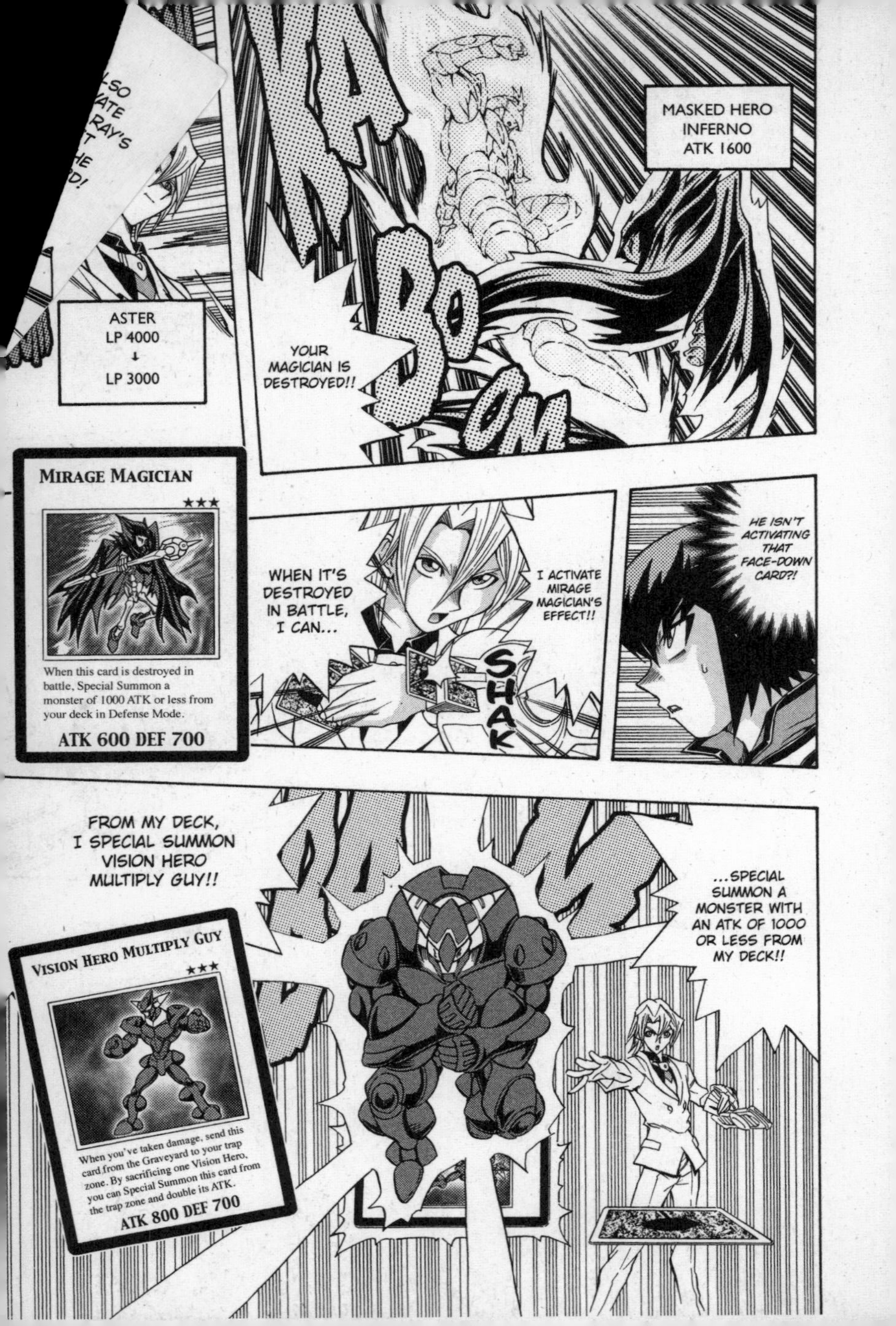
MASKED HERO INFERNO ATK 1600
BOOM
YOUR MAGICIAN IS DESTROYED!!
ASTER LP 4000 ↓ LP 3000
HE ISN'T ACTIVATING THAT FACE-DOWN CARD?!
I ACTIVATE MIRAGE MAGICIAN'S EFFECT!!
WHEN IT'S DESTROYED IN BATTLE, I CAN...
SHAK
MIRAGE MAGICIAN
★★★
When this card is destroyed in battle, Special Summon a monster of 1000 ATK or less from your deck in Defense Mode.
ATK 600 DEF 700
...SPECIAL SUMMON A MONSTER WITH AN ATK OF 1000 OR LESS FROM MY DECK!!
FROM MY DECK, I SPECIAL SUMMON VISION HERO MULTIPLY GUY!!
VISION HERO MULTIPLY GUY
★★★
When you've taken damage, send this card from the Graveyard to your trap zone. By sacrificing one Vision Hero, you can Special Summon this card from the trap zone and double its ATK.
ATK 800 DEF 700

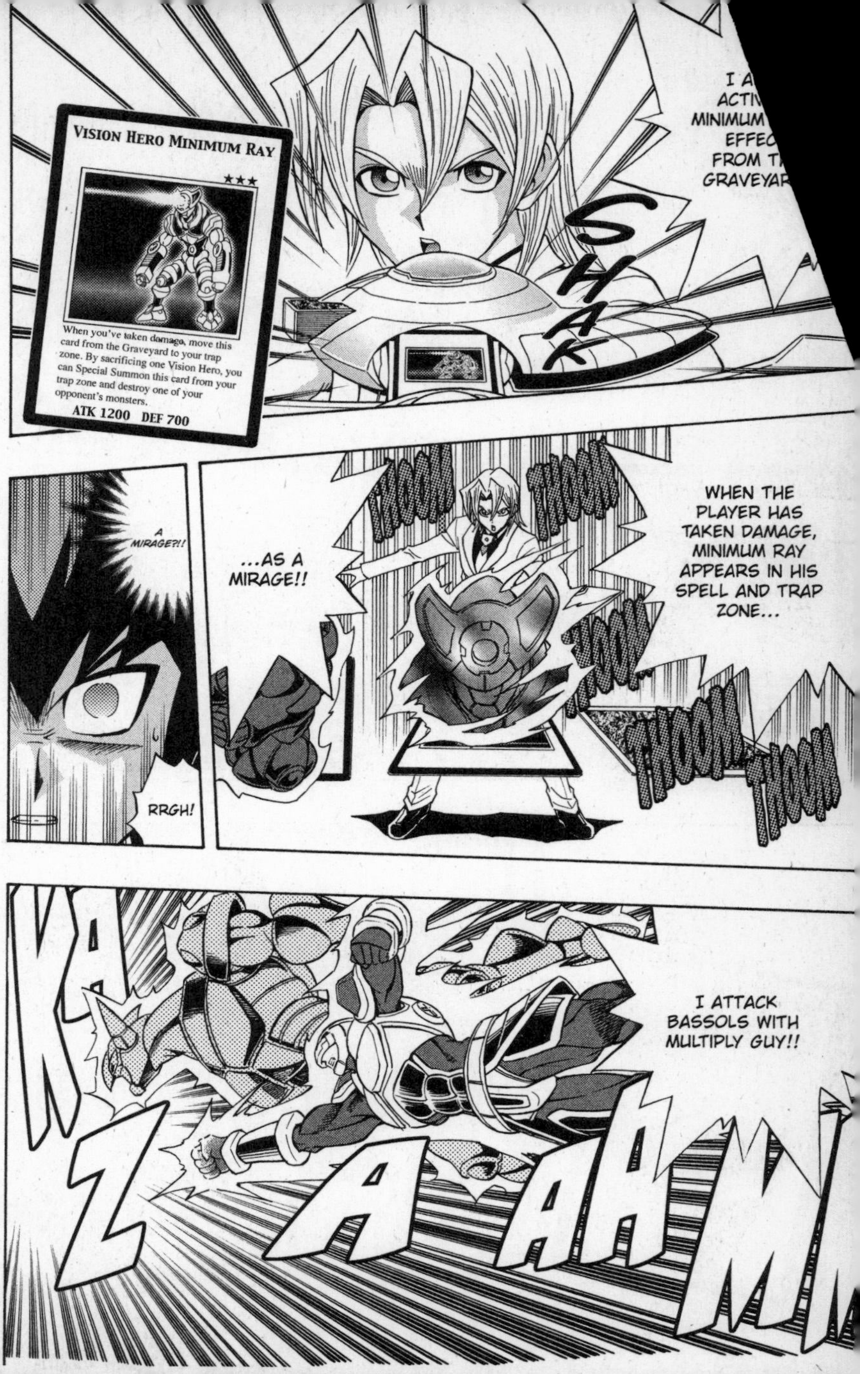
I A
ACTIV
MINIMUM
EFFEC
FROM T
GRAVEYAR
SHAK
VISION HERO MINIMUM RAY
★★★
When you've taken damage, move this card from the Graveyard to your trap zone. By sacrificing one Vision Hero, you can Special Summon this card from your trap zone and destroy one of your opponent's monsters.
ATK 1200 DEF 700
WHEN THE PLAYER HAS TAKEN DAMAGE, MINIMUM RAY APPEARS IN HIS SPELL AND TRAP ZONE...
THOOM THOOM THOOM THOOM THOOM THOOM
...AS A MIRAGE!!
A MIRAGE?!!
RRGH!
I ATTACK BASSOLS WITH MULTIPLY GUY!!

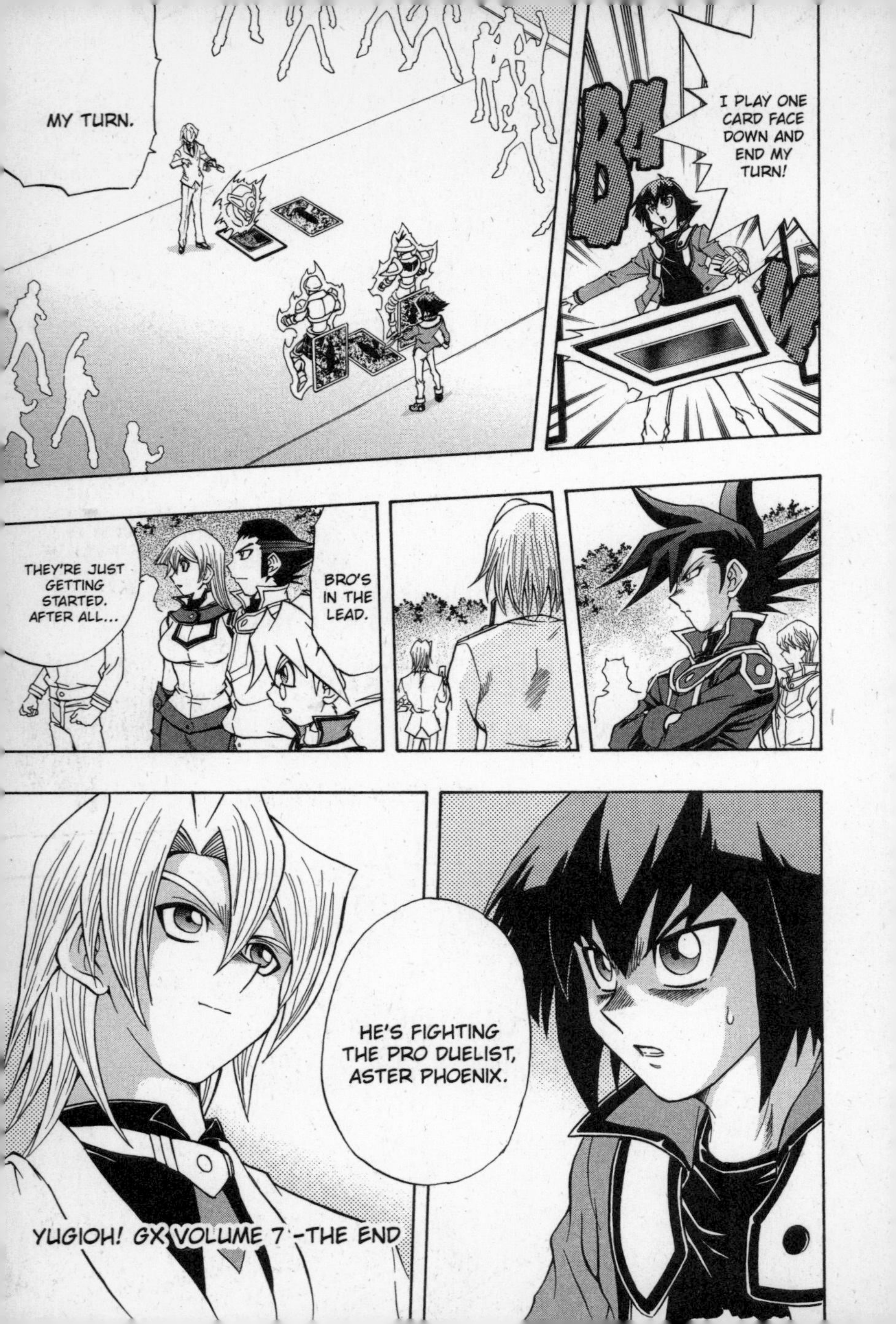
BA
I PLAY ONE CARD FACE DOWN AND END MY TURN!
MY TURN.
BRO'S IN THE LEAD.
THEY'RE JUST GETTING STARTED. AFTER ALL...
HE'S FIGHTING THE PRO DUELIST, ASTER PHOENIX.
YUGIOH! GX VOLUME 7 -THE END

STAFF

MASAFUMI SATO

YUJI KOIKE

JUNYA UCHINO

DAIJI FUKUZAWA

AKIRA ITO

DUEL COMBINATION COOPERATION

MASAHIRO UCHIDA

COLORING

NABETARO

EDITOR

DAISUKE TERASHI

MASTER OF THE CARDS

Jaden Yuki and the rest of the next generation of Duelists have introduced their own cards into the *Yu-Gi-Oh!* TCG, which also make their first appearance here in the seventh volume of the *Yu-Gi-Oh: GX* manga! As with all original *Yu-Gi-Oh!* cards, names can differ slightly between the Japanese and English versions, so we're showing you both for reference. Plus, we show you the card even if the card itself doesn't show up in the manga but the monster or trap does! And some cards you may have already seen in the original *Yu-Gi-Oh!*, but we still note them the first time they appear in this volume anyway!

First Appearance in This Volume	Japanese Card Name	English Card Name <<!>> = Not yet available in the TCG.
p.12	代償の風圧	Wind Pressure Compensation <!>
p.12	スパウン・アリゲーター	Spawn Alligator
p.14	シンセサイズ・スフィア	Synthesize Sphere <!>
p.15	エアースフィア	Air Sphere <!>
p.16	退化する翼	Regressing Wings <!>
p.17	*The tyrant NEPTUNE*	The Tyrant Neptune
p.24	大気万世	Unbroken Atmosphere <!>
p.25	クロコダイル・スケイル	Crocodile Scale <!>
p.26	死者蘇生	Monster Reborn
p.26	*The* アトモスフィア	The Atmosphere
p.30	パワレスフィア	Powerless Sphere <!>
p.63	クリスタル・ガール	Crystal Girl <!>

p.64	封印獣ボア・ボーラン	Sealed Beast Boa Bolan <!>
p.65	アイス・ブロック	Ice Block <!>
p.66	尾長黒馬	Long-Tailed Black Horse <!>
p.67	苦痛のマントラ	Mantra of Agony
p.68	ホワイト・パピオン	White Papillon <!>
p.69	ブリザード・プリンセス	Blizzard Princess
p.73	アイス・ドール	Ice Doll <!>
p.73	カーテン・オブ・ヘイル	Curtain of Hail <!>
p.74	封印獣チャルムジュル	Sealed Beast Dharmjul <!>
p.74	封印の真言	Sealed Mantra <!>
p.76	神の氷結	The Ice-Bound God <!>
p.77	ダイダラボッチ	Daidara-Bocchi <!>
p.80	奇奇怪怪	Phantasmagoria <!>
p.82	真言の呪縛	Mantra's Curse-Binding <!>
p.85	ローズ・パピヨン	Rose Papillon <!>
p.88	生者の末路	Fate of the Living <!>
p.88	化け狸の葉っぱ	Leaf of the Transforming Tanuki <!>
p.89	馬頭鬼	Mezuki
p.90	雪ダルマン	Snowman <!>

p.91	封印獣ブロン	Sealed Beast Bronn <!>
p.94	氷結界	Ice Barrier <!>
p.95	妖魔の援軍	Ghostly Reinforcements <!>
p.95	ヌリカベ	Nurikabe <!>
p.96	昆虫の大群	Insect Horde <!>
p.96	蝶の妖精	Butterfly Fairy <!>
p.97	アイス・ドール・ミラー	Ice Doll Mirror <!>
p.108	聖なるバリア・ミラーフォース・	Mirror Force
p.119	アリ・ソルジャー	Alli-Soldier <!>
p.120	タンクロイド	Tankroid <!>
p.121	エレクトロ・ガンナー	Electro Gunner <!>
p.122	エレクトロニック・モーター	Electronic Motor <!>
p.123	クロコダイル・スケイル	Crocodile Scale <!>
p.124	援軍出撃	Support Mission <!>
p.124	ミサイルロイド	Missile Roid <!>
p.127	ハリケイン・ドラゴン	Hurricane Dragon <!>
p.127	バーニング・ドラゴン	Burning Dragon <!>
p.127	竜の嗅覚	Dragon's Scent <!>
p.132	ダーク・アリゲーター	Dark Alligator <!>

p.141	レプティア・エッグ	Reptia Egg <!>
p.142	ヘリロイド	Heliroid <!>
p.143	マーチ・オブ・ロイド	March of the Roids <!>
p.143	ミサイルロイド	Missile Roid <!>
p.146	スネア	Snare <!>
p.148	エレクトロ軍曹	Sergeant Electro
p.149	メカニック魂	Mechanic's Soul <!>
p.151	スチール・ドラグーン	Steel Dragon <!>
p.152	カモフラージュ	Camouflage <!>
p.153	エレクトリック・ショック	Electric Shock <!>
p.154	アリゲーター・ベイビー	Alligator Baby <!>
p.159	不死の竜	Immortal Dragon <!>
p.160	旧型出陣	Old Model to the Frontline <!>
p.161	ランチャーロイド	Launcher Roid
p.191	***M・HERO*** 烈火	Masked Hero Inferno <!>
p.193	幻影の魔術士	Phantom Magician
p.194	***M・HERO*** バソール	Masked Hero Bassols <!>
p.195	***V・HERO*** マルティプリ・ガイ	Vision Hero Multiply Guy <!>
p.196	***V・HERO*** ミニマム・レイ	Vision Hero Minimum Ray <!>

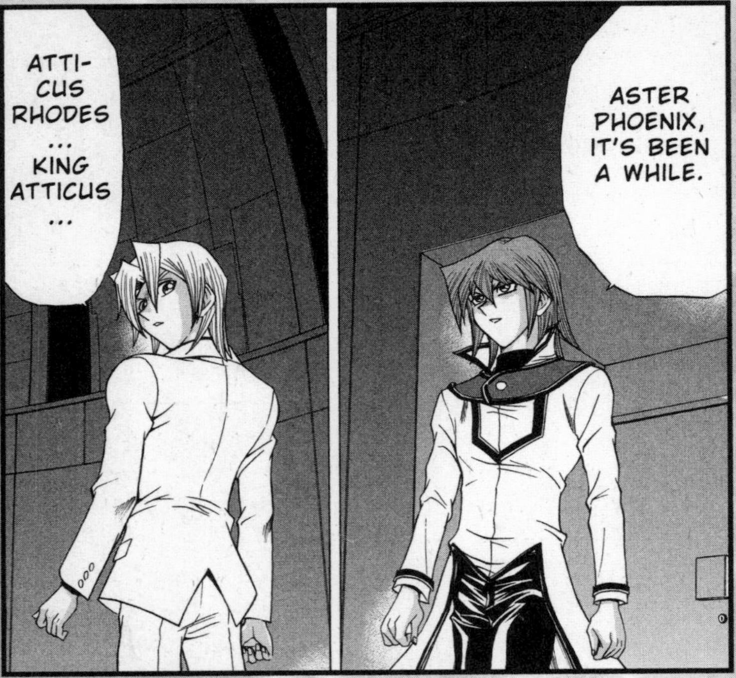
ASTER PHOENIX, IT'S BEEN A WHILE.
ATTICUS RHODES ... KING ATTICUS ...

IN THE NEXT VOLUME...

The next series of duels at Duel Academy are about to begin, and Reggie Mackenzie's father, possessed by an evil spirit determined to wreak havoc, makes his move. By manipulating members of the group of visiting duelists from America, Mackenzie plants the seeds of destruction on Duel Academy Island. When Jaden takes on his next opponent, will he realize the evil he faces, or will an ancient spirit's scheme to resurrect itself go forward?

COMING JANUARY 2012!

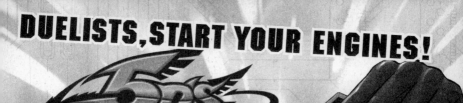
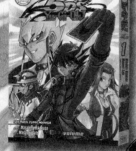

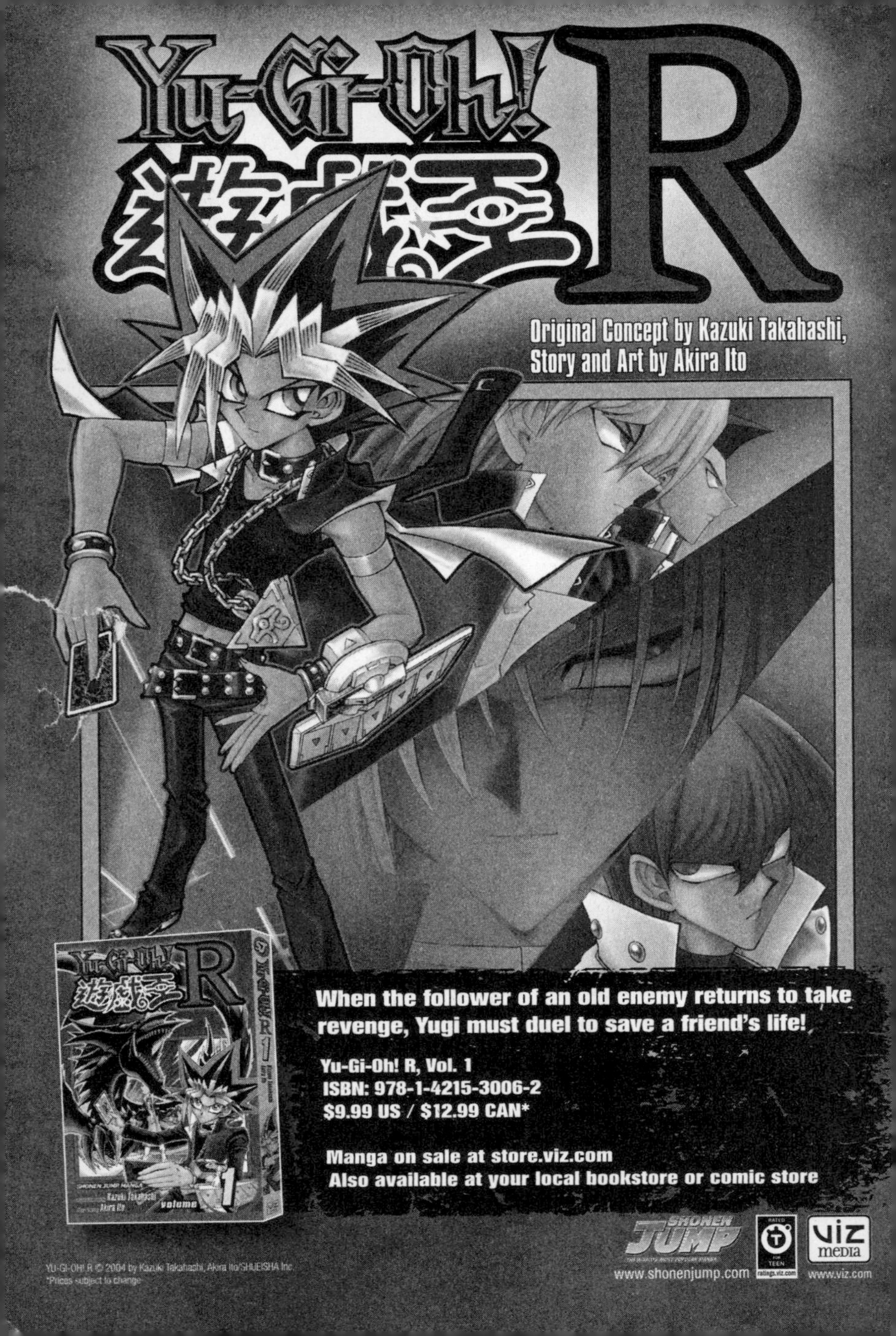
Yu-Gi-Oh! 遊☆戯☆王 R
Original Concept by Kazuki Takahashi, Story and Art by Akira Ito
When the follower of an old enemy returns to take revenge, Yugi must duel to save a friend's life!
Yu-Gi-Oh! R, Vol. 1
ISBN: 978-1-4215-3006-2
$9.99 US / $12.99 CAN*
Manga on sale at store.viz.com
Also available at your local bookstore or comic store
SHONEN JUMP
www.shonenjump.com
RATED T FOR TEEN
ratings.viz.com
viz media
www.viz.com
YU-GI-OH! R © 2004 by Kazuki Takahashi, Akira Ito/SHUEISHA Inc.
*Prices subject to change

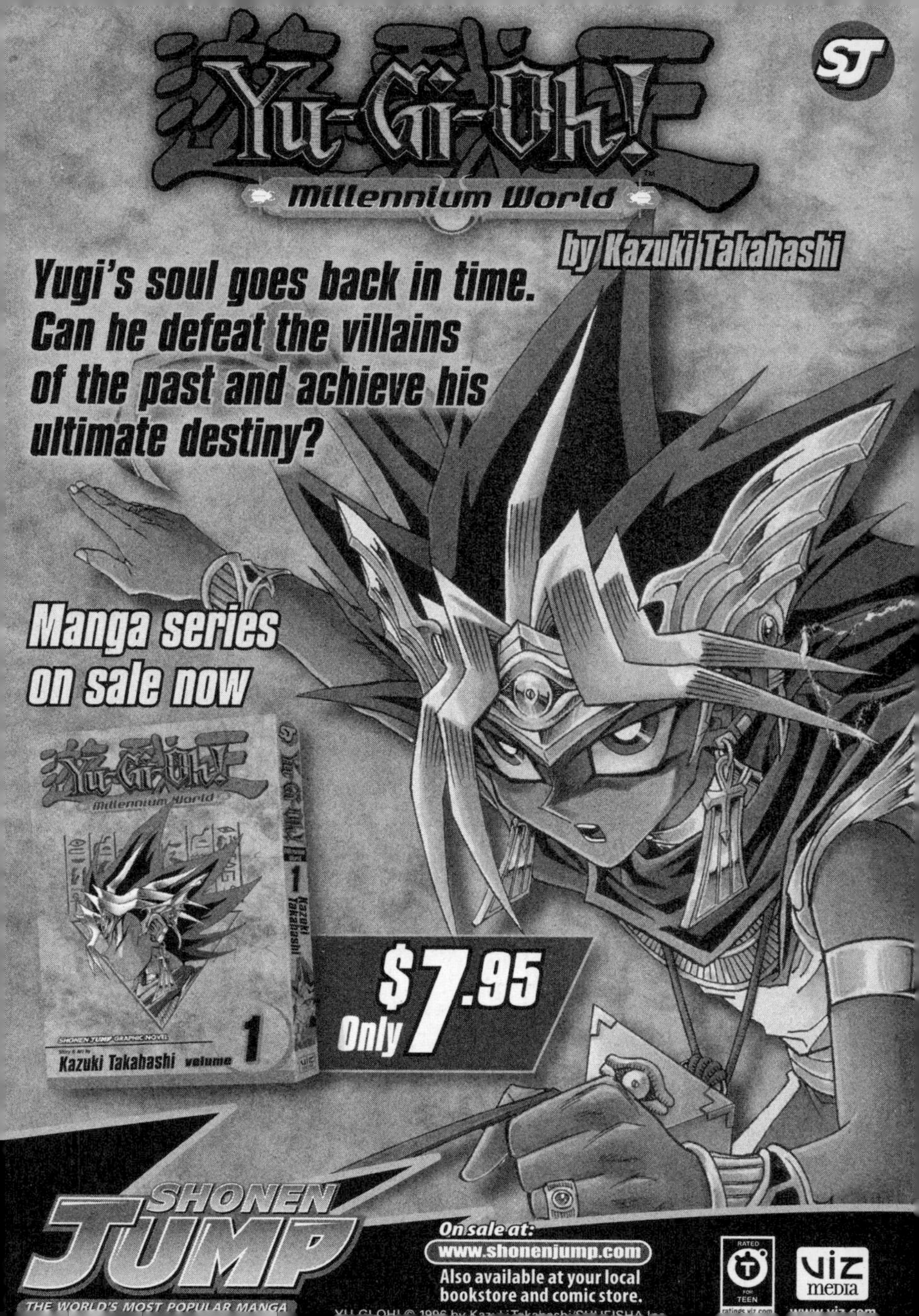

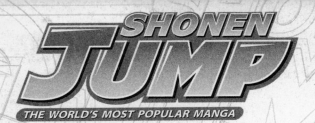
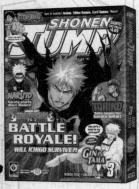
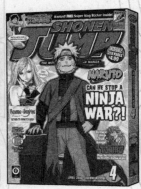
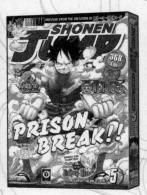